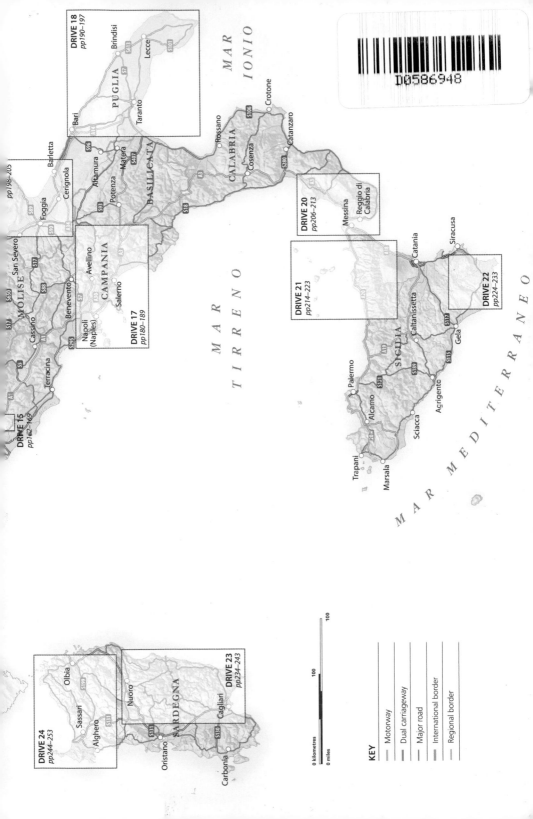

DRIVE 18
pp190–197

Brindisi
Lecce

PUGLIA
S7

Bari
Taranto

MAR IONIO

pp198–205

Barletta
Cerignola
Altamura
Matera
Potenza
BASILICATA
S407
S96
S53
S18
A3

San Severo
MOLISE
Foggia
S90
S17
S650
S88
Cassino
Benevento
Terracina
S87
S6
A1

CAMPANIA
Avellino
Napoli (Naples)
Salerno

DRIVE 17
pp180–189

DRIVE 15
pp1 –169

Rossano
CALABRIA
Cosenza
Crotone
Catanzaro
S106
S280

DRIVE 20
pp206–213

Messina
Reggio di Calabria
S18

MAR TIRRENO

Catania
Siracusa

DRIVE 21
pp214–223

DRIVE 22
pp224–233

Palermo
Alcamo
Trapani
Marsala
Sciacca
Agrigento
Gela
Caltanissetta
SICILIA
S117
S115
S121
S113

MAR MEDITERRANEO

DRIVE 24
pp244–253

Olbia
Sassari
Alghero
Nuoro
SARDEGNA
Oristano
Carbonia
Cagliari
S131

DRIVE 23
pp234–243

0 kilometres   100
0 miles   100

KEY

—— Motorway
—— Dual carriageway
—— Major road
—— International border
—— Regional border

D0586948

EYEWITNESS TRAVEL

BACK ROADS
ITALY

EYEWITNESS TRAVEL

BACK ROADS
ITALY

CONTRIBUTORS

Ros Belford, Judy Edelhoff, Adele Evans,

Tamara Thiessen, Christine Webb,

Marius Webb, Celia Woolfrey

DK

LONDON, NEW YORK,
MELBOURNE, MUNICH AND DELHI
www.dk.com

PUBLISHER
Douglas Amrine
LIST MANAGER
Vivien Antwi
MANAGING ART EDITOR
Jane Ewart
EDITORIAL
Michelle Crane, Alastair Laing,
Georgina Palffy, Hugh Thompson,
Jane Ellis, Vicki Allen
ART EDITORS
Shahid Mahmood,
Kate Leonard
PRODUCTION CONTROLLER
Linda Dare
PICTURE RESEARCH
Ellen Root
DTP
Jason Little, Jamie McNeill
CARTOGRAPHY
Uma Bhattacharya, Casper Morris
Suresh Kumar, Stuart James, Sachin
Pradhan, Lovell Johns Ltd
JACKET DESIGN
Tessa Bindloss, Meredith Smith
ILLUSTRATIONS
Arun Pottirayil, Pallavi Thakur,
Dev Datta

Printed and bound in China by
South China Printing Co Ltd

First published in the UK in 2010
by Dorling Kindersley Limited,
80 Strand, London
WC2R 0RL

12 13 14 15 16 10 9 8 7 6 5 4 3 2 1

Reprinted with revisions 2013

Copyright 2010, 2013 © Dorling
Kindersley Limited, London

A Penguin Company

Front cover: Porto di Tremosine, Lake Garda, Italy

MIX
Paper from
responsible sources
FSC™ C018179
www.fsc.org

CONTENTS

Above The Costa Smeralda, Sardinia, famous for its sandy beaches and clear water

Below The pretty town of Courmayeur in the Valle d'Aosta, Northern Italy

Below Clearly marked signs – found even on the smaller back roads in Italy

ALBA 15
BAROLO 2
DOGLIANI 11
NOVELLO 3

Above Gardena Pass in northern Italy's Dolomites, Trentino-Alto Adige

Above Typical lush, fertile landscape of the Val d'Orcia in central Tuscany

Above Bronze statue at the heart of impressive Piazza San Carlo in Turin

Below Fishing village on the Arcipelago della Maddalena, Sardinia **Below right** Art imitating nature – typical floral decoration in Tuscany

Title page: Summer landscape of olive trees and vines at Villa a Sesta in Tuscany **Half-title page:** A quiet flower-lined street in an Umbrian hill-town

About this Book

The 24 drives in this book capture the diversity of the Italian peninsula, stretching from the snow-capped mountain ranges it shares with France and Austria to the sun-baked beaches and scirocco-scorched towns of the south, where Africa seems only a breath away. A modern, industrialized nation with its finger on the financial pulse of Europe, Italy is also a country where traditional Mediterranean values hold and the pace of life is still refreshingly slow outside the cities.

These drives do not shun Italy's world-famous art towns, but rather than treating them as isolated spots on a weekend break, they are included in tours that allow a wider exploration of the history, culture and landscape that gave birth to them. Other drives go completely off the beaten track – to remote mountain outposts, wild sandy beaches, hidden rocky coves, and to rarely visited archaeological sites and towns – allowing visitors to explore facets of Italy that many never experience.

Getting Started

The guide begins with the practical information needed to plan and make the most of exploring Italy by car: how to get to Italy; whether to bring your own vehicle or hire one; and the documentation required. The guide offers motoring advice, from the quirks of Italian driving and road-signage to where to buy petrol and what to do if the car breaks down. Health, money and communications are also covered and there is an overview of dining and accommodation options. A language section at the back lists essential words and phrases, including key driver-related vocabulary.

The Drives

The main touring section of the guide is divided into leisurely drives, ranging in duration from one to five days. Most of the roads are paved, and where they are not, they are good-quality roads, which should present no difficulties to a standard vehicle.

The drives have been chosen to encompass every region of Italy. To help visitors choose and plan a trip, each drive begins with a list of highlights and a clearly mapped

itinerary. There is advice on the best time of year to do the drive, road conditions, market days and major festival dates. The drive pages contain detailed descriptions of each sight and activity, linked by clear driving instructions. Side panels offer information on places to stay and eat. Tinted boxes feature suggestions for extra activities and background information. These might be details of a local festival or speciality; tips for a wine-tasting tour; or where to find the quietest beach. Each drive also features at least one mapped town or countryside walking tour, designed to take a maximum of three hours at a gentle pace with stops along the way.

The flexible nature of the tours means that some can be linked to create a longer driving holiday; or simply dipped into to plan day trips while based in one particular region.

Using the Sheet Map

A pull-out road map of the entire country is attached at the back. This map contains all the information you need to drive around the country and to navigate between the tours. All motorways, major roads, airports – both domestic and international – plus all the ferry ports are easily identified. This makes the pull-out map an excellent addition to the drive itinerary maps within the book. The pull-out map has a comprehensive index to help you find the places, and is further supplemented by a clear distance chart so you can gauge the distances between the major cities.

Top left The Cinque Terre town of Manarola, in Liguria **Top Right** Wisteria pergola in the La Foce Estate Garden, Tuscany **Centre left** Rustic cart and bottles in a Sesto vineyard **Centre right** Hilltop town of Montefolonico, Tuscany **Below left** Classic Fiat 500 in Greve, Chianti **Below right** The beautiful rolling landscape of Tuscany

Above Driving along the quiet roads of Umbria

Introducing Italy

The best way for visitors to discover the real Italy is to slow down, leave the busy *austostrada* and explore the countryside via its back roads. Italy's traditions, cuisine and culture have evolved over thousands of years of working closely with the land and its natural resources. And they are best appreciated close up, too. Driving along a back road to swim in the crystal waters of a remote beach, there are fishermen grilling fresh anchovies; stop at a vineyard and meet a prize-winning wine maker who will happily give an opinion and a taste of his new wines. See flamingoes en route for Africa on a salt lake in a protected reserve. Whether driving through the lemon groves of Siciliy, the rugged hillsides of Lombardy or the fertile farmlands of Umbria, the visitor will never be far from beautiful towns rich in culture and history, evocative landscapes and gourmet delights. Travelling the back roads reveals the Italy that many thought had ceased to exist half a century ago – it is still alive and well, and as alluring as ever.

When to Go
Each of the drives suggests the ideal times to make the trip. This may be because the scenery is at its best or that rivers are at their highest and most spectacular or perhaps the cherry blossom is in flower. There might be a local festival taking place or it could be that a certain food is in season. The weather, of course, is also a factor, as is how busy the area is likely to be at certain times of year.

The long, narrow Italian peninsula has a varied climate falling into three distinct geographical zones: in the north, expect cold Alpine winters and warm wet summers; in the vast central Po valley summers are arid and winters damp, foggy and freezing. The rest of Italy enjoys a pleasantly clement climate, with long hot summers and mild winters.

The best times to visit Italy are spring and autumn, ideally between April and June or September and October. At this time, the climate should be mild, without being too hot, and it is generally much less crowded than in high summer.

Times to Avoid
Driving anywhere in the first days of August or in the days immediately before and after Ferragosto (August 15), the national summer holiday, should be avoided. The beginning of other school holidays also sees a great surge in traffic levels. Schools

break up for summer in mid-June (a week earlier in Sicily and the south) and resume in mid-September. The Easter holidays usually begin on the Thursday before Easter and end on the Wednesday after Easter. Days around public holidays (see right) can also be very busy on the roads.

Festivals
Festivals and fairs take place all over Italy throughout the year. As well as the Easter and Christmas festivities, every town and village has a patron saint and each one marks its saint's day with special celebrations.

Spring and autumn are the best times for *sagras*, festivals celebrating local foods. Mushroom, sausage, olive oil, bread and wine *sagras* are common in autumn, while spring *sagras* are often devoted to seasonal fruits such as strawberries and cherries or delicacies such as capers.

Carnevale (February) sees masked parades take over many towns and villages – most famously Venice.

Public Holidays
New Year's Day (1 Jan)
Epiphany (6 Jan)
Easter Sunday and Monday
Liberation Day (25 Apr)
Labour Day (1 May)
Republic Day (2 Jun)
Ferragosto (15 Aug)
All Saints' Day (1 Nov)
Immaculate Conception of the
  Blessed Virgin Mary (8 Dec)
Christmas Day (25 Dec)
Santo Stefano (26 Dec)

Left Roadway through farmland in Tuscany with a typical line of cypress trees

Above Fruit and vegetable stalls in Cannobio, Lake Maggiore

Getting to Italy

The increase in low-cost flights has revolutionized travel to and within Italy. Flights are cheaper and many provincial airports are now open to international flights from other major European cities. Arriving at a small airport, where queues for immigration and baggage are short, and where a hire car can easily be collected (often at a discount rate through the airline company) is generally the best start to a driving holiday in Italy. Travellers from outside Europe may find it cheaper to fly via London to take advantage of the many low-cost flights available from the UK.

Above Decorative ceramic tile entrance to a perfumery in Capri, Campania

DIRECTORY

AIRLINES

Air Italy
www.airitaly.it

AirOne
www.flyairone.it

Alitalia
www.alitalia.com

blu-express
www.blu-express.com

British Airways
www.ba.com

easyJet
www.easyjet.com

Emirates
www.emirates.com

Jet2
www.jet2.com

Malaysia Airlines
www.malaysiaairlines.com

Ryanair
www.ryanair.com

WindJet
www.volawindjet.it

Arriving by Air

Alitalia's sole hub is now Rome Fiumicino since Milan's twin airports of Malpensa and Linate have been downgraded to "focus" airports. There are direct Alitalia flights from London Heathrow to all three airports, but no direct flights from any UK provincial airports. Alitalia also serves about 25 domestic airports within Italy.

British Airways flies from London Gatwick to Bari, Cagliari, Catania, Genoa, Naples, Pisa, Rome Fiumicino, Turin and Verona. From London Heathrow there are flights to Milan's twin airports and to Venice. BA also fly from Manchester and Birmingham to Milan Malpensa, and also from Edinburgh to Rome Fiumicino.

From New York JFK, **Alitalia** flies to Milan Malpensa, with all other US flights going to Rome Fiumicino. Those travelling from Australia may find the best deals are often with Alitalia's business partner, **Malaysia Airlines**, which flies to Rome Fiumicino via Kuala Lumpur, or with **Emirates** which flies to both Rome and Milan via Dubai.

Many of the low-cost airlines such as **Ryanair** and **easyJet** fly from London Gatwick, Stansted, Luton and other regional UK airports to provincial Italian airports. If there are only flights to Rome from your local airport, you may find the best deals for onward flights to a provincial Italian airport from an Italian low-cost airline such as **blu-express**, **AirOne**, **WindJet** and **Air Italy**.

Italian Airports

Italy's system of naming its airports can be confusing to the uninitiated. Airports are named not only after the nearest major city, and perhaps the nearest village as well, but usually after a famous Italian, too. Rome Fiumicino, for example, is also known as Leonardo da Vinci, Palermo is known as both Punta Raisi and Falcone Borsellino (after the two Sicilian judges killed by the Mafia in 1992). Note that on road signs, an airport may be referred to by any, or a combination of its names or sometimes only the airport's international code is used.

Arriving by Rail

Countless direct services (including many sleepers) link Italy with the major European cities. Connections from Paris (and London, via **Eurostar**) run to Turin, Milan, Venice, Bologna, Florence, Pisa, Rome and Naples.

Rail services also operate from German, Swiss and other northern European cities to Milan, Turin, Venice and Verona. There are also direct services from Vienna, Spain and the south of France.

Low-cost airlines have forced the train companies to be a little more competitive. Special discount fares are often available online. As the trains can be extremely busy during peak periods (Friday and Sunday evenings, the Christmas and Easter holidays and during July and August), it is advisable to make reservations if you intend to travel at those times.

There are motorail train services to Italy from Germany and the Netherlands. There is no motorail connection from France although you can travel to Nice via motorail and drive across the Italian border.

Arriving by Road

Most roads into Italy from the rest of Europe involve Alpine crossings by tunnel or mountain passes. The exceptions are the approach from Slovenia in the northeast (on the A4 motorway) and the route along the French Riviera that enters Italy as the A10 motorway at Ventimiglia.

The most popular route from Geneva and southeast France is via the Mont Blanc tunnel and A5 motorway, entering Italy close to Aosta and Turin. Another busy approach (from Switzerland) uses the St Bernard Pass and Tunnel. The main route from Austria and southern Germany crosses the Brenner Pass and goes down to Verona on the A22 motorway via Trento and the Adige valley. Most motorways are toll-roads; pay as you exit them.

Travellers from the UK could take a car to one of the French Channel ports by ferry or on the **Eurotunnel** rail shuttle. Once there, the drive to Genoa in the north of Italy takes around 12 hours (a journey of some 1,900 km/1,200 miles). **The AA** and **Michelin** both offer reliable route planners on www.theaa.com and www.viamichelin.co.uk.

Ferry Services

A well-developed network of ferries and hydrofoils links Italy with the rest of Europe and North Africa.

There are also good connections between mainland Italy and its offshore islands. **Moby Ferries** offers routes between Italy's main ports and Sardinia. **Sardinia Ferries** has a fast service connecting Civitavecchia and Livorno with Golfo Aranci in five hours and **Tirrenia** offers a similar service from Civitavecchia and Genoa to Olbia. **Ustica Lines** and **Siremar** run throughout the year from Milazzo to the Aeolian Islands, Siremar also operates ferry routes between Palermo and Naples. If you plan to travel in July or August, book ahead. Low season services are less frequent.

Far left Modern architecture at Catania Airport, Sicily **Left** Ferries at Naples port in Campania, in front of the volcano Vesuvius **Below left** High-speed train **Below right** Alitalia airplane after unloading its baggage at Rome, Fiumicino

DIRECTORY

RAIL
Eurostar
www.eurostar.com
08432 186 186 (UK)
+ 44 01233 617 575 (outside UK)

Rail Europe
www.raileurope.com
www.raileurope.co.uk
08448 484 064 (UK)
1-800-622-8600 (US)
1-800-361-RAIL (Canada)

Motorail
(Deutsche Bahn)
www.dbautozug.de

Autoslaap Trein
www.autoslaaptrein.nl

ROAD
The AA
www.theaa.com

Eurotunnel
www.eurotunnel.com
08705 353 535

Michelin
www.viamichelin.com

FERRY SERVICES
Moby Ferries
www.moby.it
+ 39 02 7602 8132

Sardinia Ferries
www.corsica-ferries.co.uk
+ 33 0495 329 595

Tirrenia
www.tirrenia.it
+ 39 02 2630 2003

Ustica Lines
www.usticalines.it
+ 39 09 2387 3813

Siremar
For routes between Naples, Reggio Calabria and Sicily and between the Sicilian mainland and the Aeolian Islands from Milazzo.
www.siremar.it

Other Useful Sites
These websites list all the major Italian ferry companies and offer information on routes, departure times and prices.
www.directferries.com
www.aferry.co.uk

Practical Information

Italy may be trying to throw off its reputation as a country that seesaws between bureaucracy and anarchy, but many of its age-old problems remain. As a rule, things tend to be more efficient in the north than the south, but at times the chaotic happenstance of the south may be more fun and you may achieve your goal more quickly. For anything that involves bureaucracy or the state – such as going to a bank, the police, a doctor, or buying a SIM card – carry photo ID, bring a good book and have plenty of patience.

Above Pharmacy signs are lit up at night to show where to buy medicine

Passports and Visas

European Union (EU) nationals and citizens can enter Italy and stay indefinitely with a valid passport or identity card.

Citizens of the US, Canada, Australia and New Zealand can stay in the country for up to three months on production of a passport, but will need to apply for a visa at their local Italian embassy in advance if they wish to stay longer. It is not sufficient for non-EU citizens wanting to stay for longer than three months to simply cross the border into another EU country once their three-month time limit is up. All other foreign nationals need a visa.

Travel Insurance

A travel insurance policy will usually cover you for loss or theft of luggage and other property such as passports and money, as well as for personal accident, repatriation in case of severe illness, third-party damage and delayed or cancelled flights. For a premium you can even insure against cancelling the holiday yourself. You will need to take out special cover for taking part in sports and any activities that are considered hazardous. Most insurance policies also include covering legal costs, up to a specified amount, as do comprehensive motor policies.

Health

Italy is a member of the European Union and has reciprocal health agreements with the other member states. In theory all EU nationals are entitled to free treatment under Italy's public healthcare system on production of a **European Health Insurance Card** (forms available at most post offices or apply online at www.dh.gov.uk). The card is free and is valid for five years. However, in practice getting access to free medical treatment can occasionally be a little tricky. The Italian health system is severely strained and the level of care can vary hugely from one area to another. In holiday areas there may be a guardia medica, a kind of minor ailments and emergencies clinic designed to deal with the sort of accidents that befall tourists. All non-residents will be asked to pay a flat fee, usually around €15–20. And whatever kind of doctor you see, prescriptions must also be paid for upfront (unless you are staying in Italy for some time and want to register with the local health authority or USL). Before complaining, bear in mind that most Italians may have to pay for blood and urine tests, and at times, when a region's funding runs out, all Italians, except those on social security, have to pay the full price for all their prescriptions.

If you do register with the local health authority, you will need a codice fiscale, a tax identification number without which it is impossible to do anything in Italy (they are allocated at birth). You apply for one by taking your passport to the local Agenzia delle Entrate. If you are lucky, the procedure can be completed in a morning, but unless you are staying in Italy for an extensive period, it is not worthwhile.

If you are taking prescription medicines, it is a good idea to bring the packet with you in case you run out. Many pharmacists will be happy to sell you a replacement for drugs such as anti-inflammatories, antibiotics and those for blood pressure etc, without requiring a prescription. Pharmacies are signalled by a green cross, and if the one you go to is closed, there should be a notice on display telling you where to find the nearest open pharmacy.

Left European Union and American passports **Middle** An ATM or Bancomat machine **Right** The *Carabinieri* police deal with a variety of offences

If you are involved in an accident call 118 or go to the *Pronto Soccorso* (casualty department) of the nearest hospital. If you are in a major town or city, it may be possible to find an English-speaking doctor, or, at least, someone who can translate for you.

Medicare Australia has a reciprocal agreement with Italy. All other non-EU citizens should ensure the terms of their health insurance policies cover all eventualities.

No inoculations are required for Italy, but mosquito repellent may be useful in the summer.

Italy's seas have seen a marked increase in jellyfish over the past few years. None are particularly dangerous, but a sting is painful, and can even leave weals on the skin for days. To relieve the pain and swelling, either buy an ammonia stick, which you paint on the sting, or look out for several other natural remedies now widely available.

Personal Security

Italian society is generally less violent than many northern European countries. Drinking to excess is simply not a cultural norm – Italy suffers less from alcohol abuse than anywhere else in the western world – and

so drunken violence is mercifully rare. Petty crime, however, is just as rife as in any European country, particularly in inner-city and tourist areas. The most dangerous place currently in Italy is probably down-town Naples, where even the streetwise can find their wallet, passport or mobile phone has been pickpocketed. It helps a great deal if you can avoid standing out as a tourist, especially in larger towns and cities. Avoid carrying rucksacks, bum bags and money packs, which are easy targets. Keep maps and guidebooks out of sight when on the streets and try to look as if you know where you are going.

Unless you speak good Italian, it is better to report a crime in person, rather than phoning. If you are going to claim for stolen goods on your insurance, you will need a crime report. There are two crime-fighting forces in Italy, the rivalry between whom is legendary. The *Carabinieri*, the military branch, have stations in just about every village; the civil police, *Polizia Statale*, have a station known as the *Questura*, in most sizeable towns. Either can furnish you with a crime report, but English is not always spoken.

DIRECTORY

EMBASSIES AND CONSULATES

Australian Embassy
*Via Antonio Bosio 5, 00161 Roma;
www.italy.embassy.gov.au; 06 852 721*

British Embassy
*Via XX Settembre 80a, 00187 Roma;
http://ukinitaly.fco.gov.uk;
06 4220 0001*

Canadian Embassy
*Via Zara 30, 00198 Roma;
www.canada.it; 06 8544 429 11*

Embassy of the United States
*Via Veneto 119a, 00187 Roma;
http://italy.usembassy.gov; 06 46741
(switchboard); for general enquiries
call 06 4674 2420*

HEALTH

UK Department of Health
Information for travellers
www.dh.gov.uk

Medicare Australia
Information for individuals and families
www.medicareaustralia.gov.au

Below far left Pedestrian road crossing **Below left** A public ambulance **Below middle** Police women help with directions **Below right** An unusual pharmacy sign **Below far right** Police officer directs traffic

The Telephone System

In Italy the regional phone code is an integral part of every number, and always has to be dialled. Unusually, if calling Italy from abroad, the initial zero has to be retained.

There are more mobile phones per head of population in Italy than anywhere In Europe except Finland, and many people have a couple, in case they enter an area where one provider has no coverage. Consequently public phone booths are becoming a rarity and it is hard to avoid using a mobile phone. European mobile phones will work in Italy, but Americans will need a tri-band phone. Check with your provider for roaming options, and remember that if you receive a call while abroad, you have to pay for the cost of it being routed from the caller's country to Italy.

Above Popular Italian newspapers

Logo seen on Italian public phone boxes

Security measures mean that unless you have a *codice fiscale* (tax ID number) you will not be able to activate an Italian SIM card. If you do have a *codice fiscale*, it is worth considering buying an Italian SIM card when you arrive in the country. These can cost as little as five euros, and can be recharged in amounts of €10, €20, €30 or €50 either at *tabacchi* (tobacconists) advertising a SISAL terminal (also used for registering lottery numbers) or by buying a scratchable card. The main phone operators in Italy are TIM, Vodafone, Wind and 3.

Most travellers, though, will have to content themselves with hotel and public phones. There are virtually no public phones that take coins. Instead you need to buy a phone card *(scheda telefonica)* from a newsagent or tobacconist. Do not forget to snap off the corner of the card as indicated, before inserting it into the machine. If you want to make international calls, there are several types of phone card available. The best value is the EDICARD, which is available from anywhere with a SISAL terminal. These work by dialling a free number and then inserting a 12-figure PIN number – tiresome but worth it. A €10 card should buy around 350 minutes from Italy to a landline in the UK or US.

Internet

High-speed internet (ADSL) and Wi-Fi are increasingly available, and most hotels and many cafés have somewhere you can access the net. However, for security reasons, the Italian state requires you to register before going online from a computer other than your own, whether in an internet café or the hotel in which you are staying. You will need to present some photo ID.

Post

The Italian postal system, **Poste Italiane**, is somewhat erratic. It can be marvellously efficient, but also appallingly slow at times. If something is urgent, avoid sending it registered, as registered mail tends to be amassed at the collection point before being sent on – use the postal system's courier service, *Postacelere*, or, for international deliveries, *Paccocelere*

Internazionale. The latter is cheaper and more widely available outside major cities than international operators such as **DHL**, **UPS** and **Fedex** (although the service is not offered by every post office). Stamps *(francobolli)* are on sale at post offices, tobacconists and often at many shops that sell postcards.

Banks and Money

Italy is one of the many European countries using the euro. The euro is split into 100 cents, and there are seven euro notes (€5, €10, €20, €50, €100, €200 and €500) and eight coins (€2, €1, and 50, 20, 10, 5, 2 and 1 cents).

The easiest way of getting cash is with a debit or credit card from an ATM machine (Bancomat). Most cards have a maximum withdrawal amount per day (typically €250). It is essential to inform your bank that you will be using your card abroad, as many banks have introduced increased security measures.

Many banks charge high rates for withdrawals and transactions made abroad (typically 2.5 per cent), and in the case of credit cards, interest is charged from the date of withdrawal. Debit or credit cards with a PIN are increasingly accepted at larger shops,

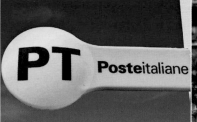

Left Regional bank of the Südtirol **Middle** Sign for a post office **Right** Modern telephone kiosks

hotels, restaurants and petrol stations, and are easy to use.

Travellers' cheques have been largely replaced by Cash Passports – a prepaid currency card that is loaded before travelling and can be used in shops and ATMs abroad. They are available from **Thomas Cook**, **Travelex** and various banks.

Banking hours in Italy are restrictive so its safest to acquire some local currency before arriving in Italy. If you want to take cash euros, you might get a better rate of exchange by using online currency operators.

Upon arrival in Italy, the best exchange rate for cash will usually be obtained at an Italian bank, but check the commission fees as they vary from bank to bank. Bureaux de change can be found in most towns, and are open all day (and in some places even late at night). Although they are easier to use, they tend to charge higher commission rates. Rates in hotels and exchange booths are rarely competitive.

General Information

Most Italian towns have a tourist information office. These can vary enormously in the service they offer. Shops are usually open Monday to Saturday 9am–1pm and 4–7pm, but many close on Saturday afternoons and Monday mornings. Most archaeological sites, museums and galleries are closed on Mondays.

Opening hours for state-run museums and most private ones are generally Tuesday to Saturday 9am until 1 or 2pm, and then for several hours in the afternoon, from any time between 3:30 and 5pm until 6–8pm, depending on the season. Sunday opening times are generally from 9am until 1pm. Many large museums now open throughout the day year round, and have late-night openings in summer (till 10pm or later Tue–Sat, or 8pm Sun). Most archaeological sites open every day, often including Sunday, from 9am until late evening – often one hour before sunset.

Time and Electricity

Like most of Europe, Italy is one hour ahead of Greenwich Mean Time (GMT), winter and summer.

Italian voltage is 220v. Plugs have either two (not earthed) or three round pins (which means they may be earthed, but not necessarily so).

Below far left One of Italy's many banks **Below left** Sign for a tourist information office **Below middle** An Italian postbox **Below right** A tobacconist's, selling stamps, SIM and phone cards

DIRECTORY

COMMUNICATIONS
Italian Post Office
www.poste.it

Directory Enquiries
1240

International Directory Enquiries
170

Operator Services
170 (also for reverse charge and calling card calls)

Italy Country Code
+39

Calling Abroad from Italy
00 followed by the country code:
UK +44, Ireland +353, USA +1, New Zealand +64, Australia +61

PRIVATE COURIERS
UPS
www.ups.com; 02 3030 3039

Fedex
www.fedex.com; 199 151 119

DHL
www.dhl.com; 199 199 345

MONEY
Thomas Cook
www.thomascook.com

Travelex
www.travelex.co.uk

TOURIST INFORMATION
Italian State Tourism Board
www.enit.it

Driving in Italy

Driving is one of the best ways of exploring the country, particularly for getting away from the crowds and reaching the more remote areas and sights. For long distances, Italy has a comprehensive motorway system, easily accessed from the rest of Europe. The condition of minor roads may vary in quality, but most are passable with care. Mountainous terrain can make for an exhilarating drive along twisty, hairpin roads, but be sure to take them at a relaxed pace.

Above Sign showing the Italian speed limits for main and secondary roads

Insurance and Breakdown Cover

In Italy it is compulsory to have third-party insurance. Check with your insurance provider that you are fully covered to drive abroad: in some cases drivers will only be covered for basic Road Traffic Accident insurance, not for theft or becoming embroiled in legal matters in the event of an accident. UK drivers can arrange full breakdown cover while abroad: some companies have a package that includes a 24-hour English language helpline.

What to Take

If you are driving your own car you should carry your vehicle insurance policy, ideally with a statement of cover in Italian (usually provided by your insurer). You will also need the vehicle registration document and a valid driving license. EU drivers need to display a country sticker on their car (unless their numberplate includes their country's euro-symbol). Also, carry spare bulbs, a warning triangle, and a high visibility jacket (to be worn if your car breaks down on a motorway and you have to leave the vehicle). The headlights of right-hand drive cars will need to be adjusted for

left-hand driving, so that the hot-spot of the beam lights up the edge of the road and does not dazzle oncoming drivers. You should also have a European Accident Statement form – if there is not one in your insurance pack, download one from www.insurance.fr/files/Accident_Form.pdf.

Road Systems

Italy was the first country in the world to build a motorway: the Autostrada dei Laghi, between Milan and Varese, was opened in 1924. It now has over 6,000 km (3,700 miles) of motorway (*autostrada*) built by both state and private companies, with several more under construction. The privately built motorways are toll roads; non toll roads are managed by ANAS. On a toll road you pick up a ticket when you enter the motorway, and pay as you exit. Tolls can be paid with cash, credit cards (Visa, Mastercard, American Express or Diners Club), or by a prepaid card called a ViaCard, available from motorway service stations and toll booth operators – worth it if you are driving in the country extensively. Validate the ViaCard at the tolls you pass so that it records your route, and pay as you exit. When you arrive at a toll station get into the correct lane,

and join the queue: for cash follow the white signs; for credit card and ViaCard look for the blue signs. A white sign displaying a couple of bank notes and coins only, is self-service; a white sign with a hand holding the bank notes means there will be an operator. Avoid the yellow telepass lanes: these are for drivers with a device in their car that registers tolls and deducts them from their bank account.

Motorway signs are green and are indicated by the letter "A" followed by a number written in white on a green background. A road prefixed with an "E" is a motorway that forms part of the pan-European system. Therefore an Italian motorway can have two numbers: say A11 and E45.

Secondary roads are known as *strada statale* (SS), *strada provinciale* (SP) or *strada comunale* (SC), which is usually very small, and maintained by the local town council. SR (rare) signifies a *strada regionale*.

There is no consistent system for the colours of roads used by different mapping companies: TCI (Touring Club Italiano, the equivalent of the AA) uses black for an *autostrada*, red for a "primary route", and yellow for everything else except the most minor roads, which are not coloured

Left Roadside mirror near Radda in Chianti **Right** Automatic lanes at a toll station on motorway

at all. The TCI also has three levels of non-asphalted roads. The AA uses red for an *autostrada*, orange for a primary route, yellow for a secondary road, and no colour for minor roads.

The privately run motorways have a website *www.autostrade.it* – get live traffic reports by clicking on a map. Note that some roads may only be named and not have a number.

Speed Limits and Fines

The speed limit for motorcycles and cars over 150cc in built-up areas is 50 km/h (30 mph). On secondary roads the limit is 90 km/h (55 mph), on main roads it is 110 km/h (70 mph) and on motorways it is 130 km/h (80 mph). Speed limits are lower if you are towing (*see p20*), or if you have held a licence for less than two years. Limits are also lower if there is fog or heavy rain.

The motorway speed limit is sometimes disregarded but speed cameras are on the increase. If you incur a fine, and are driving a rental car, the fine will go to the rental company, who will deduct the money from your credit card: speed fines can range from around €150 to over €300. Tourists who are stopped by the police for speeding may be asked to

pay 25 per cent of the total fine on the spot. A receipt will be issued.

The use of mobile phones in cars (except hands-free) is prohibited. Seat belts are compulsory for both front- and rear-seat passengers if fitted, although alarmingly, many Italians do not wear seat belts, even when driving on motorways. Never drink and drive – the alcohol limit is 0.05 per cent.

Driving with Children

Some Italians may (illegally) allow their children to ride in the car without seat belts or car seats, but it is unlikely that you will want to. Infant and child seats and booster seats can all be hired when you book your rental car. Remember to check that there is no airbag fitted if you intend to put one of your children on the passenger seat. Some companies also have portable DVD players for rent, which might make life less stressful on long journeys. Baby-changing facilities are virtually non-existent in service stations, though toys and sweets are inevitably prominently displayed in service station bars. There is unlikely to be anywhere for kids to let off steam safely at a motorway service station.

Below far left Signage in Petrolo, Siena **Below left** Filling up at a petrol station **Below middle** One-way, no parking and tow-away signs **Below** The spa town of Pré-Saint-Didier in the Valle d'Aosta **Below right** Road signage for Citerna

Left A truck negotiates the small lanes of Montisi **Right** Map of cross-country ski area, Valbruna, and signs for walking trails and historic sights

Rules of the Road

Take care to always drive on the right. Most visitors who come from a country where they drive on the left get used to it pretty quickly, but roundabouts and crossroads can be disorientating at first, as can turning from a one-way street onto a road with two-way traffic, especially if it is empty!

Italians rarely use the rear-view mirror: they concentrate on the cars in front of them and those to the side, and if there is a space in front of them, they fill it. The common wisdom that you should allow one car's length distance between vehicles for every 16 km (10 miles) per hour is never followed. Quick wits and swift reactions are a must.

Unless road signs indicate otherwise, you should give way to any vehicle joining your road from the right. On motorways and dual carriageways use dipped headlights at all times. Failing to do so can attract a hefty fine. Do not use the horn except in emergencies. This may come as a surprise in a country where weddings and football victories are celebrated by a convoy of cars sounding their klaxons. If a car flashes its headlights it is telling you to get out of its way. It is best not to argue.

The British foreign office offers advice on driving abroad on the "Know Before You Go" section of its website.

Buying Petrol

Petrol *(benzina)* stations are frequent, and most are open from early morning until lunchtime and from 3pm till around 7pm. Outside those hours you will usually find an automatic pump that functions by either credit/debit card or bank notes. Petrol stations on motorways tend to be open 24-hours a day. Unleaded petrol *(senza piombo)* is universally available, as are diesel *(gasolio)* and LPG *(PLG)*.

Road Conditions

Italy's motorways often flow freely, although rush hours and summer holidays can see the kind of long tailbacks common to most of Europe. The busiest times are at weekends in July, and at the beginning and end of August. Travel of any kind either side of the national summer holiday, Ferragosto (15 August) should be avoided at all costs. Sunday is usually a good day to travel if you have a long distance to cover, as the lorry drivers are safely at home eating lunch with their families.

Road maintenance is a major issue. Italian roads have a lot to contend with, from freezing winters in the mountains, landslide-inducing rainstorms and baking hot, tarmac-melting summers in the south, to say nothing of the roads skirting the active volcanoes of Vesuvius and Etna. "White roads", known as *strada bianche* have only a gravel surface, though these are still marked on road maps.

Mountain Roads

Reaching some of Italy's most spectacular viewpoints and mountain passes will inevitably involve tackling some steep narrow roads, hairpin bends and sheer drops, such as those on the route through the valleys of the Ortles mountain range. In spring, road surfaces may have been eroded by heavy winter snow, snow-melt and frost, and it can take some time for repairs to be undertaken, especially off the beaten track. In southern Italy there may also be cracks and fissures in the road caused by volcanic activity.

Generally, unless you are accustomed to driving in snow and ice, it is better to avoid mountain areas in the snow, especially on unfamiliar roads. In certain areas,

Left Signs for a church and palace, Malborghetto **Right** Winding mountain road between La Thuile and Col du Mont Cenis

snow chains will be recommended in mid-winter, and it would be foolish to ignore such advice. For advance weather warnings that might affect your journey always check one of the Italian weather websites such as www.meteo.it or www.ilmeteo.it.

Taking a Break

Service stations on motorways are less frequent than in the UK and other parts of Europe, so if you are getting tired, it may be worth leaving the motorway and taking a break in the nearest town or village. Italian service stations were once judged by the AA to be the worst in Europe. The most basic will have a toilet (often a sole toilet, and often less clean than you would wish) and a bar where you can get a coffee and a heated-up pre-frozen pastry or a toasted sandwich. Service stations with fast-food restaurants are on the increase, though this is not necessarily a good thing. It is probably better to bring your own food if you want to stop at a service station, and limit yourself to drinking the coffee.

Driving along the back roads, you are more likely to find a pretty village with a bar where you can have a good coffee or snack at a fair price.

Breakdown and Accidents

In the event of a breakdown or accident, switch on your hazard warning lights and place a warning triangle 50 m (160 ft) behind your car. If you do breakdown and do not have any pan-European breakdown cover you will need to call the **ACI**, the Italian Automobile Club. This service offers free tows to anyone driving in Italy with foreign numberplates. If you are in a hire car, call the rental company and follow their advice. The ACI should offer a free tow, providing you can produce your rental contract and your flight tickets. If you have pan-European cover, your provider will contact the nearest garage and make arrangements for you.

If you are involved in an accident, depending on its severity, call one of the emergency services listed in the Directory. If there is any damage to a vehicle or passengers calling the police is obligatory. You will need to fill out a **European Accident Statement** (http://european-accident-statement. accidentsketch.com) and take the contact details and vehicle registration number of any other cars involved. If you have a camera it is a good idea to take photos of the accident from all angles before any vehicles are moved.

DIRECTORY

GENERAL DRIVING INFORMATION
The AA
www.theaa.com

ACI (Italian Automobile Club)
www.aci.it

Autostrade per l'Italia
www.autostrade.it

Foreign and Commonwealth Office
www.fco.gov.uk/en/travelling-and-living-overseas/staying-safe/driving-abroad

RAC
www.rac.co.uk

Touring Club Italiano
www.touringclub.it

EMERGENCIES

Police (Carabinieri)
112

Polizia Statale
113

Fire Brigade
115

Roadside Assistance
116

Medical Emergency, Ambulance
118

Below far left Street mirror for a narrow road in Petroio, Siena **Below left** Symbol of a major petrol company, Agip **Below middle** The fertile Val d'Orcia, Tuscany **Below** Colourful street in Oneglia

Parking

Parking in an Italian town or city can demand a great deal of time and patience. When kerb space is limited, drivers tend to park everywhere and anywhere – on pavements, at bus stops or blocking private entrances. The anarchy of Italian parking notwithstanding, it is unwise to follow suit: parking attendants are on the increase, as are *zone di rimozione* (tow-away zones).

Above Camper van parked at the Rifugio Citelli in view of the summit of Etna Nord

In cities double parking is common, triple parking becoming more so, and in an attempt to reduce traffic volume several cities have introduced schemes whereby cars with even-numbered plates are allowed to drive in the city one day, those with odd-numbered plates the next. This being the case, and there being more odd-numbered days in the year than even, odd-numbered registrations are more popular. And naturally, if a family has two cars, they will ensure that one has an odd, and the other an even-numbered plate. Rental cars are currently exempt. Towns and villages popular with tourists often have a paying car park just outside the centre, and many towns now operate a colour-coded zoned parking scheme, with the type of zone indicated by the colour of the lines on the side of the road. Blue-zone parking spaces have a maximum stay of between one or two hours, and cost around €1 an hour, though they will sometimes be free after 8pm and on Sundays. There will occasionally be a meter or an attendant; at other times you need to buy a scratch card from a tobacconist. White zone areas are free, and yellow zone areas are for residents only. If there is a time limit, but no parking fee, Italian cars (including rental cars) come equipped with a mini clock dial that you set with your time of arrival and display in the window. If you do not have one, you may be able to get one from the local tourist office.

When parking, do not leave any valuables in your car and it is wise not to leave your luggage visible. Virtually all Italian cars have removable car radios, which Italian drivers inevitably take with them when they park. Secure, indoor car parks in cities are usually very expensive.

Disabled drivers displaying the new blue badge can park in designated disabled spaces.

Car Hire

All the major international car rental companies operate in Italy – such as **Avis**, **Maggiore**, **Hertz** and **Europcar**. It is worth doing an internet search before you decide who to use, as well as investigating any deals offered by your airline. Low-cost airlines have some particularly good deals. You could compare the deals you have found yourself with those of a reliable car rental broker such as **Holiday Autos** or **AutoEurope**.

To rent a car in Italy you generally need to be over 20 and to have held a full licence for one year. Be sure that your policy includes CDW, collision-damage waiver, and Theft Protection, as well as unlimited mileage. Child seats need to be booked in advance. Automatic cars are becoming more widely available with the increase of congested city centres.

You will need to produce your passport, driving licence and a credit card (from which an impression will be taken as a security deposit) when you collect the vehicle. Cars are usually supplied with a full tank of petrol, and it is wise to return it refilled, as if not, you will be charged at an inflated rate for filling the tank.

Motorbikes and Scooters

Italy is the land of the Vespa, and 10 per cent of the population have a motorbike or scooter. Two-wheel transport makes sense for navigating the labyrinth of streets that form many city centres – not designed for modern traffic. It is much easier to negotiate on two wheels than four – and you will usually find somewhere (free) to park a bike, even in the busiest city.

For keen and experienced bikers, Italy is an exhilarating country to

Left Mountain peak in France, over the border from La Thuile **Right** Reception for a camp site in Milazzo, Sicily

explore by bike, with plenty of roads twisting up and down mountains and along dramatic coastlines, unmade "white" roads to explore, and a landscape that changes constantly.

If you are on a motorbike or scooter, a helmet is compulsory for both driver and pillion, a rule now enforced with increasing frequency. A driving licence or motorbike driving licence is required for all vehicles over 49cc. Motorcycles must use dipped headlights during the day at all times.

Caravans, Motorhomes and RVs

Caravans and motorhomes are becoming increasingly popular in Italy. There is usually designated space in larger camp sites for caravans and facilities are generally good. In peak season book in advance.

In quieter areas free camping is on the increase, but overnighting wherever you feel like it, is more likely to incur local hostility. To avoid offending local sensibilities (or ruining other peoples' views) ask advice from the local traffic police (*vigili*) before parking up for the night.

The speed limit for driving with a caravan or trailer in built-up areas is 50 km/h (30 mph), on secondary and main roads it is 70 km/h (45 mph), and on motorways it is 80 km/h (50 mph).

Camper van or mobile home holidays are slowly becoming popular in Italy. Prices are usually around €1,000 for a four-berth vehicle for a week in mid-season, with unlimited mileage – companies to try include **Italy Motorhome Hire** or **Blurent**.

Maps and Satellite Navigation Devices

The best maps for long journeys and overall planning are the AA Road Atlas Italy (1:250,000) or the Touring Club Italiano Atlante Stradale d'Italia (also 1:250,000). Regional maps by Touring Club Italiano (1:200,000) are invaluable for local exploring, but even they will not have every country lane and unsurfaced track marked. Touring Club does, however, occasionally produce 1:50,000 maps of certain small areas of particular interest, such as national parks. These are rarely sold in shops, but available at park offices.

Satellite Navigation devices – such as **TomTom** or **Garmin** now come with good maps that cover Europe too. Some car rental firms often offer these devices as an extra.

DIRECTORY

CAR HIRE
AutoEurope
www.autoeurope.com

Avis
www.avis.com

Europcar
www.europcar.com

Hertz
www.hertz.com

Holiday Autos
www.holidayautos.co.uk

Maggiore
www.maggiore.com

CAMPER VAN HIRE
Italy Motorhome Hire
www.italy-motorhome-hire.com

Blurent
www.blurent.com

SATELLITE NAVIGATION DEVICES
Garmin
www.garmin.com

TomTom
www.tomtom.com

Below far left Parking signs in Panzano, Chianti **Below left** Camp site in summer **Below middle** Tourist information sign in Randazzo **Below** Iconic Italian scooter **Below right** Bicycles and signs in Parco Nazionale del Gran Paradiso, Cogne

Where to stay

Italy has some of the most memorable places to stay in Europe, ranging from grand hotels oozing *belle époque* glamour to boutique hotels on the cutting edge of contemporary design. The *agriturismo* scheme, which allowed the owners of country estates, vineyards and farms to convert historic palaces, villas and barns into rooms and apartments, and the vibrant bed-and-breakfast scene, has made it easier for visitors to avoid the impersonality of service found in so many traditional hotels and *pensioni*.

Above Balcony of Hotel Nevada, Tarvisio in Friuli-Venezia Giulia

B&Bs

Since legislation came into force allowing ordinary people to offer bed and breakfast in their homes, hundreds of "B&Bs" have opened in Italy over the last decade. The best of these can offer excellent value for money, as well as the opportunity to experience exceptional Italian hospitality, whether consisting of a couple of rooms in a simple city apartment, or a glamorous suite in a historic palace. The rule is that B&Bs should have no more than five rooms and that the owners have to live on the premises, although some establishments may not fully adhere to these rules. In the most genuine places, breakfasts are fantastic affairs, with home-made jams and cakes, fresh croissants, and fruit; in the worst, you are handed a cellophane-packed croissant and a juice box the night before.

If you are looking for a B&B on spec, ask if there are any staff on the premises, and, if not, how to contact the owner should the need arise. Also check if breakfast is served in the B&B, or whether they have an arrangement with a local café. Occasionally B&Bs may allow you free use of the kitchen.

Boutique Hotels

The international trend for boutique hotels has found fertile ground in Italy given the plethora of historic buildings as well as the Italian sense of lifestyle, food, contemporary design and hospitality. Some boutique hotels are run by hospitality-trade professionals, others by passionate newcomers, often from the worlds of architecture and design. Visitors will find plenty of boutique hotels recommended in this book, but websites such as **i-escape** and **Think Sicily** are also well worth a browse.

Hotels

Italian hotels are given an official rating of between 1 and 5 stars (though the 7-star Town House Galleria has opened in Milan – *www. sevenstarsgalleria.com*) based on a checklist of facilities, not cleanliness, charm or standards of service. The number of stars is based solely on facilities and services, such as the number of rooms with ensuite bathroom or telephone, if there is a restaurant on site, and whether there is 24-hour service. This means that the star rating is no guide to the subtler, more subjective charms of hotels, such as the style of decor or

the friendliness or helpfulness of staff. If such things are important to you, then the accommodation recommendations made in this book should guide you towards the kind of place you are looking for.

Agriturismi

The *agriturismo* scheme began in the 1980s, to enable farmers and landowners to boost falling revenues by renting out converted farm buildings to tourists. They can range from cool, state-of-the-art country hotels, to simple down-to-earth self-catering apartments. Some serve food for guests made from home-grown produce, others have full-blown restaurants. Many offer activities such as horse riding, and some have developed into little country resorts with swimming pools, tennis courts and mountain bikes to rent.

Booking

It is wise to book well in advance if you are travelling in July and August or around Easter and the various springtime public holidays. Hotels in coastal and lake resorts often close between October and Easter. Reservations can often be made online, though not all sites belonging

Left Bathing establishment along the coast near Porto Maurizio **Right** Stylish bedroom in the Hotel Greif, Bolzano, *see p54*

to individual hotels are secure, which may be a little unsettling if credit card details are requested as a guarantee. You can mimimize risk by booking over the phone or using a hotel-booking site with a secure website such as **Trip Advisor** or **i-escape**.

Facilities and Prices

Double rooms in Italian hotels usually have a double bed *(matrimoniale)* so if you prefer twin beds *(due letti)*, it is wise to request that when you book. Single rooms are rare, and you will often end up having to pay for a single-use-of-double. Bathrooms, even in 4-star hotels, do not always have bathtubs and in the cheapest hotels, bathrooms will be outside the room, and shared. Many B&Bs have rooms without an ensuite bathroom, but frequently there will be a bathroom across the corridor for your sole use.

Rates in hotels are quoted per room, and in B&Bs per person. The more expensive B&Bs will usually cost the same as a 2- or 3-star hotel, but you tend to get more for your money in terms of service and surroundings. You will often find rooms at a reduced price on the internet, at one of the accommodation broker sites or on the hotel's own website. Weekend rates in city hotels are often a bargain.

Camping

Camping is becoming increasingly popular in Italy and there are plenty of sites on the coast and in the mountains. They are usually open from April to September, though some sites stay open all year in the south and Sicily. Sites often have bungalows, sleeping up to six, if you do not have your own tent, and there is normally space for caravans and camper vans.

Self-catering

If you want to concentrate on exploring a single region of Italy, it might be worth renting a villa or rural house for a week or two. There are lovely places to be found all over Italy, ranging from simple rustic retreats and seaside apartments, to palatial places with pools, maids, chefs and masseurs. Though the widest choice can be found in Tuscany and Umbria, Puglia and Sicily have also become highly popular villa destinations, with many properties in exquisitely restored ancient country houses.

Below far left A relaxing guest lounge **Below left** Hotel room at Castel Fragsburg, Merano, *see p54* **Below middle** Doorway of a B&B in the quiet town of Castelmuzio **Below** Town Hall of Foza in the Altopiano, *see p63* **Below right** Pool and terrace of the Royal Hotel, San Remo, *see p84*

DIRECTORY

B&BS

BB Planet
www.bbplanet.it

AGRITURISMI

Official *agriturismo* **website**
www.agriturismo.it

BOUTIQUE HOTELS

i-escape
www.i-escape.com

Think Sicily
www.thinksicily.com

HOTELS & SELF-CATERING

Italy by Italy
www.italybyitaly.it

Travel Sicilia
www.travelsicilia.com

Trip Advisor
www.tripadvisor.com

CAMPING

Italian camp sites website
www.camping.it

PRICE CATEGORIES

The following price bands are based on a standard double room in high season including tax and service:

inexpensive – under €100
moderate – €100–€200
expensive – over €200

Where to eat

One of the greatest pleasures of travelling in Italy is discovering the vast variety of delicious food and wines available. Whether a sophisticated trattoria or a simple pizzeria, restaurants rarely serve anything other than Italian specialities and it is not necessary to spend a fortune to find good food. Each drive provides the chance for visitors to sample regional specialities: whether it be the fish and pine-nut delights of Liguria, the black truffles, hams and salamis of Umbria or the classic Mediterranean vegetable and lamb dishes of the south. Below is a basic guide to the typical kinds of eating places you will find in Italy.

Above Sign for a Cinque Terre restaurant offering typical seafood cuisine

Practical Information

Breakfast is usually a croissant (*cornetto*) and coffee taken in a bar. The coffee available comes in a staggering variety of modes from a short, sharp shot (*un caffè*) to long and milky (*latte macchiato*). An espresso diluted with hot water to make it resemble American filter coffee is an *Americano*, and an espresso with a blob of frothy milk is a *caffè macchiato*. In summer, there is usually iced coffee, *caffè freddo*.

The main meal is lunch, normally served in restaurants from noon until 2pm, though in summer resorts most restaurants keep their kitchens open right through to dinner. Dinner is usually served from 8pm to 10:30pm. Most restaurants are closed one day a week and display their *giorno di chiusura* in the window. In holiday resorts, restaurants are normally open between Easter and October. Outside those months, you could easily arrive and find nowhere to eat.

In cities and major towns credit cards are widely accepted, but in smaller places and in the country it is wiser to carry cash. Tax and service

are included in the bill by law, and there is often a small cover charge (*coperto*). Tipping is becoming more common and 10 per cent is usual.

Italians rarely dress down, so dressing reasonably smartly will fit the bill. Only in the most exclusive restaurants is dress formal, and men required to wear a tie and jacket. Children are welcome (and common) in restaurants, even late at night.

Meals begin with an *antipasto*, or starter, followed by the *primo*, or first course, most commonly pasta, risotto or, in winter, a *minestra* (hearty soup). The *secondo* is the meat and fish course, with the *contorno* (vegetables or salad) usually served on a separate dish alongside. Finally there is the *dolce*, or dessert. House wines can vary in quality from region to region. Local wines are always on the menu.

Ristoranti, Trattorias and Osterias

These are the three main terms for a restaurant in Italy, and until some years ago they were quite distinct. A *ristorante* was a "proper" restaurant, with linen tablecloths and waiters in

uniform. A *trattoria* was usually a more basic, homely sort of place: the menu was often scrawled on a blackboard and there were sheets of newsprint to cover the tables and on which to write the bill. *Osterias* were unpretentious country or city hostelries, offering a few cold cuts and cheese, and maybe a simple pasta dish to accompany a glass of the local wine. However, that has all changed and the choice of name for an establishment these days depends more on the tradition the place identifies with, rather than price, decor or ambience. *Ristorante* is now a neutral, generic term that could apply to anything from a Michelin-starred mecca to a seaside joint where mass-catering is the order of the day. Although there are *trattorias* and *osterias* that have existed for half a century, today the terms can as easily apply to the best restaurant in town: *trattoria* often implies an interest in reviving and reinventing traditional dishes; *osteria* that there is an emphasis on sourcing the very best primary ingredients and wines, as promoted

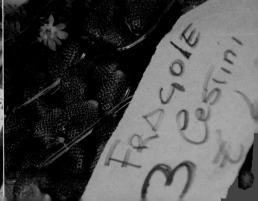

Left *Gelateria* in Nemi selling ice cream made with local strawberries **Right** Caffè degli Specchi on Piazza dell'Unità d'Italia, Trieste

by the **Slow Food movement**, and, often, a rather more minimalist/non interventionist approach to cooking.

Pizzerias

Pizzerias are found throughout the country, and, contrary to popular myth, it is only too easy to find doughy, substandard pizza. You have more chance of striking gold if you go to a pizzeria with a wood-burning oven *(forno a legna)* from which the pizzas should emerge bubbling, scorched and blistered. Pizzerias are almost always informal places, and pizza is usually only served in the evening. The classic accompaniment to pizza is a cold draught beer.

Cafés and Bars

These range from grand cafés with chandelier lit interiors and terraces fringing some of the most spectacular piazzas in Italy, to modest local bars with zinc counters, steaming coffee machines, football posters and dusty plastic flowers. These unpretentious neighbourhood bars often have standing room only and are places to come for breakfast, a quick toasted sandwich or a swift shot of coffee. Some have a few tables outside for a more leisurely breakfast or apéritif, though you should find time at least

once on your trip to dawdle over a Campari soda and olives in a traditional pavement café watching life pass by.

Picnics

There is no better way of sampling local produce than to plan a picnic. It should not be hard to find a decent delicatessen *(alimentari)* where you can buy delicacies such as rosemary-spiked hams, salamis, cured tuna and swordfish, fresh ricotta, mature gorgonzola, olives, capers and sundried tomatoes, along with a decent bakery *(il forno)*, and a greengrocer *(fruttivendolo)* or market *(mercato)* packed with seasonal fruits and vegetables.

Mountain regions often have picnic areas with massive outside grills, a great way of sampling a Chiavenna steak or a freshly caught red mullet. Look out as well for bars advertising a *tavola calda* (literally hot table). Here you can buy hot ready-prepared dishes, which will inevitably include a *pasta al forno* (oven-baked pasta).

Below far left Black truffles at the Sansepolcro market **Below left** Strawberries for sale at Nemi **Below middle** Dining in Piazza del Cisterna, San Gimignano **Below** l'Antica Bottega Food Emporium, Rocca Priora **Below right** Norcineria (a butcher's shop) in Genzano di Roma

DIRECTORY

RESTAURANT GUIDES AND ASSOCIATIONS
Gambero Rosso
www.gamberorosso.it

L'Espresso
http://espresso.repubblica.it/food

Michelin Guides and Maps
www.michelin.co.uk

Slow Food movement
www.slowfood.it

PRICE CATEGORIES

The following price bands are based on a three-course meal for one, including a half-bottle of house wine, cover charge, tax and service:

inexpensive – under €25
moderate – €25–€45
expensive over €45

THE
DRIVES

DRIVE **1**

In the Shadow of the Alps

Asti to Castello di Rivoli

Highlights

- **Gourmet Piedmont**
  Sample Barolo, the king of Italian wines, taste the famous truffles of Alba and visit Bra, the birthplace of the Slow Food movement

- **Royal Turin**
  Admire the sweeping boulevards, elegant hunting lodges and pleasure palaces of this aristocratic city

- **Strategic mountain passes**
  Walk in the footsteps of some of history's greatest armies – Hannibal, Augustus and Napoleon all marched through the Alps near Aosta

- **Paradise park**
  Explore Italy's first national park, the Parco Nazionale del Gran Paradiso, and see ibex, chamois, marmots, and magnificent golden eagles

View of the Valle d'Aosta seen en route to the Col du Mont Cenis

In the Shadow of the Alps

The rolling hillsides around Turin produce some of the world's most delectable wines and prized gourmet delicacies, such as the famous white truffle from Alba. Encircled by palaces and former hunting lodges, Turin is well-endowed with beautiful architecture as well as cutting-edge design, set against the amphitheatre of the snow-capped Alps. The tour then passes through the dramatic landscape of the Valle d'Aosta and the Gran Paradiso – the highest mountain entirely within Italy – to the spectacular Monte Bianco ("white lady"), Europe's loftiest peak, and to the towns at her feet.

Above Driving cows along the winding road from La Thuile to Col du Mont Cenis, *see p38*

0 kilometres 20

0 miles 20

ACTIVITIES

Follow the gourmet trail around the truffle areas of Alba and the winelands of Barolo and Asti

Ride up to the top of Turin's iconic Mole Antonelliana to view the towering mountains backing the city

Discover a wilderness paradise in Italy's first national park, the Gran Paradiso

Hike in the mountains and then take a chairlift or cable car from Courmayeur or La Thuile up to the highest peaks in Europe

Take the healthy waters in the thermal spa town of Pré-Saint-Didier

Follow in the footsteps of Hannibal and his elephants on the border between Italy and France

KEY

🚗 Drive route

Below Stunning green and fertile farmlands in the Valle d'Aosta, *see pp36–7*

Above Remains of an aqueduct, some of the remarkable Roman ruins at Susa, *see p39*

PLAN YOUR DRIVE

Start/finish: Asti to Castello di Rivoli.

Number of days: 5 – allowing half a day to explore Turin.

Distance: 680 km (422 miles).

Road conditions: Generally well paved and signposted but there is steep terrain in the Valle d'Aosta, which is often snowbound in winter; drivers are required to have winter tyres fitted and carry snow chains Jun–Oct. Col d'Isardo closed Oct–Jun.

When to go: The winter months are cold and prone to high snowfall, especially in the Valle d'Aosta area. Late spring and autumn are the most comfortable months for travelling.

Opening times: Shops tend to open Mon–Sat 9am–1pm and 4–7:30pm or 8pm (some shops are shut Mon am or Wed pm, but city supermarkets often stay open for the siesta). Churches and museums are usually open 8 or 9am–noon and 4–7 or 8pm. Many museums are closed on Mondays.

Main market days: Turin: Porta Palazzo, Mon–Fri am & Sat all day; Aosta: Piazza Cavalleri di Vittorio Veneto, Tue.

Shopping: Gourmet produce such as nougat, mushrooms and truffles, cheeses made from mountain milk and, of course, wine. Other good buys include textiles in Biella and cuckoo clocks in Aosta and the mountain areas.

Major festivals: Asti: Wine fair and Palio, Sep; **Alba:** White Truffle fair, Oct; **Turin:** Cultural heritage week, Apr; Classical music festival, Sep; Slow Food fair, Oct (biannually); Luci d'Artisa illuminations Nov–Jan.

DAY TRIP OPTIONS

Those interested in architecture will find a treasure trove to explore in **Turin** with the works of Baroque architect Juvarra, and impressive museums and churches. **Outdoor enthusiasts** can take the **mountain air** in historic **Aosta**; see the fantastical castle at **Fénis** and enjoy the natural glory of the **Parco Nazionale del Gran Paradiso**. For full details, *see p39*.

Above Romanesque-Gothic style Cattedrale di Santa Maria Assunta, Asti

WHERE TO STAY

ASTI

Hotel Aleramo *moderate*
Attractive hotel with emphasis on contemporary design where the 43 rooms are pleasingly decorated.
Via Emanuele Filiberto 13, 14100; 0141 595 661; closed 3 wks Aug

AROUND ALBA

Hotel Agriturismo Villa La Meridiana Ca' Reiné *inexpensive*
Attractive Liberty-style villa set in peaceful grounds with great views over the Colline delle Langhe. In autumn, truffle hunts can be organized and "grape cures" and wine tastings enjoyed during the harvest.
Localita Altavilla 9, 12051 (1 km/ ½ mile east of Alba along Viale Cherasca); 0173 440 112

AROUND POLLENZO AND BRA

Hotel Albergo dell'Agenzia *moderate–expensive*
Conveniently located for Bra, the hotel has 47 stylishly decorated and comfortable rooms. There is a good restaurant, too, specializing in seasonal and local produce.
Via Fossano 21 (2 km/1 mile southwest of Pollenzo on Via Einaudi, SP7); 0172 458 600; www.albergoagenzia.it

① Asti
Asti, Piemonte; 14100
This city of narrow streets, medieval towers and graceful churches is primarily famous as the home of Asti Spumante – the sweet fizzy wine from Moscato grapes. But wine-lovers will find there is more to Asti than just Spumante, as the town is at the heart of Italy's most important wine-making region. Every September the local Wine Fair here is accompanied by the Palio d'Asti in Piazza Alfieri, when the town resounds to the thundering of horses' hooves in a daredevil race with feats of extraordinary horsemanship. The 14th-century **Cattedrale di Santa Maria Assunta** *(open daily)* has some remarkable 17th-century frescoes and a lovely portico of brick and tufa. Asti's most central car park is at Piazza Vittorio Alfieri.

🚗 *Follow the SS231 (Corso Savona) south, then take the A33, returning to the SS231 to reach Alba Centro. Park in Piazza Giuseppe Garibaldi.*

② Alba
Cuneo, Piemonte; 12051
Set in the vine-covered hills of Le Langhe, Alba was a Roman town that became powerful in the Middle Ages. Today it is a quiet country town, which bursts into life in October/ November during the market for Alba's highly prized white truffles. On the site of the old Roman forum, the Piazza Risorgimento is dominated by the Lombard-Gothic **Cattedrale di San Lorenzo** *(open daily)*. Its façade is decorated with the symbols of the four Evangelists – Matthew, Mark,

Luke and John. Their respective symbols – *angelo* (angel), *leone* (lion), *bue* (ox) and *aquila* (eagle) – make up the name of the town ALBA. Via Vittorio Emanuele II is the main street, full of shops selling delicacies such as truffles, oils, salami, wines, cheeses and, of course, chocolates: the Ferrero Rocher factory is nearby.

🚗 *Follow Viale Torino to join the SP3bis, signposted Barolo, Grinzane Cavour. Park by the castle.*

③ Grinzane Cavour
Cuneo, Piemonte; 12060
Set on a hill, Grinzane's main sight is the **Castello di Grinzane Cavour** *(open Wed–Mon)*. This medieval castle was the former country mansion of the Count of Cavour, one of the leading figures in the movement towards Italian Unification in the 19th century. The Mask Room is worth a visit for its portraits and fantasy monsters and the Ethnographic Museum showcases some of Cavour's belongings. There is also information on the local wines and the white truffle – the castle is the site of the autumn auction (invitation only), when huge sums of money are exchanged. However, the Enoteca Regionale Piemontese Cavour (also within the castle) has an excellent wine cellar, open to all. For those with a sweet tooth, **Gallo**, the more industrial lower town, is Piedmont's largest producer of nougat (*torrone*). Try the **Gallo Wine Gallery** *(Via XX Settembre 3, La Morra; 0173 509 838)* for great nougat, wine and goodies.

🚗 *Continue southwest on the SP3 to Barolo.*

Right Medieval Castello di Grinzane Cavour is the town's principal site

4 Barolo

Cuneo, Piemonte; 12060

Surrounded by vine-cloaked slopes and medieval fortresses, Barolo is home to one of Italy's best red wines. The story of Barolo began at the **Castello dei Marchesi Falletti di Barolo** (open M–Wed). This castle, dating back to the 10th century, was the home of the Falletti family, the last of whom was the Marquesa Juliette Colbert. As well as helping the poor, she, along with compatriot Louis Oudart, applied French vinification expertise to the local wine. She then presented the resulting wines in oak casks to King Carlo Alberto to his great pleasure – and it became the "wine of kings and the king of wines". There is an *enoteca*.

🚗 *From Via Roma turn left on SP3 signed La Morra, right on SP3, at roundabout take 1st exit, SP58 to La Morra, and follow signs to Pollenzo/Bra on SP58 and SP7. After Pollenzo, turn left on SS231 to Bra.*

Barolo Wine

The king of Italian red wines, Barolo is made from the prized Nebbiolo grape with its raspberry and violet scents. After maturing for at least three years, and often much longer, the wine is powerful, complex and expensive. Barolo's best vintages are 1995 (rare), 1996 and 1997, with 2000 and 2001 also being good years.

5 Pollenzo and Bra

Cuneo, Piemonte; 12060

Lying midway between Cuneo and Turin, Bra and Pollenzo are at the edge of the Colline delle Langhe, close to the Tanaro river. Bra is the birthplace of the Slow Food movement (founded in 1986 by Carlo Petrini), dedicated to countering the global spread of fast food. In 2003 the movement founded the **University of Gastronomic Science** *(Piazza Vittorio Emanuele II)* at Pollenzo. It is the first institution to treat food and drink as an academic discipline, with degree courses on educating the palate. The campus is a restored palazzo, and the town is worth a look for the Baroque **Chiesa di Sant'Andrea e Santa Chiara** with its lovely Rococo façade designed by Bernardo Antonio Vittone (1748). Look out for the Roman baths and amphitheatre.

🚗 *From Bra take SS231, then SS661 to A6 towards Torino. Take the Tangenziale Sud A55, then take the exit for Stupinigi.*

6 Palazzina di Caccia di Stupinigi

Piazza Principe Amedeo 7, Nichelino; 10042

Recognizable by the stag icon on the central copper dome, this was the favourite hunting lodge of the Savoys – a rich family, originally from the Swiss Alps, who went on to rule Italy. Designed by Filippo Juvarra in the Rococo style, the lodge is more like a palace, in huge grounds with roaming deer, and is reached by a grand, tree-lined avenue. The **Museo di Storia, Arte e Ammobiliamento** (Museum of History, Art and Interior Design) *(closed Mon)* features exquisite frescoes, chandeliers and marquetry. The Hall of Mirrors (Saletta degli Specchi) has Turin's first marble bath, owned by Napoleon's sister, Paolina Borghese.

🚗 *Head northeast on the SS23/Viale Torino. Follow Corso Unione Sovietica to "centro". Park under Piazza Vittorio.*

Above left Medieval town of Barolo **Above right** Rococo Palazzina di Caccia di Stupinigi

Below (clockwise from top left) The grand Piazza San Carlo; the Roman Palatine Gate; former bedroom in the Palazza Madama; exterior of the Palazza Madama in the Piazza Castello; dome of the Chiesa di San Lorenzo

❼ Turin
Torino, Piemonte; 10100

It put the "T" into Fiat (*Fabbrica Italiana Automobili Torino*) and the "Italian" into the classic car film *The Italian Job,* but there is more to Turin (Torino) than cars. With the Alps as a glorious backdrop, it has squares, palaces, castles and boulevards fit for a king. Indeed, it was the first capital of the Kingdom of Italy (1861). Today, it is the country's design and contemporary art capital. And, for a taste of the *dolce vita*, Turin is a gourmet paradise, and the birthplace of Italian cinema.

A three-hour walking tour

From Piazza Vittorio Veneto, walk up the Via Po to the centre of town. The porticoes on the way give relief from the heat – or rain. Turn right into Via Montebello to reach the unmissable **Mole Antonelliana** ①. Topped with a 167-m (550-ft) spire, this is a symbol of the city and home to the excellent **Museo Nazionale del Cinema** *(closed Mon)*. The Italian film industry was born in Turin and it was the film production capital of the world 1906–16. The museum re-creates the story of cinema with many classic film clips, including the car chase in *The Italian Job* and plenty of props. Do not miss a ride in the glass lift to the viewing platform on the spire for fabulous views over the city towards the white peaks of the Alps. Next, turn right and

Madonna and child, Palazzo Madama

then left into the wide Corso San Maurizio and left into the Giardino Reale. Continue through the park to the far corner and the **Palazzo Reale** ② *(closed Mon)*. This is one of Turin's most splendid Baroque buildings, dating to the 1640s, and was the official Savoy residence. The opulent interior is graced with chandeliers and chinoiserie, frescoes, gold, velvet and tapestries. Next door to the palace is the Piazza Castello, at the heart of which is the Palazzo Madama which houses the **Museo Civico d'Arte Antica** ③ *(closed Mon)*. Highlights include Roman foundations in the basement, Juvarra's sinuous staircase and atrium, and *The Portrait of a Man* by Antonella da Messina (1476). Two of Turin's most famous cafés are in the piazza – Baratti & Miliano, and Mulassano – both are atmospheric and delightful.

Above Elegant colonnaded walkway along Via Roma, Turin

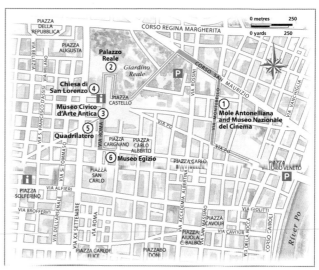

On the western corner of Piazza Castello stands the **Chiesa di San Lorenzo** ④ *(open daily).* Although plain on the exterior, inside it is a Baroque fantasy of sculptures, stucco, gilding and marble. There is also a full-size replica of the Turin Shroud *(Sindone)* – supposedly the sheet in which Christ's body was wrapped after his crucifixion (the original is in the Duomo). Walk west from the piazza to the **Quadrilatero** ⑤ – the gridded area that recalls the old Roman settlement. The cobbled streets are full of bars and cafés as well as markets and historic churches. Return to Piazza Castello and walk down Via Roma and, close to Piazza San Carlo, turn right into the Via Accademia delle Scienze and the **Museo Egizio** ⑥ *(Egyptian Museum: open Tue–Sun).* Highlights include its collection of papyri, a black granite statue of Ramses II (13th century BC), many sarcophagi and mummies and the tomb of Kha and Merit (c.1430 BC), complete with furniture and vases of food and unguents for the afterlife.

🚗 *From Piazza Vittorio Veneto, cross Ponte Vittorio Emanuele I, turn left onto Corso Casale, right at Strada Comunale di Superga, left at Piazzale Alberto Geisser and onto Strada Comunale della Basilica di Superga.*

⑧ Basilica di Superga
Torino, Piemonte; 10020
This grandiose mausoleum, holding the tombs of over 50 members of the Savoy family, is spectacularly perched on a hill, visible for miles around – its magnificent dome is 65 m (215 ft) high. Duke Vittorio Amedeo engaged

Filippo Juvarra to build it in 1717 after defeating an invading French army in 1706. In the grounds, a large plaque commemorates the tragic loss of the Grande Torino football team, when their plane crashed into the hillside in 1949. There is a museum, Museo del Grande Torino, displaying the team's memorabilia. The Basilica is open daily.

It is also possible to take the funicular from Sassi station (just below) up to the Basilica, which is always popular with children.

🚗 *Head west to pick up SS590/Via Torino, then SS11 through Chivasso to Cigliano, then the SS593 to Cavaglia and SR143 to Biella.*

EAT AND DRINK IN TURIN

L'Osteria del Corso *inexpensive*
Simple, good family-run fish place. Good-value lunch buffet.
Corso Regina Margherita 252/b, 10144; 011 480 665; www.osteriadelcorso.it; closed Sun

C'era Una Volta *moderate*
Welcoming restaurant with local fare and an excellent *menu degustazione.*
Corso Vittorio Emanuele II 41, 10125; 011 655 498; www.ristorantecerauna volta.it; dinner only; closed Sun

Ristorante del Cambio *expensive*
Turin's most famous restaurant serves authentic *bollito misto* – a mix of cooked meats. Booking essential.
Piazza Carignano 2, 10123; 011 546 690; www.ristorantedelcambio.it; closed Sun

Above The Basilica di Superga, built to commemorate the liberation of Turin from the French

Eat and Drink: inexpensive, under €25; moderate, €25–€45; expensive, over €45

Above The fortress Il Melograno, Issogne, originally built in 1480

WHERE TO STAY

AOSTA

Hotel Europe *moderate*
Set in the heart of the old town, this comfortable hotel *albergo* is both elegant and welcoming. Its 63 rooms are decorated to a high standard and there is a pleasant restaurant. *Piazza Narbonne 8, 11100; www.hoteleuropeaosta.it; 0165 236 363*

AROUND AOSTA

Agriturismo l'Arc en Ciel *inexpensive*
This genuine farm has five pleasingly furnished rooms. Home-grown produce is served in the fine restaurant. Extremely good value. *Frazione Vert 5, Sarre; 11010 (Leave Aosta on Via des Régions and follow signs to Frazione Vert, 7 km/4 miles west); 0165 257 843; www.agriturismelarcenciel.it*

COGNE

La Madonnina del Gran Paradiso *inexpensive–moderate*
A family-run small and welcoming hotel set in a panoramic position on the mountainside. Its 22 rooms are clad in pine and there is a warming, wood-burning oven in the restaurant. *Via Laydetré 7, 11012; 0165 740 78; www.lamadonnina.com*

⑨ Biella

Biella, Piemonte; 13900
At the centre of "Textile Valley", Biella is famous as a major centre for high-quality wool and yarn production, and Italian designer names such as Zegna and Loro Piana have close links with the town. More than 50 factory outlets line the industrial approach roads – many of which are on the SS230 – look for *spaccio* on signs, meaning "outlets". There are also outlets in Biella *(see right)*. The town has a compact, attractive centre and highlights include the Renaissance basilica and cloister of **St Sebastian**, with lovely frescoes inside. A funicular goes up to the beautiful medieval village of Piazzo.

🚗 **Head southwest, then take the SS338/Via Ivrea and turn right on the SS419. Fork right on SP73, then the SP72 to the SS26 before turning off onto the SR4 to Issogne.**

⑩ Issogne

Aosta, Valle d'Aosta; 11020
The Valle d'Aosta is full of castles and medieval forts. Many were pure fortresses, while others were more palatial, such as **Il Melograno** *(open daily)*. More château than fort, its name comes from the fountain in the courtyard with an iron pomegranate tree *(Il Melograno)*. Much restored over the years, it has vivid frescoes of 15th-century street life, along with period furniture and artifacts. Nearby, the village Champdepraz (just north on the A5) is the access point for the **Parco Naturale del Mont Avic** *(open daily; www.montavic.it)* whose lakes, marshes and Alpine bogs are home

Piedmontese fare

Local cuisine matches robust flavours with French flair, reflecting the area's relationship with the House of Savoy. The woods, especially near Alba, are truffle- and mushroom-rich and any dish with *salsa di tartufi bianchi* will be a delicious. *Bagna cauda* is a warm, aromatic dip made with oil, anchovies, garlic and cream. Blue gorgonzola is the best known cheese – *dolce* (creamy) or *piccante* (slightly tangy), but look for soft cheeses, too, such as *caprini, fontina,* and *raschera,* made with goat, sheep and cow's milk. Fondue *(fonduta)* is often made with *fontina* – delicious with Alba's white truffles.

to nearly 1,000 species of flowers which attract clouds of butterflies.

🚗 **Head north, signposted Champdepraz , turn right at SR6, left at SS26 towards Aosta and follow signs to Chambave-Fénis.**

⑪ Fénis

Aosta, Valle d'Aosta; 11020
The most famous and spectacular of all the castles in the Valle d'Aosta is the **Castello di Fénis** *(open: Mar–Sep, daily; Oct–Feb, Wed–Mon)*. Set on a grassy knoll, backed by a chestnut forest, it is every inch a fairytale medieval castle, bristling with towers and turrets, keeps and crenellations. Its origins date to the 13th century, but what is visible today is largely the 1340 creation of Aimone de Challant, who belonged to a noble family linked to the Savoys. It has a pentagonal layout and the keep is enclosed by a double perimeter wall, with watchtowers linked by a walkway. The inner courtyard has a

Above The remarkably well-preserved Castello di Fénis, watching over the Val d'Aosta

Where to Stay: inexpensive, under €100; moderate, €100–200; expensive, over €200

semicircular staircase and wooden balcony, decorated with exquisite frescoes of Saint George killing the dragon and a group of wise men and prophets, holding scrolls. There is also a small museum of local furniture inside.

🚗 *Take the SR13, then left onto the SS26 west to Aosta. There is a car park at Piazza Arco d'Augusto.*

⑫ Aosta
Aosta, Valle d'Aosta; 11100

Named after Emperor Augustus, Aosta was once a mini-Rome in the centre of its own valley and is the regional capital. The triumphal Arco d'Augusto now sits on a traffic island and from it runs the Roman Via Sant' Anselmo, a pedestrian precinct. To the right, outside the city walls, is an impressive series of ancient church buildings around the **Collegiata di Sant'Orso** *(open daily)*, dedicated to the patron saint of Aosta. Sant'Orso itself has a Gothic (15th-century) façade, a 12th-century Romanesque bell tower and elegant cloister. At the end of the Via Sant'Anselmo, where all kinds of souvenirs can be purchased – from cuckoo clocks to local gourmet delights – is the Porta Praetoria, the two thick, arched walls forming the impressive stone entrance to the city. Inside, on the right, lie the remains of a Roman theatre *(open daily)*. Just to the north, accessed through the Convento di San Giuseppe, is the **Amphitheatre** *(open daily)*. In the old town, the Cattedrale in Piazza Giovanni XXIII dates from the 12th century and contains within it some of the best Christian art treasures from the area in the **Museo del Tesoro** *(open Sat & Sun 3–5:30pm)*. Next to the cathedral is the Roman Forum with a supporting arcade *(cryptoporticus)*.

🚗 *Leave Aosta on the SS26 and bear left onto the SR47 heading south to Cogne.*

⑬ Cogne
Aosta, Valle d'Aosta; 11012

This is an excellent base for exploring the **Parco Nazionale del Gran Paradiso**, Italy's first national park. Originally a Savoy hunting reserve, 21 sq km (5,200 acres) were donated by King Vittorio Emanuele III in 1929 to form the present park. Today, it is home to endangered ibex, and to chamois, marmots, ptarmigans and golden eagles. Maps of the footpaths and routes are available from the tourist information centre, *(Via Bourgeois 34, 11012; 0165 74040)*. A path meanders south to Valnontey where the **Giardino Alpino Paraseia** *(1st Sat Jun–1st Sat Sep: open daily)* has a fine collection of more than 1,000 species of Alpine flora. The best time to see these is from late June to mid-July.

🚗 *Head northeast on SR47, then turn left onto the SS26. This road becomes the Avenue du Géant (Champex) leading into Courmayeur.*

Above left Near the Parco Nazionale del Gran Paradiso, Cogne **Above right** Bikes – a favourite way to explore Aosta's national park

EAT AND DRINK

AOSTA

Vecchio Ristoro *expensive*
This Michelin-starred restaurant is centrally located and combines rustic charm with elegant dining. Chef Alfio Fascendini is a master of innovation and seasonal specialities.
Via Tourneuve 4, 11100; 0165 33 238; www.ristorantevecchioristoro.it; closed Sun, Mon lunch, June

COGNE

Lou Ressignon
inexpensive–moderate
Well-established family-run inn specializing in authentic Valdostano specialities. At weekends, music complements feasting. Also has rooms.
Via des Mines 23, 11012; 0165 74034; www.louressignon.it; closed Mon, Tue (low season), May, Nov

Bar a Fromage *moderate*
Splendid little restaurant with a warm, intimate atmosphere where cheese is definitely king. Visitors can also buy some excellent produce in the shop.
Rue Grand Paradis 22, 11012; 0165 749 696; closed Thu

SHOPPING IN BIELLA

While there are many outlets just outside town, within Biella itself is **Fratelli Cerruti** *(Via Cernaia 40; open daily)*, selling men and women's classic clothes with 30 per cent plus discount, and sportswear specialist **Fila** *(Via Cesare Battisti 28, closed Mon am)*

Far left Glorious Romanesque fresco in Aosta's cathedral **Left** A *salumeria* packed full of treats on Via Sant'Anselmo, Aosta

Above Climbers traversing an icy path in the mountains, Courmayeur **Above right** Museo Alpino Duca degli Abruzzi, Courmayeur

VISITING COURMAYEUR

Parking
There is a large car park by the cable car to Plan Checrouit, on the southern edge of town.

Tourist Information
Piazzale Monte Bianco 8, 11100; 0165 842 060; www.regione.vda.it/turismo

WHERE TO STAY

COURMAYEUR

Hotel Auberge de la Maison
moderate
Warm and welcoming, this homely mountain hotel and restaurant is rustically decorated. There are 33 individually designed rooms, together with a sauna, solarium and Turkish baths. The restaurant is noted for its excellent food and service.
Via Passerin d'Entreves 16, 11013 (4 km/ 7 miles north of Courmayeur); 0165 869811; www.aubergemaison.it

Grand Hotel Royal e Golf *expensive*
Set on the main street of Courmayeur, this prestigious hotel is noted for its charm and good service. There is a small wellness centre with swimming pool and solarium and splendid views of Monte Bianco. There is also a very pleasant restaurant.
Via Roma 87, 11013; 0165 831611; www.hotelroyalegolf.com

⑭ Courmayeur
Aosta, Valle d'Aosta; 11100
In the majestic shadow of Monte Bianco (Mont Blanc), Courmayeur is a popular year-round resort and a joy to explore. The main hub, Via Roma, is traffic free and full of designer shops and gourmet gems. The **Museo Alpino Duca degli Abruzzi** *(Piazza Abbé Henry 2; 0165 842 064; closed Wed am)* tells tales of dramatic mountain rescues. Just north of Courmayeur at Entrèves, a cable car leads to Punta Helbronner – at 3,462 m (11,360 ft) the views are literally breathtaking.
🚌 *Take the SS26 to Pré-Saint-Didier.*

⑮ Pré-Saint-Didier
Aosta, Valle d'Aosta; 07021
At just over 1,000 m (3,280 ft) high, the picturesque village Pré-Saint-Didier is famous for its warm thermal waters. The spring is at a constant 36°C (98°F) at the point where the River Thuile forces its way through the narrow gorge into the Dora Valley. There is a well-known spa in the town **Allée des Thermes Pré-Saint-Didier** *(0165 867 272; open daily)*. The waters are said to have detoxifying, toning and anti-inflammatory properties.

Nearby **La Thuile** (reached via the SS26; closed in winter) was once a mining area and is now a picturesque skiing and hiking town, and more of a family resort than chic Courmayeur. In summer chairlifts allow access to heights of 2,400 m (7,900 ft) for some spectacular walking and trekking.
🚌 *Take the SS26, entering France on the D1090. Take the D84, then D902 past Val d'Isere, followed by the D1006 to Col du Mont Cenis. (Use the Fréjus tunnel in winter).*

⑯ Col du Mont Cenis
Lanslebourg-Mont-Cenis, 73480; France
Col du Mont Cenis (Cenisio in Italian) is a 2,084-m (6,831-ft) high mountain pass in the Alps on the French-Italian border. It was an important invasion route and Napoleon I built a road there in 1810. It is also believed by some to have been Hannibal's pass when he marched his army and elephants over the Alps against Rome during the Second Punic War (218– 203 BC). The picturesque Lac du Mont Cenis is frozen usually until the end of May. The **Jardin Alpin** *(open daily)* has over 120 flower species.
🚌 *Take the D1006 south. Enter Italy following the SS25, then SS24 to Exilles.*

⑰ Exilles
Torino, Piemonte; 10050
Overlooking the Valle di Susa, the little medieval town Exilles is spectacularly located and dominated by a splendid fort. **Exilles Fort** *(Via degli Alpini; 0122 58270; closed Mon)* is not only one of the oldest monuments of the valley, but is also a great example of military architecture. A fort has kept watch over this passage between France

Right Lac du Mont Cenis on a key invasion route in Italian history **Far right** The French-sounding Italian skiing village of La Thuile

Where to Stay: inexpensive, under €100; moderate, €100–200; expensive, over €200

and Italy since the 12th century, although what is visible today is mainly from the 19th century. It is said that from 1681–87, the "Man in the Iron Mask", a prisoner whose face and identity remain a mystery to this day, was incarcerated within these walls. Many have theorized as to his identity, most famously Alexander Dumas who postulated that he was Louis XIV's identical twin brother. Highlights include the Knights' Courtyard and the Staircase of Paradise leading to the Prison Courtyard. The fort's museum charts its long history and the story of Italy's Alpine troops. From the roof there are splendid views of the upper Valle di Susa.

🚗 *Take the SS24 heading northeast.*

⑱ Susa

Torino, Piemonte; 10059
Known in Roman times as Segusium, Susa is a pretty mountain town with much evidence of its earlier existence. In the old town, at Piazza Savoia, the Porta Savoia gateway dates originally from the 4th century AD, although it was reconstructed in the Middle Ages. There is also a **Roman amphitheatre** *(open daily)*, aqueduct arches and the remains of some Roman baths. The remarkably well-preserved marble triumphal Arco di Augusto (Arch of Augustus) was built in the first century BC by Gallic chieftain Cottius to commemorate the alliance with the ruling Romans. In the medieval historic centre, the Romanesque **Cattedrale di San Giusto** *(open daily)*, dating from the 12th century, has lovely frescoes and a fine campanile. The town is noted, too, for its shops full of gourmet delights.

🚗 *Head north, turn right onto SS25, signposted Avigliana, then Rivoli. Follow signs to car park at Castello.*

⑲ Castello di Rivoli

Rivoli, Piemonte; 10098
Set on a hill with splendid views, this castle was one of the Savoys' country residences. It is an imposing Baroque building bearing the classical French trademark style of master architect Filippo Juvarra *(see pp34–5)*. Inside, the **Museo d'Arte Contemporanea** *(closed Mon)* has works by Gilbert and George and Jeff Koons, while Maurizio Cattelan's stuffed horse is suspended from the ceiling – making a dramatic and inspiring contrast between modern and ancient. The museum often has excellent temporary exhibitions and there is a good café, as well as the highly acclaimed cuboid Combal.Zero restaurant.

Above left The honeycomb façade of the 4th-century Porta Savoia, Susa **Above** The fort of Exilles, strategically located in the Valle di Susa **Below** In the Museo d'Arte Contemporanea, Castello di Rivoli

EAT AND DRINK

SUSA

Zizi
This shop offers free tastings and low-price local alcoholic beverages. Established in 1945, the shop draws customers from all over the area. *Corso Inghilterra 52, 10059; 0122 622 717; closed Sun*

CASTELLO DI RIVOLI

Combal.Zero *expensive*
Michelin-starred restaurant in the Museum of Contemporary Arts, featuring classic Piemonte dishes but with very creative twists – a variant of molecular gastronomy – under the expert eye of chef Davide Scabin. Traditional meets ultra-modern. *Museo d'Arte Contemporanea, Piazza Mafalda di Savoia, 10098; 011 956 5225; www.combal.org; dinner only; closed Sun and Mon*

DAY TRIP OPTIONS

For visitors based in Turin the first trip makes a good day out, whilst for those based in Aosta, the amazing mountain scenery is easy to explore.

Baroque architecture tour
In Turin ⑦, see the beauty of the work of the great Baroque architect Filippo Juvarra (1678–1736) in his façade and staircase for the Palazzo Madama, as well as the other architectural and historical sights of the city. Then head out to the grand hunting lodge Palazzina di Caccia di Stupinigi ⑥ and the magnificent Castello di Rivoli ⑲ – filled with thought-provoking modern art.

Head south on the SS23 to Stupinigi. Then take the E70 north (Tangenziale Sud) turning left on to the SP7 to Castello.

Art and castles in paradise
Based in Aosta ⑫ take a trip to the fairytale castle in Fénis ⑪. Next head to Cogne ⑬ to visit Parco Nazionale del Gran Paradiso for an invigorating walk amongst breath-taking scenery.

Aosta is located on the SS26. For Fénis take the SS26 and SR13. To get to Cogne take the SS26 and then the SR47.

The Northern Lakes

Stresa to AlagnaValsesia

Highlights

- **Palatial splendour**
  Be entranced by the palaces and
  gardens of Isola Bella and Isola Madre
  and pretty little Isola Superiore

- **Jewels of Lago d'Orta**
  Wander around the lovely medieval
  town of Orta San Giulio and its
  enchanted island, Isola di San Giulio

- **Heavenly ascent**
  Admire the 45 chapels of the region's
  oldest *sacro monte* at Varallo – now a
  UNESCO World Heritage Site

- **Land of the Walsers**
  Explore these high-altitude villages
  where German is still spoken and
  traditional customs are maintained

View of Lake Maggiore from the Giardino
Alpino, Monte Mottarone

The Northern Lakes

Snaking through the lakes and mountains of Piedmont, the route starts at Stresa on Lake Maggiore, a genteel resort whose streets are lined with Art Nouveau buildings, overlooking the enchanting Isole Borromee. Nearby the gardens of Villa Pallavicino and Villa Taranto are botanical delights and the panoramic view from the top of Monte Mottarone should be savoured. Continue then to the jewel-like Orta San Giulio, following the "Way of Silence" on the town's own little island in the midst of Lago d'Orta. The route continues to Varallo, site of the amazing UNESCO World Heritage Sacro Monte high on the hillside, before heading up through Walser country to picturesque Alagna dotted with traditional wooden houses.

ACTIVITIES

Stroll along the waterfront in Stresa

Take a boat trip to the three wonderful Isole Borromee from Stresa

Pet and feed the goats in the lovely gardens and zoo at the Parco della Villa Pallavicino

Take the cable car from Stresa to Monte Mottarone for gardens, stupendous views and pleasant walks

Wander the winding medieval alleys of flower-filled Orta San Giulio

Go shopping in the Alessi factory outlet, north of Lago d'Orta to bag some designer household articles

Walk the trails of the Walsers in the Valsesia

Above Walser house in Alagna with balconies for drying crops, see p47 **Right** Façade of the basilica at Varallo, see p47, the most famous Sacro Monte sight

KEY

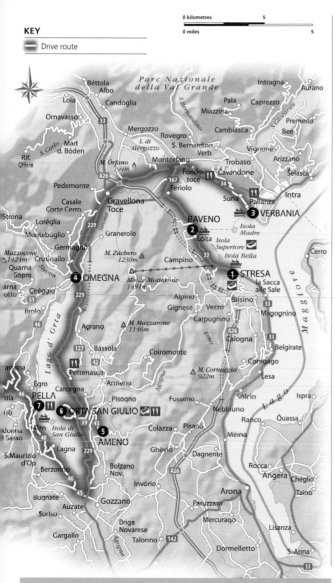

Drive route

0 kilometres   5

0 miles   5

PLAN YOUR DRIVE

Start/finish: Stresa to Alagna Valsesia.

Number of days: 3 days.

Distance: Approx. 119 km (74 miles).

Road conditions: Generally good with some steep terrain around Alagna. The scenic roads at lakes Maggiore and Orta can get very busy in high season.

When to go: May, June and September are ideal months. July and August are busy and best avoided. Alagna's roads are prone to high snowfall in winter.

Opening times: Shops tend to open Mon–Sat 9am–1pm and 4–7pm or 8pm (city supermarkets often stay open for the siesta). Churches and museums vary enormously but usually open 8 or 9am–noon and 4–7 or 8pm. Many museums are closed on Mondays.

Main market days: Stresa: Fri; Verbania: Sat; Omegna: Thu; Orta San Giulio: Wed.

Shopping: There are boutiques in Stresa near Piazza Cadorna and local gourmet treats in Orta San Giulio, near the main piazza. Omegna's centre has some good shops, however, most visitors to the area are drawn to the town's factory outlets of designer kitchenware and those in nearby Crusinallo. Look out for woodcarving around Pettenasco, just to the north of Orta San Giulio.

Major festivals: Stresa: Settimane Musicali, classical music from Jul–Sep (www.settimanemusicali.net); **Pallanza:** Camellia Festival, Apr; **Orta San Giulio:** World Fireworks Championship, last two weeks of Aug.

DAY TRIP OPTIONS

Spend a day exploring **Stresa's** sights and the beautiful **Isole Borromee** of **Lake Maggiore**. Or enjoy Ameno's **art museum**, beautiful **Orta San Giulio** and calm **Isola di San Giulio**. See the **Sacre Monte** at Varallo before heading into the **mountains** and pretty **villages**, where the **Walser** people settled after a long migration. For full details, see p47.

Left The fantastical Isola Bella, see p44, one of Lake Maggiore's Borromean Islands

Top Cable car descending from Monte Mottarone to Lake Maggiore **Above** Flowers in the Giardino Alpino, Monte Mottarone

VISITING STRESA

Parking
Main car park on waterfront with four more close by and one at Viale Lido at the far end of town (direction Baveno).

Cable car, ferries and the *trenino*
The Monte Mottarone cable car departs Piazzale Lido 8. Isole Borromee ferries sail every half hour from Piazza Marconi – visit all three with a day pass. The *trenino* (tourist train) goes to Villa Pallavicino, 9:30am–4:30pm Mar–Sep from the Piazzale Imbarcadero di Stresa.

Tourist Information
Piazza Marconi 16, 28838; 0323 30150; www.stresaturismo.it

WHERE TO STAY IN STRESA

Albergo Ristorante Verbano *moderate*
This restaurant and inn is best savoured after the crowds have gone. There are 12 charmingly old-fashioned rooms with lovely views over the lake.
Via Ugo Ara 2, Isola Superiore, 28838; 0323 30408; www.hotelverbano.it

Villa Aminta *expensive*
Sheer luxury in a chic boutique hotel full of vintage charm. Set at the lake's edge, the elegant villa also has a lovely terrace and outdoor swimming pool.
Via Sempione Nord 123, Stresa, 28838; 0323 933 818; www.villa-aminta.it

Grand Hôtel des Iles Borromées *expensive*
Super-grand hotel overlooking the lake and the islands with *belle époque*-style rooms, swimming pools, spa and a wellness centre.
Corso Umberto I 67, Stresa, 28838; 0323 938 938; www.borromees.it

① Stresa
Verbano-Cusio-Ossola; Piemonte 28838

One of Italy's most elegant 19th-century resorts, Stresa may be a little past its prime today, but still has grand hotels and a lovely waterfront and is the departure point for ferries and steamers across Lake Maggiore. Italy's second largest, the lake has always been popular with royalty, politicians, artists and writers such as Ernest Hemingway who featured Stresa's Grand Hôtel des Iles Borromées in *A Farewell to Arms*. Behind the waterfront is the café-lined Piazza Cadorna which has some good shops. A cable car from the Lido makes regular 20-minute ascents to Monte Mottarone, stopping halfway at the **Giardino Botanico Alpinia** *(open daily 9:30am–6pm Apr–Oct)* before continuing to the summit and spectacular views.

The main attractions, however, are the views from the bustling waterfront at Piazza Marconi to the **Isole Borromee** (Borromean Islands) set in the middle of the lake, and visits to the islands themselves. Once barren outcrops, the three islands are the stars of the lake, graced with villas, palaces and beautiful gardens. Each has a different character, but all have belonged to the noble Borromean family since Renaissance times. Today, the wealthy Borromeans are still the owners of these islands: **Isola Bella**, one of the family's many homes, is a showy Baroque pleasure palace set among crisply terraced gardens peppered with statues and fountains. The folly is completed by a series of grottoes dripping with nymphs and shells and a shell-shaped amphitheatre – the perfect setting for outdoor summer concerts. **Isola Madre** resembles a floating, enchanted garden where white peacocks and wildly coloured exotic birds strut among the prized botanic specimens. Highlights include Europe's largest Kashmiri cypress and, in spring, spectacular blooms of camellias, magnolias and giant rhododendrons. **Isola Superiore** (also known as Isola Pescatori) is the smallest of the three

Statuary on Isola Bella, Isole Borromee

and is a prettified fishing village where the little alleys, whitewashed walls draped with fishing nets and sleepy cats basking in courtyards conjure up a romantic idyll.

A short distance from Stresa, east along the SS33 in the direction of Novara/Milano, is **Il Parco della Villa Pallavicino** *(open daily Mar–Oct)*. Shady arbours, botanical and "English" gardens, pergolas and terraces are the setting for this villa – although the villa itself is closed to the public. There is also a good zoo with around 40 different species of animals, many of which roam freely among the visitors. Children are able to pet the Tibetan goats. Other animals include kangaroos, llamas, zebras, flamingoes, deer, parrots and peacocks.

🚗 *From Stresa head northeast on the SS33 for 4.5 km (3 miles) to Baveno.*

Below Isola Superiore seen from Stresa, Lake Maggiore

② Baveno
Verbano-Cusio-Ossola; Piemonte 28831
Once a favourite of Queen Victoria and Winston Churchill, today the resort is a quieter version of Stresa. Full of elegant villas, fringed by an attractive waterfront and beaches, it also has a lovely backdrop of Monte Camoscio (890 m/2,919 ft), famous for its pink granite. This was used to build both Milan's Galleria Vittorio Emanuele II and St Paul's Basilica in Rome. In town, the 11th-century parish church **Santi Gervasio e San Protaso** was also built from the local stone and has a splendid Romanesque bell tower, façade and octagonal baptistry. To the north (via SS33 and then SS34), is the **Riserva Naturale di Fondo Toce** covering an area of 741 acres (300 hectares) and a favourite stopping spot for migratory birds.

🚗 *Take SS33, left on SS167, then SS34. Villa Taranto is by the lake at Pallanza.*

③ Verbania
Verbano-Cusio-Ossola; Piemonte 28900
Verbania gets its name from the Roman for Lake Maggiore, Lacus Verbanus, after the *verbano* (vervain) plant that grows here. Along the lakeside, the town merges with Pallanza, forming one of Maggiore's best-known and cosmopolitan resorts, beautifully located at the foot of Monte Rosso. The highlight here is the gardens at **Villa Taranto** *(open Easter end Oct)* – with over 20,000 plant species, it is one of Italy's richest collections of subtropical flora. The gardens were laid out by a retired Scottish captain Neil McEacharn, who devoted 33 years to them and bequeathed them to the Italian state on his death in 1964. Whatever the season, the gardens are blooming.

🚗 *Head north to join the SS34, cross autostrada E62, then head south on the SS229 to Omegna (17 km/11 miles).*

④ Omegna
Verbano-Cusio-Ossola; Piemonte 28887
At the northern end of Lago d'Orta, bustling Omegna is the largest town in the area. It lies on the two banks of the Nigoglia, an outflowing river and, curiously, Italy's only north-flowing river. The heart of the old town is the pedestrianized Via Felice Cavallotti.

There is some good shopping to be had here and along Via Alberganti, also known as Via dal Buter, after the old butter and cheese market that was held along this street. Designer household articles are the good buys in Omegna, as the town is home to design guru Alessi as well as Calderoni, Bialetti and Lagostina – all big names in the Italian kitchen. To the north at Crusinallo is the Alessi headquarters and factory shop *(see right)*.

From Omegna it is worth making a quick detour to the town of **Quarna Sopra**, a further 8 km (5 miles) along the SP51, for splendid views over the mountain pastures from its castle.

🚗 *From Quarna retrace the route to Omegna, then go south on SS229. Turn off on SP39 and take SP43 to Ameno.*

⑤ Ameno
Novara; Piemonte 28010
A tourist resort since the 18th century, Ameno is 500 m (1,640 ft) above sea level and a great base for trekking in beautiful scenery overlooking Monte Rosa. The town is dotted with grand villas with gardens, such as Casa Calderara, the former home of painter Antonio Calderara (1903–78) – now a museum-gallery. The **Collezione Calderara di Arte Contemporanea** *(open mid-May–mid-Oct: Tue–Fri 3–7pm, Sat & Sun 10am–noon & 3–7pm)* features contemporary paintings and sculptures by European, American, Chinese and Japanese artists. Walk southwest 1.5 km (1 mile) to the lake past pretty gardens to sandy Miami Beach *(entrance fee)* for waterside fun.

🚗 *Retrace route to SS229, then turn off for Orta San Giulio. The main road is Via Panoramica or Strada Nuova.*

Above The terraced gardens at the delightful Villa Taranto, Verbania-Pallanza

EAT AND DRINK

AROUND BAVENO

Piccolo Lago *expensive*
With glorious views over the Lago di Mergozzo and close to the Fondo Toce nature reserve *(see left)*, this two-Michelin-starred restaurant is a haven of gourmet delight. Has rooms too.
Via Filippo Turati 87, Fondotoce, 28924; 0323 586 792, www.piccololago.it, dinner only except Sat and Sun; closed Mon, Jan and Feb

VERBANIA

Osteria dell'Angolo *moderate*
This little restaurant has a delectable menu of Piedmontese cuisine and lake specialities.
Piazza Garibaldi 35, Verbania-Pallanza, 28922; 0323 556 362; closed Mon & Nov

AROUND OMEGNA

Il Giardinetto *moderate*
Lakeside setting with an awning-shaded veranda (part of a hotel). Light, creative dishes and traditional local specialities.
Via Provinciale 1, Pettenasco, 28028 (8 km/5 miles south of Omegna on lakeside road, SS229); 0323 89118; www.lagodortahotels.com; closed Mon lunch, Nov–Mar

SHOPPING IN OMEGNA

Alessi factory shop
This outlet sells Alessi's range of pasta pots and the original coffee pots – fun as well as useful and well crafted.
Via Alessi 6, Crusinallo, 28887 (3 km/ 2 miles north of centre); 0323 868 611

Omegna Forum
This cultural centre and retail outlet showcases local designer goods.
Parco Pasquale Maulini 1, Omegna, 28887; 0323 866 141; www.forumomegna.org

Eat and Drink: inexpensive, under €25; moderate, €25–€45; expensive, over €45

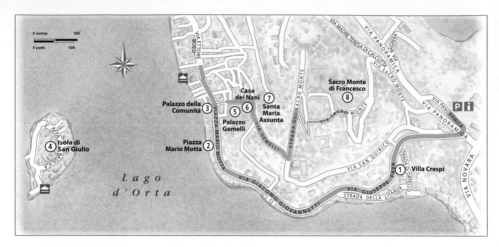

Lago d'Orta

VISITING ORTA SAN GIULIO

Parking
Use the car park by the tourist office (Via Panoramica). From here a tourist train heads to the centre and Sacro Monte.

Tourist Information
Via Panoramica, 28016; 0322 905 163; www.distrettolaghi.it; closed Mon–Tue

WHERE TO STAY

ORTA SAN GIULIO

Hotel Ara Coeli *moderate*
Central, quirky minimalist hotel with themed rooms. Glorious lake views.
Piazza Motta 34, 28016; 0322 905 173; www.ortainfo.com

VARALLO

Sacro Monte *moderate*
Handy for the site of pilgrimage above Varallo, this small hotel has a pleasant old-fashioned aura and verdant gardens.
Sacro Monte 14, 13019; 0163 54254; www.sacromontealbergo.it

ALAGNA VALSESIA

Residence Mirella *inexpensive*
This charming, good-value, family-run establishment offers simple, cosy rooms.
Piazzale Funivia, 13021; 0163 91286; www.residencemirella.com

⑥ Orta San Giulio
Novara; Piemonte 28016

Impressive frescoed peach- and cappuccino-coloured houses with galleries, wrought-iron balconies and gates line the cobbled alleys of this gorgeous little medieval town, the jewel of Lago d'Orta.

A three-hour walking tour

From the car park and **tourist office** walk south along Via Fava to the Moorish fantasy hotel **Villa Crespi** ① (luxury at a price – *www.villacrespi.it*). Follow the lakeside road to the main square, **Piazza Motta** ②, with cafés, restaurants, shops and hotels and a weekly market since 1228. The 16th-century town hall, **Palazzo della Comunità** ③ holds art shows and nearby, **Rovera** (*Largo de Gregori 15; 0322 90123*), is an Aladdin's cave of local treats and wines. From the piazza, take a boat to **Isola di San Giulio** ④. Legend has it that, in AD 390 Giulio, a Christian preacher, rid the island of its dragons and serpents and built the Romanesque **Basilica di San Giulio** (*open daily*) – his remains are in the crypt. The only street, Via del Silenzio, becoming the Via della Meditazione, leads past the Benedictine convent,

Palazzo dei Vescovi, home to about 60 nuns. The abbess has put up signs encouraging contemplation and self-renewal on "the island within".

Back at Piazza Motta, take the Salità della Motta, a stepped lane past the late-Renaissance **Palazzo Gemelli** ⑤ and other elegant palazzi such as the **Casa dei Nani** (House of Dwarfs) ⑥. Orta's oldest house, dating from the 14th century, this home takes its name from the four tiny windows. Passing by other houses in a profusion of architectural styles, head up to the 15th-century Baroque church **Santa Maria Assunta** ⑦. From here take Via Gemelli and turn left to the **Sacro Monte di Francesco** ⑧ (*open daily*). Spectacularly set on a hillside above the lake with views to Isola di San Giulio, this is a devotional path with 21 chapels illustrating the life of St Francis of Assisi. The chapels, built between 1591 and 1750, alternate Baroque and Renaissance styles and hold 376 sculptures and 900 frescoes. There is a good restaurant here, with a picturesque ivy-clad terrace. Return to the car park on the tourist train.

🚗 *Head south on SS29, turn right at Gozzano on SP45, turn right on SP46 and again on SP48.*

Left The tiny island of Isola di San Giulio, a short boat ride from Orta San Giulio

❼ Pella

Novara; Piemonte 28010

This lakeside village is a pleasant place for a stroll and an ice cream from the Gelateria Antica Torre. Towering above the village, on a granite outcrop, is the **Santuario della Madonna del Sasso** *(open daily pm)*, accessible on a winding road from the SP48/46/49. This sanctuary, with Baroque church, bell tower and hermitage, was built in 1730–48. Inside there are some fine frescoes and a 17th-century crucifix, but the highlight is the great view – encompassing almost the entire lake.

🚗 *Take SP49, then SP46, left on SP50, then SP88 and SP78. Turn right on SP8.*

❽ Varallo

Vercelli; Piemonte 13019

Varallo is a picturesque town, but the focal point is the **Sacro Monte** *(open daily)*. Representing the Stations of the Cross, the site was chosen in 1481 by a Franciscan friar who wanted to create a miniature Holy Land. Today there are 45 chapels with statues and frescoes. In front of the basilica, a fountain takes the place of the 44th chapel, hewn out of one rock, crowned by a statue of the Risen Christ, with five spouts symbolizing the wounds of Christ. A steep walk from town, the site can also be reached by car and cable car.

🚗 *Take the SS299 to Riva Valdobbia.*

❾ Riva Valdobbia

Vercelli; 13020

With good views of Monte Rosa, this is a pretty village of the Walsers, a German-speaking people – note their wooden houses with balconies for drying hay, hemp or rye. Originally a chapel of the Holy Virgin (1473), the town church was rededicated to St Michael in 1640. The original bell tower has a figure of St Christopher, protector of pilgrims. It holds various art works, a marble altar and wooden choir from the Sacro Monte of Varallo.

🚗 *Continue for just over 3 km (2 miles) on the SS299 to Alagna Valsesia.*

❿ Alagna Valsesia

Vercelli; Piemonte 13021

This pleasant hiking centre has strong connections with the hardy Walsers who colonized the area around Monte Rosa in the 13th century. On the edge of Alagna, at Pedemonte, is the **Museo Walser** *(open Sep–Jun: Sat & Sun; Jul: daily pm; Aug: daily)*. This 17th-century wood-slatted house gives an insight into Walser life, with the *stube* (stove), built-in cattle stall, furniture and workshops. Drive (or just walk) through town, past a car park, to the track that goes 2 km (1 mile) up to a mountain café – there are waterfalls nearby and it is just perfect for hiking.

🚗 *Retrace the route to Alagna.*

Above left River valley and ruined chapel on the drive to Varallo. **Above centre** Fresco on St Michael's church, Riva Valdobbia **Above right** Wooden Walser house in front of St Michael's church

EAT AND DRINK

ORTA SAN GIULIO

La Bussola *moderate*
Amazing views from the terrace and fish specialities including trout.
Via Panoramica 24, 28016; 0322 911913; closed Oct–mid-Mar

Leon d'Oro *moderate*
Dine by the water on lake fish.
Piazza Motta 43, 28016; 0322 911 991; www.albergoleondoro.it; closed Jan

Other options
For cakes, snacks and drinks try **Bar Pasticceria Arianna** *(Via Domodossola 10/12, 28016; closed Mon)*.

PELLA

Antica Torre *inexpensive*
Great ice-cream and pancake stop.
Via Lungo Lago 8–10, 28010

VARALLO

Delzanno *moderate*
This well-respected family-run restaurant provides good simple dishes.
Località Crosa 8, 13019; 0163 51439; www.ristorantedelzanno.it; closed Mon

ALAGNA VALSESIA

Pressmel Ristorante *moderate*
In the Hotel Cristallo, this airy restaurant specializes in Piedmontese cuisine.
Piazza degli Alberghi, 13021; 0163 922 822

DAY TRIP OPTIONS

This drive offers aquatic, meditative or mountainous day-trip options around lakes Maggiore and Orta or Varallo.

Family fun
Park near the waterfront at the Lido in Stresa ❶ and take the cable car to the top of Monte Mottarone before hopping across on the ferry to the **Isole Borromee**. Then drive out to the park and zoo at **Villa Pallavicino**. *Travel east on the SS33 for 5 km (3 miles) from Stresa to Villa Pallavicino.*

A day of meditation
At Ameno ❺ contemplate modern art at the **Collezione Calderara di Arte Contemporaneo**, then take a walk around Orta San Giulio ❻ and a boat to **Isola di San Giulio**. Finish at peace on the Via della Meditazione.

The main road to use is the SS229.

Climb every mountain
At Varallo ❽ walk to the **Sacro Monte**, before driving to the little Walser village of Riva Valdobbia ❾. Continue to Alagna Valsesia ❿ and the **Museo Walser** to learn about the Walsers before enjoying a short walk in the beautiful mountains.

Travel on the SS299 through the valley.

Eat and Drink: inexpensive, under €25; moderate, €25–€45; expensive, over €45

Across the Roof of Italy

Bormio to Rovereto

Highlights

* **Designer hotels and spas**
  Relax at chic alpine retreats, fed
  by thermal waters enjoyed since
  Roman times

* **High-altitude challenge**
  Take on the 82 hairpin bends of the
  Passo dello Stelvio and be rewarded
  with awe-inspiring views of the Alps

* **Award-winning wine producers**
  Stop for tastings in the oldest wine
  region of the German-speaking world

* **Avant-garde MART**
  Grapple with modern art at one of
  Italy's most exciting new galleries

Winding route to the Passo dello Stelvio, one of the
highest passes in the Alps

Across the Roof of Italy

Road signs in Italian and German, spaghetti and schnitzel on the menu – this is a fascinating frontier land that has passed back and forth between ruling powers for centuries. Stupendous alpine scenery is matched by warm hospitality – it is not unusual to find hotels that have been in the same family for generations. After crossing the vast Ortles mountain range at the beginning of the drive, the route follows a well-established wine road, with vines strung on wide pergolas on either side of the road as in Roman times.

[Map showing the drive route across northern Italy, including place names such as:]

P. Saldura 3433m, Madonna d. S. (Unserfrau in S.), Tiro (Dorf Tirc, Mülles V. (Mals i. V.), Tanai (Thanai), Val d'Senales (Schnalsta), Certosa (Karthaus), MERANO (MERAN), Láudes (Laatsch), Sluderno (Schluderns), Spondigna (Spondinig), Silandro (Schlanders), Compaccio (Kompatsch), Naturno (Naturns), Monte San Vigilio, GLORENZA (GLURNS), 40, 41, 4, 38, Müstair, Prato a. S. (Prad a. S.), Lasa (Laas), Val Venosta, Láces (Latsch), Adige (Etsch), S. Pancrázio (St. Pancraz), Sta Maria im M., 28, Gomagoi, 38, 522, Pso d'Balade (Gampenjoch) 1512m, Lago di Cancano, Pso d. Umbrail 2503m, Trafoi, Parco Nazionale dello Stélvio (Stilfserjoch), PASSO DELLO STELVIO (STILFSERJOCH), 3, Solda (Sulden), S. Gertrude (St. Gertraud), Provés (Proveis), Castelfond, Valdidentro, 301, Bagni Vecchi, BORMIO, 1, 300, Arnoga, Val Viola, Rif. Val Viola, Rif. Federico V in Dosdé, VALFURVA, VALLE DEI FORNI AND VAL DI GÁVIA, 2, S. Caterina Valfurva, Valle dei Forni, Bordolona, Samónico, Bagni di Rabbi, Brésimo, Revò, LOMBARDIA, le Prese, M. Gávia 3223m, Péjo, Cima Mezzana 2845m, Caldés, Lago di S. Giustina, Sanzeno, Malè, 42, Sóndalo, 38, Passo di Gávia 2621m, Mezzana, Dimaro, Tuenno, Dermulo, Fusino, Pezzo, Fucine, M. Péller 2320m, 43, Vervò, Grosotto, Sorottini 2967m, Pso d. Tonale 1883m, Val Vermiglio, Marilleva, Tirano, Ponte d. Legno, Vione, TRENTINO-ALTO-ADIGE, Rov, Cima Presanella 3558m, Madonna di Campiglio, Mezzocorona, Bédole, Cima Grostè 2901m, A22, 12, M. Cádria 2254m, Val Génova, Pinzolo, Molveno, Andalo, Lavis, 239, L. di Molveno, Gruppo di Brenta, Terlago, Vezzano, 239, Terme di Comano, Lasino, 11, TREN, 45b, Garniga, A22, M. Cádria 2254m, Dro, Drena, Nomi, Arco, Tenno, Calliano, Bezzecca, Folga, Riva d. Garda, Törbole, Mori, 12, ROVERETO (MART), 12, Limone S. G., Brentónico, 249, Val Laga, 46, Lago di Garda

KEY

🚗 Drive route

0 kilometres — 15
0 miles — 15

ACTIVITIES

Plunge into thermal waters at Bormio's unique Bagni Vecchi, a spa since Roman times

Stretch your legs on exhilarating walks in the Valfurva and Val Viola, or just drive up for the views

Enjoy café life in the historic towns of Trento and Bolzano

Get a bird's-eye view of the Dolomites by taking the cable car to summer pastures on the Alpe di Siusi

Join the locals for autumn Törggelen, the time to sample grape juice and new wine, ham and chestnuts

Above High pastures around Compaccio in the Alpe di Siusi, looking across to the Sasso Lungo massif of the Dolomites, *see p56*

Below The world-renowned Giardini di Castel Trauttmansdorf at the spa town of Merano, *see p54*

PLAN YOUR DRIVE

Start/finish: Bormio to Rovereto.

Number of days: 3–4 days.

Distance: Approx. 330 km (205 miles).

Road conditions: Generally well-paved and signposted. Mountain routes can be slow, with steep twists and turns. Roads through the Valfurva, Valle dei Forni and Val di Gavia are narrow and potholed. Late snow may keep the Passo dello Stelvio closed into July. Look out for signs on the approach roads or call 0471 999 999 (Mon–Fri 9am–7pm) for information. There are no fuel stops between Bormio and Prato.

When to go: Best time is late Jun–late Sep, when the passes are open, the summer hiking season is in full swing and cable cars are running.

Opening times: Museums and shops in northern Italy now tend to open 9am–7pm, with a lunch break of one to three hours, shutting earlier on Sundays and in the winter. Many places are closed on Mondays. Churches commonly open 7am–12:30pm and 4–7pm.

Main market days: Bormio: 1st and 3rd Tue of the month; Bolzano: Mon–Sat fruit and vegetable market at Piazza Erbe/Obstplatz; 1st weekend each month, arts and crafts market, Piazza del Grano; Trento: Thu am.

Shopping: Look out for "Trehs" spa products made from Sarntal pine, fine wines, rhododendron honey and buck-wheat pasta.

Major festivals: Across region: Törggelen, Sep–Nov; Bormio: Easter parades; Lasa/Laas in Val Venosta: Marmor e Marillen (Marble & Apricots), Aug; Merano: Easter horse races & Grapefest, late Oct; Bolzano: speck festival, May; Strada del Vino: wine festival, May–Jun; Trento, Merano, Bolzano & Appiano: Christmas markets.

DAY TRIP OPTIONS

Using Bormio as a base offers day trips to **mountain passes, ancient spas** and medieval Glorenza. Stay in and around Bolzano for the **wine road, modern art** and access to the Dolomites. For full details, *see p57*.

WHERE TO STAY

BORMIO

Sertorelli Reit *moderate*
Several of the smallish rooms have a Jacuzzi, balcony and rooftop views. Discount available for local spa.
Via Monte Braulio 4, 23032; 0342 910 820; www.hotelmeublebormio.com

Bagni Nuovi *moderate*
Grand Neo-Classical hotel complete with ballroom and its own spa, as well as use of the Bagni Vecchi.
Via Bagni Nuovi 7, 23038, N of Bormio; 0342 910 131; www.bagnidibormio.it

PASSO DELLO STELVIO

Bella Vista *moderate*
This stylish mountain retreat run by Olympic skier Gustav Thöni offers guided excursions and a wellness centre.
Trafoi, 39029 (before the pass on SS38); 0473 611 716; www.bella-vista.it

GLORENZA (GLURNS)

Grüner Baum *moderate*
A traditional inn on minimalist lines in the village centre – a mix of antique and modern.
Piazza Città/Stadtplatz 7, 39020; 0473 831 206; www.gasthofgruenerbaum.it

Below Church of San Gervasio and San Protasio on Piazza Cavour, Bormio **Below right** Road passing by a turquoise mountain lake on the Passo di Gávia **Below left** The summit of Passo dello Steelvio

① Bormio
Lombardia; 23032

A popular winter ski resort, this ancient mountain village has a strong cultural life distinct from tourism. It is a fascinating place simply to wander: justice was once dispensed from the canopied **Kuerc'** in the main square and buildings such as the fine 15th–16th-century clock tower and collegiate church of **San Gervasio and San Protasio** *(open daily)*, with its richly decorated interior, attest to the town's wealth. The burghers of Bormio filled their coffers from purchase taxes – the town was a trading post between Venice and Switzerland – and the spa industry, which has thrived since medieval times.

Bormio's thermal baths, the **Bagni Vecchi** *(open daily, Sat & Sun till 10pm)*, lie 2 km (1 mile) north on the SS38, clearly signposted on the left and with parking outside. Visitors have enjoyed a session at these baths since Roman times, if not before. Pliny the Elder, Leonardo da Vinci and Giuseppe Garibaldi are among the great and the good to have wallowed in the nine hot springs here. The entrance fee allows visitors to stay all day, so leave enough time

to enjoy the various indoor pools and cascades; the natural sauna in a cave 50 m (165 ft) inside the mountain that gets steadily hotter like Dante's *Inferno*; the fragrant, pine-clad dry-heat room; and a beautiful open-air pool with a view of the mountain peaks.

🚗 *Leave Bormio on the SS38 towards Tirano. At the hotel Baita dei Pini, turn left on the SS300 to Santa Caterina Valfurva. At Santa Caterina turn left into the Valle dei Forni, drive up until the road ends and park below the Rifugio-Albergo Ghiacciaio dei Forni.*

② Valfurva, Valle dei Forni and Val di Gavia
Lombardia; 23030

A traditional way of life still goes on in these valleys at the base of the Ortles (Ortler) mountain range, with hay-making in the meadows and animals being led up to high pasture in summer beneath vast glaciers stretching from the Ghiacciaio dei Forni to Monte Cevedale. From the refuge car park, take the gently sloping track 28B up to Rifugio Pizzini (1½–2 hrs), a good place for lunch. Then pick up a short section of the **Sentiero della Pace** (Path of Peace), a long-distance path running the

length of the World War I battlefront here, back to the car park (1½ hrs). Return to Santa Caterina and follow signs for the beautiful **Passo di Gavia** (2,621 m/8,600 ft) to see further reminders of the Great War.

🚌 *Retrace steps to Bormio. Skirt town on SS38 and follow signs for Passo dello Stelvio (Stilfserjoch).*

③ Passo dello Stelvio (Stilfserjoch)
Lombardia & Alto Adige; 39020

As the highest road pass in Italy, the Stelvio pass makes an awesome drive, although it is well within the average driver's capabilities if taken slowly. Each hairpin bend is numbered – there are 34 from Bormio up to the pass and 48 back down to Prato – and the grandeur of the landscape increases with every turn. A knot of hotels and cable cars at the top (2,757 m/9,045 ft) serve

---

Optional Walk in the Val Viola

For a long, fairly demanding walk, through lush meadows, waterfalls and boulder-strewn terrain, **drive** west from Bormio along the SS301 to Arnoga. Stop at the small, free car park on the left-hand side of a sharp bend. Parking obligatory Jul/Aug, at other times cars allowed on the track to the valley head. **Walk** along the woodland footpath signposted to Rifugio Federico V in Dosdé, a handy stop for lunch. Return to the car the same way or via the road (half a day). For a full day's walk, from the *rifugio* in Dosdé follow the red-and-white trail no. 2 markers past a series of small mountain tarns to Rifugio Val Viola, close to the Swiss border. Return via the track to the car park.

---

summer ski slopes (*May–Nov*) on the glacier of "King Ortler". For more views, head up to **Cima Garibaldi**, a 20-minute climb by foot from the pass.

🚌 *Continue along the SS38 towards Spondigna. At Prato allo Stelvio, turn left and continue until you reach Glorenza (Glurns). Park outside the city walls in one of the four car parks.*

④ Glorenza (Glurns)
Alto Adige; 39020

For an idea of what cities looked like in medieval times, head for Glorenza, a tiny fortified town encircled by well-preserved walls, with three ancient gateways allowing traffic in and out. Its small-scale perfection and fewer than 900 inhabitants have led to it being known as "the smallest city in the Alps". The cafés in the main square make a good pit stop.

🚌 *Take SS41 to Sluderno and turn right to join the SS40/38 towards Merano. Follow signs for central Merano and use the car park at the roundabout by the Terme Merano.*

WALKING AROUND BORMIO

Kompass walking maps show footpaths, their level of difficulty and steepness of terrain. Trails are numbered and paths marked by red-and-white blazes painted on rocks and trees. Mountain refuges (*rifugi*) offer good food and drink en route.

EAT AND DRINK

BORMIO

Notte e Dì *moderate*
Simple trattoria with a varied menu, including carpaccio of *oca* (goose).
Piazza Cavour 15, 23032; 0342 903 339; closed Wed, May, Oct

Latteria Sociale
Shop selling local cheeses such as *Scimudin*, fresh ricotta and honey.
Via de Simoni 22, 23032; 0342 901 437

AROUND BORMIO

Azienda Agricola Rini *inexpensive*
Family-run dairy farm offering a five-course set menu of Valtellinesi dishes.
Via Cav. Pietro Rini 2, Bormio, 23032 (3km/2 miles on SS38); 0342 901 224; www.rini.it

Fior d'Alpe *inexpensive*
Popular for its buckwheat flour pizzas and deep-fried *Sciatt* (savoury donuts).
Via Madonnina 6, Valdidentro, 23038 (3 km/2 miles on SS301); 0342 929 269

AROUND PASSO DELLO STELVIO

Yak & Yeti *moderate*
Himalayan climbs inspired Reinhold Messner's yak farm and restaurant.
Forststraße 55, Solda (Sulden), 39029 (SS38 15 km/9 miles after pass, then right onto SS622); 0473 613 266; closed Mon

Above A church on the eastern lower reaches of the Passo dello Stelvio **Below** Medieval fortified walls and towers, Glorenza

Where to Stay: inexpensive, under €100; moderate, €100–€200; expensive, over €200

Right Beautifully preserved Castel Roncolo
in its valley setting **Far right** Former *Kurhaus*
(Spa House) in the centre of Merano

WHERE TO STAY

AROUND MERANO

Castel Fragsburg *moderate*
Originally a 17th-century hunting
lodge, this is a small 4-star hotel with a
fine restaurant suspended high above
the Adige (Etsch) valley. Notable
features are the open-air pool and the
little hut for naked sunbathing.
*5 km (3 miles) east of Merano (Meran)
at Fragsburgerstrasse 33, 39012; 0473
244 071; www.fragsburg.com*

Zur Goldenen Rose *moderate*
Snug bolt hole in Certosa (Karthaus),
with its famous church and cloister
where monks lived from 1326 to 1725.
Runs its own mountain refuge
restaurant on the Schnalstal glacier.
*Karthaus 29, Senales (Schnals), 39020;
0473 679 130; www.goldenerose.it*

Vigilius *expensive*
This luxury eco-spa has won top
environmental awards. Built from larch
wood, it is an ultra-relaxing place to
stay – swimming in the quartzite-lined
pool is like floating through treetops.
*Monte San Vigilio (Vigiljoch), 39011,
reachable only by cable car (15 min
from Lana); 0473 556 600;
www.vigilius.it*

BOLZANO

Greif *expensive*
The Black Griffin inn first opened its
doors 500 years ago and is now a chic
4-star haven decorated with Biedermeier
furniture and original artworks.
*Via della Rena 28, 39100; 0471 318
000; www.greif.it*

⑤ Merano (Meran)
Alto Adige; 39012
Tourists started flocking to Merano
at the turn of the 19th century after
Empress Elizabeth of Austria – known
as Sissi – chose the town for her
winter cure. A resort of *fin-de-siècle*
hotels and riverside promenades
evolved, with one of Sissi's holiday
castles now at the centre of the
Giardini del Castel Trauttmansdorf
(open daily, mid-May–mid-Sep until 9pm).
From central Merano, follow signs for
Scena (Schenna) and the gardens and
car park are signposted on the right.
A surprise gem within the gardens is
the imaginative **Turiseum** *(as gardens)*,
a hands-on museum with exhibits on
tourism in the South Tyrol and the
influences that helped shape it, from
Romantic poets to Napoleon, the
railways and the first mountaineers.
🚗 *Leave Merano on the SS38 towards
Bolzano. Take the Valle Sarentina
(Sarntal) exit and continue to Piazza
Gries. There, follow signs for Funivia S
Genesio and Castel Roncolo. Cross the
river to the car park.*

⑥ Castel Roncolo (Schloss Runkelstein)
Bolzano, Alto Adige; 39100
Giants and dwarfs, the legendary
lovers Tristan and Isolde and the
world of chivalry all feature in the
medieval frescoes of Castel Roncolo
(open Tue–Sun), which are some of the
finest of their kind. Not for nothing
did director Pier Paolo Pasolini
choose this 13th-century castle as a
location for his film *Decameron*
(1971), based on the medieval story
cycle by Giovanni Boccaccio. In the
Sala del Torneo, look out for the
fresco of a fishing party: in the
background, a noble is offering a fish
to a lady, the medieval equivalent of
an indecent proposal.
🚗 *Follow the road signs for Bolzano
(Bozen) centre. See "Visiting Bolzano",
opposite, for parking options.*

Below left Statue of Walther von der Vogelweide
in Piazza Walther, Bolzano **Below** Detail of fine
wall fresco in Chiesa dei Domenicani, Bolzano
Bottom Gothic cathedral of Bolzano, restored
after bomb damage in World War II

❼ Bolzano (Bozen)

Alto Adige; 39100

A part of the Austrian Empire until the end of World War I, this distinctly Germanic market town is famous for its arcades and the mortal remains of a 5,000-year-old Ice Man.

A two-hour walking tour

This walk can be done anytime, though Sunday is best avoided as the shops tend to be closed. From any of the car parks, head towards the spire of the cathedral to reach the main square, **Piazza Walther** ①. Passing the monument to Walther von der Vogelweide (1170–1230), one of the greatest German poets of the Middle Ages, walk into **Piazza del Grano** ②. The lovely Casa della Pesa (1634) is on the northern side of this square. Head along Via Argentieri. A right turn onto Via Goethe will bring you to the busy **food market** ③ on Piazza Erbe. On one corner stands the **fountain of Neptune** ④ (1745), known locally as Gabelwirt (Innkeeper with a Fork). Walk past this and head up Via dei Francescani to the **Chiesa dei Francescani** ⑤ (open daily) dating back to the first half of the 14th century and with a superb Gothic wooden altar.

Backtrack a little to the top end of the market and take a left along **Via Dr Streiter** ⑥ which has a number of small design shops. Continue to Via dei Bottai, where a right turn comes

to **Piazza Municipio** ⑦, lined with beautiful Rococo façades. Another right finds **Portici** ⑧, a Baroque porticoed shopping street.

Leave plenty of time for the **Museo Archeologico dell'Alto Adige** ⑨ (closed Mon except Jul, Aug & Dec). The prize exhibit here is Ötzi, a Copper Age man, preserved in ice and discovered in 1991. Cross the River Talvera, taking a left at the **arch on Piazza della Vittoria** ⑩, commissioned by Mussolini in 1928. Cross over the new bridge downstream to the **Museion** ⑪ (open daily), with a vast collection of avant-garde art on show.

Return to the centre via **Chiesa dei Domenicani** ⑫ (closed Sun) with 15th-century frescoes in the cloisters and Giotto School frescoes in the chapel. Go back to Piazza Walther and the 13th-century **Duomo** ⑬ (open daily) with its steep, lozenge-pattern roof.

🚗 *Leave via SS12 in Renon/Bolzano Nord direction. Follow signs to Chiusa and Bressanone. At Prato Isarco (Blumau) enter tunnel and keep on left to Fié allo Sciliar (Völs am Schlern) and Siusi (Seis). Park at cable car station.*

Peppers for sale

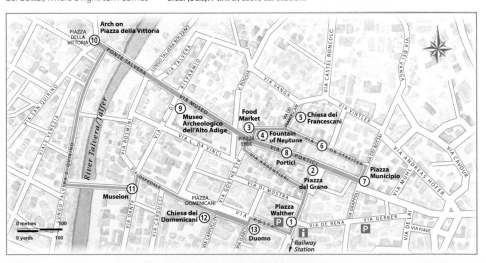

WINE TASTING

Two of the many new-school producers to visit are **Manincor** (*S Giuseppe al Lago 4, Caldaro, 39052; 0471 960 230; www.manincor.com*) and **Elena Walch** in Termeno (Tramin), the village that gives Gewürztraminer its name (*Via A Hofer 1, Termeno, 39040; 0471 860 172; www.elenawalch.com*).

WHERE TO STAY

ALPE DI SIUSI

Seiser Alm Urthaler *moderate*
Beautiful wooden hotel built using sustainable methods. Guests are exempt from the ban on cars.
Compaccio (Compatsch), 39040; 0471 727 919; www.seiseralm.com

AROUND ALPE DI SIUSI

Briol *inexpensive*
This Bauhaus-designed guesthouse, in a superb position high above the Isarco valley (1,310 m/4,300 ft), offers spectacular views over the Dolomites. Expect basic mod cons, good food and a warm welcome.
On mountainside above Tre Chiese (Dreikirchen), 39040; by foot/4-wheel-drive taxi from Barbiano; 0471 650 125; www.briol.it

Bad Dreikirchen
inexpensive–moderate
Family-run hotel in a 14th-century chalet halfway up a mountain, with big fluffy duvets and an outdoor pool.
Tre Chiese 12, 39040; by foot/taxi from Barbiano; 0471 650 055; www.baddreikirchen.it

TRENTO

America *inexpensive–moderate*
This friendly, efficient central hotel is strong on service and has a restaurant.
Via Torre Verde 52, 38100; 0461 983 010; www.hotelamerica.it

Top right Jagged peak of Sciliar rising above the meadows around Compaccio **Below** Vine-covered slopes along the Strada del Vino **Below right** Neptune fountain with the cathedral behind, Trento

Trentino-Alto Adige Wine

After mass producing easy-drinking reds from the Vernatsch grape in the 1970s and 80s, the region is remarketing itself as a fine wine region. Exceptional local Lagreins, Cabernets and Merlots win plenty of prizes, as do whites from Sauvignon Blanc and Gewürztraminer. The most famous whites are the Pinot Grigios and Chardonnays, the basis for superb traditional-method sparkling wines.

⑧ Alpe di Siusi (Seiser Alm)
Alto Adige; 39040
This alpine plateau 2,000 m (6,500 ft) above sea level is closed to traffic between 9am and 5pm. Instead, ride the cable car from Siusi (Seis) to the peaceful summer pastures around the hamlet of **Compaccio** (Compatsch). Take the chair lift from Compaccio to Restaurant Bullaccia for a superb view of the Dolomite mountains: from flat-topped Sciliar (Schlern), emblem of the Dolomites, to the saw-toothed Sasso Lungo (Langkofel). Return to Compaccio on foot or by chair lift.
🚗 *Retrace the route back to Bolzano on the SS12. Cross the Ponte Druso and keep going straight. Then take the SS42*

for Appiano (Eppan) and the Strada del Vino (Weinstraße). Take minor road on left signposted Castello Firmiano (Sigmundskron). Continue to car park on the right. The castle is a 15-minute walk uphill on a path through woods.

⑨ Castello Firmiano (Sigmundskron)
Bolzano, Alto Adige; 39100
Commanding the junction of two valleys, Firmiano has been fought over by forces north and south of the Alps for at least 1,000 years. The castle is now record-breaking climber Reinhold Messner's flagship **Mountain Museum** (*open 1st Sun Mar–3rd Sun Nov, closed Thu*) focusing on what mountains symbolize in global culture. A trail leads up through towers and battlements, passing an eclectic selection of art including a Tibetan prayer wheel, and an Inuit-style stone man.
🚗 *Rejoin Strada del Vino (Weinstraße) and stop in Caldaro (Kaltern). Park in the sign-posted car park on Goldgasse.*

⑩ Strada del Vino (Weinstraße)
Alto Adige; 39052
The Wine Road stretches between Bolzano and Trento, winding through the idyllic Adige valley on quiet country roads. Well-signposted, there are *enoteche* (wine shops) and small producers offering tastings in almost every village, but the main focus is **Caldaro** (Kaltern). Wines have been cultivated on its south-facing slopes since before the Romans, and although Alto Adige is one of the smallest wine regions in all Italy, it produces more DOC wines than any other in the country. Around 80 of them can be sampled from 17 local producers at the wine bar and

information point **Punkt** *(closed Mon)* on Caldaro's main square. A stroll around the village reveals much 16th-century Uberetsch architecture – a style that combines Gothic and southern Renaissance details.

🚗 *Follow the Strada del Vino (Weinstraße) to Salorno and join A22 towards Trento/Verona at the S Michele/Mezzocorona junction. Exit at Trento Centro. Free parking in Area ex Zuffo park-and-ride next to motorway exit (shuttle bus Mon–Sat) or pay at Garage Torre Verde, Autosilo Buonconsiglio or Centro Europa, all near the train station in the centre.*

⑪ Trento
Trentino; 38100
Frescoed palaces line the main square of this thoroughly pleasant town, at the centre of

Window box, Trento

which is a playful 18th-century fountain of Neptune with his trident (the town's Roman name was Tridentum). Trento is still best known as the venue for the Council of Trent (1545–63), a series of debates among Catholic church leaders over how best to respond to the Reformation in Protestant Europe. The main debates took place in the **Duomo**

(open daily), which is built over a medieval crypt and early Christian basilica. Next door, the **Palazzo Pretorio** *(open daily)* – all fishtail battlements and flags – has good views over the historic centre. Also of interest is the 13th–15th-century **Castello di Buonconsiglio** *(closed Mon)*.

🚗 *Take the A22 motorway towards Verona and exit at Rovereto Nord. Follow the signs for the centre. Park on Via Manzoni; MART is a 5-min walk.*

⑫ Rovereto (MART)
Trentino; 38068
Opened in 2002, MART *(Corso Bettini 43, closed Mon, open Fri till 9pm)* is recognized as one of Italy's foremost galleries of modern art. It is particularly strong on American Pop Art and 1920s Futurist art by local artist Fortunato Depero, whose paintings and collages celebrating the machine age have developed an international reputation. Displays vary but expect to see works by Metaphysical artists Giorgio de Chirico and Giorgio Morandi, the Arte Povera artists and Pop Art by Warhol and Lichtenstein, as well as cutting-edge temporary exhibitions.

Above left Spectacular entrance rotunda of MART, Rovereto **Above** Frescoes on the exterior wall of a palace in the centre of Trento

EAT AND DRINK

STRADA DEL VINO
Ansitz Pillhof *moderate*
Hundreds of bottles of the best wine from South Tyrol are on display in the *enoteca* (wine shop) here. Bistro has a short menu offering home-made pasta. *Via Bolzano 48, Frangart, Appiano, 39050 (take SS42 north for 8 km/5 miles from Caldaro); 0471 633 100; www.pillhof.com; closed Sat pm & Sun*

Castel Ringberg *expensive*
Housed in a 17th-century castle with a view of Lago di Caldaro, this restaurant offers imaginative versions of Italian favourites and fantastic desserts. *San Giuseppe al Lago 1 (take SP14 south for 5 km/3 miles from Caldaro), 39052; 0471 960 010; closed Tue*

Zur Rose *expensive*
Michelin-starred food and a well-stocked wine cellar of 600 labels *Josef Innerhoferstrasse 2, San Michele Appiano, 39057 (take SS42 north for 5 km/3 miles from Caldaro, then continue through Appiano to San Michele); 0471 662 249; www.zur-rose. com; closed Sun, Mon am*

DAY TRIP OPTIONS
To break up the tour into day trips it is best to choose either Bormio (off SS38) or Bolzano (off A22) as a base.

Hiker's relief
The valleys and passes extending out from Bormio ❶ are classic hiking country. Get an early start and recover in the afternoon with

a muscle soak at the thermal waters of the Bagni Vecchi.

Access Valfurva on the SS300 and Val Viola on the SS301.

Avant-garde practitioners
Get a taste for cutting-edge wine along the Strada del Vino ❿ then be inspired by revolutionary art in Rovereto at MART ⑫.

Take it slowly along the Strada del Vino then head down to Rovereto on the A22.

Castles and councils
History buffs can soak in the medieval atmosphere of Castel Roncolo ❻ then visit the scene of the momentous Council of Trent ⑪.

Head for the SS38 after Castel Roncolo which joins with the A22 to Trento.

Where to Stay: inexpensive, under €100; moderate, €100–€200; expensive, over €200

The Veneto

Bassano del Grappa to Venice

Highlights

- **Palladian villas**
  From Villa di Maser to the Riviera del
  Brenta, visit the 16th–18th-century
  villas inspired by Classical architecture

- **Bassano del Grappa**
  Stroll around this pretty, historic
  town with its pastel buildings,
  Renaissance art, piazzas and palaces

- **Fortified towns**
  Explore medieval walls, churches, and
  castles from Marostica through to
  Castelfranco Veneto

- **Riviera del Brenta**
  Picnic along this semi-rural waterway
  meandering from Padova to Venice

- **Venice**
  Discover the art and architecture of
  this mesmerizing canal city

A peaceful view of the River Brenta at
Bassano del Grappa

The Veneto

Extending from the Alps to the coast across seven provinces, the Veneto is a region of contrasting landscapes. Follow the mountain-kissed highlands down through the flat plains of the Brenta valley, past castles and villas to the Adriatic maritime jewel of Venice, which for centuries has been the political and cultural centre of the entire region. Splendid rural villas are a highlight of the drive – many of them along the riverbanks leading into Venice, in the historic aristocratic holiday playground of the Riviera del Brenta.

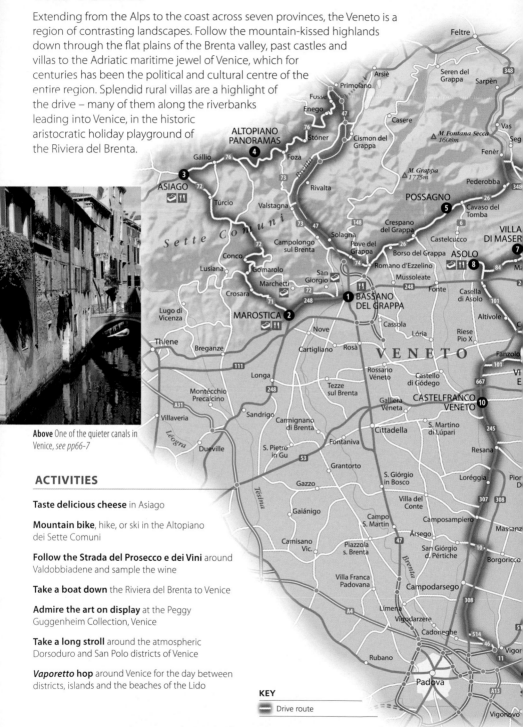

Above One of the quieter canals in Venice, see pp66–7

ACTIVITIES

Taste delicious cheese in Asiago

Mountain bike, hike, or ski in the Altopiano dei Sette Comuni

Follow the Strada del Prosecco e dei Vini around Valdobbiadene and sample the wine

Take a boat down the Riviera del Brenta to Venice

Admire the art on display at the Peggy Guggenheim Collection, Venice

Take a long stroll around the atmospheric Dorsoduro and San Polo districts of Venice

Vaporetto hop around Venice for the day between districts, islands and the beaches of the Lido

KEY

Drive route

VALDOBBIADENE

Above View of the lush countryside surrounding Asolo, see *p64*

Above View from the road between Possagno and Asolo, *see pp63-4*

0 kilometres 5

0 miles 5

PLAN YOUR DRIVE

Start/Finish: Bassano del Grappa to Venice.

Number of days: 4 days, allowing a day in the region around Bassano del Grappa, half a day on the Riviera di Brenta and a full day in Venice.

Distance: 249 km (155 miles).

Road conditions: In the mountainous area of the Veneto some roads may not be in good condition. The drive could be hazardous after heavy snow, and winter tyres or chains are required by law from November to April. Take the bends cautiously on the Altopiano dei Sette Comuni.

When to go: June to September for warm weather; winter is good for skiing, snow-capped mountain views, and fewer crowds in Venice.

Opening times: Museums and shops open 10am–7pm, shutting earlier on Sundays and in the winter. Many are closed on Mondays. Churches tend to open 7am–12:30pm and 4–7pm.

Main market days: Bassano del Grappa: Via del Mercato, Mon–Sat; Marostica: Piazza Castello, Tue; **Asiago:** Thu–Sat; **Valdobbiadene:** Mon; **Asolo:** Sat; Castelfranco Veneto: Piazza Giorgione, Tue & Fri am; **Venice:** Campo S Margherita, daily; **S Polo** Rialto: Campo della Pescaria, daily; **Cannaregio:** Rio Terrà S Leonardo, daily.

Major festivals: Bassano del Grappa: Mestieri in Piazza, Sep; **Marostica:** Spring Festival, 1 May; Cherry Festival, end May–early Jun; Partita a Scacchi (human-chess tournament, bi-annual even-numbered years), mid-Sep; St Simeon Fair, last Sun Oct; **Asolo:** International Art Film Festival, Aug; Asolo Musica (chamber music), Aug–Sep; **Venice:** Carnevale, Feb; Regata Storica, first Sun Sep; 120 regattas, Apr–Sep.

DAY TRIP OPTIONS

Lovers of architecture and art can take the route between Bassano del Grappa and Castelfranco Veneto; the Altopiano is perfect for **family nature outings** or a day of skiing; while Venice is the obvious magnet from the Riviera del Brenta. For full details, *see p67*.

Above Scalinata dei Carmini, left, and the Chiesa del Carmini, Marostica

VISITING BASSANO DEL GRAPPA

Parking
On entering the town, head for the car park near Piazza Cadorna.

Tourist Information
www.comune.bassano.vi.it

WHERE TO STAY

AROUND BASSANO DEL GRAPPA

Villa Brocchi Colonna *moderate*
A small *agriturismo* surrounded by olive trees and vineyards. Free Wi-Fi.
Contrà San Giorgio 98, 36061 (2 km/ 1 mile from centre across the Brenta on Viale Diaz); 0424 501 580; www.villabrocchicolonna.it

MAROSTICA

Albergo Due Mori *expensive*
This 18th-century Venetian building has original features set with modern chic.
Corso Mazzini 73, 36063; 0424 471 777; www.duemori.com

AROUND MAROSTICA

La Rosina *moderate*
A small hillside hotel with an inexpensive restaurant serving traditional dishes.
Contrà Marchetti 4, Località Valle San Floriano (3 km/2 miles north of centre), 36063; 0424 470 360; www.larosina.it

ASIAGO

Golf Hotel Villa Bonomo *moderate*
Rustically elegant hotel with golf course, ski area and walking trails.
Via Pennar 322, 36012; 0424 460 408; www.hotelvillabonomo.it

❶ Bassano del Grappa
Vicenza, Veneto; 36061
This town is renowned for the production of grappa. Its landmark bridge, the **Ponte degli Alpini**, which can be seen on arrival into town, was designed by Andrea Palladio in 1571 and rebuilt in 1948. Enter the old walls through **Porta Dieda** and head up Via Roma, past **Museo Civico** *(closed Mon)*, which has works by the 19th-century sculptor Canova, to the splendid adjacent city squares, Piazza della Libertà and Piazza Garibaldi. The first is home to the **Palazzo del Comune** and the **Chiesa di San Giovanni Battista** *(open daily)*, the latter to the 13th-century **Torre Civica** *(open mainly summer weekends)* and the 11th-century Romanesque-Gothic **Chiesa di San Francesco** *(open daily)* with its pastel façade. Admire the views from Piazza del Terraglio and visit the medieval shell of the **Castello Superiore** and the **Viale dei Martiri** (pathway of the martyrs), dedicated to 31 Resistance fighters hung by the Nazis in 1944.
🚗 *Exit the centre of Bassano, following the "tutte le direzioni" signs, then at the main roundabout take SP248 direction Marostica. Park by the old city walls, near Porta Vincenza. There are 11 car parks near the historic centre.*

❷ Marostica
Vicenza, Veneto; 36063
Driving along the valley beneath the hills of the Colline Bassanesi, fairy-lights lead to the city's upper castle, **Castello Superiore**, where the Venetian government representative

lived for three centuries of rule. At the foot of the *Pausolino*, castle hill, is the **Castello Inferiore** *(open daily)* and one of three of the old city entries, **Porta Vicenza**, where the tourist office is located *(Piazza Castello 1)*. The castle opens onto the colonnaded city square, Piazza Castello, which is inlaid with a giant stone chessboard used during the bi-annual festival. At the far end of the square the **Palazzo Doglione**, once the armoury of the castle, has held the daily market since 1930. Cross the main palazzo-lined street, Corso Mazzini, from where a stone pathway, Sentiero Panoramico, leads up through olive groves to **Castello Superiore** – its walls and main gate can be explored at will. The footpath back to Marostica is reached via the steps of Scalinata dei Carmini (good walking shoes are essential).
🚗 *Take the SP71, with signs marking the way up to Asiago. Pass through Gomarolo and Conco, then take the SP72. There is ample street parking and free car parks in Asiago.*

❸ Asiago
Vicenza, Veneto; 36012
The picturesque regional capital lies at the heart of the "Sette Comuni", at 1,000 m (3,280 ft) altitude. The town is renowned all over Europe for its cheeses, and advertising billboards for the "formaggio di Asiago" skirt the country roads. Some cheese farms are open for visits. The medieval buildings of the town hall square, Piazza Risorgimento, were either fully re-built or re-clad after World War I.

Below The Ponte degli Alpini across the River Brenta at Bassano del Grappa

Where to stay: inexpensive, under €100; moderate, €100–€200; expensive, over €200

Above left The cupola and Doric colonnades of Tempio Canoviano at Possagno **Above** The centre of Asiago – Piazza Risorgimento

🚗 *Exit Asiago and turn left into the SP76, direction Gallio/Enego.*

④ Altopiano Panoramas
Vicenza, Veneto; 36052

The road from Asiago to Enego cuts through several communities of the Altopiano. Gallio is the main sports resort and has ski circuits and a forested ice-track. The tiny 1830s **Santuario della Madonna del Buso** church was rebuilt after World War I, when the Altopiano became the frontline of the Italian Resistance. Events will be held in 2014 to mark the war's centenary. **Foza** is a tiny village, perched on an escarpment with views of the northern Alps. **Enego** is the last stop before the road descends on the other side of the tableland. At 800 m (2,625 ft) altitude, the austere, greystone houses of the town are encircled by the Dolomites mountain chain.

House sign in Gallio, Altopiano region

🚗 *Take the SP76 through Fosse in the direction of Bassano del Grappa. On the valley floor, head south on the SS47, passing Cismon del Grappa, Valstagna and Solagna. After Solagna, turn left onto the SP74 to Romano d'Ezzelino, then right onto the SP26 for Possagno. Park outside the Tempio Canoviano.*

⑤ Possagno
Treviso, Veneto; 31054

The **Tempio Canoviano** (closed Mon; www.museocanova.it) dominates the town in which sculptor Antonio Canova (1757–1822), was born. He designed this Neo-Classical temple which was completed in 1832. The design is a hybrid of inspirations with Pantheon-like columns and the raised apse of a Christian basilica. In Via Canova, the **Museo Gipsoteca Canoviana** (closed Mon) has several rooms of paintings and sculptures, and is set in parkland alongside the 17th-century oil-painting filled **Casa del Canova**, where the artist lived.

🚗 *Continue on SP26 to Pederobba; turn left onto SR348 towards Feltre and right onto SP38, becoming SP29 and SP36, cross the river, following signs for Valdobbiadene. Car parks are signed; there is also street parking.*

⑥ Valdobbiadene
Treviso, Veneto; 31049

Overlooking the valley of the River Piave, this town is the capital of Italy's Prosecco and Cartizze spumante wine-making industry. The Piazza Guglielmo Marconi is lined with Palladian Neo-Classical buildings including the **Duomo** (open daily), the 18th-century campanile and town hall. Also here are Prosecco boutiques, fine pasticceria and grand old Art Nouveau cafés such as Caffè Vittoria.

🚗 *Take the SP2 south, passing through Covolo-Levada, then the SP84 to Maser. The Villa di Maser is signposted all the way up to the road leading into it.*

Strada del Prosecco

The Prosecco and Wine route, the *Strada del Prosecco e dei Vini dei Colli Conegliano e Valdobbiadene* winds its way through the hills and villages around Valdobbiadene. On the outskirts of town, wine makers beckon passers-by into their cellars with signs. (For more information visit www.prosecco.it).

EAT AND DRINK

BASSANO DEL GRAPPA

Pulierin *inexpensive–moderate*
There are 300 wines on the list and the restaurant prepares traditional, local dishes from farm produce.
Strada Soarda 26, 36061; 0424 566 785; www.pulierin.it; closed Sun

Ristorante Trevisani *moderate*
A convivial restaurant serving hearty dishes of pasta, meat and fish. *Piazzale Trento 13, 36061; 0424 522 201; www.ristorantetrevisani.it; closed Sun*

MAROSTICA

Osteria Madonnetta *inexpensive*
Sit at chunky wooden tables for simple dishes such as local cheeses, *fegato alla veneziana* (Venetian liver) and *baccalà alla vicentina* (Vicenza salt cod).
Via Vajenti 21, 36063; 0124 758 59; www.osteriamadonnetta.it; closed Thu

ASIAGO

Locanda Aurora *moderate*
Family-run restaurant using regional produce for dishes like ravioli – with Asiago cheese and Rotzo potato, or Asiago speck (lean cured ham) – and *gnochetti* with Asiago cheese and speck.
Via Ebene 71, 36012; 0424 462 469; www.locandaaurora.it; closed Mon

SHOPPING FOR CHEESE AND WINE

Caseificio Pennar Asiago is a cooperative selling cheeses made with milk from the Altopiano dairy farms.
Via Pennar 313, Asiago, 36012; 042 446 2374; www.caseificiopennar.it

Nino Franco Spumanti produces and sells several different styles of Prosecco and dessert wine, from Prosecco Brut to the outstanding, sweeter Cartizze.
Via Garibaldi 147, Valdobbiadene, 31049; 042 397 2051; www.ninofranco.it; Book for winery visits and tastings

---

Eat and Drink: inexpensive, under €25; moderate, €25–€45; expensive, over €45

Above Rooftops and panoramic views across the hills, Asolo **Top right** The Albergo Al Sole, Asolo **Right** Villa Emo's Classical Greek frontage

VISITING VILLA DI MASER

Via Cornuda 7, 0423 923 004; www.villadimaser.it; open Apr–Oct: Tue–Sun; Mar, Jul & Aug: Tue, Thu, Sat & Sun; check the website first as times can vary.

WHERE TO STAY

ASOLO

Albergo Al Sole *expensive*
An elegant 16th-century palazzo close to the main town square, with chic bar and views over the *città vecchia*.
Via Collegio 33, 31011; 0423 951 332; www.albergoalsole.com

RIVIERA DEL BRENTA

Hotel Villa Alberti
inexpensive–moderate
Restored 18th-century Venetian villa in classical gardens and peaceful woods. Restaurant, parking and free Wi-Fi.
Via Ettore Tito 90, Dolo, 30031; 041 426 6512; www.villalberti.com

Hotel Villa Franceschi *moderate*
Villa set in park of trees, sculptures and gardens. Some rooms have river views. Buffet-style breakfast.
Via Don Minzoni 28, Mira, 30034; 041 426 6531; www.villafranceschi.com

Hotel Villa Goetzen *moderate*
On the banks of the River Brenta, this hotel is furnished with antiques and high-tech fittings. Delicious breakfast.
Via Matteotti 2/c, Dolo, 30031; 041 510 2300; www.villagoetzen.it

⑦ Villa di Maser
Maser, Treviso; Veneto; 31010
This UNESCO-listed villa and its splendid gardens are alongside the road in Maser. Both were designed by 16th-century architect Andrea Palladio who transformed the ruins of the medieval palazzo of Maser into a Renaissance masterpiece. Palladio's designs were inspired by the values of ancient Greek and Roman Classical architecture. Six rooms in the villa are decorated in a typically Palladian style with frescoes by Paolo Veronese and stuccoes by Alessandro Vittoria.

🚗 *Continue down the SP84, turn right into the SP248 and follow the signs to Asolo città vecchia (old town) for parking. The main car park is in Piazza Garibaldi.*

⑧ Asolo
Treviso, Veneto; 31011
The historic heart of this hillside town is Piazza Garibaldi whose fountain still draws water from the underground aqueducts that fed the ancient Roman baths. Piazza Garibaldi spills out over the main street and the steps to the **Cattedrale**. At Piazzetta Pio X explore the art and archaeological collections in the **Museo Civico** *(open Sat–Sun only)*. On Via Browning **Casa Tabacchi** is where English poet Robert Browning (1812–1892) wrote *I Versi di Asolando*. The **Giardino di Villa Freya** showcases flowers loved by English writer Freya Stark; the ruins of the **Teatro Romano** are also here. An old city door on Via Collegio leads to a scenic pathway up to the 14th-century castle, **La Rocca** *(open Sat–Sun only)*, on top of Monte Ricco. The medieval **Castello della Regina** *(grounds open daily; castle open Sat–Sun)* has unmissable views of Asolo and the surrounding countryside.

🚗 *Follow the SP101 to Fanzolo where Via Boscalto leads into Via Stazione. Villa Emo is a short way along this road.*

⑨ Villa Emo
Fanzolo di Vedelago, Treviso, Veneto; 31050
Another of Palladio's masterpieces set in a large park, the villa was built for Count Leonardo Emo in the 1550s. Composed around a central flight of marble steps and four Greek temple-like columns, the long rectangular building is framed on each side by large storage barns typical of a Venetian villa. Well-preserved 16th-century frescoes by Giovanni Battista Zelotti decorate the porch and the central salon – depicting the Veneto

Above Classical statues mark the entrance to the grounds and ornate house of Villa di Maser

Where to stay: inexpensive, under €100; moderate, €100–€200; expensive, over €200

region's agricultural history with agrarian motifs such as festoons of flowers, fruits and crops.

🚗 *Head to the centre of Fanzolo, and take the SP101 following the signs for Castelfranco, then turn left onto the SR667. Follow signs to the car park at Piazza Giorgione.*

⑩ Castelfranco Veneto
Treviso, Veneto; 31033

From the old market square, Piazza Giorgione, walk around the medieval 17 m (56 ft) high red stone walls to the semi-ruined **Castello**, then through the western **Porta Cittadella**. The hub of the historic centre is the Piazza del Duomo with its mid 18th-century Palladian-inspired **cathedral** *(open daily)* and the **Oratorio Madonna della Grazie** *(open daily)*. Exit through the eastern **Porta Davanti** to see the adjacent clock tower, **Torre dell'Orologio**. Medieval frescoes adorn the castle's walls, the town's ancient arcades and the palazzi along Corso XXIX Aprile.

🚗 *Leave town on the SR245, following the signs for Padova. Pass Resana and follow the SR307. Turn left onto the SP10 towards Borgoricco, then take the SR308 towards Cadoneghe. Come off the slip road on the SR514 which becomes the SP46. Approaching Stra on the SR11, turn left into Via Doge Pisani and the entry of the Villa Pisani.*

⑪ Riviera del Brenta
Venezia, Veneto; 30039

The Riviera del Brenta became a rural haven for wealthy Venetian merchants and aristocrats in the 14th century. Their splendid country homes were built in Palladian, Neo-Classical or Renaissance style with lavish interiors and sculpture-filled gardens. Today many of the houses are open to visitors and contain museums, parks, restaurants and hotels. From Stra to Mira, the "Naviglio del Brenta" (Brenta Canal) meanders its way past dozens of splendid villas.

The first villa of note is the **Villa Pisani**. Dating from 1700, this is the grandest villa on the Brenta. Venetian doges and European monarchs once

stayed in the 114-room residence. It is now a museum of 18th- and 19th-century art, furniture and interiors. The French-style gardens and surrounding park are scattered with statues.

Continue along Via Riviera del Brenta to reach **Villa Foscarini Rossi**. Built in the mid-1600s, this was the residence of Marco Foscarini, Venice's procurator and future doge. Part of the villa is now the **Museo RossiModa della Calzatura**, which has a collection of fine footwear by one of the most prestigious Italian shoe manufacturers for designers such as Yves Saint Laurent, Givenchy and Christian Dior. Head back onto the SR11 to the medieval town of **Dolo**, once a vital midway point between Venice and Padova. Among Dolo's several villas, the gardens of **Villa Ferretti-Angeli** are now a large public park. Continue on the SR11 to **Mira** and the **Villa Widmann Rezzonico Foscari**. This exquisite Baroque villa has ground floor salons with silk-panelled walls and lavish Murano glass chandeliers. It also houses the **Information Point of the Riviera del Brenta**. Mira's other villa attraction is the frescoed mid-18th-century guest quarters of the **Barchessa Valmarana**.

🚗 *Continue on the SR11/SS11, then take the SS309 and follow signs to the "stazione" for the car parks at Mestre. A regular train runs from here to Venice, making it a good option for those who want to avoid driving into Venice. Alternatively, to drive into Venice take the SR11 and park at Piazzale Roma.*

Mosaic detailing, Asolo

Above Detail of fresco featuring allegorical figures, Villa Foscarini Rossi

VISITING VILLA EMO

Via Stazione 3, 31050; 042 347 6334; open Apr–Oct: Mon–Sat pm, Sun am; Nov–Mar: daily pm; check first as times may vary.

VISITING THE VILLAS ALONG THE RIVIERA DEL BRENTA

Villa Pisani
Via Doge Pisani 7, Stra; 30039; 049 502 074; www.villapisani.it; open Apr–Sep: daily

Villa Foscarini Rossi
Via Doge Pisani 1/2, Stra; 30039; 049 980 1091; www.villafoscarini.it; open Apr–Oct: daily except Mon am & Sat pm; Nov–Mar: Mon–Fri am

Villa Widmann Rezzonico Foscari
Via Nazionale 420, Mira; 30034, 041 424 973; www.turismovenezia.it; open Mar–Oct: Tue–Sat; Nov–Feb: Sat–Sun

Villa Barchessa Valmarana
Via Valmarana 11, Mira, 30034; 041 426 6387; www.villavalmarana.net; open Mar–Oct: Tue–Sat; Nov–Feb: Sat–Sun and for large groups by appointment

EAT AND DRINK

ASOLO

Antica Osteria Al Bacaro *inexpensive*
A rustic inn with excellent wines and simple pasta dishes. Finish off with a honey strudel.
Via R Browning 165, 31011; 042 355 150; closed Wed

Osteria Ca' Derton *expensive*
In a 17th-century building, it serves many pasta and soup dishes, as well as meat and fish mains.
Piazza Gabriele d'Annunzio 11, 31011; 042 352 9648; www.caderton.com; closed Sun & Mon lunch

RIVIERA DEL BRENTA

Trattoria Nalin *moderate–expensive*
This trattoria in an 18th-century villa serves seafood and fish dishes, as well as pasta and risotto dishes and home-made desserts.
Via Novissimo Argine Sinistro 29, Mira, 30034; 041 420 083; www.trattorianalin.it; closed Sun pm & Mon

Ristorante Villa Goetzen *expensive*
Serves a regularly changing menu of seafood dishes and weekly specials. In summer, the restaurant extends onto a romantic canal-floating pontoon. *Via Matteotti 2/c, Dolo, 30031; 041 510 2300; www.villagoetzen.it; closed Thu & Sun eve*

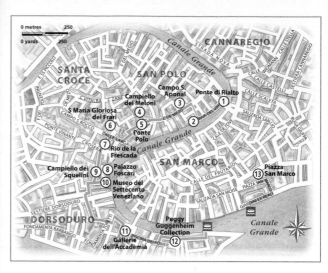

Above *Vaporetto* travelling along the Grand Canal, Venice

VISITING VENICE

Parking
Close to the Santa Lucia train station, there are several car parks at Piazzale Roma. *www.veniceparking.it*

Getting Around
The best way of getting around Venice is by *vaporetti* (waterbuses). The main *vaporetto* route is along the Grand Canal, though waterbuses also connect to the outskirts of Venice and islands in the lagoon. *www.hellovenezia.it*

Tourist Information
Santa Lucia train station; 041 719 078; open daily 8am–6:30pm; Piazza San Marco; 041 522 6356; open daily

WHERE TO STAY IN VENICE

Ca' Pisani *moderate–expensive*
This 14th-century Venetian palace has Art Deco furnishings, marble bathrooms and high-tech facilities. Free Wi-Fi. *Dorsoduro 979/A, 30123; 041 240 1411; www.capisanihotel.it*

Pensiona La Calcina
moderate–expensive
This 17th-century inn and café was the haunt of bohemian artists. Buffet breakfast, rooftop deck, bar and a floating café. *Dorsoduro 780, 30123; 041 520 6466; www.lacalcina.com*

Al Ponte Antico Hotel *expensive*
A quixotic 9-room hotel in a small 16th-century Venetian palace, with balcony views over the Grand Canal and Rialto Bridge. *Calle dell'Aseo, Cannaregio 5768, 30131; 041 241 1944; www.alponteantico.com*

Right One of the many minor waterways in Venice with houses crammed along its edge

⑫ Venice
Venezia, Veneto; 30100

One of the world's greatest enigmatic beauties, floating on a labyrinth of waterways and bridges. Few visitors do not find themselves totally lost in Venice. Before heading to its main tourist hub and most evocative square, Piazza San Marco, with the marble-walled Palazzo Ducale (Doge's Palace), try taking a stroll through some of the more peaceful *sestieri* (districts).

A two-hour walking tour
Catch a *vaporetto* to the **Ponte di Rialto** ① – the most famous of the city's 350 bridges and, until the mid-19th century, the only one across the Grand Canal. Cross the bridge and turn immediately left into **Riva del Vin** ② to soak up the atmosphere of the Grand Canal – the 3.5 km (2-mile) long "main road" of Venice and its principal transport artery. Stop at a café and watch passing gondolas. Turn right into Rio Terà San Silvestro (o del Fontego) and take the passageway

Calle di Mezo to the **Campo S Aponal** ③ in San Polo. This, the smallest district, is full of old craft ateliers and shops; some streets, squares and rivers are named after the goods once sold there. The **Campiello dei Meloni** ④ is a small marketplace where melons were sold – continue through here, over the Rio dei Meloni, following the signs/arrows to the *Ferrovia* (station), to reach the Campo San Polo. Cross the Rio Polo, across **Ponte Polo** ⑤, and take Calle Larga to the Campo dei Frari with its

RIO DE LA TOLETTA

minor basilica, **S Maria Gloriosa dei Frari** ⑥. Take the Calle Fianco de la Scuola across the bridge behind the church – over the **Rio de la Frescada** ⑦ – to reach the art-rich Dorsoduro neighbourhood. At the sign pointing to Ca' Rezzonico turn left and continue along Calle Largo Foscari, cross the Rio di Ca'Foscari, and on to the **Palazzo Foscari** ⑧, rumoured to be the birthplace of the great Doge Francesco Foscari, who ruled from 1423–57. Continue through the peaceful square **Campiello dei Squelini** ⑨ and head to the Ca' Rezzonico – a Gothic palazzo once owned by English poet Robert Browning's son in the 1880s, which now houses the **Museo del Settecento Veneziano** ⑩ (closed Tue).

Cross the Rio di San Barnaba to Campo San Barnaba and take the Calle della Toletta to the **Gallerie dell'Accademia** ⑪ (open daily) in

Campo della Carità. This former Palladian convent has a priceless collection of 15th–18th-century Venetian paintings, including works by Giorgione, Carpaccio, Bellini, Titian and Tintoretto.

Italy's leading treasure-chest of early 20th-century art lies a short distance along the canal, over the Rio de San Vio: the **Peggy Guggenheim Collection** ⑫ (open daily) is housed in her former home, the Palazzo Venier dei Leoni, and includes major works by Giacometti, Dalí, Picasso and Pollock. The museum has sculpture-filled gardens and wonderful views from the terrace over the Grand Canal.

Mooring post, Grand Canal

From here it is a short walk across the Rio della Furnace to Campo della Salute and the vaporetto stop of Salute, which goes across to the historic hive around **Piazza San Marco** ⑬.

Above left The Danieli Palace, one of Europe's most celebrated hotels Left Gondolas on the Grand Canal Above One of the arcades around Piazza San Marco

EAT AND DRINK IN VENICE

Il Refolo *inexpensive*
A buzzing, canal-side pizzeria in a typical Venice square. Pizza toppings include pumpkin flower and *porcini* mushrooms. *Santa Croce 1459, Campiello del Piovan, 30135; 041 524 0016; closed Tue lunch*

La Mascareta *moderate*
A wine bar-*osteria* endorsed by Italy's Slow Food movement. Choose from a handful of mains: squid with polenta, meat stews and mixed seafood platters. *Castello, 5183, Calle Lunga Santa Maria Formosa, 30122; 041 523 0744; open Tue–Fri eve*

Vino Vino *expensive*
A few steps from Piazza Marco, with 330 wine labels; daily specialities such as salted cod (*baccalà*), quail with polenta and home-made sweets. *San Marco 2007/A, 30124; Via XXII Marzo; 041 2417 688; www.vinovino.it*

DAY TRIP OPTIONS

The Altopiano provides an array of activities for outdoor enthusiasts. It lies north of Marostica and Bassano del Grappa, and is easily reached from both. Drive up to Asiago and down to Enego on the other side of the Altopiano, or return directly from Asiago or Gallio. The Strada dell'Architettura can be accessed from Bassano, Marostica, Asolo or Castelfranco Veneto. A day in Venice is not to be missed for those based along the Riviera del Brenta.

Altopiano dei Sette Comuni
The Altopiano ❹ is a massive outdoor amphitheatre: trek over its rugged terrain or in winter, try the

ski circuits and ice tracks in Gallio, immersed among the peaks and valleys. Visit Asiago ❸, the pretty regional "capital" for lunch and to sample some of its famous cheese.

The SP71 from Marostica and SP72 from Bassano del Grappa both lead to Asiago, meeting at Conco about mid-way up the plateau.

Strada dell'Architettura
Follow this route of architectural wonders – magnificent Palladian villas, museums, churches and medieval walled towns – north-east from Bassano del Grappa ❶ to Possagno ❺, Valdobbiadene ❻, down to Villa di Maser ❼ and

Asolo ❽, through to Villa Emo ❾ and Castelfranco Veneto ❿.

Follow the driving instructions in the itinerary between these stops.

Venice
From the Riviera del Brenta ⑪, take a scenic trip to Venice ⑫ on a tourist boat. Highlights include the treasures of Piazza San Marco, a stroll along the Grand Canal, Ponte Rialto, the Accademia art gallery and the Peggy Guggenheim Collection of modern art.

The SS11 leads from Mestre to Venice or alternatively take a train. Once there, day-tickets can be bought on the vaporetto for multiple water trips.

Eat and Drink: inexpensive, under €25; moderate, €25–€45; expensive, over €45

Mountains and Lakes

Laghi di Fusine to Trieste

Highlights

- **Scenery of the Alpi Giulie**
  Admire the national parks and pretty alpine villages in the Alpi Giulie

- **Cultural capital of Udine**
  Wander past the ancient palazzos and loggias of the Friuli region's old capital

- **The farms and vineyards of Collio**
  Zig-zag around the low-lying hills, thick with vineyards, farms and country inns, close to the Slovenian border

- **Rustic food**
  Feast on delicious homely cuisine washed down with top-quality wine from this overlooked area of Italy

- **Trieste**
  Tour the Roman ruins, grand palazzos and coffee houses of the seaside capital of Friuli-Venezia Giulia

The 14th-century Castello Duino, on the road from Gorizia to Trieste

Mountains and Lakes

Bordering Austria and Slovenia, Friuli-Venezia Giulia has a complex history, reflected in the patchwork of languages and ethnic minorities of the region. Its Tarvisiano area has passed between Austrian and Italian rule over the centuries and sits in a valley gouged by rivers and lakes and surrounded by the high peaks of the Alpi Giulie. The mountains form an undulating border south through the plains of the Friuli Grave, the winemaking and ham-curing area scattered with castles, west of the small art city of Udine. To the east are two wine-growing regions, the Colli Orientali and the Collio, the latter literally a stone's throw from the Slovenian border. In the lower part of Gorizia, the dramatic colours and limestone landscape of the karst plateau unroll to the Adriatic and the spirited maritime capital of Trieste.

Above The remains of the colonnaded Roman forum in front of the medieval Castello di San Giusto, Trieste, *see p77*

ACTIVITIES

Walk the loop of the lower Lago di Fusine

Hear the call of the wild with some dog-sledding in Tarvisio

Cross-country ski in winter (or walk in summer) through the beautiful Valbruna countryside

Ascend to the spiritual heights of Monte Lussari by cable car

Scare yourself with the mummies in the Duomo, Venzone

Explore the Collio hillside wineries and farms near Cormons on the Strada del Vino e delle Ciliege

Play golf under the mountains at San Floriano del Collio

Picnic by the River Isonzo enjoying the region's gourmet specialities

Spend a day in museums in the "museum quarter", Trieste

KEY

━ Drive route

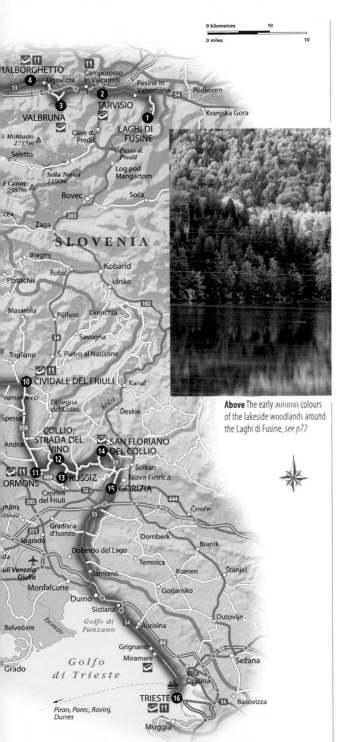

0 kilometres 10

0 miles 10

Above The early autumn colours of the lakeside woodlands around the Laghi di Fusine, *see p72*

PLAN YOUR DRIVE

Start/finish: Laghi di Fusine to Trieste.

Number of days: 5 days – 2 days for sport and relaxation in the mountains; a day for Udine; a day touring the Friuli wine region and a full day in Trieste.

Distance: Approx. 201 km (125 miles).

Road conditions: The road is very narrow to and from Laghi di Fusine, though most of the alpine routes are wide. Signage is generally good but particularly scarce in the Gorizia area and on the tiny Collio hillside roads. Snow chains are obligatory during winter.

When to go: Tarvisiano's autumn hues are glorious and it will be free of summer trekkers and winter skiers. Udine and the wine region are best visited May Oct. Maritime Trieste can be mild – but also windy any time of the year.

Opening times: Shops tend to open Mon–Sat 9am–1pm and 4–8pm (some are shut Mon am or Wed pm). Churches and museums vary but usually open 8 or 9am–noon and 4–7 or 8pm. Many museums are closed Mon.

Main market days: Tarvisio: daily; Gemona del Friuli: Centro Storico, Fri; Udine: Via Zanon, daily; Via Redipuglia, Sat; Cividale del Friuli: Sat; Cormons: Fri; Trieste: Mon–Sat.

Shopping: Look out for salt-cured, air-dried ham in San Daniele del Friuli and organic wines from the Castello di Arcano estate along the Strada dei Castelli e del Prosciutto.

Major festivals: Tarvisio: Krampus (St Nicholas Eve), 5 Dec; Venzone: Festa della Zucca, last weekend Oct; Udine: Friuli DOC food and wine, 2nd or 3rd weekend Sep; Trieste: Barcolana regatta, 2nd Sun Oct; Palio di Trieste: Carnevale, late Jan to mid-Feb.

DAY TRIP OPTIONS

From Tarvisio, walk in the **mountains** around **lakes** and ride in **cable cars** to hilltop **churches**. Enjoy the **cured ham** of San Daniele, and ancient **castles** and **cities** rebuilt after **earthquakes**. Take a **tour of the vineyards** of Collio, before visiting **lively and cultured Trieste**. For full details, *see p77*.

Above The picturesque hamlet of Valbruna, in the shadow of the Alpi Giulie

GETTING TO LAGHI DI FUSINE

Starting from Tarvisio, take the SS54 east through Fusine in Valromana and take the small Via dei Laghi right about 1.5 km (1 mile) to the two lakes.

WHERE TO STAY

TARVISIO

Edelhof *inexpensive–moderate*
At the edge of the forest, this grand residence has 16 rooms, a restaurant, bar, wellness centre and free Wi-Fi.
Via Diaz 13, 33018; 0428 40081; www.hoteledelhof.it

VALBRUNA

Valbruna Inn *moderate*
This village inn has rooms with balcony views of the Alpi Giulie and the forested valley. Free Wi-Fi.
Via Alpi Giulie 2, 33010; 0428 660 554; www.valbrunainn.com

MALBORGHETTO

Casa Oberrichter *inexpensive*
A B&B in a wood-beamed 15th-century Brandenburg palace with a restaurant on the first floor. Free Wi-Fi.
Via Superiore 4, 33010; 0428 41888; www.casaoberrichter.com

SAN DANIELE DEL FRIULI

Hotel Alla Torre *inexpensive*
A family-run 3-star hotel in the historic centre with helpful and efficient staff. The interior is modern yet sober, with classical decor and furnishings.
Via del Lago 1, 33038; 0432 954 562; www.hotelallatorrefvg.it

① Laghi di Fusine

Udine, Friuli-Venezia Giulia; 33018
The two glacial-formed lakes of Fusine, the Lago Inferiore and Lago Superiore, are set amid dense forests of red fir trees, framed by curving hills and a crown of alpine summits. The colours of the mirror-surface lakes vary from sapphire to turquoise, clear to milky as the seasons and light change – in autumn the forests are afire with intense colours. Walk a circuit of the lakes on the Sentiero del Rio del Lago.

🚗 *Head onto the SS54, and follow the sign to Tarvisio. Parking in Tarvisio can be tricky as it gets extremely busy – use on-street parking.*

② Tarvisio

Udine, Friuli-Venezia Giulia; 33018
In the far northeast of Friuli-Venezia Giulia, where Italy, Slovenia and Austria meet, Tarvisio, the capital of the region flies the flags of the three border communities. Nestled in an amphi-theatre of valleys and peaks, the town is charming and very alpine-oriented – the local hero is Julius Kugy, who climbed the Alpi Giulie (Julian Alps) in the early 1900s. Ski shops and neon-signed hotels line the high street. Alpine sports – snow-boarding, skiing, dog-sledding and snow-shoeing – are the attraction, so visit the **Tourist Office** *(Via Roma 14, 33018; 0428 2135)* for information. But enjoy, too, the village ambience, the daily market in **Piazza Mercato**, and the restaurants which, oddly, specialize in fish.

🚗 *Take the SS13 direction Udine, and turn left into Via Fassinelle for Valbruna.*

③ Valbruna

Udine, Friuli-Venezia Giulia; 33010
This delightful alpine hamlet in the Val Canale opens onto a natural world of mountain meadows and vales – habitats for roe deer and myriad birds. From spring to autumn it is the place for nature lovers. A network of walking trails leads into the valley, to mountain peaks, and to the 1,790-m (5,872-ft) high church bells of the **Santuario Monte Lussari** *(open daily mid-Jun–mid–Sep)* (about three hours' walk, or take a cable car from neighbouring Camporosso). In winter, the plains of Valbruna transform into a fabulous cross-country ski domain, right alongside the village, with a huge network of trails extending through the upper Val Saisera.

🚗 *Return to the SS13, direction Udine, then turn right into Malborghetto.*

④ Malborghetto

Udine, Friuli-Venezia Giulia; 33010
The main street of Malborghetto is tucked along the edge of a valley, skirted on both sides by a ridge of mountain peaks. A sign points out the village's two main historic sights: the 13th-century **S Maria della Visitazione** *(open daily)* on the town hall square near the Municipio, and down the street, the dashing 17th-century **Palazzo Veneziano** *(closed Mon)* which houses a **Museo Etnografico** with displays on local geology, prehistory, ethnology and forestry.

🚗 *Return to the SS13, direction Udine. Turn off to Venzone. Park outside the walls or near Piazza Municipio.*

Below Hotels with geranium-festooned balconies near the centre of alpine Tarvisio

Above Late 19th-century fountain at the centre of the town square, Venzone

5 Venzone
Udine, Friuli-Venezia Giulia; 33010
This medieval town prospered due to its position on an old trading route linking the Veneto to Corinthia (Austria), Kranjska Gora (Slovenia) and Bavaria. In 1976 an earthquake killed 3,000 people and destroyed most of the buildings. However, the citizens rallied and rebuilt it and the city is now an historic monument. Admire the skilful renovation of the walls, tower and old gate, **Porta San Genesio**; the Romanesque-Gothic 14th-century **Duomo Sant'Andrea Apostolo** (open daily), with mummified corpses in its **Capella di San Michele** – and the loggia on **Piazza Municipio**, around the Venetian-Gothic town hall.

🚗 Continue south on the SS13 and turn left to Gemona del Friuli. Follow signs to "centro storico" up to the car park near Piazza del Municipio.

6 Gemona del Friuli
Udine, Friuli-Venezia Giulia; 33103
The sloping, mountain-flanked old town of Gemona was also largely rebuilt after the 1976 earthquake. From the Piazza del Municipio and its Renaissance Palazzo Comunale, explore the boutiques and bookshops tucked into the ancient porticoed arcades which line both sides of Via Bini. Dominated by the **Castello**, the main street ends at the medieval doorway, **Porta Udine**. Here stands the intricate façade of the Romanesque-Gothic **Duomo di Santa Maria Assunta** (open daily), with its splendid central rose window and huge 7-m (23-ft) high statue of St

Christopher, protector of travellers. Inside, there is a reminder of earthquake damage in the inclination of the pink marble columns supporting the naves. Rising behind the cathedral are the peaks of the Parco Naturale delle Prealpi Giulie, gateway to the Alpi Giulie.

🚗 Head back onto the SS13, then take the SS463 through Osoppo, following the signs for San Daniele del Friuli.

7 San Daniele del Friuli
Udine, Friuli-Venezia Giulia; 33038
Dominating the plains of central Friuli from its hilltop, San Daniele is the area's cultural hub and famous for a prosciutto to rival that of Parma – connoisseurs say it is slightly sweeter. The main street is packed with shops and restaurants selling and serving the prized salt-cured, air-dried ham. From Piazza Vittorio Emanuele a graceful stairway leads up to the **Duomo di San Michele Arcangelo** (open daily), built around a medieval campanile in the early 1700s. Next door is the Palazzo Comunale (built in 1415 but with later additions) housing one of Italy's oldest libraries, the 15th-century **Civica Biblioteca Guarneriana** (open Tue & Fri). **Chiesa Sant'Antonio Abate** has Renaissance frescoes by Pellegrino da San Daniele (1467–1547), whose real name was Martino da Udine.

🚗 Head south in the direction Rive d'Arcano on the SP66, left into Loc. San Mauro, right into Via Castello d'Arcano, following signs to Castello Superiore. Take the SP66 to Fagagna, then the Via Fagagna and finally the SS464 to Martignacco.

SHOPPING FOR PROSCIUTTO

There are plenty of shops specializing in salt-cured, air-dried ham in San Daniele del Friuli, but try **Bottega Del Prosciutto** on Via Umberto Primo, 33038, or **Prosciutteria DOK Dall'Ava** on Via Gemona 29, 33038.

EAT AND DRINK

AROUND TARVISIO
Ristorante Hotel Bellavista moderate
Daily changing menu: starters of home-made pasta and soups, and mains of stews, game and grills.
Via Sella 61, Camporosso, 33010 (4 km/ 2 miles west of Tarvisio on SS13); 0428 63010; www.sporthotelbellavista.com

MALBORGHETTO
Antica Trattoria Da Giusi moderate
Revealing the culinary link between alpine Italy and Austria: mountain cheeses, smoked meat with sauerkraut, gnocchi with prunes and apricots.
Via Bamberga 19, 33010; 0428 60014; www.dagiusi.it

AROUND VENZONE
Hotel Ristorante Carnia moderate
Highly feted, this restaurant is bright and contemporary, with a menu based on seafood and classic Friulian dishes.
Via Canal del Ferro 28, Loc. Carnia, 33010 (6 km/4 miles north of Venzone on SS13); 0432 978 013; www.hotelcarnia.it

SAN DANIELE DEL FRIULI
Da Scarpan moderate
This simple cosy bistro serves excellent regional food – prosciutto, smoked trout and home-made pasta and sweets.
Via Garibaldi 41, 33038; 0432 943 066; www.dascarpan.it

Below left Prettily decorated lavender shop in Venzone **Below** Striking façade of Duomo di Santa Maria Assunta, Gemona del Friuli

Eat and Drink: inexpensive, under €25; moderate, €25–€45; expensive, over €45

Loggia del Lionello and Renaissance Loggia di San Giovanni. The **Torre dell'Orologio** (clock tower) where the main castle gate once stood is part of another portico. From here, take the path to the old castello, whose **Musei della Provincia di Udine** *(closed Mon & Sun pm)* houses valuable frescoes in the Galleria d'Arte Antica. Piazza Matteotti, with its 1543 fountain, is the heart of the city's elegant café and shopping zone – reached by the old market street, Via Mercatovecchio. Lastly, pass in front of the Palazzo del Comune and head to the Piazza del Duomo to see the Latin cross-shaped **cathedral** *(open daily)* whose foundations date to 1335. Masterful 18th-century frescoes by Tiepolo can be seen in the **Museo Diocesano** *(closed Mon & Tue)*, housed in the Palazzo Arcivescovile (Archbishop's Palace).

🚗 *Take the SS54 northeast following signs for Cividale del Friuli.*

Above Piazza della Libertà, Udine, filled with statuary and porticoes **Top right** The fertile vineyards and valley of the Rive d'Arcano **Bottom right** Piazza Paolo Diacono, site of the daily market, Cividale del Friuli

WHERE TO STAY

AROUND UDINE

Scacciapensieri *moderate*
Set on the Marina Danieli winery in the Buttrio hills, this agriturismo has six rooms with antique rustic furnishings and balconies for rural landscape views.
Via Morpurgo 29, Buttrio, 33042 (take SS56 south 25 km/16 miles to Buttrio); 0432 674907; www.marinadanieli.com

CIVIDALE DEL FRIULI

Locanda al Pomo d'Oro
inexpensive–moderate
Near the cathedral and located in a medieval inn, this place still serves its original purpose of providing travellers with shelter, tasty food and good wine.
Piazzetta San Giovanni 20, 33043; 0432 731 489; www.alpomodoro.com

Locanda al Castello *moderate*
Close to the *centro storico*, this inn oozes historic and bucolic allure, while offering luxury-hotel services such as an indoor pool, wellness centre and gardens.
Via del Castello 12, 33043; 0432 733 242; www.alcastello.net

CORMONS

Albergo Ristorante Felcaro *moderate*
A fine antique-filled villa combining a traditional style with modern frills: gym, sauna, swimming pool, tennis courts and free Wi-Fi. The wine bar serves wines made in the family's vineyard.
Via S Giovanni 45, 34071; 0481 60214; www.hotelfelcaro.it

⑧ Strada dei Castelli e del Prosciutto
Udine, Friuli-Venezia Giulia; 33034–33035
The hills of Friuli are dotted with ruins of castles built to ward off invaders. The Strada dei Castelli e del Prosciutto (Castles and Ham Route) leads from the prosciutto centre of San Daniele through the Rive d'Arcano, past misty moors and hillsides to Fagagna and Martignacco. Obelisks mark the turn-off to the **Castello Arcano Superiore** – a high medieval castle with a double wall, surrounded by vines. As well as pig farms there are many wineries in the area with tasting rooms – the rich soil yields quality white wines and makes stopping off at one or two a good idea. Organic production is popular here – the **Castello di Arcano** estate bottles wines from five organic grape-growing estates in the Friuli Grave and Colli Orientali di Friuli areas.

🚗 *From Martignacco take the SR464 to Udine.*

⑨ Udine
Friuli-Venezia Giulia; 33100
Midway between the mountains and seaside, Udine is a small powerhouse of art, architecture and gastronomy. Start out from **Piazza della Libertà**, cited as "the most beautiful Venetian square on dry land", with its sweep of 15th–17th-century buildings with elaborate lacework façades of arches and porticoes: the Venetian-Gothic

⑩ Cividale del Friuli
Udine, Friuli-Venezia Giulia; 33043
The Romans first built a fortification here on the banks of the Natisone river in 53 BC which Julius Caesar christened Forum Julii, from where the name Friuli comes. In AD 568, it became capital of the feudal Duchy of Lombard; later, like much of Friuli, it fell under the dominion of the mighty Venetian Republic. Cividale del Friuli has treasures from all of these epochs concentrated around the historical heart of the city and the eclectic (15th–17th century) cathedral **S Maria Assunta** on Piazza del Duomo. Opposite is the 8th-century fresco- and stucco-filled **Tempietto Lombardo** and, in front of it, a wonderful panorama of the Ponte del Diavolo and the River Natisone. Nearby is the 16th-century **Palazzo dei Provveditori Veneti** – attributed to the master architect Andrea Palladio – which houses the **Museo Archeologico Nazionale** *(closed Mon pm)*. From here take the antiquated pedestrianized Corso Mazzini: the main street leads up to the Piazza Paolo Diacono where a daily vegetable market is held between the pretty fountain and sweep of tall ochre-coloured houses.

🚗 *Take the SR356 south following the signposts to Cormons – park on-street.*

Where to Stay: inexpensive, under €100; moderate, €100–200; expensive, over €200

⑪ Cormons

Gorizia, Friuli-Venezia Giulia; 34071
This small peaceful town sits at the foot of Monte Quarin, in the heart of the hillside Collio vineyards. Its long main street, lined with miniature palaces and noble residences, loops around from the Piazza XXIV Maggio, home to the **Palazzo Locatelli**. This Palladian-style building houses the tourist office. It also conveniently doubles as an *enoteca* serving and selling local produce and wines. Maps of the wine routes are also available. Cormons was part of the Austrian Empire from 1497 to 1918, and its architecture and the statue of Maximilian I are testimony to the strong Habsburg memory. The town still toasts the Austrian Emperor Franz Joseph (1830–1916) on his birthday (18th Aug). The ruins of Castello di Cormons can be seen on the slopes of Monte Quarin.

🚗 *Take Via Roma, then the SR409 – turn right into Localitá Zegla.*

⑫ Collio: Strada del Vino

Gorizia, Friuli-Venezia Giulia; 34170
The *Collio* is the colloquial name given to the sloping Isonzo hills in northern Gorizia. Wedged between Cormons and the Slovenian border, the narrow belt is patchworked with vineyards and orchards and laced by a network of tiny roads forming the signposted Strada del Vino e delle Ciliegie (Wine and Cherry Route). Between the mountains and sea, the microclimate and ponka soils (clay and limestone) help create many celebrated DOC white wines Pinot Grigio, Sauvignon, Traminer Aromatico and Malvasia Istriana. An illustrated map by the roadside on the way out of town, replicated in tourist brochures, marks out the wineries with tasting rooms. Two vineyards on the way are **Azienda Agricola Bordo del Tiglio** and **Venica & Venica**. Pay close attention to the maps and signs as a wrong turn could lead you to Slovenia.

🚗 *From Zegla take Loc. Giasbana to Russiz di Sotto, then along Via Cesare Battista to Capriva del Friuli.*

⑬ Russiz

Capriva del Friuli, Gorizia; 34070
The Strada del Vino e delle Ciliegie follows a spidery trail of narrow roads that wind through the hills. Follow signs to Russiz – a tiny yet glorious wine-growing region spread over the hillsides. The splendid estate of **Villa Russiz** *(open Mon–Fri)*, founded in 1869 by French Count Theodore de la Tour was one of the first wineries in Friuli to use French vine varieties. The villa has some tasting rooms *(see right)*, a park, a chapel and a small mausoleum whose tiled cupola perches above the rows of vines. The mausoleum was built in 1894, on the death of the count, by his wife. From Russiz continue towards Capriva del Friuli, passing by the **Castello di Spessa** *(open daily)*. This medieval castle was altered in the 1880s and is now the centrepiece of a huge complex – a winery, golf course and hotel.

🚗 *Up Via Preval to Loc. Giasbana then right to Loc. Valerisce, left into Loc. Uclanzi and left into Loc. Bivio. San Floriano is well signposted.*

Below left The curving main street of Cormons, lined with grand residences **Below right** Hillside vineyards on the wooded Strada del Vino

WINERIES

One of the highlights of this drive is the wineries that can be visited, offering the chance to taste local vintages. On the Strada dei Castello e del Prosciutto try **Castello di Arcano***(Loc. Arcano Superiore 11/c, Rive d'Arcano, 33030; 0432 809 500; www.castellodiarcano. it)*. On the Strada del Vino e delle Ciliegie try **Azienda Agricola Borgo del Tiglio** *(Via San Giorgio 71, 34070, Cormons; 0481 62166; www.borgodeltiglio.it)* and **Venica & Venica** *(Loc. Cerò 8, Gorizia, 34070, Dolegna del Collio; 0481 61264; www.venica.it)*. In Russiz stop off at **Villa Russiz** *(Via Russiz 6, 34070, Capriva del Friuli; 0481 80047)* or **Castello di Spessa** *(Via Corona 62, 34071, Cormons; 0481 60445)*.

EAT AND DRINK

UDINE

La Clacarade *moderate*
This wood-beamed dining room has a handful of tables plus a long bar for drinking and dining. Enjoy smoked trout, cheese fritters with onion and *prosciutto cotto d'oca all'arancio* – orange-flavoured goose prosciutto. *Via S Francesco 6/A, 33100; 0432 510 250; closed Tue eve*

CIVIDALE DEL FRIULI

Enoteca De Feo *moderate*
In an appealing side street, this place exudes chic rustic charm. Enjoy a glass of wine with quality hams, salamis and cheeses, or more elaborate dishes. *Via Adelaide Ristori 29, 33043; 0432 701 425; www.enotecadefeo.it; closed Mon*

CORMONS

Caramella Osteria *Inexpensive*
Informal, authentic and charming small inn. Enjoy fresh minestrone, *insalatone* (hearty salad) and *crostini*. *Via Matteotti 1, 34071; 0481 639 341; closed Thu*

Eat and Drink: inexpensive, under €25; moderate, €25–€45; expensive, over €45

VISITING TRIESTE

Driving and Parking
Narrow streets and the one-way system make driving in Trieste difficult. There are few car parks, although many hotels have undercover parking (at extra cost). Park in the car park on Riva Nazario Sauro or on-street in the residential area between the historic centre and the cathedral/castello. Check that it is not a tow-away zone.

Tourist Information
4b Piazza dell'Unità; 040 347 8312

WHERE TO STAY

SAN FLORIANO DEL COLLIO

Hotel Castello Formentini *expensive*
This ancient castle (1520) has refined rooms and is run with simplicity and discretion – golf course, pool and gardens with views. Exquisite wine list.
Via Oslavia 2, San Floriano del Collio; 0481 884 051; www.golfhotelformentini.com

TRIESTE

Hotel Miramare *expensive*
Near the Castello di Miramare, this grey slate, metal and glass hotel is modernist and minimalist. Rooms have sea-facing terraces and high-tech essentials. There is also a beach bar and restaurant.
Viale Miramare 325/1, 34136; 040 224 7085; www.hotelmiramaretrieste.it

Urban Hotel Design *expensive*
Sleek and arty hotel in historic city location: the 18th-century stone and chunky ceiling beams are offset with contemporary art installations.
Androna Chiusa 4, 34100; 040 302 065; www.urbanhotel.it

⑭ San Floriano del Collio
Gorizia, Friuli-Venezia Giulia; 34070

The wine route winds through a series of hills before finishing in this medieval border village with stunning alpine views. The 15th-century **Castello Formentini** has a pine-filled garden and hotel-restaurant. At the golf club of **San Floriano** *(open May–Dec; 0481 884 252)* guests can hit balls into Slovenia. There is a wine estate in the village – **Azienda Agricola Simon Komjanc** *(www.colliowines.com)*. The road to Gorizia passes the Parco di Piuma Isonzo nature reserve by the Isonzo river, an ideal spot for a picnic.

🚗 *Take the SP17 to Gorizia – park at the Castello.*

⑮ Gorizia
Gorizia, FVG; 34170

The 11th-century **Castello di Gorizia** *(closed Mon)* hilltop district is an enclave of medieval history: the ethereal castle is one of the most splendid in Italy, with glorious views. The hilltop quarter of Santo Spirito is also home to the

Gothic **Chiesa di Santo Spirito**, and the **Musei Provinciali** *(closed Mon)* housing exhibitions on World War I and regional history. In the mesh of medieval, Baroque and 19th-century architecture in the city below, there are walkways along the Isonzo river and fine villas, such as the **Palazzo Coronini-Cronberg** *(closed Mon)*, set in magnificent parkland.

🚗 *Take the SS55 south, turn left onto the coastal SS14 at the sign for Duino, past Miramare on to Trieste.*

⑯ Trieste
Trieste, Friuli-Venezia Giulia; 34100

Once the third city of the Austrian Habsburg Empire after Vienna and Prague, Trieste is now a complex hilly cluster of Roman, Eclectic-style, Art Nouveau and Neo-Gothic architecture. From the bay and waterfront promenades to the top of San Giusto Hill, Trieste retains an international atmosphere among the the salty breezes washing in from the Adriatic.

A two-hour walking tour
From the car park, head up Riva 3 Novembre towards **Piazza dell'Unità dell'Italia** ①. The grand sweep of façades include the 1870 Palazzo Comunale, Palazzo del Governo, Palazzo del Lloyd Triestino – the shipping company's headquarters – and Casa Stratti, home to Caffè degli Specchi, an 1839 coffee house.

Visit the Tourist Information Office for maps, before heading northeast, through the small Piazza Verdi to the bottom of Corso Italia, the main road referred to locally as "Corso". Cross over and take the small Via Cassa di Risparmio to Via G Mazzini. Turn left and rejoin the waterfront avenue, Riva 3 Novembre: on the corner is the Neo-Classical **Chiesa Greco-Ortodossa di San Nicolò** ②. Continue along to the picturesque warehouse-lined strip

Map labels:
0 metres 100
0 yards 100

CORSO CAVOUR
VIA FABIO SEVERO
VIA TRENTO
VIA MILANO
VIA VALDIRIVO
VIA DEL CORONEO
Canal Grande ③ ④ Via Rossini
② Chiesa Greco-Ortodossa di San Nicolò
⑤ Chiesa di San Spiridione
PIAZZA VERDI
① Piazza dell'Unità dell'Italia
CORSO ITALIA
⑥ Teatro Romano
VIA DEL MONTE
⑦ Tor Cucherna
⑬ Chiesa di San Silvestro
Monumento ai Caduti ⑫ ⑧ ⑨ Foro Romano
Arco di Riccardo
⑩ Castello di San Giusto
⑪ Cattedrale di San Giusto
RIVA NAZARIO SAURO

Where to Stay: inexpensive, under €100; moderate, €100–200; expensive, over €200

of the **Canal Grande** ③: dug in 1756 to allow ships to unload inside the city. The canalside **Via Rossini** ④ is animated by restaurants, bars and markets and leads to the Ponterosso, with its James Joyce statue. The Irish writer lived in Trieste for more than a decade. Cross the bridge to the Piazza Ponterosso and head for the church, the **Chiesa di San Spiridione** ⑤, a Neo-Byzantine Serbian Orthodox church. Take Via Dante Alighieri back to the Corso Italia, and cross over to the gaping pit of the **Teatro Romano** ⑥, a Roman amphitheatre built by Emperor Augustus around 30 BC.

Take the steps alongside the Teatro, following signs to the **Tor Cucherna** ⑦, the ruins of a medieval tower, with fantastic views from the street above. From here, take the Treppe Giuseppe Rota stairway for the final climb up to the hilltop of San Giusto. Named after one of the city's patron saints, this area has Roman relics, medieval churches, public gardens and viewpoints. The piazza around the **Monumento ai Caduti** ⑧, a World War I memorial, is a popular romantic spot with terrific views. Carry on through the colonnaded **Foro Romano** ⑨ and on to the 14th–16th-century **Castello**

di San Giusto ⑩ *(open daily).* Across Piazza delle Cattedrale stands the Gothic stone lacework and trilobite arches of **Cattedrale di San Giusto** ⑪, a fusion of two 15th-century churches – hence its asymmetrical façade. Look to the right of the rose window for two huge cannon balls wedged into the wall. Head downhill on Via Cattedrale into suitably windy Via della Bora (north-east street) and on to the **Arco di Riccardo** ⑫, a crumbling 1st-century BC Roman gateway. Turn right and trace the walls of the Chiesa Santa Maria Maggiore perched on a ledge over the old town – alongside the small **Chiesa di San Silvestro** ⑬. A wide stairway leads down to the Via del Teatro Romano. Cross the street and head back to Piazza dell'Unità past the pretty sqaure of Piazza Piccola. Museum-lovers may wish to see the unofficial museum quarter – near Piazza Hortis – with three museums: the Civico Museo di Storia ed Arte e Orto Lapidario (archaeology), the Civico Museo di Storia Naturale (natural history) and the Civico Museo Sartorio (art and culture) *(all closed Mon).* Return to the car park via Via F Venezian.

Opposite The Isunzo river in the Parco Puma Isonzo natural reserve **Above left** The lively Canal Grande in the historic heart of Trieste **Above** Outside Caffe degli Specchi, a grand Viennese-style coffee house, Trieste

EAT AND DRINK

TRIESTE

SaluMare *inexpensive*
This gem of a restaurant offers a wealth of simple fishy treats: bruschetta topped with smoked puréed cod, anchovy butter or smoked salmon, as well as more substantial fish-filled panini and salads of octopus, squid and sardines. *Via di Cavane 10; 040 304 044; www.salumare.it; closed Sun & Mon*

Osteria da Marino *moderate*
A 1925 tavern serving simple, tasty Mediterranean staples such as mozzarella with tomatoes and Ligurian olives, washed down with lots of wine, in a jovial, gritty ambience. *Via del Ponte 5; 040 366 596; www.osteriadamarino.com; closed Sat & Sun lunch*

Pepenero Pepebianco Ristorante *moderate–expensive*
Modernist in atmosphere and food, the dishes here are fragrant and innovative; vegetarian options available. A convenient walk for those staying in the Piazza della Libertà and central station area. *Via Rittmeyer 14/a; 040 760 0716; www.pepeneropepebianco.it; closed Sun and Mon*

DAY TRIP OPTIONS

Incredibly varied landscape makes three desirable day trip options from Tarvisio, Udine or Gorizia:

Alpine village tour
From Tarvisio ②, walk a loop of the Laghi di Fusine ①, then on to Valbruna ③, stopping to take the cable car from Camporosso to Monte Lussari, and finish in Malborghetto ④.
Use the SS54 east to the lakes and the

SS13 west to the other alpine villages.

Strada dei Castelli e del Prosciutto
From Udine ⑨ head northwest on the Prosciutto & Castello route ⑧, to San Daniele del Friuli ⑦, the capital of cured ham. Then visit the renovated towns of Gemona del Friuli ⑥ and Venzone ⑤ for their architecture.

Take the SS464, the SP66, the SS463 and the SS13 to Venzone.

Vineyards to the coast
From Gorizia ⑮ visit Russiz ⑬ and Collio ⑫ winding through pretty vineyards – and stopping for a taste on the way – to Cormons ⑪. Then its off to Trieste ⑯ and the coast for an afternoon walk around the city and possibly an evening's entertainment.

Roads in the wine area are narrow and winding – use the SS55 then autostrada A4 (E70) to Trieste to save a little time.

Eat and Drink: inexpensive, under €25; moderate, €25–€45; expensive, over €45

The Italian Riviera

Dolceacqua to Cervo

Highlights

- **Medieval mountain villages**
  Explore the villages, castles and
  churches of the Val Nervia

- **Rustic flavours**
  Enjoy strong country flavours in bread,
  olives, pesto, pasta, chestnut honey;
  vegetable pies and boar with polenta

- **Flowers and villas**
  Admire the prettily decorated villas of
  the flower-painted Riviera dei Fiori

- *Belle époque* **San Remo**
  Parade along the elegant palm-lined
  waterfront boulevards and marinas

- **Fishing villages**
  Tour the Imperia coast via a string of
  fishing villages and seaside bastions
  from Porto Maurizio to Cervo

The Oratorio di San Bartolomeo and Palazzo
Comunale (Town Hall), Apricale

The Italian Riviera

From the palm-shaded *belle époque* villas and gardens of the bustling riviera towns to the ancient history and wild beauty of the hinterland valleys, the Imperia region in western Liguria is a land of incredible contrasts. Protected from climatic rigours by the Alpi Ligure, Val Nervia's villages are so sun-soaked that olive crops flourish even at altitude – Dolceacqua, Perinaldo and Apricale form the Strada dell'Olio (Olive Route). These medieval clusters of castle ruins and stone houses along the River Nervia are packed with narrow shady lanes, small piazzas, and Baroque churches full of valuable artworks and frescoes. Along the coast, produce from the fishing villages of the Riviera dei Fiori is vital in the flavoursome, fragrant and colourful Ligurian cuisine.

Above A walking trail near Dolceacqua, along the banks of the Rio Peitavino, *see p82*

ACTIVITIES

Buy olive oil direct from the source along the Val Nervia's Strada dell'Olio

Taste the local brews – Rossese di Dolceacqua red wine or Apricale's beer

Shop for pottery crafts in Dolceacqua and Apricale

Take an engraving or ceramic class in Apricale

Mountain bike or hike on Monte Ceppo in the Val Nervia

Take a ramble along the banks of the River Nervia

Walk or bike the coastal trail between Sanremo and Bussana Vecchia

Go whale watching from Imperia (www.whalewatch.it)

Above Colourful façade of the Chiesa di Sant' Antonio Abate in Dolceacqua, *see p82*

KEY

— Drive route

0 kilometres 2.5

0 miles 2.5

Below The beautiful village of Apricale, basking in the sun, *see p83*

PLAN YOUR DRIVE

Start/finish: Dolceacqua to Cervo.

Number of Days: 2–3 days allowing at least half a day in Sanremo, a day in the Val Nervia and a day between Imperia's beaches and fishing villages.

Distance: Approx. 97 km (60 miles).

Road conditions: Excellent, barring the odd winding road in the Val Nervia (notably Pigna to Perinaldo). The coast road (SP1) can be a slowly moving traffic jam in Jul–Aug and at rush hour.

When to Go: For fewer crowds, but loads of sunshine, flowers and flavours, opt for May–Jun and Sep–Oct. The Riviera dei Fiori makes a great destination in winter, when oranges and lemons are in season.

Opening times: Shops tend to open Mon–Sat 9am–1pm and 4–7pm or 8pm (city supermarkets often stay open for the siesta). Churches and museums vary enormously but usually open 8 or 9am–noon and 4–7 or 8pm. Many museums are closed on Mondays.

Main market days: Dolceacqua: Thu am; **Perinaldo:** Wed am; **Sanremo:** Tue and Sat am; **Cervo:** Thu am; **Oneglia:** Wed & Sat; **Porto Maurizio:** Mon & Thu.

Major festivals: Riviera dei Fiori: Festa di Primavera (spring festival), Jan–May; Fiori & Giardini di Riviera, end Jan; Sanremo: Festival della Canzone Italiana (Italian song festival), Feb/Mar; Piazza Nota 1: Concertino del Venerdì (classical music), Mar–Dec, Fri, Corso Garibaldi; Festival della Scienza, Oct–Nov; Festival dei Sapori (flavours), late Nov–early Dec; **Imperia Region:** Un Mare da Scoprire, mid-Mar; Vele d'Epoca (historic yachts), Sep; OliOliva, late Nov; **Cervo:** Basil festival, early May; Festival Internazionale di Musica da Camera, Jul–Aug.

DAY TRIP OPTIONS

Explore the Val Nervia for **medieval history**, maquis-covered **mountains**, ancient **churches, olive groves**, **vineyards** and **wild rivers**; families and sun-worshippers will want to target the **beaches**, **bathing establishments** and boulevards of the western Riviera – and the odd **museum** and **palazzo** for non-swimmers. For full details, *see p85*.

VISITING THE VAL NERVIA

Getting to Dolceacqua
From Ventimiglia, follow the Corso Genova parallel to the sea and turn left into the Corso della Repubblica/SP64 inland to Dolceacqua and the Val Nervia. After entering the town, turn right over the flat bridge for parking.

WHERE TO STAY

DOLCEACQUA

Talking Stones *moderate*
With charming interiors, this medieval B&B's studios have kitchens, claw-feet baths, and balconies with views over the Castello dei Doria and Val Nervia.
Via San Bernardo 5; 18035; 0184 206 393; www.talkingstones.it

PIGNA

Grand Hotel Pigna Antiche Terme *moderate–expensive*
Chill out at this mountain spa washed by sulphurous spring waters. Rooms are light with mountain or valley views.
Regione Lago Pigo, 18037, Pigna; 0184 240 010; www.termedipigna.it

APRICALE

Apricus Locanda *moderate*
Five gorgeously refined rooms with little balconies over the village and forests. This spotless village-centre home offers a warm welcome, rustic chic and excellent breakfasts.
Via IV Novembre 5, 18035; 0184 209 020; www.apricuslocanda.com

Below Steep medieval cobbled alleyway in the *Téra* quarter, Dolceacqua

➊ Dolceacqua
Imperia, Liguria; 18035
The **Castello dei Doria** ruins sit high on a hill over the mass of red roofs of Dolceacqua. A humped bridge spans the River Nervia which separates the original medieval quarter, **Téra**, from the **Borgo**, built several centuries later. Follow the signed historic trail which links the two and leads into the countryside. The Téra houses are up to six storeys high, in a labyrinth of steep cobbled alleyways. The **Palazzo della Caminata** stands out among the buildings, its portals decorated with the ruling Doria coat of arms. A good series of short, signed walking trails starts near the castle: the Sentiero Rio Peitavino reveals glimpses of the valley and riverside gardens. Relax afterwards with a glass of Maixei Rossese di Dolceacqua from the local cooperative wine cellar *(Piazza G Mauro 3).*

🚗 *Take the SP64 north all the way to Pigna – parking on the street.*

➋ Pigna
Imperia, Liguria; 18037
Pigna's main streets are laid out in concentric circles linked by steep paths and narrow alleys called *chibi*. These wind their way up to the *colla* – the highest part of the village with wonderful valley views. Admire the old town's Romanesque steeples and medieval fountains and spot the monograms of the land-owning families on the walls of the houses, showing their

Above The village of Bajardo, set at the top of a 900 m (2,950 ft) hill

privileged social position. The main Piazza Vecchia is rich in history: with the *campanile* (bell tower), Baroque **Oratorio di Sant'Antonio** and Roman **Chiesa di San Bernardo** graced with 15th-century frescoes by painter-priest Giovanni Canavesio. The main highlight is the **Chiesa Madre di San Michele Arcangelo**, its façade sculpted from local dark stone – *pietra nera* – and embellished with a white marble rose window and a stained-glass window.

Fountain sculpture, Dolceacqua

🚗 *Continue east on the SP65. Watch for right fork, SP64, to Castel Vittorio. Follow road around town to a square where it exits towards Bajardo.*

➌ Bajardo
Imperia, Liguria; 18031
At the end of the Val Nervia, many of the roads follow old carriageways and mule paths, and the alpine passes that connect the area to the coast are

Below View of Dolceacqua's graceful bridge over the river Nervia

recent additions. The hills are covered with woods of chestnut, pine and oak trees, and in the shadier parts olive trees and alpine pastures. Bajardo – at 900 m (2,950 ft) above sea level – has the highest olive plantations in Europe. Set on a rocky spur encircled by stone-walled crops, its red roofs and church steeples are almost as high as the neighbouring mountain. The medieval centre is full of small streets and great views from eastern Liguria to the French Alps. Mountain bike and hiking enthusiasts head for the 1,627-m (5,300-ft) Monte Ceppo, reached by crossing over the Ghimbegna pass from Bajardo.

🚗 *Take the SP63 south in the direction of Apricale.*

④ Apricale

Imperia, Liguria; 18035

High on a sun-soaked slope and surrounded by olive trees, Apricale – from the Latin for sunny – is one of Italy's most beautiful villages. A tradition of ceramic art, which started in the 1970s, has seen the village walls progressively covered in bright murals. The main piazza, Vittorio Emanuele, contains many treasures: stone arches, a trough and fountain, ochre logglas, a 13th century bell tower and a Baroque palazzo. The hanging gardens of the restored **Castello della Lucertola** (closed Mon; Jul–Aug open daily) form the backdrop for many artistic and cultural events. Its Art Nouveau-style frescoed rooms house a museum, with collections of old paintings and antiques. The micro brewery **Piccolo Birrificio** (Via IV Novembre 20) serves local beer.

🚗 *Head east on the SP63, soon forking right into the SP62 into Perinaldo.*

⑤ Perinaldo

Imperia, Liguria; 18032

Stretched along the crest of a hillside of terraced crops, Perinaldo is easily visible from a distance, especially the white bell tower of the Baroque **Chiesa di San Nicolò**. Fittingly, for a place whose ancient roofs are closer to the sky than most, the village was the birthplace of 17th-century astronomer, Gian Domenico Cassini. The observatory is in the **Convento di San Sebastiano**, a former Franciscan convent. (Some weekend nights in

summer at 9pm there are guided tours of the night sky.) Opposite is the town hall and church **Sant'Antonio da Padova** with its unique triangular-based bell tower. Stop, too, at **Castello Maraldi**, said to be the birthplace of Cassini and home to Napoleon and General Massena during the French Emperor's Italian campaign in the 1790s. On Piazza San Nicolò, the church of the same name houses the Renaissance painting, *Tela delle Anime (Cloth of Souls)*. On the façade of the **rectory** and former summer residence of the Marchesi Doria di Dolceacqua, is a sundial, built to the specifications of Cassini's grandson, the astronomer Gian Domenico Maraldi.

🚗 *Take the SP61, then turn right onto the SP59 to the coast. Take the SP1 through Vallecrosia and Bordighera to continue to San Remo.*

Above Bell tower and steps of Sant'Antonia da Padova, Perinaldo

Above View from the south facing – and sunny – village of Apricale

EAT AND DRINK

DOLCEACQUA

Ristorante Gastone *moderate*
Surrounded by café terraces and park benches full of chatty locals, this colourful-shuttered restaurant serves Ligurian food – tuna pasta, *tortino di patate* (mushroom and potato pie), stuffed ravioli, *faro* (spelt) lasagna with piquant *peperoncino* pesto – plus farm-fresh beans, lamb and cheeses and many vegetarian choices. Finish off with a traditional custardy dessert such as *zabaglione*.
Piazza Giuseppe Garibaldi 2, 18035; 0184 205 038

APRICALE

Ristorante Apricale Da Delio *moderate*
Inspired by dishes cooked up by his grandmother and mother, Delio serves Apricale ravioli stuffed with herbs and meat; pappardelle pasta made from chestnut flour and filled with *porcini* mushrooms; pan-fried rabbit, and aubergine, mushroom and potato pie.
Piazza Vittorio Veneto 9, 18035; 0184 208 008; www.ristoranteapricale.it; closed Mon & Tue (except Jul & Aug), Christmas

La Capanna da Bacì *moderate*
In an old stone cavern, this restaurant with a panorama over the valley serves typical country dishes of the Val Nervia. The fixed-price menu includes entrees of home-made pasta and main dishes of roast beef *carpaccio* and wild boar with polenta. The Terrazzone dell'Amore balcony is set up for candlelit romantic dinners. The owners also run a wine bar, **Grotte del Locanda** (Via Roma 1), with an *enodegustazione* (wine taster) menu – wine accompanied by small, lighter dishes. *Via Roma 14/16, 18035; 0184 208 137; closed Mon eve, Tue*

Eat and Drink: inexpensive, under €25; moderate, €25–€45; expensive over €45

Above Exotic palms and pretty flowers on Corso Matteotti, Sanremo

VISITING SANREMO

Parking
On the waterfront at Corso Imperatrice and along the Lungomare delle Nazioni.

Tourist Information
Largo Nuvoloni 1, 18038; 0184 59 059; www.visitrivieradeifiori.it

WHERE TO STAY

SANREMO

Hotel Paradiso *inexpensive–moderate*
A motel-style white building with sea-facing verandas. An excellent choice for those seeking 4-star comfort in an ideal location at a good-value price.
Via Roccasterone 12, 18034; 0184 571 211; www.paradisohotel.it

Belsoggiorno *moderate*
Considerate management, spacious and modern rooms and a big breakfast are major positives of this small 3-star hotel. There is a car park, too.
Corso Matuzia 41, 18038; 0184 667 631; www.belsoggiorno.net

Royal Hotel *expensive*
This 1872 hotel drips with Art Nouveau bronzes and paintings; glass walls reveal lush gardens and a pool. A terrace looks out to sea and there is an excellent spa.
Corso Imperatrice 80, 18038; 0184 5391; www.royalhotelsanremo.com

ONEGLIA

Hotel Rossini al Teatro
moderate–expensive
A high-tech hotel built around an 1863 theatre with deluxe stylish rooms. The service is switched-on and there is a spa and outdoor terrace.
Piazza Rossini 14, 18100; 0183 74000; www.hotel-rossini.it

⑥ Sanremo

Imperia, Liguria; 18038

With its casino, palm-lined seaside promenade and faded villa façades, Sanremo, the capital of the western Ligurian riviera, recalls the French Côte d'Azur. This air of early 20th-century *belle époque* lingers around the grand hotels, flower-gardened marina area and beachfront *corsos*, while the historic town centre – Pigna – is a living vestige of the past.

A one-hour walking tour

Start along the waterfront stretch of **Corso Imperatrice** ① part of the "new" city developed in the 1800s. The wide seaside avenues are planted with exotic plants – as is the **Parco Marsaglia** ②. Next to the park is the **Tourist Information Office** ③, housed in the former Riviera Palace Hotel. Behind it, the **Chiesa Russo-Ortodossa di Cristo Salvatore** ④ looks more like a lollipop-coloured palace than a religious edifice. The city's **Casino** ⑤ *(open daily)* marks the intersection of Corso Imperatrice and Corso Matteotti: built in 1905 but later expanded to its current cruise ship form. Opposite, the old train station is a hub of future urban regeneration. Continue along Corso Matteotti past the 1924 Art Deco **Ariston Theatre** ⑥, once frequented by Italian writer Italo Calvino. Next are the sea-facing façades of the 1720s **Palazzo Roverizio** ⑦ and elegant 1667 **Palazzo del Commissario** – sculpted with the Sanremo coat of arms.

Pass through the old city gateway off Via Palazzo, to the Chiesa di Santo Stefano and art-filled 17th-century Jesuit convent, **Convento dei Padri Gesuiti** ⑧ on Piazza Cassini, and enter the walled medieval town of **Pigna** ⑨.

A community still thrives in Pigna's covered passages, small squares, alleys stairways and tunnels known as *vallai* – from the Latin *vallum* for protection. Continue up pretty Via Moreno to the 14th-century fountain **Funtanassa** ⑩, which supplied the town's water until the 1900s. Cross the eastern fortified doorways, the **Porta del Roglio** and **Porta Bugiarda** ⑪ and climb up Via Roglio: past Sanremo's oldest church, the 1297 **Chiesa San Costanzo** ⑫ on Piazza San Costanzo. Carry on up to the hilltop gardens **Giardini Regina Elena** ⑬, where there is a lookout (avoid early or late in the day, if alone). Walk through the gardens to reach the cupola-topped Baroque **Santuario della Madonna della Costa** ⑭.

Return to the old town through **Porta di Santa Maria** ⑮, pass through **Piazza Capitolo** ⑯ and descend Via Capitolo. Turn right, and end the walk on Pigna's most beautiful square, **Piazza dei Dolori** ⑰. Sit at one of the cafés and admire the crested façades of the Genovese style Palazzo Pretorio and Palazzo Gentile Spinola. Return to the car park on Corso Imperatrice.

🚗 *From Corso Imperatrice head east on SP1 to Porto Maurizio, which is merged with Oneglia into Imperia.*

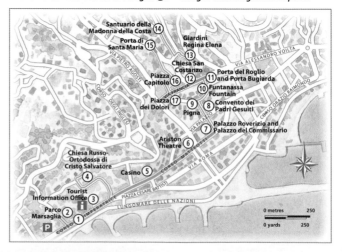

Above A view of the old town of Porto Maurizio on Paraiso Hill

⑦ Porto Maurizio

Imperia, Liguria; 18100

A once-thriving medieval trading centre managed by Benedictine monks, Porto Maurizio boasts Baroque oratories, palazzi and the loggias of **Convento di Santa Chiara**, skirting the old city walls with views over the Golfo di Imperia. The domes of the grandiose Neo-Classical **Basilica di San Maurizio** – Liguria's largest church – tower over the Piazza del Duomo, where there is also a **naval museum**. Stroll along the *lungomare* past the ruined **Torre di Prarola** and town beaches. On the western pier of Porto Maurizio, the bathing establishment **Spiaggia d'Oro** (Golden Beach) has a fine 1913 Art Nouveau entrance.

🚌 *Take the SP1, turning right onto the lungomare to Oneglia. Find a car park or meter by the port or in the centre.*

Above Elegantly decorated façade of the chiesa San Giovanni Battista, Cervo

⑧ Oneglia

Imperia, Liguria; 18100

Via Bonfante runs through the *centro storico*, with porticoed arcades full of independent shops, next to the busy Piazza Dante and its fine palazzo. Stroll along the marina, past the fishing cottages and the **Palazzo dei Doria** of old Oneglia. At the eastern edge of the town, in Via Palestro, there are traces of the 17th-century city walls. For a lesson on the history of olive oil, head to the **Museo dell'Olivo** (*Via Garessio 11; www.museodellolivo.com; open daily*). Above Oneglia, the Baroque fantasy **Villa Grock** (*Via Fanny Roncati Carli; 0183 704 211; open weekends*) is the 1920s villa of Swiss clown Adrien Wettach, a folly of fountains and gardens.

🚌 *Continue on coastal SP1 through Diano Marina to Cervo.*

⑨ Cervo

Imperia, Liguria; 18010

Set on a hillock, Cervo's houses form blocks of colour leading down to the sea. The blue and yellow Baroque façade of **San Giovanni Battista** (*open daily*) rises elegantly above its surroundings. Built in the 18th century from fishing industry profits, the church looks onto a courtyard used for the Festival Internazionale di Musica da Camera in summer. Higher up is the crenellated **Castello dei Clavesana** (*open daily*) housing an ethnographic museum. From the Piazza Castello, walk through olive groves to **Ciappà Park** for views over the Golfo di Diana.

EAT AND DRINK

SANREMO

Vino Panino & Co *moderate*
This enoteca has high benches and a street-side terrace. A big list of wines by glass and bottle, plus light snacks of panini, cheese and salami. Puts on weekend jazz evenings
Corso Mombello 56–8, 18038; 0184 524 290; closed Sun

Le Quattro Stagione *expensive*
Serving seafood, this restaurant offers a pleasant, welcoming atmosphere in the old city centre. Excellent wine list from its cellar-bar, Cantina Vini.
Via Corradi 83, 18038; 0184 573 262; closed Sun, Mon lunch

ONEGLIA

Ristorante Pizzeria Storie di Mare e... *inexpensive–moderate*
A big choice of traditional Ligurian dishes on Oneglia's portside restaurant row: fish, pasta, salads, grills and pizzas.
Calata Gian Battista Cuneo 41, 18100; 0183 291 719; closed Mon

Didù *moderate–expensive*
Part of Italy's Slow Food movement, the restaurant's ethos is authentic cooking with local produce. Expect quality food with home-made breads in an elegant minimal dining room.
Viale Giacomo Matteotti 76, 18100; 0183 273 636; www.ristorantedidu.it; dinner only; closed Sun and Mon

---

DAY TRIP OPTIONS

There are two obvious day trips possible – one through the Val Nervia via the ancient inland villages and the other along the sunny coastal riviera.

Through the Val Nervia
From Sanremo ⑥ (worth a day's investigation itself) drive to the high village of Perinaldo ⑤ to learn about astronomer Cassini, then visit the hilltop Apricale ④ for its plentiful charm and beauty before stopping at Dolceacqua ① for some olive oil and a walk along one of its historic trails. Then loop back to Sanremo.

From Sanremo take the SP1 then SP59 and SP61 to Perinaldo; then loop on the SP62, SP63, SP64 and back.

The Western Riviera
Staying at Oneglia ⑧ visit the olive oil museum before whizzing off to Porto Maurizio ⑦ for a walk along its promenade. Enjoy a swim before returning to Oneglia for a long lunch. Refreshed, set off to Cervo ⑨ for a stroll and, if lucky, a concert.

Take the SP1 all the way along the coast.

Eat and Drink: inexpensive, under €25; moderate, €25–€45; expensive over €45

The Cinque Terre

Varese Ligure to Montemarcello

Highlights

- **Val di Vara**
  Explore breathtaking rural scenery dotted with ancient stone churches, castles and villages

- **Cinque Terre Park**
  Hike in this UNESCO-listed natural gem with its pastel-coloured villages and sublime coastal views

- **Cinque Terre seafood**
  Taste fresh lobster, calamari, octopus, stuffed mussels and anchovies, all prepared from delicious local recipes

- **Golfo dei Poeti**
  Enjoy the sparkling Golfo di La Spezia whose rocky coves and fishing ports were immortalized by English poets

Manarola, one of the oldest villages in the Cinque Terre, nestled into the Ligurian cliffs

The Cinque Terre

The Val di Vara in eastern Liguria is named after the river that flows through it from Monte Zatta to the coast. Here the valley is dotted with *borghi rotondi* (round villages), named after the defensive circular layout of streets and piazzas. Along the coast, the Cinque Terre Park protects the five famous coastal villages – Riomaggiore, Manarola, Corniglia, Vernazza and Monterosso al Mare – as well as hamlets, wineries and sanctuaries in the hills above. The dazzling Golfo di La Spezia (known as the Golfo dei Poeti) stretches from Portovenere to Lerici, through the region's maritime capital, La Spezia, and is encircled by a backdrop of hills and a foreground of islands.

Above Pignone, nestling into the forested hillside, *see p92*

ACTIVITIES

Surf the rolling waves at Levanto, Italy's premier surfing centre (www.occhioblu.it/en/surf.html)

Sample the local *sciacchetrà* white wine in Vernazza

Hike or bike the *sentieri* – walking trails – in the beautiful Cinque Terre Park

Take the ferry from Portovenere along the Cinque Terre coast for the best views of its pretty towns

Enjoy a boat trip around the Golfo dei Poeti (Gulf of Poets) from La Spezia

Walk the "Castello to Castello" trail from San Terenzo to Lerici

Plant yourself on a beach in Fiascherino near Lerici

Go mountain biking in the forests and hills around Montemarcello

Below A view of the marina at La Spezia, *see p96*

Above Portovenere in the shadow of the huge Genovese fort, Castello Doria, see p95

KEY

━━━ Drive route

PLAN YOUR DRIVE

Start/finish: Varese Ligure to Montemarcello.

Number of days: 4–5 days allowing at least half a day in the Val di Vara; 2 days to explore the Cinque Terre area and about 2 days between the Golfo di La Spezia and Montemarcello.

Distance: Approx. 113 km (70 miles).

Road conditions: Roads in the Cinque Terre are narrow, winding and steep – some are single lane with infrequent passing places. Local signs often only point the way to the next village, and roads are rarely numbered.

When to go: Visit from April to October, but to avoid excessive heat skip July and August, when busy roads may also be impassable. June and September are best for cooler days and smaller crowds.

Opening times: Shops tend to open Mon–Sat 9am–1pm and 4–7pm or 8pm (city supermarkets often stay open for the siesta). Churches and museums vary enormously but usually open 8 or 9am–noon and 4–7 or 8pm. Many museums are closed on Mondays.

Main market days: Varese Ligure: Tue; **Levanto:** Wed; **Monterosso al Mare:** Thu; **La Spezia:** Fri am; **Lerici:** Sat am.

Shopping: Excellent organic salami and cheese in Varese Ligure; lemon liqueur, pesto and honey.

Major festivals: Varese Ligure: Sagre a Varese Ligure, Aug; **Levanto:** Festa del Mare, mid-Jul for a week; **Monterosso al Mare:** Sagra dei Limoni, May; Torneo di Noci, Sep; **Manarola:** Presepe di Manarola, mid-Dec–end Jan; **La Spezia:** Cadimare Sapori e Colori del Golfo, Aug; Palio del Golfo, end Jul–start Aug; Festival Internazionale del Jazz, mid-Jul; **Lerici:** Sagra della Lumaca (snails), late Aug; **Tellaro:** Film Festival, Aug.

DAY TRIP OPTIONS

For **medieval architecture**, **rural charm** and **farm produce** head into the Val di Vara for the day; the upper Cinque Terre area offers **hillside hamlets**, **sea views** and **hiking**; while the area around Lerici is best for its **pretty beaches**. For full details see p97.

Above The heavily fortified Castello dei Fieschi at the heart of Varese Ligure

VISITING THE CINQUE TERRE

National Park Office
The main office is in Riomaggiore. The park's website has useful information.
Via Telemaco Signorini 118, Riomaggiore, 19017; 0187 760 31; www.parconazionale5terre.it

Parking
The Cinque Terre villages are car-free zones. There are car parks (close at 10 or 11pm) at the tops of the villages and parking further away on the roadsides.

Surfing
There is a surf school in Levanto.
Via Rimembranza 14, 0187 808764

WHERE TO STAY

VARESE LIGURE

Hotel Amici *inexpensive*
Family-run hotel – with excellent bistro attached – and 26 tasteful rooms.
Via Garibaldi 80, 19028; 0187 842 139; www.albergoamici.com; closed mid-Dec–Jan

AROUND VAL DI VARA

Agriturismo Ca' du Chittu *inexpensive*
Small, quiet and welcoming eco-haven in the heart of the Val di Vara.
Isolato Camporione 25, Pavareto; 19012, (15 km/9 miles from Val di Vara on the SP566, then turn left onto the SP50 Strada Comunale per Agnola towards Pavareto); 0187 861205; www.caduchittu.it

LEVANTO

Stella Maris *moderate–expensive*
Old World grace in an 18th-century villa surrounded by a beautiful garden.
Via Marconi 4, 19015; 0187 808 258; www.hotelstellamarislevanto.com

MONTEROSSO AL MARE

Hotel La Colonnina *moderate*
A 3-star family-run hotel near the main square and church. Enjoy sea views from the rooftop terrace.
Via Zuecca 6, 19016; 0187 817 439; www.lacolonninacinqueterre.it

1 Varese Ligure
La Spezia, Liguria; 19028
Built under the fiefdom of the Fieschi family, this colourful collection of porticos, arcades and squares forms the most beautiful *borgo rotondo* (round village) of the upper Val di Vara. At the heart of the spectacular merry-go-round of houses sits the 14th-century **Casa del Capitano** and the mighty towers of the Fieschi family castle (privately owned) built on the site of a former Roman fort.

Across the main piazza sits the Baroque **Chiesa di San Filippo Neri e Santa Teresa d'Avila** *(open daily)*. Close by, the yellow and white Baroque **Oratorio dei Santi Antonio e Rocco** *(open daily)* is a real jewel with an elaborate interior of stucco, gold lanterns, frescoes and 18th-century paintings. Next door is the colonnaded 16th-century **Chiesa di San Giovanni Battista** *(open daily)* with plenty of frescoes, paintings and statues that testify to the generosity and wealth of the local nobles.

Buy some organic cheese or salami, or arrange a farm/factory tour at the **Cooperativa Casearia Val di Vara** *(Loc Perazza, Varese Ligure, 0187 842108)*. Ask at the tourist office, on Piazza Castello, about free guided tours of the town between 11am and 5pm.

🚗 *Take the SP523 south to San Pietro Vara, continue on the SP566 in the direction of La Spezia, then Carrodano-Levanto, turn off at the sign Carrodano "centro".*

Above Pastel-coloured houses in Piazza Chiesa Carrodano, Val di Vara

2 Val di Vara
Carrodano, Liguria; 19020
The drive through the forests of the Val di Vara passes river crossings, castle ruins and church steeples. From the villages of San Pietro Vara to Carrodano, the narrow streets are full of houses dating back to Roman

Valley of *Borghi Rotondi*
The tightly packed houses of Val di Vara's medieval *borghi rotondi* (round villages) were designed around a central hub such as a castle or church with few external windows to thwart enemy attacks. The upper floors were used as living quarters, while the ground level rooms were used as warehouses.

Below Carrodano Inferiore and the Chiesa Santa Felicità, facing out over the Val di Vara

Above The *lungomare* (promenade) and grand seafront villas backed by the Castello di Levanto

times. Take a break at **Carrodano Inferiore** – the lower village – and walk through the arched passageways to pastel façades and the Chiesa Santa Felicità in Piazza Chiesa. The upper village, **Carrodano Superiore** offers views over the entire valley and coast. Several well-marked walking trails pass near to Carrodano: one links to the upper trail of the Via delle Cinque Terre, Sentiero 5T which starts in Levanto and ends at Monte Zatta.

Take the SP566d all the way to Levanto; plenty of parking: meters are best for access to the waterfront.

3 Levanto
La Spezia, Liguria; 19015
Named after its location on the Riviera di Levante, east of Genoa, the town is also an entry point to the Cinque Terre Park and shares the same spellbinding mix of mountain and Mediterranean scenery. Popular with Benito Mussolini in the 1920s and 30s, Levanto has some fine Renaissance palazzos and villas overlooking the wide bay. On the main square, Piazza Cavour, the 13th-century **Chiesa Sant'Andrea** has a striking striped Genovese Ligurian façade of green serpentine and white marble. Admire also the medieval arcades on the **Piazza della Loggia**, the clock tower, ancient city walls and 13th-century **Castello di Levanto**. The area is known for its wines and extra virgin olive oil, and in the countryside there are many old olive oil mills, or *mulini*.

Take the Via Nuova Stazione Ferroviaria, turn right on the SP43 and right on the SP370 towards Monterosso. Car parks are at both sides of town.

4 Monterosso al Mare
La Spezia, Liguria; 19016
The **Torre Aurora** (Dawn Tower) stands on a rocky promontory between the old village beach and the newer Fegina beach and *bocce* (bowls) court. Above town stands the ruins of the **castello** built by the Lagneto family in 1201 to ward off pirate attacks. At the heart of old Monterosso, on Piazza Garibaldi, is the Genovese-Gothic church, **Chiesa di San Giovanni Battista** (1220) with its white marble and serpentine stripes. Stroll west to the end of the beach to appreciate the 14-m (46-ft) statue of **Neptune**, nicknamed *Il Gigante*. The **Convento Cappuccini** on San Cristoforo hill in the old town has unbeatable views. Franciscan wooden altars and fabulous paintings – most notably *The Crucifixion* – by 16th-century Flemish artist Anthony Van Dyck.

Go back up the SP370, turn right on to the SP38 and right on the SP51. At Foce, turn left on the SP38 for Pignone. Park inside the walls at Piazza Marconi.

VARESE LIGURE

La Taverna del Gallo Nero *moderate*
On the main square, this small rustic inn has just a few choices on the menu.
Piazza Vittorio Emanuele 26, 19028; 0187 840 513; closed Mon, Jan

LEVANTO

La Vineria *inexpensive*
An alfresco wine bar offering light bites and good choice of wines. Try the local *guttafin* fried ravioli of seasonal herbs.
Piazza Staglieno 28, 19015; 0187 800 141

Trattoria Cavour *moderate*
Tasty fare in an old tanner's studio.
Piazza Cavour 1, 19015; 0187 808 497; www.trattoriacavour.it; closed Mon, mid-Dec–Jan

Other options
Moderately priced family restaurant, with authentic seafood, pasta and pizza, **L'Oasi** (*Piazza Cavour, 19015; 0187 800 856; closed Wed, mid-Nov–mid-Dec, mid-Jan–mid-Feb*). Shop selling delicious organic foods, run by an organization of local producers, **Sapori di Levanto** (*Piazza Cavour 10, 19015; 0187 80221; www.saporidilevanto.it; closed Sun*)

MONTEROSSO AL MARE

Ciliegio *moderate*
Serves all kinds of seafood but especially *acciughe* – anchovies. Great views.
Località Beo 2, 19016; 0187 817 829; closed weekends

Enoteca Internazionale *inexpensive*
Good local food – focaccia, acciughe di Monterosso (anchovies) and torta di verdure (vegetable pie) – and wine.
Via Roma 62, 19016; 0187 817 278; www.enotecainternazionale.com; closed Dec–Mar

Below The 16th-century Torre Aurora, Monterosso al Mare

Eat and Drink: inexpensive, under €25; moderate, €25–€45; expensive, over €45

Above View of Pignone's 16th-century bridge and gate, Porta Maestra Above right Brightly painted houses in pretty Vernazza

BIKING IN THE CINQUE TERRE

It is possible to make reservations to hire bikes at the Cinque Terre Park information offices located at train stations, or by telephone. Bikes can be hired for a half or a full day. *Volastra: 0187 760 523; Montenero: 0187 760 528*

WHERE TO STAY

VOLASTRA

Il Vigneto *inexpensive*
Green travellers will be pleased to know that this cute little B&B with a lovely terrace comes with the Cinque Terre Park's stamp of eco-quality. *Via Pasubio 64, 19017; 0187 185 2377; www.ilvigneto5terre.com*

Albergo Luna di Marzo *moderate*
An airy, relaxed, comfy hillside home with large functional bedrooms and good organic breakfasts. *Via Montello 387c, 19017; 0187 920 530; www.albergolunadimarzo.com*

MANAROLA

Hotel Ca' D'Andrean
inexpensive–moderate
In the pedestrian zone, this is a small family-run hotel in a typical Cinque Terre village house with a few fragrant lemon trees. The 10 rooms are simply furnished, spotless and spacious. *Via Discovolo 101, 19010; 0187 920 040; www.cadandrean.it*

⑤ Pignone

La Spezia, Liguria; 19020
Straddling the ridge which divides the Cinque Terre from the Val di Vara, Pignone is an archetypal village of the *entroterra* (hinterland). Its stone houses lean against each other in a huddle and the granite Ponte Vecchio (Old Bridge) has a statue of the Virgin Mary in a niche. Of the original three fortified gateways, the imposing **Porta Maestra** is the only one still standing; a medieval loggia encircles the small piazza and its 14th-century **Chiesa Santa Maria Assunta**.

War memorial, Piazza Marconi, Pignone

🚗 *Return to Foce and turn left into the SP63, direction Vernazza.*

⑥ Vernazza

La Spezia, Liguria; 19018
One of Italy's most beautiful villages, Vernazza's rows of tall ochre-, yellow- and apricot-painted houses are stacked up around the cliff sides of a crooked ocean promontory with the ruins of an 11th-century lookout tower – the **Torre di Avvistamento** – perched out on its bulbous tip. The sweep of coloured window shutters and washing on its main square forms a backdrop to the

Country Flavours

Ligurian specialities include ravioli with mushroom sauce; *croxetti* – flower-shaped pasta with pine-nut or walnut salsas, and chestnut-flour tagliatelle with pesto or fresh ricotta. For dessert, try *torta di verdure* – a sweetened vegetable pie – or some *castagnaccio* (chestnut flour) cake, both featuring pine nuts and raisins.

miniature fishing port (*porticciolo*). At the sea's edge stands the salmon-pink 1318 **Chiesa Santa Margherita di Antiochia**, with its beautiful dove-grey tiled dome and bell tower with arched windows and colonnaded upper balcony. Vernazza's maritime history is evident in the boating symbols, marine boutiques and fishermen's taverns that dot its narrow streets. In 1170, the town helped the Republic of Genova combat and vanquish the Pisans – the fortified walls and hilltop **Castello Doria** are among the remains of its once mighty medieval defence system. In those days, Vernazza was the main stopover and market centre along the coastal trading route now famous as the Cinque Terre walkway.

🚗 *Head east on the SP61, then turn right towards the coast on the SP30.*

Above Niche with statue of the Virgin Mary on the Ponte Vecchio, Pignone

❼ Corniglia

La Spezia, Liguria; 19018

Topping a spectacular ocean-jutting cape and surrounded by terraced olive groves and vineyards, this is the only Cinque Terre village inaccessible from the sea. Its narrow lanes and boxy stone houses are packed along the main street Via Fieschi. From the medieval tower there are excellent views of all the capes and curves of the Cinque Terre coastline. For a good workout descend the *Lardarina* (377 steps) that links the town centre to the train station below and leads to the Guvano beach and promenade, along the lower cliffs through to Manarola.

🚗 *Take the SP30 and turn right on SP61, at Fornacchi, turn right on SP51 to Volastra. The car park is free.*

❽ Volastra

La Spezia, Liguria; 19017

On a hill 350 m (1,150 ft) above sea level and a little way inland, this village was a horse-changing station for the coastal Via Romana. Locals believe its circular layout pre-dates the Romans, and the *menhirs* – standing stones – on nearby Monte Capri bear witness to even earlier human presence. The 13th-century Romanesque church **Santuario di Nostra Signora della Salute** (Our Lady of Health) lies on Via dei Santuari, a pathway that links several hilltop sanctuaries from Riomaggiore to Monterosso. At the heart of the Cinque Terre's dry-stone wall terrain and hilltop walks, the village is a hub for hiking and mountain biking.

🚗 *Continue along the SP51, at the first roundabout turn right on the SP59 to Manarola. Park just outside the town.*

❾ Manarola

La Spezia, Liguria; 19010

Manarola's historic jewel is the **Chiesa di San Lorenzo**, a tiny tabernacle with three naves and an ornate *rosone* (rose-shaped window). Located in Piazza Papa Innocenzo IV, its creamy stone bell tower – the Campanile Bianco – was a 12th-century defence lookout. The other key attraction lies in Manarola's mix of community atmosphere and picturesque scenery: the upper village perches on the cliff face above the marina which laps at the lower village. There are walking trails through the vineyards on the hills, or swimming in the harbour.

🚗 *Go back up the SP59; at the roundabout turn right on the SP370. Turn right on the SP32 and follow signs to Riomaggiore. Park at the top of the village.*

Above left Manarola catching the last of the evening's sun **Top right** Façade of the 14th-century Chiesa di San Lorenzo, Manarola **Above right** Looking down to Corniglia stretched along its rocky promontory

EAT AND DRINK

PIGNONE

Trattoria Medinelli *inexpensive*
A rustic eatery in a verdant setting; try the wild boar or mushroom tagliatelle
Via del Campanile 139 (heading towards Levanto), 19020; 0187 887 950; www.locandadamarco.it

VERNAZZA

Other options
Get a taste of the sea in one of Vernazza's old fishermen's taverns, **Antica Osteria Il Baretto** *(Via Roma 31, 19018)* or **Enoteca Sciacchetrà** *(Via Roma 19, 19018)*

CORNIGLIA

Enoteca Il Pirun *inexpensive*
A hole-in-the-wall wine bar stuffed with memorabilia and charm.
Via Fieschi 115, 19018; 0187 812 315

VOLASTRA

Ristorante-Bar Gli Ulivi *moderate*
Excellent dishes in convivial restaurant-bar. Try the seafood antipasti.
Via N S della Salute 114, 19017; 0187 760 020

MANAROLA

Marina Piccola *moderate*
This open-air restaurant offers good local cooking (and has 3 rooms).
Via Lo Scalo 16, 19010; 0187 920 923; www.ristorantemarinapiccola.it; closed Tue

Above The huddled houses of Corniglia, one of the quieter Cinque Terre villages

Eat and Drink: inexpensive, under €25; moderate, €25–€45; expensive, over €45

HIKING IN THE CINQUE TERRE

As well as the famous Sentiero Azzurro (Blue Trail), linking the five villages, the network of well-marked trails or *sentieri* connects hilltop hamlets, monasteries, and other sights in the Cinque Terre Park. These areas are more rural, without the crowds that sometimes clutter the villages. Cinque Terre Park has trails ranging in length and difficulty. Pick up a footpath map from any information point or tourist office.

WHERE TO STAY

TRAMONTI DI CAMPIGLIA

Piccolo Blu *moderate*
Bright and cool B&B cottage, with sea view balconies and personal touches.
Piazza della Chiesa 4, 19025; 0187 758 517; www.piccoloblu.it

PORTOVENERE

Belvedere *moderate*
Set in a *palazzina* – the best rooms have bay views and balconies.
Via G Garibaldi 26, 19025; 0187 790 608; www.belvedereportovenere.it

Hotel della Baia *expensive*
In quieter Le Grazie, 2 km (1 mile) along the winding coastal road, this hotel offers spacious rooms, a pool and dining terrace.
Via Lungomare 111, Le Grazie di Portovenere, 19025; 0187 790 797; www.baiahotel.com

⑩ Riomaggiore and the Cinque Terre Park
Riomaggiore, Cinque Terre; 19017

This pretty 12th-century village, named after the Rio Major (Main River) that once flowed beneath it, looks as though it has tumbled down the hillside towards the sea. It serves as the gateway to the Cinque Terre for many visitors who head out from here on the trail linking it to the other four villages. This featured walk from Riomaggiore to Montenero and back follows Sentiero 3 (Trail 3) away from the more crowded coast, taking in coastline panoramas, olive groves and the hilltop Santuario di Montenero, which can only be reached by foot. The 4-km (2½-mile) round walk can be comfortably finished in about 2 hours, allowing time for exploring the village at the start and enjoying the views on the way.

A two-hour walk from Riomaggiore to Montenero

This trail starts from the upper village, alta Riomaggiore, close to the car park. But warm-up the muscles first with a 30-minute stroll around the steep streets of Riomaggiore.

The bustling **Via Colombo** ① is lined with bright houses – *case torri* (tower houses). The murals by Silvio Benedetto in the lower village near the train station depict locals building the *muretti a secco* – the dry-stone walls of the Cinque Terre landscapes.

To reach the **marina** ② take the stairway at the very bottom of Via Colombo, (opposite the passage to the train station), down through a grotto. After taking in the wonderful views, climb back up Via Colombo and follow the road to the **Chiesa di San Giovanni Battista** ③ through a

series of graceful, wide stairways. The 1340 basilica is set into the ridge of the hill, its Gothic doorways – the façade was remodelled in the 19th-century – enclosed by pilasters and decorated with small statuettes.

Walk back along Via Colombo, turn sharp right onto Via di Loca and continue until it meets **Via Don Minzoni** ④. This road crosses the Rio Major near the hamlet of Lavac and is where the Sentiero 3 starts out from. At the outset there is a fork in the walking trail: take the higher path up Via della Liberta through hillsides of vine terraces.

Follow the well-marked trail along a *mulattiera* – mule track – and cross a stone bridge over the Rio Major, before tackling a steep stairway. Coastal views start opening up as the path curves around a cemetery,

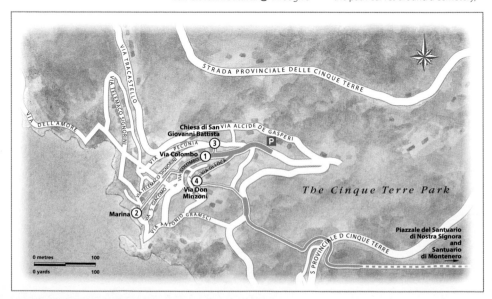

Far left Via del Amore coastal path leading from Riomaggiore **Left** The pretty harbour at Riomaggiore **Below** Tramonti di Campiglia overlooks a stunning coastline

BOAT TRIPS AND FERRIES

Regular passenger ferries run along the coast between Portovenere and the Cinque Terre villages. Boat trips are available from La Spezia too.
Consorzio Marittimo Turistico 5 Terre, Via Minzoni 13, La Spezia; 0187 732987; www.navigazionegolfodeipoeti.it

EAT AND DRINK

RIOMAGGIORE

Trattoria La Lanterna *moderate*
Cheerful service in an old anchovy-salting warehouse.
Via San Giacomo 46, 19017; 0187 920 589; www.lalanterna.org; closed Tue in Nov

Other options
Cavern for seafood and wine **La Grotta Bar Trattoria** (*Via Colombo 247, 19017; 0187 920187*) Dining room with a view **Ristorante Colle del Telegrafo** (*Colle del Telegrafo, 19133; 0187 760 561; closed Thu*)

TRAMONTI DI CAMPIGLIA

Ristorante La Lampara *moderate*
Good food in a bright restaurant with coastal views and home-made wine.
Via Tramonti 4, 19025; 0187 758 035; closed Jan–Mar

PORTOVENERE

Bacicio Bar-Restaurant *inexpensive*
Soak up the pirate-inspired decor.
Via Capellini 17, 19025; 0187 792 054; closed Thu

Locanda Lorena *expensive*
Excellent seafood worth the boat trip.
Via Cavour 4, Isola Palmaria, 19025; 0187 792 370; www.locandalorena.com; closed Wed

---

along a ridge and up to the provincial road. Cross the road, and follow it some 200 m (650 ft) to concrete steps which lead back onto the mule track through the vineyards and on through the valley.

As the trail nears Montenero, a picture of the Madonna di Montenero and a drinking fountain greet walkers before they reach the **Piazzale del Santuario di Nostra Signora**.

The **Santuario di Montenero** lies amid pine forest and Mediterranean grasses and shrubs at an altitude of 341 m (1,120 ft) with fantastic views. The Santuario has a restaurant/café for a recuperative meal or snack, before the return walk to the car park.

For energetic walkers, the path carries on to the Colle del Telegrafo (making a 9-km/6-mile round trip in total). Instead of walking back, there is a bus service with stops in other villages along the way. Check the bus timetable at the Riomaggiore tourist office at the train station.

🚗 *Exit on the SP32 and turn right onto SP370. At roundabout/intersection take turn onto the SP530 to Marola and follow signs to Campiglia.*

⑪ Tramonti di Campiglia
La Spezia, Liguria; 19025

Campiglia sits above the Cinque Terre coast in a beautiful location amid sea cliffs, saffron crops and old olive oil mills. It lies at the heart of a network of walks along old mule tracks, along the coast and through the woods. The pathway that leads down to Punta Persico (Sentiero 11) and its pebbly beach was for centuries the only link the locals had with the outside world, before the road was built in the 1950s. The longest coastal walk, Sentiero 1, passes in front of the church, on its way from Portovenere to Levanto.

🚗 *Return to Marola and turn right into the SP530. Pass through the port of La Grazie and on to Portovenere.*

⑫ Portovenere
La Spezia, Liguria; 19025

On the western peninsula of the Golfo di La Spezia, Portovenere was named after a Roman temple to Venus that once stood here. The tall pastel-coloured houses along the quayside, once medieval defence towers, are now a lively run of restaurants and craft shops. Wander the narrow streets between the harbour and the hilltop and climb the main artery, Via Capellini, to the mighty 13th-century **Castello Doria**. At the end of the promontory sits the striped 13th-century Genovese **Chiesa di San Pedro**. In the cliffs below, the **Arpaia Grotto** is known as Byron's Grotto, in memory of the poet's swim to Lerici. Boats leave the port for the nearby islands of Palmaria, Tino and Tinetto, to the Cinque Terre villages and to Lerici.

🚗 *Return to Marola and take the SP530 all the way to La Spezia.*

Eat and Drink: inexpensive, under €25; moderate, €25–€45; expensive, over €45

VISITING LA SPEZIA

Parking
There is a car park at Via Alessandro Manzoni or street parking close to the train station.

WHERE TO STAY

LA SPEZIA

Hotel Ghironi *moderate*
A good-value hotel in the port area with period furnishing, spacious rooms and air conditioning. Also offers private parking and a shuttle to the train station and ferries. *Via del Tino 62, 19126; 0187 504 141; www.hotelghironi.it*

Hotel Firenze e Continentale *moderate*
A most personal 4-star hotel, with a refined interior – wood panelling, marble and quality upholstery. *Via Paleocapa 7, 19122; 0187 713 210; www.hotelfirenzecontinentale.it*

Other options
A 16th-century convent, **Hotel Relais Al Convento** is 10 km (6 miles) from La Spezia. *(Take the SP1, then left onto the SP330 and right onto the SP16; Piazza Regina Margherita 1, Vezzano Ligure; 19020; 0187 994 444; www.hotelalconvento.com)*

LERICI

Doria Park Hotel *moderate*
Five minutes from town, this hotel has a good restaurant and rooftop terrace. Comfortable modern rooms and suites some with terrace views over the sea. *Via Carpanini 9, 19032; 0187 967 124; www.doriaparkhotel.it*

Il Nido *moderate*
Cloaked in pine and olive trees, this 3-star yellow-and-white striped hotel with a private beach is an oasis of calm. There is also a roof terrace, garden and spa. *Via Fiascherino 75, 19030; 0187 967 286; www.hotelnido.com*

Locanda del Lido *expensive*
Designer hotel over a private beach strip in Lerici centre. Fantastic breakfast of fresh fruit and home-made jams and pastries. Also has free internet. *Lungomare Biaggini 24, 19032; 0187 968 159; www.locandadellido.it*

13 La Spezia

La Spezia, Liguria; 19100
Italy's leading naval port is a small pleasant city with wide boulevards, good shopping and fine food. Stroll through the **Giardini Pubblici**, along the Constantino Morin, where boats depart for trips around the Gulf (operated by Consorzio Marittimo Turistico, *see p94*). Next walk along the elegant stone arcades of Via Chiodo to Piazza Chiodi, near the Naval Arsenal. Here also are the **Museo Tecnico Navale** *(closed Sat)* and **Centro d'Arte Moderna e Contemporanea** *(closed Mon)*. Do not miss the wavy-roofed market on Piazza del Mercato in the town centre. In nearby Via del Prione, the shopping area, the **Museo Amedeo Lia** *(closed Mon)* has many 13–15th-century Florentine paintings. Finally, climb the stairway, the *Scalinate Spallanzani*, to the fortified hilltop, Poggio, where there is a monastery, convent and fabulous views.

🚗 *Head east around the port, along Viale San Bartolomeo onto the SP331 and follow signs for San Terenzo/Lerici.*

14 San Terenzo

La Spezia, Liguria; 19032
The beachfront at San Terenzo looks out over the Baia di Lerici – the stunning landscape that inspired the English poet Percy Shelley. The white porticoed **Villa Magni**, part of a former monastery, is where he and his wife lived. Take the coastal promenade to the cliff side, medieval **Castello** *(closed Mon)*: it is now a cultural centre with exhibitions, events and a display about the Shelleys. The 2-km (1-mile) "Castello to Castello walk" links the castles of San Terenzo and Lerici.

Above The 16th-century Oratorio di San Rocco, Piazza Garibaldi, Lerici

🚗 *Return to the SP331 and turn right into the Galleria Primacina, following the signs for Lerici.*

15 Lerici

La Spezia, Liguria; 19032
On the eastern Golfo dei Poeti, Lerici is a mix of chic jet-setters' port and salty maritime village. It was at the heart of a tug of war between the republics of Genova and Pisa. The Pisans took the town in 1241 and built the **Castello**, which was later expanded by the Genoese. The castle's pentagonal

Right The lush gardens of the Giardini Pubblici, La Spezia

tower encloses the 12th-century **Cappella di Sant'Anastasia** and a **Museo di Geopaleontologico** *(closed Mon,).* From the grand harbour square, Piazza Garibaldi, Via Cavour passes the 16th-century **Oratorio di San Rocco** with Baroque façade and Romanesque bell tower and climbs up a narrow street of craft studios and 17th- and 18th-century villas with ornate iron balconies.

🚗 *Leave on the Galleria Primacina, turn right on the SP331, then follow the SP26 along the coast to Tellaro.*

🔟 Tellaro

La Spezia, Liguria; 19032
Along the coast from Lerici, the road dips down to Tellaro, a cluster of houses huddled round a small church and clinging to an outcrop of rock. It was built in the 17th century as a stronghold to protect nearby Barbazzano and its valuable olive oil crops from Saracen pirates. A walking trail leads from the church square along an old mule track to the hilltop ruins of Barbazzano castle. Even in high summer, the little local beaches, such as Fiascherino can be pleasantly quiet and secluded.

🚗 *Head back on the SP26, turn right into Via Giacomo Matteotti, then right at Località Narb-Ostro. Follow SP28 to Montemarcello. Park on street.*

🔟 Montemarcello

La Spezia, Liguria; 19031
In the **Parco Naturale Regionale di Montemarcello-Magra** and up on a wooded promontory, Montemarcello's grid of streets recalls its past history as a Roman fort. There are also remnants of 13th-century defences – the old walls and the watchtower. The 15th-century **Chiesa di San Pietro** was given a Baroque face-lift in the 17th century – note its marble altarpiece and triptych. On the peak of Monte Murlo, the **Orto Botanico** provides a guide to local flora and fauna, as well as views over the Val di Magra and the stark Alpi Apuane mountains.

On the SP28 to Ameglia, the 12th-century **Convento dei Carmelitani Scalzi** (Convent of the Barefoot Carmelitans) is where the poet Dante Alighieri supposedly once stayed.

Above left Harbourfront piazza in the small fishing village Tellaro **Above right** Quiet and colourful Montemarcello

EAT AND DRINK

LA SPEZIA

Enoteca La Cambusa *inexpensive*
Enjoy traditional food and a hefty wine list in this 2-roomed gastro wine cellar. *Viale San Bartolomeo 471, 19100; 0187 503 083; closed Sun*

Il Ristorantino di Bayon *moderate–expensive*
Intimate restaurant serving flavoursome seafood dishes and delicious desserts, with a serious wine list. *Via Felice Cavallotti 23, 19121; 0187 732 209; closed Sun, Jan*

LERICI

Ristorante Pizzeria Bontà Nascoste *inexpensive*
A traditional restaurant – try the chickpea flatbread *(farinata)* speciality and home-made *focaccia*. *Via Cavour 52, 19032; 0187 965 500; www.bontanascoste.it; closed Tue*

2 Corone *expensive*
Relaxed dining space with bay views and excellent seafood dishes. *Via Vespucci 1, 19032; 0187 967 417; www.duecorone.com; closed Tue, Wed lunch*

DAY TRIP OPTIONS

La Spezia, the Val di Vara, Cinque Terre and the Fiascherino coast are all suitable bases for day trips.

Borghi Rotondi **tour**

On a day trip to the *borghi rotondi* of the Val di Vara, there are stone villages, forests and rivers to be seen. Visit the towns of the Val di Vara **2** and on up to Varese Ligure **1**, probably the prettiest of the round villages.

The quickest way into the valley from La Spezia, is due north on the SP1, direction Borghetto di Vara; then take the SP566, pass through San Pietro Vara and continue north on the SP523, following the signs for Varese Ligure.

The Cinque Terre

Get a flavour of the pretty clifftop and seaside hamlets of the Cinque Terre by visiting Manarola **9** and Riomaggiore **10** in the morning, before hiking up one of the Park's famous trails to the excellent views at Santuario di Montenero.

From La Spezia take the SP530, then right on the SP370 (Via Litoranea) to the turn off for Manarola (passing Riomaggiore on the way out, but visiting it on the way back).

Fiascherino beaches

Families will enjoy spending a few hours at the beach between visits to San Terenzo **14**, Lerici **15** and Tellaro **16** for ice cream and refreshments. There are several coves and beaches along the stretches of coast between the towns.

From La Spezia or Lerici, pass through Pugliola on the SP28 to Fiascherino. The beaches are on the right hand side of the road, along the coast.

Eat and Drink: inexpensive, under €25; moderate, €25–€45; expensive, over €45

Remote Hills of North Tuscany

Lucca to Forte dei Marmi

Highlights

- **Patrimony of Lucca**
  Circle this glorious city's walls and wander its ancient Roman street plan

- **Mountain meals**
  Savour traditional cuisine in the sleepy Garfagnana

- **Castles in the sky**
  Explore the castles of the Malaspina, protecting high mountain passes and ancient byways

- **Michelangelo's inspiration**
  Visit the blistering white marble mountains of Carrara, home of quarrymen and sculptors

The beautifully preserved town of Barga, one of many that line the Valle del Serchio

Remote Hills of North Tuscany

Tucked in a remote corner of Tuscany are some of the wildest valleys and stunning terrains of the Apennine Mountains. A massive volcanic movement compressed limestone, creating the valued white marble of Carrara and raising the Alpi Apuane, leaving deep valleys and a narrow coastal strip. This drive takes visitors across the plain of Lucca, up the Valle del Serchio and the Garfagnana, over a mountain pass into the Lunigiana, and across the ranges into the marble mines of Carrara. The drive ends at the sophisticated beach resort of Forte dei Marmi. The area's simple food now graces tables around the world, and its natural beauty is offset with ancient castles and hamlets.

Above View of the Torre dei Guinigi with holm-oak trees growing on its roof from the Torre delle Ore, Lucca, *see p102*

ACTIVITIES

Join the locals for a bike ride around the walls that circle the town of Lucca

Take in a Puccini concert at the Chiesa di San Giovanni in Lucca

Sample gourmet delights at one of the food shops or restaurants in Castelnuovo di Garfagnana

Follow one of the hiking trails at Foce Carpinelli

Visit sculpture studios and the marble museum, Museo Civico del Marmo, in Carrara

Swim in the sea at the resort of Forte dei Marmi

Right Beach lined with parasols at the resort of Forte dei Marmi, surrounded by dramatic mountains, *see p107*

KEY

Drive route

0 kilometres | 5

0 miles | 5

Above Detail of the fountain *Il Gigante*, meaning "the Giant", sculpted by Bandinelli, Carrara, *see p107*

PLAN YOUR DRIVE

Start/finish: Lucca to Forte dei Marmi.

Number of days: 4–5, allowing half a day to explore Lucca.

Distance: Approx. 275 km (171 miles).

Road conditions: Well-sealed roads and good signposting. In winter chains or winter tyres are mandatory.

When to go: June and July when the mountains are at their best. August can be crowded. In October and November there are numerous food festivals.

Opening hours: Major museums are usually open 10am–6pm Tue–Sun and most smaller museums close 12:30–3pm. Shops tend to open 9am–1pm and 3:30–8pm. Most shops are closed on Monday mornings and Sundays, and food shops are closed on Wednesday afternoons. Churches tend to open 9am–12:30pm and 3:30–6pm but are closed to visitors during Mass.

Main market days: Lucca: Wed; Barga: Sat; Castelnuovo di Garfagnana: Thu; Pontrémoli: Wed, Sat; Bagnone: Mon; Forte dei Marmi: Wed, Sun.

Shopping: Look out for gourmet products made of *farro* (spelt), *biroldo* (blood sausage flavoured with herbs), *castagnaccio* (a type of sweet cake), and *Balsamo Clementi* (alcoholic tonic).

Major festivals: Lucca: Puccini e la sua Lucca, year round; Luminara di Santa Croce, 13 Sep; Barga: Jazz Festival, Aug; Garfagnana and Lunigiana: chestnut festivals, Oct–Nov.

DAY TRIP OPTIONS

This drive is easily divided into three sections. Gourmet Garfagnana should satisfy **food-lovers'** appetites. **Families** with young children will enjoy visiting the castles in the Lunigiana, and those interested in **local history and art** can see how the stunning white marble of Carrara is produced and sculpted. For more details *see p107*.

VISITING LUCCA

Parking
Inside each of Lucca's five *porte* (gates) is paid parking. Outside the walls, free parking is at Piazzale Don Franco Baroni.

Tourist Information
The main office is at *Piazza Santa Maria 35, 55100; 0583 919931; www. luccaturismo.it; open daily.*

Bike hire
Bikes can be hired from *Cicli Bizzarri, Piazza Santa Maria 32, 55100; 0583 496682; www.ciclibizzarri.net*

WHERE TO STAY

LUCCA

Residence Santa Chiara *inexpensive*
Basic rooms with tiled floors in palazzo. *Via Santa Chiara 12, 55100; 0583 491349; www.residencesantachiara.com*

Casa Biancalana *moderate*
This 13th-century monastery has been converted into apartments and rooms. *Via SS Annunziata 1070, 55100; 0583 572108; www.casabiancalana.it*

Hotel Noblesse *expensive*
Restored palazzo with exquisite interiors. *Via S Anastasio 23, 55100; 0583 440275; www.hotelnoblesse.it*

AROUND LUCCA

Fabbrica di San Martino *moderate*
One of the famous Lucchese villas, now an elegant B&B. *Via Pieve S Stefano 2511, San Martino in Vignale, 55100 (take SP1 N out of town; turn left immediately after bridge); 0583 394284; www.fabbricadisanmartino.it*

Below The exterior of Basilica di San Frediano, with its striking 13th-century mosaic, Lucca

Above left View of Via Fillungo, Lucca's main pedestrian street from the Torre delle Ore
Above right Di Simo Caffè in Via Fillungo, Lucca, once frequented by the composer Puccini

❶ Lucca
Toscana; 55100
Ringed by massive walls, Lucca sits on the fertile plain of the River Serchio. The city's architecture includes nearly every era in Italian history: a Roman amphitheatre, superb Romanesque churches and delicate Art Nouveau façades. Today Lucca is resplendent in shopping streets and fine dining, underscored by the ever-present genius of opera maestro Giacomo Puccini, who was born here.

A two-hour walking tour
Set off early in the morning from the car park at Piazzale Don Franco Baroni and enter the walled town at Baluardo S Frediano for Piazza del Collegio. Walk down Via Battisti, Via del Moro, Via S Lucia, Via Beccheria and turn right into Piazza San Michele in the heart of Lucca where the weekly market is held. Lucca's original street grid is still evident where the Roman *cardo* (running from north–south) and the *decumanus* (east–west) streets cross here.
San Michele in Foro ① *(open daily)*, which stands in the piazza, has a beautiful façade, with a unique assortment of marble columns, Romanesque in the lower part and Gothic in the upper part. The interior houses a 15th-century fresco *Saints Helena, Jerome, Sebastian and Roch* by Filippino Lippi. Just off this piazza is Via di Poggio, which leads to Corte San Lorenzo and the **Museo Casa Natale di Giacomo Puccini** ② *(closed Tue)* at no. 9. The museum houses portraits of the composer, and the piano he used to compose *Turandot*.

Inlaid marble, Duomo di San Martino

Head back to Piazza San Michele, and then walk south along Via Vittorio Veneto to the Piazza Napoleone. Flanking this tree-lined piazza is **Palazzo Ducale** ③, once the ancient citadel and seat of power, though today it hosts travelling exhibitions. Head east through Piazza del Giglio and along Via del Duomo to Piazza San Martino where **Duomo di San Martino** ④ *(open daily)* stands. The largely Romanesque cathedral with a Gothic interior, commenced in 1063, houses some of Lucca's most important religious works: the *Volto Santo*, a Byzantine crucifix; and the *Funereal Monument to Illaria del Carretto* by sculptor Jacopo della Quercia.
Head northwest through a succession of small streets that lead to **Via Fillungo** ⑤, the main pedestrian street, which is home to cafés and boutiques. On the corner of Via Fillungo and Via dell'Arancio is **Torre delle Ore** ⑥ *(closed Nov–Feb)*, built in 1490. Visitors can climb the 207 wooden steps of the clock tower for a spectacular panorama of the town. At Via Fillungo 58 is **Di Simo Caffè** ⑦,

Giacomo Puccini

Lucca's most famous son was born in a house in Corte S Lorenzo in 1858. After studying in Milan, Puccini spent most of his time at Torre del Lago (28 km/17 miles west of Lucca) where he composed *La Bohème* (1896), *Tosca* (1900) and *Madama Butterfly* (1904). Puccini died in 1924 and is buried in a chapel at Torre del Lago.

where intellectuals, artists and even the great composer Puccini would gather in the 1880s. Further along to the left at no. 95 are the unusual display casements of Carli, jewellers since 1655.

To the right off Via Fillungo is Via dell'Anfiteatro, circling the oval-shaped **Piazza Anfiteatro** (8), a ring of houses built from stone salvaged from the site of a Roman amphi-theatre. Crossing to the other side of Via Fillungo at Viale San Frediano is the Romanesque **Basilica di San Frediano** (9) *(open daily)* with a huge late 13th-century mosaic on its façade. Inside is a superb Lombard baptismal font from the 12th century. Head back to Baluardo S Frediano and take the path to the car park.

🚗 *Head north on Via del Brennero/SS12, towards Abetone. Veer right towards Marlia at Via dei Ceccotti, which becomes Via Fraga Alta. Parking for Villa Reale at the end of this road.*

② Villa Reale di Marlia
Lucca, Toscana; 55014

Created in 1805 by Napoleon's sister Elisa Baciocchi, this villa provided a suitable residence for an Imperial Highness. While the villa is not open to the public, sights within the grounds include the Bishop's Villa, Pan's Grotto – a folly with fountains that played on unsuspecting visitors – and a theatre made of green hedging. Allow an hour to wander the extensive garden *(open Mar–Nov; closed Mon, except public hols)*, which includes natural parkland, a lemon garden and contemplative pools with Roman-style statuary.

🚗 *Turn right onto SP29 (not signed), right at the SS12 towards Garfagnana. Left over the bridge at Borgo a Mozzano, right onto the SP2. Park at the bridge.*

③ Ponte della Maddalena
Lucca, Toscana; 55023

Known as *Il Ponte del Diavolo* (Devil's Bridge), this stone bridge across the River Serchio dates from the 1300s. Legend has it that a pact was made with the devil to build the bridge in exchange for the first soul who crossed it. The devil built the bridge overnight, but the locals went back on their word and substituted an animal.

🚗 *Continue on the SP2, turn right at Calavorno crossing the river then left onto the SS445. Turn right for Barga onto the SP7. Follow signs to "centro" for the main car park outside the walls.*

Above Formal sunken garden at Villa Reale di Marlia, outside Lucca

EAT AND DRINK IN LUCCA

Di Simo Caffè *inexpensive*
Try one of the splendid coffees at this historic café. *Via Fillungo 58, 55100; 0583 496234*

Antica Drogheria *inexpensive*
Sample local cooking, pizza and salads at this eatery with a buzzy atmosphere. *Via Elisa 5, 55100; 0583 467732; www.anticadrogheria.eu*

Buca di Sant'Antonio *expensive*
Lucchese specialities such as *coniglio farcito al forno con sformato di fagiolini* (stuffed rabbit with a bean mousse). *Via della Cervia 3, 55100; 0583 55881; www.bucadisantantonio.it; closed Mon, Sun pm; book ahead*

Osteria Via S Giorgio *expensive*
Serves fresh seafood with local cuisine. *Via S Giorgio 26, 55100; 0583 953233; www.osteriasangiorgio.it*

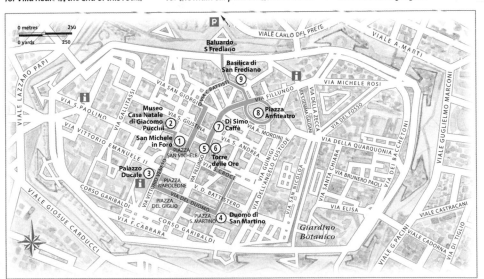

Above Winding medieval cobbled street lined with potted flowers, Barga

WHERE TO STAY

BARGA

Casa Fontana *inexpensive*
B&B located in the heart of the historical centre with simple, clean rooms. *Via di Mezzo 77, 55051; 0583 724524; www. casa-fontana.com; open Apr–Oct*

Below The 11th-century Rocca Ariostesca in Castelnuovo di Garfagnana **Below right top** Sign advertising local specialities for sale, Castelnuovo di Garfagnana **Below right bottom** The medieval stone bridge outside Castiglione di Garfagnana

❹ Barga
Lucca, Toscana; 55051
This ancient Longobard town is one of the best preserved in the region. Enter through the Porta Mancianella and follow the winding streets to Barga's hub, the Piazza Angelio with its **Galleria Angelio** *(open daily; closed for lunch)* featuring contemporary art. The magnificent Gothic **Duomo San Cristoforo** *(open daily)* at the top of the town offers spectacular views and at sunset the 13th-century travertine glows golden. Inside, the enormous marble pulpit, regarded as one of the finest, dates from the 13th century.

🚗 *Leave Barga on the road to Castelnuovo. At the bottom of the hill turn right onto the SS445 towards Castelnuovo. Park on Via della Fabbrica.*

❺ Castelnuovo di Garfagnana
Lucca, Toscana; 55032
The lively market town of Castelnuovo di Garfagnana sits on the confluence of the River Serchio and fast-flowing River Secca. Visitors will find plenty of the gourmet produce for which the area is famous, and the food shops that line Piazza delle Erbe are worth browsing, particularly **Angelo Abrami Alimentari** and **Bottega da Roberto**. The town is dominated by an elegant fortress, **Rocca Ariostesca**, begun in the 11th century, and named after the

poet who lived there in the 16th century. Today it houses the **Museo Archeologico del Territorio della Garfagnana** *(open daily in summer; Sat–Sun in winter)* displaying archaeological excavations dating back to the Stone Age and artifacts of Ligurian settlers from the 3rd–2nd centuries BC.

🚗 *Head north on the SP72 to Castiglione di Garfagnana. There is good parking outside the castle walls.*

Gourmet Garfagnana
The Garfagnana is well-known for its regional products. The centuries-old cereal *farro* (a type of spelt) is used in salads, combined with legumes in soup and also brewed as a beer. Maize and chestnuts are used to make *polenta*, a set porridge often grilled and served with meat or mushrooms. *biroldo*, a pressed meat, is made from fat, blood and the flesh of a pig's head, flavoured with herbs.

❻ Castiglione di Garfagnana
Lucca, Toscana; 55033
The most impressive part of this castle is its intact walls. Once a Roman *castra* protecting the valley leading to the Passo San Pellegrino, Castiglione di Garfagnana was repeatedly besieged and rebuilt. Visitors can almost completely circumnavigate the walls with stopping points and stunning views across the valley to the Alpi Apuane. A short way along the road towards *località* Mulino is a medieval bridge that should not be missed.

🚗 *Retrace the route back to Castelnuovo di Garfagnana and take the SP69 in the direction of Caréggine.*

❼ The chestnut forests of the Garfagnana
Lucca, Toscana; 55030
The road from Castelnuovo di Garfagnana to Caréggine weaves through some of the most spectacular chestnut woods in Tuscany. St Michael's Day (29 September), marks the beginning of the chestnut season when dried chestnuts are ground into flour and baked as *castagnaccio*, a sweet slice made with pine nuts or *necci*, soft wafers filled with ricotta.

🚗 *Continue along the SP69 until Caréggine. There is plenty of parking on the approach into town.*

Above Foce Carpinelli with the marble peaks of the Carrara mountains in the background

8 Caréggine
Lucca, Toscana; 55030

This mountain village was once walled, although today only two ancient gates remain. The Romanesque church of **Pieve di San Pietro** (open daily) has an elegant portico and bell tower, the oldest in Garfagnana. Many of the town houses built from local stone have double verandas, typical of the area. Some 12 km (7 miles) from Caréggine the artificial **Lago di Vagli** is drained every 10 years, revealing the startling spectacle of the drowned village of Fabbriche di Caréggine. The next event is in 2016.

🚗 Head to Póggio on the SP49. Turn left at the junction with the SS445 towards Aulla. Stop at Foce Carpinelli after 19 km (12 miles). Parking is on the left.

9 Foce Carpinelli
Lucca, Toscana; 55034

The pass here divides the Garfagnana on one side and the Lunigiana on the other. Breathtaking views of mountain meadows against a backdrop of the marble peaks of Carrara make this a perfect place to stop and there are plenty of picnic areas and walking trails accessible from the road. Look out for birds of prey such as eagles and falcons, especially in spring.

🚗 Continue on the SS445 until the road meets the SS63 just after Gassano. Turn right for Fivizzano and park inside the western gate.

10 Fivizzano
Massa Carrara; 54013

Located in a valley, this attractive town was once called the "Florence of the Lunigiana", when in 1540 Cosimo I, the Grand Duke of Tuscany, built a wall around the town (ask at the Pro Loco, Piazza Garibaldi 10 to visit) and appointed Fivizzano his seat of government. The town has a wide central, **Piazza Medicea** dominated by a fountain donated by Cosimo III. In 1849 Fivizzano was given the title "Noble City" and boasted intellectuals, poets and the first typewriter (1802), celebrated at the **Museo della Stampa** (open daily May–Sep). The local wood-fired bread is the best in the area and **Antica Farmacia Clementi** (Via Roma 109) is renowned for its Balsamo Clementi (alcoholic tonic), developed in 1886.

🚗 Follow directions to Aulla on SP63, then A15. Keep right on the tollway for Parma. Exit at Pontrémoli, right at the tollway exit (signed Pontrémoli). Left onto SS62. After 1.7 km (1 mile), left over bridge. Park on the banks of the river.

11 Pontrémoli
Massa Carrara, Toscana; 54027

First mentioned in AD 990, Pontrémoli was a free comune from the 12th century, controlling the important passes of the Brattello, Cisa and Cirone. Enter the town by crossing a huge medieval bridge and climb through the complex of medieval alleyways to the highlight of the area, the **Castello del Piagnaro** housing the **Museo delle Statue Stele** (closed Mon). Some of the menhirs (standing stones) date from 3000 BC.

🚗 Head back to the SS62 and turn right (direction Aulla). Turn left onto the SP30 for Bagnone, and turn left onto Via del Canaletto for Castello Malaspina di Malgrate. Parking is on the right.

Above Piazza Medicea's distinctive fountain was donated by Cosimo III, Fivizzano

EAT AND DRINK

BARGA

Caffè Capretz inexpensive
A pleasant place for sipping cocktails on the balcony with splendid views. Piazza Salvi 1, 55051; 0583 724 567; closed Mon

Da Riccardo moderate
Local dishes are served at this restaurant located just outside the walls of the Old Town. Via Guglielmo Marconi 8, 55051; 0583 722 345; www.trattoriadariccardo.it; closed Tue

CASTELNUOVO DI GARFAGNANA

Osteria Vecchio Mulino moderate
Ebullient host Andrea Bertucci shares his passion for local cuisine in bite-sized delicacies and excellent wines. The osteria also sells gourmet produce. Via Vittorio Emanuele 12, 55032; 0583 62192; www.vecchiomulino.info; closed Mon

Below Sweeping views of Pontrémoli, seen from its castle's walls

Above The striking exterior of Castello Malaspina di Malgrate with its trapezoidal wall

WHERE TO STAY

AROUND BAGNONE

Giunasco *inexpensive*
An *agriturismo* in the nearby village of Orturano. Mountain bikes and scooters are available for rent to explore the surrounding countryside.
Località Orturano– Bagnone, 54021 (follow winding road for 2 km/1 mile); 0187 427019; www.giunasco.it; open Apr–Nov

AROUND CARRARA

Agriturismo La Battilana *inexpensive*
This *agriturismo* offers bed and breakfast with the possibility of guided horse rides for guests.
Via Pontrémoli 9, Località Battilana, 54033 (3km/2 miles towards Marina di Carrara on Viale 20 Settembre, then right at roundabout 1a on Via Aurelia, SS1, and follow signs to left); 0585 53960; www.fattoriabattilana.com

FORTE DEI MARMI

Grand Hotel Imperiale *expensive*
Set in parkland close to the beach this luxurious 5-star hotel has elegant rooms, a fitness spa, an outdoor swimming pool and an excellent restaurant.
Via Mazzini 20, 55042; 0584 78271; www.grandhotelimperiale.it

Villa Roma Imperiale *expensive*
This hotel villa in a splendid oasis is a luxurious retreat in the most exclusive area of Forte dei Marmi. Stylish rooms with some opening onto the garden.
Via Corsica 9, 55042; 0584 78830; www.villaromaimperiale.com; open Easter–Oct

Right The famous marble quarries at Fantiscritti, Carrara **Above right** The wheel, symbol of Carrara, carved out of marble **Below right** Carrara's Accademia delle Belle Arti, housed in a former Malaspina fortress

⑫ Castello Malaspina di Malgrate
Massa Carrara, Toscana; 54028
A classic medieval fortress *(closed Mon except Aug)* with characteristic round towers, Malgrate's fortifications were built in the 13th century and the central body of the complex turned into a palazzo in 1641. The complex is surrounded by a trapezoidal wall, with Guelph battlements and scarps, loopholes, angular turrets and a rampart walk, which dates back to the 14th century. The old town is gradually being restored.
🚗 *Return to the SP30 and turn left for Bagnone. Park on Via della Fontanella.*

⑬ Bagnone
Massa Carrara, Toscana; 54021
This vibrant market town sits on a bend of the Bagnone torrent which cascades alongside the main **Piazza Roma**, home to several bars and pizzerias. Founded in the mid 1400s, Bagnone became one of the great marketplaces in the valley. Heading through the double porticoes on either side of the old market, the road leads up to the Malaspina castle, **Castello Bagnone** *(closed to the public)* and the parish church **Chiesa di San Nicola**, first recorded in AD 981.
🚗 *From the Castello Bagnone, head south to Castiglione on the SP21. Turn left at Via della Costa-Castiglione, which leads up to the castle.*

The Malaspina
Lunigiana is distinguished by castle towers which seem to compete with the surrounding mountains for dominance. They were built by the Malaspina family, who rose to power in the 13th-century, ruling their prestigious feudal estates for nearly five centuries. The Malaspina name allegedly originated in AD 540. The story goes that a young noble used a thorn to avenge the death of his father by slashing the throat of the King of the Franks who gasped "Ah! Mala Spina" (bad thorn).

⑭ Castello di Castiglione del Terziere
Castiglione Frazione di Bagnone; 54021
The winding road through the rambling agrarian countryside passes the **Castello di Castiglione del Terziere** *(open by appointment; 0187 429 100)*, originally constructed on the site of a Byzantine (7th-8th-century) fortified stronghold. The castle has a high square watchtower, from around the 12th century, and the interior features marble lancet windows and restored frescoes. The surrounding countryside affords some beautiful views of the valley.
🚗 *Return to SP21, pass through Licciana Nardi. Keep on SP21, follow signs for Fivizzano. Right onto SP18, follow signs to Bigliolo, then Aulla. After a railway crossing take a left onto SS63, follow signs for Fosdinovo on SS446.*

⑮ Fosdinovo

Massa Carrara, Toscana; 54035

This rocky outcrop of a town is dominated by the Malaspina castle **Castello di Fosdinovo** *(open Sat–Sun & public hols for guided tours)*. Thought to be haunted, the fortress is said to be riddled with lethal trapdoors. An evil *marchesa* even had one for unwary lovers at the end of her bed.

🚗 *Head east on SS446 towards Carrara. Parking is off Via del Cavatore.*

⑯ Carrara

Massa Carrara, Toscana; 54033

The ancient Romans quarried white Carrara marble, Michelangelo would use nothing else, and today the town is still the hub of the marble industry. Explore Carrara starting at the **Accademia delle Belle Arti** *(open to the public on special occasions)* in the Malaspina castle, where sculptors train. Walk through Piazza Gramsci and left down the hill to the 11th-century **Chiesa di S Andrea** *(open daily)* and through the old town to Piazza Alberica. On the outskirts of Carrara the **Museo Civico del Marmo** *(Viale XX Settembre, open daily)* shows different types of marble, production methods and art works.

Sign for an artist studio, Carrara

🚗 *Turn left onto Via del Cavatore from the car park, stay on this road until signs for Miseglia/Fantiscritti. The car park is beyond the museum to the right.*

⑰ Fantiscritti

Massa Carrara, Toscana; 54033

The quarry of Fantiscritti has a ramshackle private museum **La Cava Museo** *(open daily)* explaining the history and process of quarrying, and

includes a tour inside the mountain. The drive through the tunnel is a one-way loop from the car park. A Roman carving of angels was discovered here in 1863 and is now housed in the Accademia delle Belle Arti in Carrara.

🚗 *Head down the mountain, left at Via Cavour, right at Via 7 Luglio, and left for Massa on the SS446. Then proceed to Via Aurelia (SS1) towards Lucca. Turn right at Viale Marina (SP1), and left to Forte dei Marmi.*

⑱ Forte dei Marmi

Lucca, Toscana; 55052

In the 19th and early 20th centuries marble was shipped from the pier at Forte dei Marmi. Nowadays people come to enjoy a stroll along the coast, where the beaches teem with parasols. The town is the choice of well-heeled tourists for dining, nightclubbing and shopping on **Via Duca d'Aosta**. Visitors can either pay the day rate for a well-maintained private beach with bar service or try the free beach at Montignoso, with a reserve protected by the World Wildlife Fund. There are daily boat tours *(Jul–Sep)* to the **Cinque Terre** from here.

Above left The imposing Castello di Fosdinovo towering above the town **Above right** The main shopping street at the resort of Forte dei Marmi

---

EAT AND DRINK

CARRARA

Cibart08 *inexpensive–moderate*
A cheerful restaurant where local artists display their ceramics. The fare includes *crepes*, *focaccia* and panini. *Via Ulivi 1, on the corner of Piazza Alberica, 54033; 0585 70210*

FORTE DEI MARMI

La Barca *moderate*
Regional innovative cuisine is served here including seafood and some meat dishes with seasonal variations such as mushrooms and truffles. *Viale Italico 3, 55042; 0584 89323; www.labarcadelforte.it; closed Mon, Tue lunch (summer), Tue (winter)*

Lorenzo *expensive*
One of the area's most acclaimed restaurants specializing in fresh seafood simply served. *Via Carducci 61, 55042, 0584 89671; www.ristorantelorenzo.com; dinner only Jun–Sep; closed Mon, Tue, mid-Dec–Jan; booking essential*

DAY TRIP OPTIONS

The fastest approach to Lucca is along the A11. The following day trips are all within easy access from Lucca or Bagnone.

Epicurean Garfagnana

For an epicurean feast drive past the fields of *farro* at Castiglione di Garfagnana ⑥; lunch in the historic centre of Castelnuovo di Garfagnana ⑤ and visit its gourmet shops.

Follow the SP2 and take the SP72 to Castelnuovo di Garfagnana. Back on SP72 to Castiglione di Garfagnana.

Castle hopping

Families will enjoy the Malaspina castles. Begin with Castello di Fosdinovo ⑮, then head to Castello Malaspina di Malgrate ⑫ and finally end up at Castello di Castiglione del Terziere ⑭.

Fosdinovo is reached from the SS446,

and Malgrate and Castiglione del Terziere are accessible from Bagnone.

Monumental artist

Drive around the marble mountain in the morning, visiting the quarry of Fantiscritti ⑰. Head for Carrara ⑯ in the afternoon before ending the day with a relaxing stroll along the beach at Forte dei Marmi ⑱.

Take the Carrara exit off the A12. From Carrara follow signs to Forte dei Marmi.

Eat and Drink: inexpensive, under €25; moderate, €25–€45; expensive, over €45

Chianti Vineyards

Siena to San Casciano

Highlights

- **Medieval Manhattan**
  Look up at the stone towers of
  San Gimignano, remnants of a
  fascinating feudal past

- **Villa of beauty**
  Visit the beautiful gardens of
  Villa Vignamaggio, home to the
  original Mona Lisa

- **Gentle Greve**
  Take time to wander the lanes and
  shop at the market in this
  stylish, easy-going town

- **World-class wine**
  Sample the local speciality at any
  number of family-run vineyards

A typical Chianti landscape of rolling hills cloaked
with vines and topped by grand villas

Chianti Vineyards

The gentle hills and valleys of Chianti sit snugly between the great art cities of Siena and Florence and are host to some of Italy's best vineyards. Forests of oak give way to open pasture, while easy country roads lead to remote abbeys and hilltop castles. This is an area for the meandering drive and the curious traveller. Morning markets in vibrant piazzas, picnic lunches with the best local produce and wine tasting in ancient cellars are what Chianti is all about. With no big towns to speak of, it is one large glorious garden to wander through at leisure.

Above Traditional straw-covered, rounded Chianti *fiaschi* (flasks) stored on an old cart in a vineyard at Villa a Sesta, *see p113*

ACTIVITIES

Swap the car for a bike and pedal past olive groves and vineyards on quiet country roads

Follow in the footsteps of Benedictine monks and take a walk up the Arno Valley by the Badia a Coltibuono

Stock up on "La Cinta Senese" sausages, made from the local breed of swine, at a famous butcher's in Panzano

Be a *barone* for a day and sup from the world-class cellars of several castles-turned-wineries

KEY

━━━ Drive route

Left The medieval towers of San Gimignano rising high above the hilltop town, *see p115*

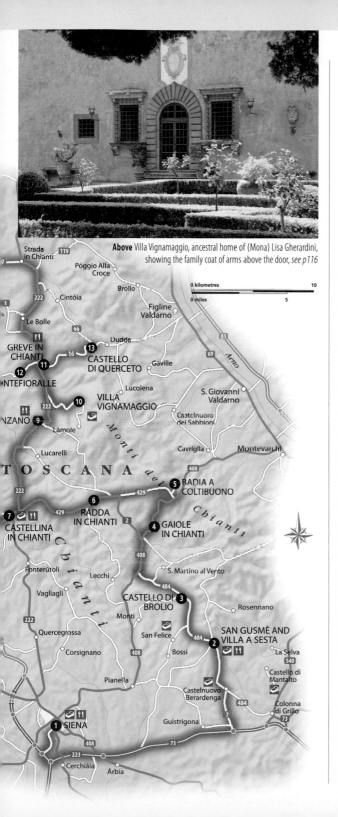

Strada
in Chianti   119

Above Villa Vignamaggio, ancestral home of (Mona) Lisa Gherardini, showing the family coat of arms above the door, *see p116*

PLAN YOUR DRIVE

Start/finish: Siena to San Casciano.

Number of days: 3, allowing for a half day in Siena and a half day's side trip to San Gimignano.

Distances: 134 km (83 miles). Siena to Castellina 66 km (41 miles); side trip to San Gimignano 28 km (17 miles); Castellina to San Casciano 40 km (25 miles).

Road conditions: Mostly on well-maintained provincial roads. Be wary in rain or snow on smaller "white roads."

When to go: Spring and autumn are the best times, especially late autumn when leaf colour can be exceptional.

Opening times: Most museums open 9am–7pm and often close Mon and Sun afternoon, with shorter hours in winter. Churches can be unpredictable, and usually close noon–3 or 4pm.

Wine estate tours & tastings: Vineyards in the Chianti are working enterprises so it is best to book in advance for tours and tastings, though large operators such as Castello di Brolio are well staffed. Look out for hand-painted "Cantina Aperta" signs, which indicate that the smaller vineyards are open for tastings and purchases. Expect a charge of around €10–20 for a tour and tasting. Snacks or nibbles are often included.

Main market days: Gaiole: 2nd Mon; Radda: 4th Mon; San Gimignano: Thu; Greve: Sat.

Major festivals: Siena: Palio horse race, Jul 2nd & Aug 16th; San Gimignano: Medieval Festival, 2nd weekend Jun; Chianti: Classico Wine Festival, 2nd weekend Sep; Greve: harvest festivals across Chianti Sep/Oct.

DAY TRIP OPTIONS

The tour is easily treated as a series of day trips. **Art and history enthusiasts** can combine Siena with the castles of Chianti; **keen photographers** shouldn't miss the skyline of San Gimignano; and visiting the vineyards around Greve is a must for **wine buffs** – for full details *see p117.*

Above Siena's great tower, Torre del Mangia, looms over the fan-shaped Piazza del Campo

VISITING SIENA

Parking
Follow signs to Porta Tufi. Just inside the old city gate on the right is the turn off for Campo car park. Retain the ticket and pay on return.

Tourist Information
Piazza del Campo 56, 53100; 0577 280 551; www.terresiena.it

WHERE TO STAY

SIENA

Canon d'Oro *inexpensive*
In a perfect position near the top of Via Banchi di Sopra, this accommodation is modest but clean and cheerful.
Via Montanini 28, 53100; 0577 44321; www.cannondoro.com

Antica Torre *moderate*
Set in a 16th-century tower just inside the Porta Romana. Panoramic views from top floors. Booking essential.
Via di Fiera Vecchia 7, 53100; 0577 222 255; www.anticatorresiena.it

VILLA A SESTA

Villa di Sotto *inexpensive*
Pleasant family-run B&B villa. Sauro and Paola also provide meals.
Via S Caterina 30, Villa a Sesta, Castelnuovo Berardenga, 53019; 347 932 7090 or 0577 330 220; www.villadisotto.it

AROUND VILLA A SESTA

Castello di Montalto
moderate–expensive
Wonderful location, grand castle and very welcoming hosts.
Strada di Montalto 16, 10 km (6 miles) from Castelnuovo Berardenga on SS540, 53019; 0577 355675; www.montalto.it

❶ Siena
Toscana; 53100

Regarded by some as the most perfectly preserved medieval town in Europe, Siena is a visual feast of town-planning centred around its vast main square, Piazza del Campo ("field"), always a lively place and twice-yearly the scene of the exuberant Palio horse race.

A two-hour walking tour

From the car park, walk up the hill on Via Mattioli and turn right into Via S Agata, which becomes Via Dupre and emerges onto the Campo beside the eye-catching **Torre del Mangia and Palazzo Pubblico** ①.

The *palazzo* is still the Sienese town hall and also contains the Museo Civico *(open daily)*, which holds some excellent works of art, including a bronze she-wolf suckling the twins Romulus and Remus: legend has it that Senius, son of Remus, founded Siena. Other works not to miss are the majestic *Maestà* fresco of the Madonna enthroned, by Simone Martini, and Lorenzetti's *Allegories of Good and Bad Government* which gives a unique

Romulus and Remus statue, symbol of Siena

perspective on medieval city and country life. Climb the 388 steps of the *torre* for another splendid view of town and country. Leave the Campo along Via Rinaldini, turn left into Via Banchi di Sotto and continue to a sharp right into **Via Banchi di Sopra** ②, Siena's main shopping street. A short way along, the street opens onto the smallish piazza of the **Palazzo Tolomei** ③, a marvellous example of Sienese Gothic, now home to a Florentine bank. Further along Banchi di Sopra is Piazza Salimbeni, the headquarters of the world's oldest bank, **Monte dei Paschi di Siena** ④, founded in 1472. Turn left here and left again into Via dei Termini, a quieter walk back to Piazza dell'Indipendenza. Turn left into Via di Città and take Via

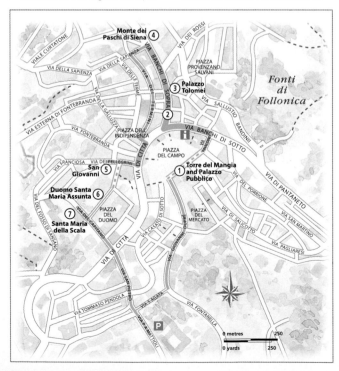

del Pellegrini to the right uphill to the beautiful baptistry of **San Giovanni** ⑤ *(open daily)*, containing art works by Florentine masters such as Ghiberti and Donatello, as well as local artist Jacopo della Quercia.

To the left of the baptistry, marble steps lead to the cathedral. One of the wonders of religious architecture and originally planned to be bigger than St Peter's in Rome, **Duomo Santa Maria Assunta** ⑥ *(open daily, Sun after 1:30pm)* is a masterpiece of Tuscan Gothic largely completed by 1215. The breathtaking façade, added after 1284, is a symphony in stone while the interior is a treasure trove of medieval and Renaissance sculpture, including some early Michelangelos. A particular highlight, in the Piccolomini Library, is Pinturicchio's 15th-century fresco cycle on Pope Pius II, an early example of naturalism in religious painting.

Opposite the Duomo is the elegantly understated **Santa Maria della Scala** ⑦ *(open daily)*. A former pilgrims' hospital dating from 1090, it is now a museum and gallery with displays ranging from Roman and Etruscan artifacts to modern art.

From Piazza del Duomo, turn right into Via del Capitano which leads back to the car park. On the way, pop along Via di Città to Antica Drogheria Manganelli and pick up some *panforte*, the local hard, spicy cake.

🚗 *Head south from the car park and take the Siena Tangenziale SS674, following signs for the A1 to Rome. Leave the motorway at signs for Castelnuovo Berardenga (SS484). Beyond Castelnuovo look for right turn up hill to San Gusmè.*

❷ San Gusmè & Villa a Sesta
Siena, Toscana; 53019

San Gusmè is a beautifully restored doll's-house of a town with miniature piazzas like elaborate opera sets framing terrific views towards Siena. A short distance along the SS484, the wine village of Villa a Sesta sits picturesquely surrounded on all sides by vineyards and olive groves. Perfectly formed around a church, square and café, the sight of brick-red geraniums against weathered stone, and traditional Chianti wine flasks, complete an idyllic rural scene.

🚗 *Continue on SS484 to Castello di Brolio. Park outside the Cantina.*

❸ Castello di Brolio
Gaiole in Chianti, Toscana; 53013

This small village takes its name from the neighbouring vineyard and castle that has been in the hands of the Ricasoli family since the 10th century. Long a Florentine stronghold, Castello di Brolio was remodelled in its current mock-Gothic medieval manner in the 19th century by Barone Bettino Ricasoli (1809–1880). Playing a key role in the Unification of Italy, Ricasoli was twice Prime Minister. Perhaps more importantly, he was also responsible for defining the composition of Chianti wine in 1870, still largely adhered to today. The *cantina* is the place to enjoy tasting Barone Ricasoli wines, which are highly regarded all over the world *(www.ricasoli.it)*.

🚗 *Follow SS484 to junction with SS408 and turn right for Gaiole.*

Below An invitation to a roadside wine tasting straight from the barrel **Below right** The mock-Gothic main building of Castello di Brolio

Above A path curves past olive trees and vines, Villa a Sesta **Left** The façade of the Santa Maria Assunta cathedral in Siena, a dazzling display of statuary and gilded mosaic

EAT AND DRINK

SIENA

Osteria Il Grattacielo *inexpensive*
Tiny, iconic *osteria*. Be prepared to share a table and enjoy a rough red. *Via Pontani 8, 53100; 0577 289 326; closed Sun*

Medio Evo *moderate*
Emphasis on the medieval, as its name implies. Great food and atmosphere. *Via dei Rossi 40, 53100; 0577 280 315; www.medioevosiena.it; closed Thu*

Osteria Le Logge *moderate*
Excellent *osteria* for sitting outside, owned by wine maker Gianni Brunelli and serving classic Tuscan food, *Via del Porrione 33, 53100; 0577 48013; www.osterialelogge.it; closed Sun*

VILLA A SESTA

La Bottega del 30 *expensive*
Sophisticated cooking in a simple, rural background. Try *carpaccio of Cinta Senese* with wild fennel seeds. *Via S Caterina 2, 53019; 0577 359 226; www.labottegadel30.it; dinner only (Sun lunch & dinner); closed Tue & Wed*

Above 11th-century Badia a Coltibuono church **Above right** Distant view of Radda set amidst fertile slopes **Below** Neo-Romanesque tower of San Salvatore church, dwarfed by Castellina's massive fortress

WHERE TO STAY

CASTELLINA IN CHIANTI

Hotel Belvedere di San Leonino *moderate*
Well-appointed, relaxed country hotel. *Loc. San Leonino, 2 km (1 mile) along SS222, 53011; 0577 740 887; www. hotelsanleonino.com*

Palazzo Squarcialupi *expensive*
Beautifully restored building with pool. *Via Furruccio 22, 53011; 0577 741 186; www.palazzosquarcialupi.com; open Apr–Oct*

SAN GIMIGNANO

Hotel L'Antico Pozzo *moderate*
Charming, unpretentious luxury. Some rooms with frescoed ceilings. *Via San Matteo 87, 53037; 0577 942 014; www.anticopozzo.com*

④ Gaiole in Chianti
Siena, Toscana; 53013
Full of life on market days, Gaiole is a pleasantly rural riverside town that first prospered when the surrounding castles and great abbeys needed a marketplace for their goods. Along with Radda and Castellina, Gaiole was one of the original members of the *Lega del Chianti* (Chianti League), established in the 14th century by the Florentine Republic as a bulwark against rival Siena. Nearby castle ruins testify to Gaiole's frontline role. In particular, the stark and splendidly solid, block-like towers of **Barbischio**, up a winding road behind the main square, and **Vertine**, above the village on the other side, keep a vigilant lookout over the landscape.
🚗 *Head north on SP408 to junction with SS429, turn off for Cavriglia/Radda. Turn off for Coltibuono is immediately after the Radda turn off, on the right.*

⑤ Badia a Coltibuono
Gaiole in Chianti, Siena; 53013
Founded by Benedictine monks, who were the first to plant vineyards in this area of Chianti, the Abbey of Coltibuono ("Good Harvest") is now a wine estate with an excellent restaurant specializing in game and local cheeses, where visitors can also sample the estate wines *(moderate; 0577 749 031; www.coltibuono.com; closed in winter).* Some of the abbey buildings date from 1050 and feature fine Romanesque architecture. The abbey church is open daily and every afternoon in summer there are guided tours of the rest of the monastery and the cellars;

Gallo Nero wine label for Chianti Classico

ring to confirm and to arrange wine tastings and cookery classes *(0577 744 81).* Marked walking trails behind the restaurant afford fine views down the Arno Valley.
🚗 *From Coltibuono turn right on to the SS429 and continue to Radda.*

⑥ Radda in Chianti
Siena, Toscana; 53017
Quaint, compact and perfectly proportioned, Radda was the capital of Chianti in the 14th century. Look for the numerous heraldic shields on the front of the town hall in **Piazza Ferrucci**, representing the noble families who would elect the ruling *podestà* (chief magistrate). Across the square is the church of **San Niccolo** whose Romanesque design is still evident despite remodelling.
🚗 *From Radda continue west along the SS429 to Castellina in Chianti.*

> **Florence vs Siena**
>
> As both Florence and Siena rose to riches and sought to expand their territory in the medieval period, clashes were inevitable. Serious rivalry began in 1260 and continued until the Sienese admitted defeat in 1554. With just the verdant hills of the Chianti between them, each side erected castles in the area around which formed towns and fortified hamlets like Montefioralle.

⑦ Castellina in Chianti
Siena, Toscana; 53011
Castellina is a lively town, deeply involved in the wine industry and full of excellent bars. The Neo-Romanesque church of **San Salvatore** in Piazza Roma contains a lovely, late 14th-century fresco by Lorenzo de Bicci. Dominating the centre is the fortress **Rocca Comunale**, commissioned by Lorenzo the Magnificent in the late 1400s and host to the Museo Archeologico del Chianti Senese *(closed Wed).* Heading east there is a fascinating covered medieval walkway, **Via delle Volte**, which has recently been revived with art galleries but retains a slightly spooky atmosphere.
🚗 *Take SS429 direction Poggibonsi. Follow signs to San Gimignano on SP1.*

❽ San Gimignano

Siena, Toscana; 53037

Built in a grandiose game of one-upmanship played out by rival aristocratic families in the 12th and 13th centuries, the 14 surviving towers of San Gimignano – from an astonishing peak of 72 – form one of the most iconic skylines in all Italy.

Via San Giovanni affords the best entrance to the town, like an extended aisle ushering in visitors to the centre. Halfway along the street, on the right, are the remains of the church of **San Franceso**, with a superb travertine and serpentine marble Romanesque façade. At no. 57 is the excellent **Galleria Gagliardi,** a gallery that showcases contemporary sculptors in Italy. At the top of the street you come to the first of the two linked piazzas that form the centre of town.

Majolica shop, Via San Giovanni

Piazza della Cisterna, named after its stone well, is surrounded by mansions with mullioned windows and towers that once had wooden balconies at the upper levels. Nearby Piazza del Duomo is flanked by the Duomo (cathedral) and the **Palazzo Nuovo del Podesta** (New Government Palace), which now houses the Tourist Information office to the left and the Museo Civico (open daily) up the stairs, where you can also ascend the 218 steps of the **Torre Grosso** for a stunning panorama. The

Below The façade of Palazzo Nuovo del Podesta, San Gimignano **Above right** View from Torre Grosso along Via San Giovanni, Gimignano

museo has several superb works such as a Maesta, by Lippo Memmi, works by Gozzoli and an altarpiece of San Gimignano holding the town in his grasp. A profane cycle of frescoes on the initiation to love was intended to raise medieval eyebrows.

The **Duomo** (daily till 4:40pm; closed Feb) dates from 1148. The highly decorated interior includes cycles of the Old Testament in the left nave and New Testament in the right, a magnificent Saint Sebastian by Benozzo Gozzoli, and a harrowing depiction of the Seven Deadly Sins. A Renaissance chapel by Domenico Ghirlandaio, Michelangelo's tutor, depicts the story of Santa Fina who was confined on a board with rats nibbling at her dress as she prayed.

Around the back of the Duomo, the **Rocca di Montestaffoli** fortress, dating from 1353, offers more great views. Nearby in Villa della Rocca is **Il Museo del Vino** (open daily) featuring the local Vernaccia wine, one of Italy's finest whites. A portal to the north leads down through parkland to Via San Matteo with its excellent shops, bars and restaurants.

🚌 **Return to Castellina, take SS222 to Panzano, follow signs to Greve/Firenze.**

VISITING SAN GIMIGNANO

Tourist Information
Piazza del Duomo 1, 53037; 0577 940 008; www.sangimignano.com

Parking
Pick from four car parks marked with blue "P" signs. Summer shuttle bus from Giubileo and Santa Lucia car parks.

Bike and Scooter Hire
See the sights by Vespa or bicycle. Bruno Bellini, Via Roma 41, 53037; 0577 940 201; www.bellinibruno.com

EAT AND DRINK

CASTELLINA IN CHIANTI

Antica Trattoria La Torre moderate
Traditional food with a copy of the great mural by Vasari on the ceiling. Piazza del Comune 15, 53011; 0577 740 236; www.anticatrattorialatorre. com; closed Fri

SAN GIMIGNANO

Enoteca Da Gustavo inexpensive
Outstanding bar for a quick bite. Via San Matteo 29, 53037; 0577 940 057

Restaurant Bel Soggiorno moderate
Local food with a twist, served in a historic building with splendid views. Via San Giovanni 91, 53037; 0577 940 375; www.hotelbelsoggiorno.it

Dorandò expensive
Cosy, elegant restaurant with creative Tuscan menu by a world-class chef. Vicolo dell'Oro 2, 53037; 0577 941 862; www.ristorantedorando.it

Above Covered walkway past the old merchants' *loggias* on Piazza Matteotti, Greve

CYCLING IN CHIANTI

Chianti offers great facilities for cyclists and enjoyable terrain. Try following the Chianti section of the Eroica bike race which is signposted all year round. *www.terresienainbici.it*

Bike Hire
Officina Ramuzzi; Via Italo Stecchi 23, Greve in Chianti, 50022; 055 853 037; www.ramuzzi.com; closed Sat pm & Sun

WHERE TO STAY

VILLA VIGNAMAGGIO

Villa Vignamaggio *expensive*
Ornate grand house in elegant grounds. A Wellness Centre offers "Wine Therapy" treatments.
Via Petriolo 5, Località Vignamaggio, Greve in Chianti, 50022; 055 854 661; www.vignamaggio.com

SAN CASCIANO

Villa Talente *expensive*
Luxurious but homely hotel in a secluded farmland setting.
Via Empolese 107, Talente 50026; 055 8259 484; www.villatalente.it

⑨ Panzano
Greve in Chianti, Toscana; 50022
Perched on a ridge, Panzano is renowned for its views down the Conca d'Oro valley. The SS222 passes the lower part of town where, just off the road to the left, is the renowned butcher's **Cecchini**, whose restaurant Solociccio is regarded by many as an essential Italian experience. Top New York chef Bill Buford came here to learn from Dario Cecchini and wrote the classic foodie memoir, *Heat*.

🚗 *Follow the SS222 downhill towards Greve. At the bottom of the hill there is a sharp right turn to Lamole. Follow the signs to Villa Vignamaggio, about 2 km (1 mile).*

⑩ Villa Vignamaggio
Greve in Chianti, Toscana; 5022
The aristocratic Gherardini family established some dominion over the region just south of Greve. They held onto their land and the delightful Villa Vignamaggio is now a wine estate offering tours and tastings *(055 854 661; www.vignamaggio.com)*. It was here that Lisa Gherardini, identified as Leonardo's Mona Lisa, was probably born and spent her summer holidays. The splendid Italianate garden and rustic glory of the villa itself provided the perfect setting for Kenneth Branagh's film *Much Ado About Nothing*.

🚗 *Head back to the main road, the SS222 and turn right towards Greve, about 2 km (1 mile). At the traffic lights turn right and follow the "P" signs to the main car park.*

Above Looking towards the church of Santa Croce at the southern end of Piazza Matteotti, Greve

⑪ Greve in Chianti
Florence, Toscana; 50022
Piazza Matteotti is the heart of Greve and its irregular shape and uneven architecture add to the charm: individual merchants were required to pay for and construct their own loggias (porticoes) so different segments are similar but not identical. The loggias now house shops, bars and restaurants, all of some distinction. On market days the square comes into its own, hosting stalls of fruit and vegetables, clothes and hardware. The statue almost in the centre of the piazza, looking down with feigned indifference, is of the explorer Giovanni di Verrazzano, who was born nearby.

🚗 *Continue on SS222 following signs for Montefioralle. Before leaving town take a sharp left uphill to Montefioralle.*

Left A distant view of Villa Vignamaggio in its bucolic valley setting

Far left A narrow cobbled street in the fortified hamlet of Montefioralle **Left** The main house at Castello di Querceto winery

EAT AND DRINK

PANZANO

Solociccia *moderate*
This welcoming restaurant is the home of a butcher. Bring your own wine.
Via Chiantigiana 5, 50022; 055 852 727; www.solociccia.it; sittings 7pm & 9pm Thu–Sat, Sun lunch

GREVE IN CHIANTI

Gallo Nero *moderate*
Old-fashioned, good value *osteria* housed in the former town stables.
Via Cesare Battisti 9, 50022; 055 853 734; www.enoristorantegallonero.it; closed Thu

Mangiando, Mangiando *moderate*
Excellent salads, light dishes and wines.
Piazza Matteotti 80, 50022; 055 854 6372; closed Mon, all Jan; www.mangiandomangiando.it

La Taverna del Guerrino *moderate*
Family-run trattoria serving local food in the age-old tradition. A rustic gem.
Via Montefioralle 39, 50022; 5 min W of Greve; 055 853 106; closed Mon & Tue

Da Verrazzano *moderate–expensive*
Splendid terrace and good choice of wines. Try the *ribollita* and *panzanella*.
Piazza Giacomo Matteotti 28, 50022; 055 853 189; www.ristorante verrazzano.it; closed Mon

Antica Macelleria Falorni
One of the best butchers in Tuscany.
Piazza Giacomo Matteotti 71, 50022; 055 853 029; www.falorni.It; closed Sat pm and Sun

Le Cantine
Tastings from over a hundred wines in the cellars of the old wine cooperative.
Galleria delle Cantine 2, 50022; follow the signs from the main square; 055 854 6404; www.lecantine.it

---

⑫ **Montefioralle**
Greve in Chianti, Toscana; 50022

Still effectively "castellated" within its original walls, this beautifully intact and much restored fortified hamlet provides an authentic medieval atmosphere with its close houses, narrow lanes and arched roadways. The tortuous and narrow road leading up to it adds to the feeling of travelling back in time.

🚗 *Return to Greve, then take SP16 opposite Greve's main square, Piazza Matteoti, towards Figline Valdarno. Park on the road outside the castello.*

⑬ **Castello di Querceto**
Greve in Chianti, Toscana; 50020

This is the perfect spot for superb wine tasting and a snack after touring the castle, all for a very reasonable price. Owned by the François family since 1897, the history of the castle goes back far longer. Call to book a wine-tasting tour *(055 859 21; www.castellodiquerceto.it).*

Chianti breed of pig on butcher's sign

🚗 *Take SP16 back to Greve. From Piazza Matteoti take SS222 north for 11 km (7 miles) to Strada in Chianti. Drive around the town and turn left for SP67. At Il Ferrone turn left onto SP3 towards Firenze. Continue 5 km (3 miles) to meet Via Cassia SR2. Turn sharp left onto SP2 and follow signs to San Casciano.*

⑭ **San Casciano**
Florence, Toscana; 50026

San Casciano is a typically well-placed hill town, retaining the buildings and streetscape of its medieval past. Just inside the town's remaining gateway, the church of **Santa Maria al Prato** is well-endowed with works of art from the 14th century, and there is an excellent central *enoteca*, Antica Fiaschetteria del Chianti *(inexpensive)* on Piazza Pierotti, serving local food and wine. Heading north, take a detour to **San Andrea in Percussina** where Machiavelli wrote *Il Principe* (The Prince) in 1513, still regarded as one of the best books on politics.

DAY TRIP OPTIONS

Chianti is not large and virtually everything is half an hour's drive away, making it easy to stay in one place and break up the tour into several days out.

Old battlegrounds

As medieval Siena grew rich a rivalry began with neighbouring Florence and the hills of Chianti became a defensive buffer zone. Spend a morning looking at the artistic and architectural treasures

that Siena ❶ produced out of this period of wealth, then visit the castellated hamlet of Montefioralle ⑫ and the castles near Gaiole ❹ for a sense of how this 300-year conflict helped to shape the landscape.

From Siena take the SS222 straight to Greve, then on to Montefioralle. Return to Siena via Gaiole.

Towers of the past

Though not strictly in Chianti, San Gimignano ❽ is an unmissable day trip for anyone staying in the area.

Be sure to stop at Castellina ❼ on the way back for an aperitivo.

San Gimignano is directly west of Castellina along the SS429.

Sampling the best wines

The perfect wine buff and gourmet's day out in Chianti starts with a tasting at Castello di Querceto ⑬, followed by a leisurely lunch in Greve ⑪, before tasting further vintages at Villa Vignamaggio ⑩.

All stops are a short drive from each other off the SS222.

Eat and Drink: inexpensive, under €25; moderate, €25–€45; expensive, over €45

On the Piero Trail

Arezzo to Urbino

Highlights

- **The sublime Piero**
  See the world-famous fresco cycle in
  Arezzo – *The Legend of the True Cross* –
  simply outstanding

- **Landscapes of the Tiber Valley**
  Cross the valley and visit the old
  towns of the Valtiberina

- **The Apennine mountain range**
  The winding road over the spectacular
  Bocca Trabaria pass provides
  sensational views over the region

- **Renaissance art and architecture**
  Marvel at the Palazzo Ducale, Piero's
  Flagellation and Raphael's *Muta*
  in Urbino – some of the finest art and
  architecture in the world

The sloping Piazza Grande, giving a flavour of
medieval Arezzo

On the Piero Trail

Piero della Francesca, an early Renaissance master, was one of the first painters to experiment with perspective, although he was subsequently overshadowed by the giants who came after him. Despite a productive lifetime, only 22 of his works have survived, but a large proportion are viewable on this drive through the picturesque region where Piero was born, lived, worked and died. The important restoration of *The Legend of the True Cross* in Arezzo has created a new opportunity to see some of his major works in sequence along the Piero Trail.

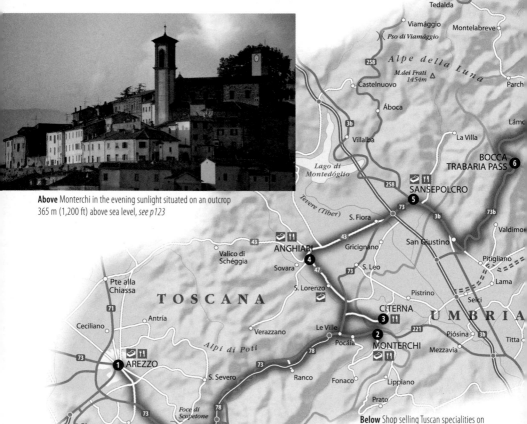

Above Monterchi in the evening sunlight situated on an outcrop 365 m (1,200 ft) above sea level, *see p123*

Below Shop selling Tuscan specialities on the Corso Italia, Arezzo, *see p122*

ACTIVITIES

See Piero's astonishing frescoes and paintings in Arezzo, Monterchi and Urbino

Picnic in the park of the Medici fortress above Arezzo

Go horse riding in the countryside around Sansepolcro

Take a walk in the wild at the Bocca Trabaria Pass

Scare yourself with the mummified corpses in Urbania

Fly a colourful kite in the hills above Urbino

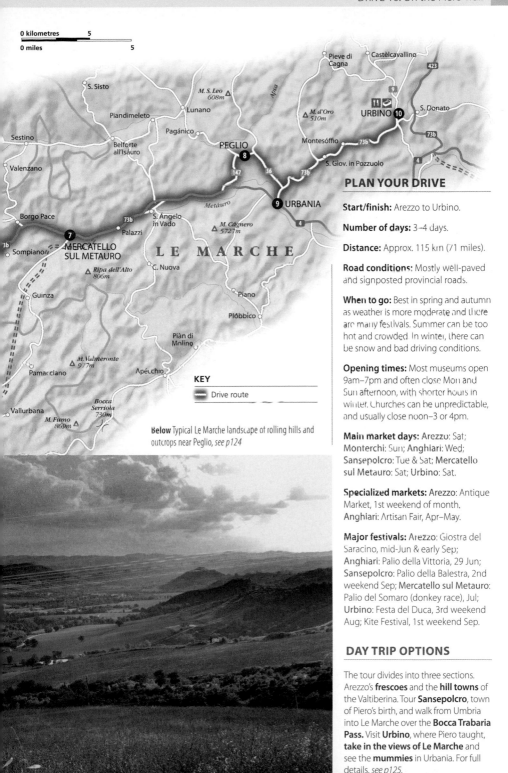

0 kilometres   5

0 miles   5

KEY

⊟ Drive route

Below Typical Le Marche landscape of rolling hills and outcrops near Peglio, *see p124*

PLAN YOUR DRIVE

Start/finish: Arezzo to Urbino.

Number of days: 3–4 days.

Distance: Approx. 115 km (71 miles).

Road conditions: Mostly well-paved and signposted provincial roads.

When to go: Best in spring and autumn as weather is more moderate and there are many festivals. Summer can be too hot and crowded. In winter, there can be snow and bad driving conditions.

Opening times: Most museums open 9am–7pm and often close Mon and Sun afternoon, with shorter hours in winter. Churches can be unpredictable, and usually close noon–3 or 4pm.

Main market days: Arezzo: Sat; Monterchi: Sun; Anghiari: Wed; Sansepolcro: Tue & Sat; Mercatello sul Metauro: Sat; Urbino: Sat.

Specialized markets: Arezzo: Antique Market, 1st weekend of month. Anghiari: Artisan Fair, Apr–May.

Major festivals: Arezzo: Giostra del Saracino, mid-Jun & early Sep; Anghiari: Palio della Vittoria, 29 Jun; Sansepolcro: Palio della Balestra, 2nd weekend Sep; Mercatello sul Metauro: Palio del Somaro (donkey race), Jul; Urbino: Festa del Duca, 3rd weekend Aug; Kite Festival, 1st weekend Sep.

DAY TRIP OPTIONS

The tour divides into three sections. Arezzo's **frescoes** and the **hill towns** of the Valtiberina. Tour **Sansepolcro**, town of Piero's birth, and walk from Umbria into Le Marche over the **Bocca Trabaria Pass**. Visit **Urbino**, where Piero taught, **take in the views of Le Marche** and see the **mummies** in Urbania. For full details, *see p125*.

VISITING AREZZO

Parking
Driving into Arezzo, follow signs to the station *(stazione)*. A main road (Viale Michelangelo) runs one way past the station – a large car park is to the left.

Tourist Information
Palazzo Comunale, Piazza della Libertà, 52100; 0575 401 945; www.apt.arezzo.it

The Legend of the True Cross
Prebook your visit and pick up your tickets – if you miss your allotted time, you'll need to buy more: *0575 352 727*

WHERE TO STAY

AREZZO

Casa Volpi *inexpensive*
Pleasant old villa with its own restaurant, at the start of the road to Sansepolcro.
Via Simone Martini 29, 52100; 0575 354 364; www.casavolpi.it

Hotel Continentale *moderate*
A modern hotel with a roof garden (and the internet). Close to major attractions.
Piazza Guido Monaco 7, 52100; 0575 20251; www.hotelcontinentale.com

Graziella Patio Hotel
moderate–expensive
An elegant hotel in the heart of town.
Via Cavour 23, 52100; 0575 401 962; www.hotelpatio.it

MONTERCHI

Palazzo Marzocchi *moderate*
Donatella Marzocchi is an outstanding hostess in a fascinating household.
Piazza Umberto I 18, 52035; 0575 966 030; www.palazzomarzocchi.com

Top Romanesque apse and loggias of the Pieve di Santa Maria, Arezzo **Right** Detail from *The Legend of the True Cross* by Piero della Francesca, in the Basilica di San Francesco, Arezzo

❶ Arezzo
Arezzo, Toscana; 52100

The provincial capital of eastern Tuscany, Arezzo is a bustling town whose prosperity derives from its gold manufacturing industry. It has been an important commercial centre since Roman times, with a beautiful medieval heart and a significant artistic patrimony, including the largest cycle of frescoes by Piero della Francesca, probably the most important painter of the early Renaissance.

A two-hour walking tour

Walk back through the station car park to the forecourt, Piazzale della Repubblica. From here, go straight ahead to the circular Piazza Guido Monaco. Continue for four short blocks to arrive at Piazza San Francesco. The main purpose in visiting Arezzo is to see the cycle of frescoes *The Legend of the True Cross* by Piero della Francesca (c. 1418–92) in the main chapel of the **Basilica di San Francesco** ❶ *(open daily)*. The extraordinary frescoes depict the story of the wood of the cross of the crucifixion, its origin and rediscovery after it had been lost. The work demonstrates the painter's mastery of perspective, colour, geometry and composition.

Arezzo's coat of arms

On leaving the church, turn right into Via Cavour. It is only one block to the **Corso Italia** ❷, Arezzo's historic main street. Now full of smart shops and ancient buildings, the Corso is the scene for the stylish *passeggiata* or evening stroll. Turn left and soon the individual and beautiful **Pieve di Santa Maria** ❸ *(open daily)*, the parish church of old Arezzo, comes into view. The façade has so many arches and loggias as to defy reason. Its bell tower was known as "the tower with a thousand holes", so pierced was it by its architectural filigree. The street beside the church leads up to Arezzo's main square, the beautiful **Piazza Grande** ❹, one of the most evocative in Italy. This is the venue for the Giostra del Saracino – a twice-yearly jousting tournament celebrating 16th-century military expertise. But the piazza is attractive at any time, so take in the atmosphere, and a coffee or an *aperitivo*, in the **Vasari Loggia** ❺ and then wander uphill to the splendid Gothic **Duomo** ❻ *(open daily)*, home to a lovely fresco by Piero of Mary Magdalene (left of the main altar). The gardens behind the Duomo and the **Fortezza Medicea** ❼ provide a perfect spot for a picnic or a walk.

Follow Via Ricasoli, which runs alongside the Duomo. Turn right into Via di Sassoverde to the **Chiesa di San Domenico** ❽. This unfinished church was begun in 1275 and is home to a number of works by Arezzo artists. The church highlights the level of artistic activity in Arezzo, with its beautiful illustrated *Crucifix* (1269) by the painter Cimabue. Next, head down Via XX Settembre to see **Casa Vasari** ❾ *(closed Tue)*. Born in Arezzo,

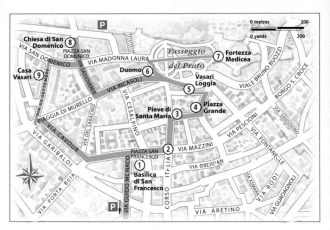

Above *Madonna del Parto*, Monterchi, painted following a request from Piero's mother

Vasari (1511–74) found fame as an architect working on projects including the elegant colonnade in the Piazza Grande. He is perhaps most famous for his biographies of Italian artists. Continue to Via Cavour and back to the Piazza San Francesco where there is a choice of two good bars. Then take Via Guido Monaco back to the station car park.

🚗 *Leave Arezzo on Viale Giotto which becomes Via Simone Martini, look for signs for Sansepolcro SS73, this becomes a motorway (E78) to Le Ville, then take the right fork for Monterchi.*

❷ Monterchi
Arezzo, Toscana; 52035
This typical hill town dates from the 10th century. Its narrow cobbled streets follow ancient mule tracks, past fine palazzos, up to the castle at the top (great views). Although little remains of the castle, Palazzo Alberti can be visited with the quirky **Museo di Bilance e Pesi** (Museum of Weights and Measures) *(closed for restoration)*. In the former schoolhouse at the south of the town is the **Museum** *(open daily; free admission for pregnant women)*, dedicated to Piero's *Madonna del Parto* (Pregnant Madonna). Piero was asked by his mother to paint the fresco for the chapel where his father, who died before he was born, was buried. This exquisitely personal depiction shows a woman full of melancholy at the thought of her child's future sacrifice, yet with a dignified nobility.

🚗 *Take the SP221 towards Arezzo, then the SS73 right to Sansepolcro. After 2 km (1 mile) turn right to Citerna.*

❸ Citerna
Perugia, Umbria; 06010
With valleys on either side of its steep ridge, Citerna enjoys its reputation as the "Balcony of the Upper Tiber", and there are splendid views from Piazza Scipione over the Valtiberina (Upper Tiber Valley) towards the Apennines and Sansepolcro. Founded in Etruscan times, due to the presence of a spring, the town's name is a corruption of *cisterna* or "well", the town symbol. The large round red-brick tower, **Il Torrione**, is 10th century and many of the public buildings date from the late Middle Ages.

🚗 *Return towards SS73. Take right to Arezzo, then right to Sansepolcro, take left at roundabout to Anghiari. Park in or above town.*

Piero della Francesca
Mathematician, scholar and painter, he is best remembered as the father of perspective in early Renaissance art. His theories were to influence the artists Perugino, Signorelli and Giovanni Santi, father of Raphael. His work spans the Gothic, where the size of figures reflected their importance, to the more modern style, when Piero started to depict subjects in a realistic picture plane with foreshortened limbs. He also embraced new painting techniques introduced by northern artists. His exquisite *Flagellation* (Palazzo Ducale, Urbino) is the pinnacle of modern technique and perspective, a feat not equalled for more than a century. Piero died in 1492, on the day Columbus discovered America, a date regarded by many as the beginning of the modern era.

TRUFFLE HUNTING IN CITERNA

In the autumn the locals go mad for truffles. Join in with Saverio Bianconi who will take you to a nearby forest with a hunter and his dogs. Later he will regale you with recipes and delicious food prepared by his wife. *www.tartufibianconi.it; 075 851 1591*

EAT AND DRINK

AREZZO

Buca di San Francesco *moderate*
In the medieval lane by the basilica, this specializes in local delicacies. *Via San Francesco 1, 52100; 0575 232/1; www.bucadisanfrancesco.it; closed Mon eve & Tue*

Il Saraceno *moderate*
Friendly, family-run restaurant just off the Corso – excellent value. *Via G Mazzini 6, 52100; 0575 27644; www.ilsaraceno.com; closed Wed*

MONTERCHI

La Pieve Vecchia *moderate*
This friendly family restaurant does an excellent fixed price lunch. *Loc. Pieve Vecchia 12, 52035 (on main road to Città di Castello); 0575 709 053; www.lapievevecchia.com; closed Tue*

Other options
Fra' Pacifico inexpensive place for light snacks next to the museum.

CITERNA

Belvedere *moderate*
Dine *al fresco* next to the piazza, or in the restaurant with its splendid view. *Corso Garibaldi 66, 06010; 075 859 2148; www.belvedererestaurant.it; closed Mon–Wed in winter*

Where to Stay: inexpensive, under €100; moderate, €100–200; expensive, over €200

Above left The medieval fortified bastion of Anghiari **Above right** Wheat fields on the plain between Citerna and Anghiari **Below right** The hill town of Peglio high above the surrounding countryside

WHERE TO STAY

ANGHIARI

Il Cardo Resort moderate
Beautifully restored old farmhouse just outside Anghiari. Turn off right by the Madonna Shrine on the approach to Anghiari from Citerna.
Loc. San Lorenzo 108, 52031; 0575 178 7767; www.ilcardoumbria.it

SANSEPOLCRO

Albergo Fiorentino inexpensive
In the heart of Sansepolcro only a few steps from the Piero frescoes.
Via Luca Pacioli 56, 52037; 0575 740 350; www.albergofiorentino.com

AROUND SANSEPOLCRO

Podere Violino inexpensive
This agriturismo is an excellent spot for horse riding and fly fishing.
Loc. Gricignano 99, 52037 (just off the main road (SS73) from Sansepolcro to Arezzo, on the left 5 km/3 miles out); 0575 720 174; www.podereviolino.it

URBINO

Albergo San Giovanni inexpensive
Not far from the main square in the old town and run by the Cecconi family, this budget hotel has an old-world feel. Breakfast not included.
Via Barocci 13, 61029; 0722 2827; www.albergosangiovanniurbino.it; closed 2nd half Jul, late Dec–early Jan

Albergo Italia moderate
Centrally located and completely modernized, this mid-level hotel is excellent for a stop-over.
Corso Giuseppe Garibaldi 32, 61029; 0722 2701; www.albergo-italia-urbino.it

Albergo San Domenico expensive
This restored monastery is opposite the Palazzo Ducale and is a comfortable place to stay in central Urbino.
Piazza Rinascimento 3, 61029; 0722 2626; www.viphotels.it

④ Anghiari
Arezzo, Toscana; 52031
This stunning town has held markets for the last 800 years, in Piazza Baldaccio, outside the old walls. Walk through the ancient gateway and into the narrow lanes and medieval houses to Piazza Mameli with the **Palazzo Taglieschi** (closed Mon), a state museum with excellent local artifacts. Higher up is Piazza del Popolo, with the Comune (Town Council) housed in a palazzo covered in stone shields.
🚗 *From the main piazza the SP43 leads straight (literally) to Sansepolcro.*

⑤ Sansepolcro
Arezzo, Toscana; 52037
Best known as the birth-place of Piero della Francesca, the **Museo Civico** (open daily) has four of his works including The Resurrection, one of the few paintings of its era to directly engage the viewer. Aldous Huxley described it as "the greatest painting in the world". During World War II, a British commander, about to bombard the town, recalled Huxley's essay and ordered a halt, thus saving the painting and the town.

The **Duomo** has a fine Ascension by Perugino and a superb carved 8th–9th century crucifix. Piazza Torre di Berte, is the town's heart with fashionable shops and Via XX Settembre runs west to the old stone gate, the Porta Fiorentina.
🚗 *Take the SS3bis to San Giustino. At the pedestrian plaza follow the blue signs to the Pesaro-Urbino SS73bis on the left, towards Urbino.*

⑥ Bocca Trabaria Pass
As the road winds up into the hills above the Valtiberina, gentle slopes of olive groves give way to wilder heaths and dramatic drops – with viewpoints.

After about 10 km (6 miles) the terrain becomes mountainous and the road steeper until the Bocca Trabaria Pass. At a height of 1,049 m (3,442 ft), this is the highest point in crossing the Apennines. There is a marked walking trail along the ridge of the pass.
🚗 *Follow the SR73bis to Mercatello – car park at the far side of town.*

⑦ Mercatello sul Metauro
Le Marche; 61040
At the town's centre is the large Piazza Garibaldi, with the fine 15th-century **Palazzo Ducale** to the north and the Romanesque **Pieve Collegiata**, with a gilded wooden Byzantine altarpiece, to the east. Along Corso Bencivenni is **La Chiesa Monumentale di San Francesco** (1235), a religious complex and gallery (closed Sun & Mon in winter) with 12th-century panels and ceilings.
🚗 *Take the SR73bis towards Urbino for 11 km (7 miles). Left onto the SS147. Follow signs to Peglio – parking on Via Montefeltro, after sign for "centro".*

⑧ Peglio
Le Marche; 61049
Once an 8th-century Lombard fortress, Peglio is perched atop a steep hill. A cantilevered walkway circles the town, giving a bird's-eye view of the valley and Urbania. Although little remains of Peglio's castle after centuries of feuding between rival factions, the medieval bell tower still stands.
🚗 *Leave following the signs for Urbania on the SP36, then rejoin the SS73bis just above Urbania.*

⑨ Urbania
Le Marche; 61049

Approaching Urbania, look out for the **Barco Ducale**, Duke Federico da Montefeltro's hunting lodge built in 1465 *(closed to the public)*. The town has a quaint historic centre and is noted for its majolica pottery. The morbidly curious will enjoy **La Chiesa dei Morti** *(closed Mon)* and its mummified corpses. They were put on display by the 19th-century brotherhood that cared for them. The **Museo Civico** *(closed Mon)* has the same fine architectural signature as the Barco Ducale.

🚗 *It is 11 km (7 miles) on the SR73 to Urbino. The SS73bis goes direct to the car park.*

⑩ Urbino
Le Marche; 61029

This enchanting city flourished under the patronage of Duke Federico da Montefeltro (1422–82). His university attracted painters, architects and mathematicians from far and wide, including Piero della Francesca.

The huge **Palazzo Ducale**, housing the **Galleria Nazionale delle Marche** *(closed Mon pm)*, dominates the approach to Urbino. The fairytale quality of the turrets that frame the balcony of the duke's private quarters belie the strength of an undefeated

military power, but in its day this was the largest building in Europe. The courtyard is a masterpiece of the classical Greek and Roman humanist ideals that would go on to become the hallmark of the Renaissance.

The gallery's most famous works are: Piero della Francesca's enigmatic *The Flagellation* (c. 1460) often cited as the world's greatest small painting; *The Ideal City*, a perspective study attributed to Piero or his students and the gorgeous *La Muta* by the 16th-century local-born painter Raphael. See also the Duke's private rooms, with inlaid wood panelling, and the kitchens and servants' quarters.

Across the square from the palace is the **Cattedrale di Urbino**, or Duomo, founded in 1062 but often rebuilt, its 18th-century Neo-Classical façade at odds with the nearby buildings.

Near the Piazza della Repubblica, **Casa di Rafaello** *(open daily)* has been preserved as a monument to Raphael since the 19th century and retains an evocative historic atmosphere. Nearby are the **oratories of San Giovanni and San Giuseppe**, the former holding paintings by the Salimbeni brothers (c. 1416). Blending International Gothic, a highly decorative narrative style, with a more natural approach, their work is an exciting presentiment of what was to come in the Renaissance.

Above left Self-portrait in Piero's *Resurrection*, Sansepolcro **Above centre** Skulls in Urbania's Chiesa dei Morti **Above right** Urbino's Duomo with its 18th-century Neo-Classical façade

EAT AND DRINK

ANGHIARI

Da Allghiero *expensive*
Quality restaurant just off main square
Via Garibaldi 8, 52031; 0575 788 040; www.daalighiero.it; closed Tue

SANSEPOLCRO

Ristorante Fiorentino *moderate*
This is a family-run and top-notch institution with traditional Tuscan fare.
Via Luca Pacioli 60, 52037; 0575 742 033; www.ristorantefiorentino.it; closed Wed

Al Coccio *moderate*
Great for local specialities.
Via Niccolò Aggiunti 83, 52037; 0575 741 468; www.alcoccio.com; closed Wed

Locanda da Ventura *moderate*
Famed for meat dishes and truffle pasta.
Via Niccolò Aggiunti 30, 52037; 0575 742 560; closed Sun eve & Mon, Jan

URBINO

Il Cortegiano *moderate*
Close to the palace this does café food on the street or serious food inside.
Via Francesco Puccinotti 13, 61029; 0722 320 307; closed Sun

Vecchia Urbino *moderate*
Good food near Piazza della Republica
Via dei Vasari 3, 61029; 0722 4447; www.vecchiaurbino.it; closed Tue

---

DAY TRIP OPTIONS
The drive is easily divided into three convenient sections:

Arezzo fresco

Piero's frescoes and Arezzo ❶ need a good half day, then tour the tiny hill towns – Monterchi ❷, Citerna ❸ and Anghiari ❹ are all very close.

The SS73 is the key road here, turning off on signposted roads to the hill towns.

Marching into Le Marche
Those seeking activity should explore Sansepolcro ❺ then, with supplies, drive to Bocca Trabaria Pass ❻ and enjoy a walk, the views and a picnic.

Apart from the start, take the SS73bis.

View from the top
Urbino ⑩ sits high on a hill with wonderful views, so make a day of it and go down to Peglio ❽ for another hill top treat, looking down on Urbania ⑨, quaint home of the petrified persons – mummies.

The SS73bis is again the key road – look for the signposted road to Peglio.

Eat and Drink: inexpensive, under €25; moderate, €25–€45; expensive, over €45

Tuscan Vistas

Buonconvento to La Foce

Highlights

- **Pilgrims' progress**
  See the stone portals of faith of Sant'Antimo and Abbazia di Monte Oliveto Maggiore on the pilgrim trail

- **Perfect Pienza**
  Marvel at the tiny but glorious piazza that heralded the beginnings of the Renaissance

- **Sublime music**
  Listen to the atmospheric and uplifting sound of Gregorian chant in the ancient abbeys

- **Sensational cheese and wine**
  Taste the region's famous sheep's cheese, served with superb local red wines

The Crete Senesi, a landscape seemingly unchanged since Roman times

Tuscan Vistas

The view over the Crete Senesi is one of the most evocative in Italy: great clay hills, eroded through time, cultivated for centuries and traversed by ancient pilgrims. This amazing landscape continues to the south in the valley of the River Orcia – a UNESCO World Heritage Site. Together they create the most harmonious panoramas and pleasant drives, passing ancient abbeys, medieval villages, healing spas and crumbling fortresses that guarded the pilgrim routes.

Above The dramatic drawbridge at the Abbazia di Monte Oliveto Maggiore, *see p130*

ACTIVITIES

Build up a head of steam on the Nature Train through the Crete Senesi from Siena, stopping at Buonconvento and other villages

Experience the thrill of a hot-air balloon at dawn from Montisi and see the amazing Crete Senesi landscape from a totally different viewpoint

Sample the two great red wines of the region: the Vino Nobile di Montepulciano and the Brunello di Montalcino

Soak in a mud bath at Bagno Vignoni and enjoy the healing effects of *fangoterapia* (mud therapy)

Above Classic Cretan Senesi view with clay hill, large farm and cypress trees, *see p131*

PLAN YOUR DRIVE

Start/finish: Buonconvento to La Foce.

Number of days: 3 days.

Distance: Approx. 130 km (80 miles).

Road conditions: Generally good with little heavy traffic – some "white roads" which are maintained but unsealed.

When to go: All-year but in autumn and winter the landscape is slightly dull and has less impact.

Opening times: Most museums open 9am–7pm and often close Mon and Sun afternoon, with shorter hours in winter. Churches can be unpredictable, and usually close noon–3 or 4pm

Main market days: Buonconvento: every Sat; San Giovanni d'Asso: 1st Mon of the month pm; Montisi: 3rd Mon of the month pm; Montepulciano: every Thu; Pienza: organic and traditional food, every Fri, 1st Sun of the month; San Quirico d'Orcia: 2nd & 4th Tue of every month; Montalcino: every Fri, 1st & 3rd Tue of the month; Castiglione d'Orcia: every 2nd Sat, 1st & 3rd Tue.

Major Festivals: Montisi: Giostra di Simone, 1st weekend Aug – medieval festival culminating in a Sunday joust; Montepulciano: International Festival of Arts, Jul; Bravio delle Botti (Wine Barrels competition), last Sun of Aug. Pienza: Fiera di Cacio, 1st week Sep – a festival celebrating the Pecorino di Pienza cheese; San Quirico d'Orcia: Festa del Barbarossa, 3rd Sat & Sun in Jun; Montalcino: Jazz & Wine, Jul; Honey Week, Sep; Thrush Festival: last weekend in Oct; Castiglione d'Orcia: May Festival, night of 30 Apr – singers parade around town.

DAY TRIP OPTIONS

There are three excellent themes on this drive – enjoy the **architecture** and **chanting** of the **abbeys** funded by the **pilgrims** on the **Via Francigena**. Settle a debate that has raged for centuries in the local **enotecas** and **vineyards** – whose **wine** is best? Enjoy the famous culinary specialities of **San Giovanni d'Asso**, **Pienza** and **Montalcino**. For further details, *see p135*.

Above Tree-lined entrance to the Abbazia di Monte Oliveto Maggiore

WHERE TO STAY

BUONCONVENTO

Podere Salicotto Country Hotel
moderate
Total comfort in a farm stay with an emphasis on luxury. Serves brunch for late risers. There is a pool and bikes, too. *Strada Prov. le Pieve a Salti, Loc. Salicotti 73, 53022 (2 km/1 mile from centre of Buonconvento); 0577 809 087; www.poderesalicotto.com*

SAN GIOVANNI D'ASSO

Hotel La Locanda del Castello
moderate
A floral theme runs through the rooms in this hotel in the historic centre of town. Restaurant serves classic Tuscan cuisine featuring local produce. *Piazza Vittorio Emanuele II 4, 53020; 0577 802 939; www.lalocandadelcastello.com*

MONTISI

La Locanda di Montisi *moderate*
Small but comfortable hotel in the historic centre with 7 rooms, tiled floors and original wooden beams. Refurbished in country-cottage style. *Via Umberto I 39, 53020; 0577 845 906; www.lalocandadimontisi.it*

La Grancia *moderate*
A farm fortress built by the Hospital of St Maria della Scala in Siena in the 14th century. Set near the historic centre, the farm has well-appointed apartments. *Via Umberto I 8, 53020; 335 660 9987; www.lagrancia.com*

① Buonconvento
Siena, Toscana; 53022
Unusually for a Tuscan town, this fortress town sits on a plain. Its huge walls recall its role as an outpost in the south of Siena, guarding the food-producing plains around. Inside the walls is a pleasant *centro storico* with a town hall and art gallery, **Museo d'Arte Sacra** *(closed Wed in summer, weekdays in winter)* which has a fine collection of religious art. The **Museo della Mezzadria** (Museum of Peasant Farming) explains local peasant life *(closed Mon, also pm in winter)*. Steam buffs will enjoy the Nature Train that slowly puffs through here on the way to other villages *(www.terresiena.it)*.

🚗 *Leaving to the northeast take the SS451 to Abbazia di Monte Oliveto Maggiore. Ample parking on site.*

② Abbazia di Monte Oliveto Maggiore
Siena, Toscana; 53041
This enduring monastic complex, first settled by Giovanni Tolomei in 1313, is a quite enchanting collection of buildings. Amid shady forests of oak and cypress, the monastery has an impressive entrance tower decorated with 15th-century della Robbia ceramics – there is even a drawbridge, but oddly no protective walls. The **Chiostro Grande** is the main reason for visiting, as the cloister contains a wonderful cycle of paintings by Luca Signorelli (1497) and *Il Sodoma*, (1505–08) on the life of St Benedict. If possible time the visit to hear the Gregorian chant sung at 6:15pm daily.

Below View over the surrounding countryside from Montisi

🚗 *Go towards Asciano on the SS451, turn right on the SP60, past Chiusure, then turn left and keep right, still on the SP60, becoming SP60b, then SP60a.*

③ San Giovanni D'Asso
Siena, Toscana; 53020
This quiet town boasts the **Museo del Tartufo**, entered via the courtyard of the **Castello Comunale** *(open Apr–Nov: Fri–Sun; Dec–Mar: Sat & Sun)*, for everything there is to know about truffles and funghi. Visitors will also not want to miss **San Pietro in Villore**, a small 12th-century chapel with an original Romanesque brick and tufa façade and a sail-like bell tower.

🚗 *Head south downhill. At the bottom of the hill turn left on the SP14 to Montisi. Park at the other end of town, at the eastern end of Via Umberto I.*

④ Montisi
Siena, Toscana; 53020
This vibrant village stretched along the road and focussed on an ancient castle keep, makes a pleasant stop for lunch and a stroll. It dates back to Etruscan times, although much of what there is to see was built at the height of the Sienese Republic (13–14th centuries). At the very top of Montisi, a small music academy is housed in the 13th-century Castello di Montisi which holds summer concerts. To get the most impressive view of the countryside, try taking a hot-air balloon flight. This should be arranged in advance – it is an early start. (For more information see *www.ballooningintuscany.com*).

Where to Stay: inexpensive, under €100; moderate, €100–200; expensive, over €200

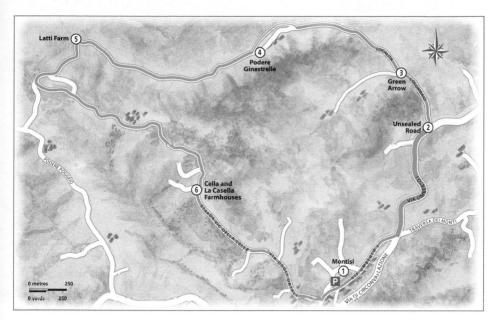

⑤ A walk through the Crete Senesi

Siena, Toscana; 53020

There is no better way to experience the traditional Tuscan beauty of the Crete Senesi than to take a walk through it. This circular walk passes a ruined castle and continues through ancient olive groves and past working and abandoned farms. Easy at first, the route crosses some rough terrain on the return to Montisi. Good walking shoes and picnic provisions are recommended. Most of the walk is marked by the Club Alpino Italiano walking group (*www.cai.it*) with a red-and-white painted blaze which will help in finding the way.

A three-hour walking tour

Set off from the car park at **Montisi** ① along the road towards Trequanda, turning left after 1.3 km (1 mile) along an **unsealed road** ② towards Colombaio. This gentle downhill road takes you past olive groves below the Castello di Montelifré, a fortified village dating back to the 11th century. It is still owned by the ancient family of Martinozzi – distant relatives of the Bourbon family. Where the hill rises slightly to a junction, take a right (a **green arrow** ③ painted on the stone wall indicates the correct path). Keep following the trail until the path comes to a farmhouse where there is a sign marking the detour "Strada Campionata". Then, circle to the right below the modern farm sheds and back up to the main trail. This farm, the **Podere Ginestrelle** ④, is typical of Crete farms bought by Sardinian

families in the 1970s. The farmyard cockerels will crow and dogs may bark but they are all very friendly, as is the farmer, Giuseppe.

The dirt road continues along a ridge of Crete fields – enjoy the classic Tuscan scenery of rolling clay hills, wooded valleys and farmed fields in a seasonal colour palette, punctuated by exclamatory cypress trees. The path then heads towards some abandoned stone buildings of the **Latti Farm** ⑤. Before reaching the farm, the track winds left, across fields and down to a small natural reserve. Watch your footing in the woods then, in the open, proceed up through the olive groves, past the farmhouses of **Cella and La Casella** ⑥ to re-enter Montisi on Via degli Ortali.

🚗 *Take Via di Circonvallazione south, and turn left onto Viale della Rimembranza towards Castelmuzio.*

Above Typical countryside of the Crete Senesi, on the walk north of Montisi

EAT AND DRINK

MONTISI

Bar il Rondò *inexpensive*
This bar at the eastern approach to the town is good for a basic bowl of home-made pasta or a plate of local cheeses. Rustic interior and garden.
Via Umberto I, 144, 53020; 0577 845 186; www.laromita.it

Da Roberto *moderate*
Specializing in organic local products, with seasonal highlights, this has a cosy vaulted interior in winter, and a veranda in summer. Located on the western approach to the town.
Via Umberto I, 3, 53020; 0577 845 159; www.tavernamontisi.com; closed Mon

Above One of the many pretty views of medieval Castelmuzio **Right** Elegant bell tower in the fortified town of Montefollonico **Below right** The Tempio di San Biagio sitting below Montepulciano

VISITING MONTEPULCIANO

Parking
Park at the lower part of the historic centre near Viale Primo Maggio or at the top near Via di Collazzi.

Tourist Information
Via di Gracciano nel Corso 59/a; 0578 757 341; www. prolocomontepulciano.it

WHERE TO STAY

PETROIO

Palazzo Brandano *expensive*
Casual Tuscan chic is the signature of this smart hotel in the historic centre. *Via di Val Gelata 18, 53020; 0577 665 169; www.palazzobrandano.com*

MONTEPULCIANO

Sant' Antonio *moderate*
This converted 12th-century Franciscan monastery offers excellent hospitality. *Via della Montagna, 6–8, 53045; 0578 799 365; www.santantonio.it*

PIENZA

Piccolo Hotel La Valle Pienza *inexpensive–moderate*
Comfortable rooms in a modern building on the outer walls of the old centre. *Via Circonvallazione 7, 53026; 0578 749 402; www.piccolohotellavalle.it*

SAN QUIRICO D'ORCIA

Palazzo del Capitano *moderate*
These elegant rooms have a central location. Spa facilities. *Via Poliziano 18, 53027; 0577 899 028; www. palazzodelcapitano.com*

⑥ Castelmuzio
Siena, Toscana; 53020

Set on a volcanic limestone hill, this almost untouched medieval village, simply called "il Castello" by the locals, has a structure typical of a fortified castle. Ringed with walls and bastions, the atmospheric hamlet merits a stroll around – there are a few shops inside the main gate and a bar/pizzeria under the campanile in the piazza.

🚗 *Head east on the SP71 to Petroio.*

⑦ Petroio
Siena, Toscana; 53020

This tiny village has for centuries been known for its terracotta pottery. In the Middle Ages it came under various feudal lordships before becoming part of the Republic of Siena and then the Grand Duchy of Tuscany. Architecturally, Petroio still echoes this period so it is worth exploring its streets and dropping into the Museo della Terracotta in the Palazzo Pretorio *(open Apr–Sep Thu, Fri pm & weekends; Oct–Mar weekends)*.

🚗 *In the direction of Sinalunga, take the SP71 (follow green Autostrade signs), turn sharp right at SP57 (for Pienza), continue on the SP15 to Osteria delle Noci. Left to Montefollonico.*

The Via Francigena

About 1,000 years ago, Sigeric, the Archbishop of Canterbury, wrote an account of his pilgrimage to Rome. This early best-selling travel guide made the route famous as the Via Francigena. The ensuing pilgrims brought riches, churches were adorned, hospices established, but plague followed, too, and the towns declined. Today the route is being revived, visit www.viafrancigena.eu.

⑧ Montefollonico
Siena, Toscana; 53049

This hamlet was originally a Sienese fortress built to keep an eye on the Florentines across the valley. The castle has evolved into a long rectangular village that still retains its old walls and gates. Its main square is enlivened by a couple of good restaurants.

🚗 *Leaving town, return to the SP15, turn left on the SS146, and left again onto the SP17 to Montepulciano.*

⑨ Montepulciano
Siena, Toscana; 53045

In this part of Tuscany, Montepulciano is second in importance architecturally and historically only to Siena. In a commanding position at 600 m (1,970 ft), the town affords spectacular views of the surrounding landscape. Its

strategic location – on an important crossroads – along with some useful tactical alliances saw Montepulciano thrive in the medieval period and afterwards, when it was conquered by Florence (1511). The walk up the hill from Porta al Prato to the central Piazza Grande is a challenging 1.5 km (1 mile). Once there, the piazza is flanked by the **Duomo** *(open daily)* and the **Palazzo Comunale** (Town Hall). The splendour and charm of the old civic buildings, and the views, make the town uniquely enjoyable. It is worth walking down again, just to see it all once more.

Most visitors will want to try the Vino Nobile di Montepulciano, a quality red wine and the first in Italy to receive the *denominazione di origini controllata e garantita* (DOCG). Many *cantine* offer their wine for tasting around Piazza Grande. The Tourist Information Office can advise on wineries and wine tours.

To the west of the town take Via di San Biagio to visit the geometrical Renaissance masterpiece, the **Tempio di San Biagio** *(open daily)*, designed by Antonio da Sangallo the Elder in 1529 🚗 *Return to the SS146 in the direction of Pienza. Follow the blue parking signs. Off-street parking is in the modern part of the town, such as Via degli Archi.*

Vino Nobile di Montepulciano
Produced exclusively in the area, this rich red wine of mainly Sangiovese grapes can trace its history as far back as the Etruscan era. In the 17th century it was in much demand throughout Europe, but popularity waned dramatically until the 1960s when modern vinification methods saw a resurgence, making it one of Italy's most prestigious wines.

🔟 Pienza
Siena, Toscana; 53026
A UNESCO World Heritage Site, this tiny gem was extensively remodelled by Pope Pius II in 1458–62, who left his mark, a crescent moon, all over town. Pienza was an architectural marvel of its time, heralding the advent of the Renaissance – the exquisite Duomo on Piazza Pio II marks the transition with its Renaissance façade and Gothic interior. See, too, **Palazzo Piccolomini** *(closed Mon)*, the Pope's former home and now an exceptional museum of opulent interiors. Pienza is also the centre for making pecorino, a sheep's cheese – visit **Zazzeri** *(Il Rossellino 6, 53026)* to see (and taste and buy) some delicious local produce.
🚗 *Take the SS146 towards Siena. On entering San Quirico, turn left down Via dei Fossi for ample parking.*

⑪ San Quirico d'Orcia
Siena, Toscana; 53027
One of the major stopping points on the ancient Via Francigena pilgrim route, San Quirico d'Orcia is ringed by walls surmounted by 14 tower houses. The medieval historic centre of the town is an easy stroll to explore. Visit the 12–13th-century **Chiesa Collegiata di San Quirico** *(open daily)* with its fine Romanesque portals and nearby looming form of the 17th-century **Palazzo Chigi** *(open for events and exhibits)*. At the other end of town, the **Horti Leoni** is a classic Italian Renaissance garden dating back to 1580 – its clipped box hedgerows and shady holm oaks allow a pleasant respite from the heat of summer. For excellent views, visit the ancient walls along the eastern side of the town.
🚗 *Head left towards Siena on the Via Cassia SS2. After about 5 km (3 miles), take the SP14 to Montalcino.*

Above left A well in the historic centre of Montepulciano **Above centre** Medieval stone building in the Crete, still used by the locals **Above right** "Everything for the home" in San Quirico d'Orcia

EAT AND DRINK

MONTEFOLLONICO
La Chiusa *expensive*
Offers very pleasant food, an extensive wine list and even accommodation.
Via della Madonina 88, 53040; 0577 669 668; www.ristorantelachiusa.it; closed Tue

MONTEPULCIANO
L'Enoteca del Consorzio del Vino Nobile di Montepulciano Wine Shop
Taste and buy wines.
Palazzo del Capitano, Piazza Grande 7, 53045; 0578 757 812; www.consorzio vinonobile.it; summer: 1–5pm; winter: by appointment

Osteria Aquacheta *moderate*
Try some home-made *pici* pasta with wild boar from the Tuscan menu.
Via del Teatro 22, 53045; 0578 717 086; www.acquacheta.eu; closed Tue

La Grotta *expensive*
Classic Tuscan restaurant beside the Tempio di San Biagio.
Via San Biagio 15, 53045; 0578 757 479; www.lagrottamontepulciano.it; closed Wed

PIENZA
Ristorante Il Rossellino *moderate*
This tiny gem serves traditional, seasonal food and superb local wines.
Piazza di Spagna 4, 53026; 0578 749 064; booking essential; closed Thu

SAN QUIRICO D'ORCIA
Bar Centrale *inexpensive*
A large, lively bar with a simple menu.
Piazza della Libertà 6, 53027; 0577 897 583

Trattoria al Vecchio Forno *moderate*
Hearty Tuscan menu with local specials.
Via Piazzola 8, 53027; 0577 897 380; www.palazzodelcapitano.com; closed Wed

Eat and Drink: inexpensive, under €25; moderate, €25–€45; expensive, over €45

Brunello di Montalcino
One of the best red wines in Italy, this is made using only the Sangiovese grape variety, and is governed by the *Consorzio del Vino Brunello* guidelines, including the use of local grapes and a minimum of six years' ageing, two of which must be in modern barrels. Try (and buy) some in Montalcino at **Enoteca Grotta del Brunello** *(Via Costa Garibaldi 3)* and **Enoteca Pierangioli** *(Piazza del Popolo 16)*. For wine tours and tastings, see the Tourist Office *(see left)* or visit www. consorziobrunellodimontalcino.it.

Above The Fortezza, Montalcino, offering fine views from the ramparts **Above right** The Abazia Sant'Antimo

VISITING MONTALCINO

Parking
There is a large car park on Via Aldo Moro, left from the main roundabout just before entering town.

Tourist Information
Via Costa del Municipio 1, 0577 849 331; www.prolocomontalcino.it

WHERE TO STAY

CASTIGLIONE D'ORCIA

Castello di Ripa D'Orcia *moderate*
Owned since 1484 by the Piccolomini family, this castle offers a stay with a difference, and more history than luxury.
Loc. Ripa d'Orcia; 53023; 0577 897 376; www.castelloripadorcia.com; open 15 Mar–31 Oct

San Simeone di Castiglione d'Orcia *moderate*
In Rocca d'Orcia, this relaxing hotel offers modern luxurious rooms and independent apartments.
Via della Chiesa 11, Rocca d'Orcia, 53023; 0577 888 984; www.hotelsansimeone.com

BAGNO VIGNONI

Hotel Le Terme *inexpensive*
The original spa house, now revamped, offers basic family accommodation.
Piazza delle Sorgenti 13, Bagno Vignoni, 53027; 0577 887 150; www.albergoleterme.it

Hotel Posta Marcucci *moderate*
This standard 3-star international-style spa hotel welcomes families.
Bagno Vignoni, 53027; 0577 887 112; www.hotelpostamarcucci.it

Hotel Adler Terme *expensive*
A 5-star, total *benessere* (wellness) resort, visitors are expected to take a health package, too. Minimum stay 3 nights.
Bagno Vignoni, 53027; 0577 889 001; www.adler-toscana.com

⑫ Montalcino
Siena, Toscana; 53024
Near the entrance to this important hill-town stands a magnificent 14th-century **Fortezza** *(closed Mon in winter)*. As the Sienese Republic collapsed in 1555, defeated by the mighty Florentine army, 600 brave souls held out in this bastion for four years. The Fortezza contains a good *enoteca* selling the famous Brunello di Montalcino wines, as well as some excellent local honey. On the way into town, visit the Sant'Agostino Convent along Via Ricasoli, now the **Museo Civico e Diocesano** *(closed Mon)*, with the work of local masters. The heart of the town is Piazza del Popolo, a lively Tuscan square with a 12th-century Palazzo Comunale and clock tower. There are wine shops around here.

🚗 *Head south on the SP55 towards Monte Amiata. In Castelnuovo dell' Abate turn off for Abbazia Sant'Antimo.*

⑬ Abbazia Sant'Antimo
Castelnuovo dell'Abate, Toscana; 53020
A paragon of Tuscan Romanesque architecture founded by the Holy Roman Emperor Charlemagne in the 9th century, this abbey is still a centre of monastic life. It is well-preserved with fine capitals decorated with Lombardy griffins, eagles and dragons. The simple interior evokes a feeling of calm, which is often further enhanced by Gregorian chant. There is a car park and shop on the access road *(www.antimo.it)*.

🚗 *Take the SP55 south for Monte Amiata. Left at the SS323. Still on the SS323 turn left up into the town at Via del Fosso. Park on Via della Rocca.*

Column capital of Abbazia Sant'Antimo

⑭ Castiglione d'Orcia and Rocca d'Orcia
Siena, Toscana; 53023
Two castle ruins are all that remain of the ancient command post that controlled the nearby byway, the Via Cassia. Castiglione d'Orcia is topped by crumbling Rocca Aldobrandesca, named after the family who ruled here from AD 714. The heart of the

Above The Rocca Aldobrandesca overlooking Castiglione d'Orcia

town is Piazza il Vecchietta, a sloping square with a travertine fountain (1618) and Municipal Palace – do not miss its Sienese fresco. It is a steep walk from the car park to the Rocca of Tentennano, a second impressive stone sentinel with spectacular views of the Val d'Orcia. The **Tower** *(open: Apr–Oct Tue–Sun; Nov–Mar Sat & Sun)* has an exhibition of the structure's history.

🚗 *Leave town on the SS323, towards Siena, left on the SR2 over the river and turn off for Strada di Bagno Vignoni. Car parks are well indicated.*

Where to Stay: inexpensive, under €100; moderate, €100–200; expensive, over €200

⑮ Bagno Vignoni
Siena, Toscana; 53027

This is the place to take advantage of the spa waters that are mineral-rich and a steamy 49°C (120°F) at source. Bagno Vignoni has retained the feeling of a resort, with a cluster of buildings around the original baths forming a piazza of water. The waters were enjoyed by the likes of Lorenzo di Medici (1449–92), the Renaissance patron, and Italy's patron, Saint Catherine (1347–80). Today the tourist village has many historic herbal shops and excellent restaurants. Take the waters in luxury at one of the spa hotels *(see left)* – it is possible to get a day ticket – or take a dip for free at the public access pools.

🚗 *Retrace route back to the SR2 for Siena, then take SP53 right. Left on the SP40 towards Chianciano Terme. Turn right for La Foce at SP88 junction. Take care on bends. Parking is signed.*

⑯ La Foce
61, Strada della Vittoria, Chianciano Terme, Siena, Toscana; 53042

This historic garden, created by 20th-century Irish-American author Iris Origo, will delight everyone, especially green-fingered garden-lovers. The **Gardens at La Foce** *(open Wed only: guided tours Apr–Oct every hour from 3–6pm; Nov–Mar 3 & 4pm; also 1st weekend Apr–Nov 10am–noon, 3–6pm)* were designed in the 1920s by Cecil Pincent in a formal Italianate style and overlook the Orcia river valley and Monte Amiata. One of Origo's most famous works is her secret diary which became *War in Val d'Orcia* (1947), a moving account of country life in Italy during World War II. There is a good restaurant here and a shop with local produce, and it is possible to rent a villa in the grounds *(www.lafoce.com)*. From the car park there is a classic view of a road zig-zagging in the Tuscan countryside.

Above left Wisteria-covered walkway in the Gardens at La Foce **Below left** The watery piazza at the heart of Bagno Vignoni

EAT AND DRINK

MONTALCINO

Fiaschetteria Italiana *inexpensive*
Café-wine bar furnished in the Liberty style popular when it opened in 1888. *Piazza del Popolo 3, 53024; 0577 849 043; www.fiaschetteriaitaliana.it; Nov–Mar closed Thu*

CASTIGLIONE D'ORCIA

Il Cassero *inexpensive*
Simple restaurant serving regional food of Monte Amiata and Val d'Orcia. *Piazza Cesare Battisti 1, 53023; 0577 888 950; www.trattoriailcassero.com; closed Tue*

BAGNO VIGNONI

La Parata *moderate*
Excellent regional fare on nice terrace. *Piazza del Moretto 40, 53027; 0577 887 508; www. termedibagnovignoni.com; closed Thu*

DAY TRIP OPTIONS

This drive has three day trip options. Visitors may wish to retrace the steps of the pilgrims, to decide which is the greater Tuscan red wine or simply enjoy the foodstuffs for which the Crete is renowned.

The pilgrim's progress
The pilgrim route from France passed this way. Visit the churches of the Abbazia di Monte Oliveto Maggiore ②, followed by the Chiesa Collegiata di San Quirico d'Orcia ⑪ and the Abbazia Sant'Antimo ⑬.

From Siena, get to the Abbazia di Monte Oliveto Maggiore on the SS408 and then the SS438 turning right before Asciano on the SP541. From the abbey, head west towards Buonconvento then take the Via Cassia/SR2 to San Quirico d'Orcia, then the SP14 for Montalcino.

Judging the best vintage
This drive covers the DOCG zones of two of Italy's greatest red wines: the Vino Nobile di Montepulciano ⑨ and the Brunello di Montalcino ⑫. Taste different vintages of both wines at the *cantine* and *enoteche* of each town and decide the best for yourself.

Montepulciano is easily reached from the A1 Autostrada along the SP17. Head west, all the way, taking the SS146 in the direction of Pienza, continuing past San Quirico d'Orcia to the north on the SS14 and staying on that road to Montalcino.

Taste the earth
The Crete Senesi are famous for many gourmet treats. Visit the truffle museum of San Giovanni d'Asso ③, the cheese shops of Pienza ⑩ and the honey sellers of Montalcino ⑫.

From Siena take the SS408 and then the SS438. From San Giovanni d'Asso, take the SP14 east for Montisi, then Castelmuzio before turning right at SP71 for Pienza. From there, head west along the SS146 for San Quirico d'Orcia then the SP14 for Montalcino.

Eat and Drink: inexpensive, under €25; moderate, €25–€45; expensive, over €45

Etruscan Journey

Orvieto to Isola del Giglio

Highlights

- **Awesome Orvieto**
  Marvel at the spectacular town and its magnificent Duomo perched high on a rocky outcrop

- **Tufa towns**
  Explore the towns and villages first carved from this rock by the ancient Etruscans

- **Cities of the dead**
  Enter the Etruscan tomb complexes and sacred temples built before the Roman Empire

- **Argentario and Isola del Giglio**
  Enjoy the marinas, old-fashioned quays and secluded beaches that dot this stunning coastal area

The tufa-built town of Pitigliano, seeming to grow organically out of the rock

Etruscan Journey

This drive enters the heartland of the mysterious, ancient civilization of the Etruscans whose legacy can be seen in the many towns they founded and in their enigmatic burial complexes or necropoli. The region is also a landscape forged by volcanic activity: lakes, hot springs and the tufa rock that the Etruscans used as building material and which, to this day, gives towns in the area their distinctive colour and look. The drive ends in the Etruscan islands and coastal strongholds, Monte Argentario and pretty Isola del Giglio, ideal places for seaside and maritime pleasures.

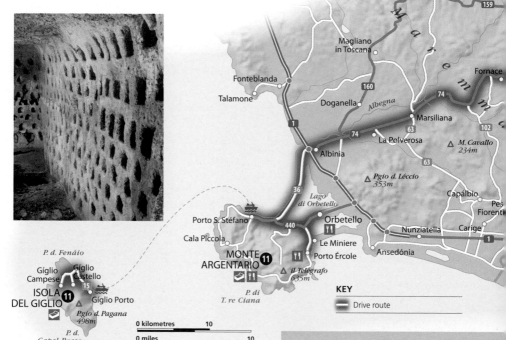

Poggioferro

Scansano

Pereta

159

Magliano
in Toscana

Fonteblanda

Fornace

160

74

Talamone

Doganella   *Albegna*

Marsiliana

63

102

1

74

La Polverosa

△ *M. Cavallo*
234m

Albinia

63

△ *Pgio d. Léccio*
353m

36

*Lago
di Orbetello*

Capálbio

Pes
Fiorenti

Porto S. Stéfano

440

Orbetello

Nunziatella   Carige

Cala Piccola

Le Miniere

Ansedónia

1

MONTE
ARGENTARIO **11**

11 Porto Ércole

△ *il Telégrafo*
635m

11

P. d. Fenáto

Gíglio   Gíglio
Campese   Castello

15

ISOLA **11**
DEL GIGLIO △ Gíglio Porto

Pgio d. Pagana
498m

*P. di
T. re Ciana*

KEY

Drive route

*P. d.
Capel Rosso*

| 0 kilometres | 10 |
| 0 miles | 10 |

ACTIVITIES

Sail, kayak or windsurf on Lago di Bolsena

Pamper yourself with a day at the Terme di Saturnia – or do it on a budget and plunge in the free cascade of healing water

Go birdwatching on Orbetello lagoon, full of rare waders, ducks and seabirds, at Le Miniere on Argentario or at the official WWF centre, 2 km (1 mile) south of Albinia – see www.wwf.it

Go scuba diving off the Isola del Giglio, one of the best diving spots in Italy – see www.giglioinfo.com

Above Cave cells carved out by the Etruscans and probably used for keeping pigeons, Vitozza, *see p141*
Right Fishermen's boats that work the still waters of Orbetello lagoon, *see p145*

TOSCANA

Selvena
Castell'Azzara
M. Civitella
1107m
M. Elmo
829m
Castell'Ottieri
Semproniano
Catábbio
San Martino
sul Fiora
Onano
SORANO
5
SOVANA
8
7
La Rotta
6
PITIGLIANO
VITOZZA
4
San Quirico
GROTTE
DI CASTRO
3
Látera
Cantoniéra
312
Lago di
Bolsena
BOLSENA

Acquapendente
2
Castèl
Viscardo
A1
Castèl Giórgio
S. Lorenzo
Nuovo
74
Casa San Biagio
Val di
Lago
2
53
ORVIETO **1**
71

TERME DI
SATURNIA
9
CITTÀ
DEL TUFA
10
MONTEMERANO
74
Poderi di Montemerano
Manciano
Poggio
Buco
Nova
Valentano
Farnese
Ischia di Castro
Céllere
Piansano
M. Bellino
516m
LAZIO
312
Canino
Tessennano
Arlena di
Castro
M. Maggiore
379m
M. Canino
516m
Fiora

UMBRIA

Gradoli
489
74

PLAN YOUR DRIVE

Start/finish: Orvieto to Isola
del Giglio.

Number of days: 3 days.

Distances: Approx. 165 km (102 miles)
from Orvieto to Monte Argentario.

Road conditions: An excellent
winding road with little heavy traffic.

When to go: High summer is busy for
the lake and coastal areas, but year-
round it's very pleasant.

Opening times: Most museums open
9am–7pm and often close Mon and
Sun afternoon, with shorter hours in
winter. Churches can be unpredictable,
and usually close noon–3 or 4pm.

Main market days: Orvieto: Thu & Sat,
with an artisan market on 4th Sun of
the month; Bolsena: Tue; Pitigliano:
Wed; Manciano & Orbetello: Sat.

Major festivals: Orvieto: end May–
early Jun, Corpus Christi, 10-day festival;
Aug, Folk Festival; Dec, food festival;
New Year period, Jazz Winter; Bolsena:
end May–Jun, Infiorata, carpet of
flowers for Corpus Christi; Pitigliano:
19 Mar, torchlight procession for St
Joseph; Giglio Castello: 15 Sep, Festival
of San Mamiliano, music and fireworks.

DAY TRIP OPTIONS

Seek a **miracle in the churches** of
lofty Orvieto and lakeside Bolsena;
explore **tufa towns and mysterious
Etruscan tombs** in Pitigliano and
Sovana; and enjoy **the pretty ports**
around Monte Argentario and the
rich birdlife of Orbetello, *see p145.*

Above The warren-like townscape of Sorano, dominated by its gigantic
fortress, *see p141*

VISITING ORVIETO

Parking
Park at the railway station (room for 450 cars) where the funicular brings visitors up to Piazza Cahen (every 15 mins).

Tourist Information
Piazza Duomo 24, 05018; 0763 341 772; info@iat.orvieto.tr.it

WHERE TO STAY

ORVIETO

Grand Hotel Italia *moderate*
Close to the centre, but in a quieter area, this refurbished large hotel offers a good choice of rooms and suites.
Piazza del Popolo 13, 05018; 0763 3423065; www.grandhotelitalia.it

BOLSENA

Hotel Royal *moderate*
This slightly formal hotel has the perfect location right on the lakeside.
Piazzale Dante Alighieri 8/10, 01023; 0761 797 048; www.hotelroyalbolsena.it

SORANO

Il Borgo di San Valentino *inexpensive*
Simple apartments in an unfussy rustic style with a great location overlooking the countryside. Includes pool, cooking facilities, indoor and outdoor eating.
San Valentino, 58010; 366 655 9328; www.ilborgodisanvalentino.com

Hotel della Fortezza a Sorano *moderate*
A hotel in a fortress – entry is via the castle forecourt. Rooms are comfortable restorations with wooden beams.
Piazza Cairoli 5, 58010; 0564 632 010; www.hoteldellafortezza.com

❶ Orvieto
Terni, Umbria; 05018

The formidable tufa cliff *(rupe)* of Orvieto was colonized nine centuries before Christ and flourished in the Etruscan period when it was known as Velzna. After a long siege the Romans took over in 264 BC, virtually destroying the town. Its fortunes didn't revive until medieval times, when it resurged as a free and powerful commune encouraged by the residence of various popes. Recent Etruscan finds and a trove of medieval and Renaissance art make Orvieto a compelling destination.

The 12th-century **Torre del Moro** (42 m/138 ft) looms over busy Via Cavour at the heart of the town. To the right a small lane leads to the 12th-century **Palazzo del Popolo** with its swallow-tailed crenellations. To the left is Via Duomo, packed with shops selling everything from tourist souvenirs to fine ceramics. Piazza Lago Barzini, with its outdoor bars, is a pleasant refreshment stop.

The Duomo or **Cattedrale dell'Assunta** *(Piazza Duomo; open daily)* is breathtaking with its stripes of white travertine and dark basalt and Italian Gothic façade (more restrained than French Gothic). Started in 1290 in honour of the Miracle of Bolsena *(see right)*, building work continued for the next 300 years. The façade is most striking with its large rose window, exquisite reliefs, gold tiles and bronzes of the four Evangelists. Note the scenes from Genesis on the façade's lower left.

Inside, don't miss the frescoes in the sanctuary and the Cappella del Corporale (left of Luca Signorelli's altar), but the star sight is the 1499 masterpiece of *The Last Judgement* in the **Capella di San Brizio** *(open daily)*. The depictions of resurrection and damnation constitute one of the finest fresco cycles of the Renaissance.

Piazza Duomo also has two excellent museums – the **Museo Archeologico Nazionale** *(closed Mon am)*, with impressive Etruscan finds, and the **Museo Archeologico Faina** *(open daily, closed Mon in winter)*, which holds artifacts such as the 6th-century BC amphorae of Exekias, thought to be one of antiquity's finest vase painters. This and other Greek vases were found in Estruscan tombs in this area.

Off Via Cavour is **Pozzo della Cava** *(closed Mon and all Jan)*. This fascinating series of underground rooms, originally dug by the Etruscans, contains pottery shards from a nearby ancient kiln. The easily excavated tufa of Orvieto is riddled with labyrinthine tunnels and secret caves; Orvieto Underground *(0763 383 1472, www.orvietounderground. it)* can arrange guided tours.

Back near the funicular at Piazza Cahen lies Orvieto's other great site

Twisting column, Orvieto's Duomo

Pozzo di San Patrizio *(open daily).* In 1527 Pope Clement VII, fleeing the sack of Rome by the Holy Roman Emperor's mutinous troops, took refuge at Orvieto and built the 62-m (203-ft) St Patrick's Well. Designed by Florentine architect Antonio da Sangallo, it took ten years to complete. The double-helix spiral allowed teams of donkeys to get down by one route and up by another at the same time. The 248 steps are lit by 72 windows.

🚗 *From Strada della Stazione, turn left and follow signs to Viterbo. Stay on the SS71, turn right for Bolsena. Park at the bottom of the hill.*

② Bolsena

Viterbo, Lazio; 01023
Set beside a volcanic lake, Bolsena is dominated by **Rocca Monaldeschi**, a 13th-century fortress and museum *(open daily).* In 1263 the town became famous – and a stop on the pilgrim road to Rome – when a confirmation of transubstantiation occurred during a Mass. Today the miracle is celebrated at Corpus Christi *(May or June, date varies)* with a procession via a 3-km (2-mile) carpet of flowers.

On the lake, boats, windsurfers and canoes can be hired at the tourist office, Piazza Matteotti 12, or the Volere Velare sailing club on the shore.

Try local fish *coregone*, oven-baked with garlic and sage or as a *carpaccio*: sliced, seasoned and served raw.

🚗 *Take the Via Cassia Nord SS2, towards Siena, past Val di Lago; fork left to SS489, then right to Grotte di Castro.*

③ Grotte di Castro

Viterbo, Lazio; 01025
Another pretty tufa town, Grotte di Castro is famous for its **Chiesa di Maria SS del Suffragio,** whose Baroque altarpiece is paraded through the streets every ten years. The town is also known for its potato festivals *(sagre),* its well-maintained shrines and old-fashioned shop signs.

🚗 *Drive through Grotte di Castro on the SS74. Still on SS74, turn right towards Pitigliano for 8 km (5 miles) and right onto the SP12 to San Quirico. Park in the town.*

Right Ancient wooded path through the Parco Archeologico degli Etruschi, Vitozza

The Etruscans

Arriving in Italy around 1200 BC, the Etruscans were influenced by ancient Greece and originally competed with the early Romans. However, their city federations were no match for the centrally organized Romans. Their language died out around 150 BC, overcome by Roman orthodoxy, so most of what we know of this skilful and sophisticated culture comes from their architecture and the art found in their necropoli (tombs).

④ Vitozza

Grosseto, Toscana; 58010
The medieval ruins and cave dwellings north of San Quirico have been turned into a large **Parco Archeologico degli Etruschi** *(open Apr–Oct daily, Nov–Mar Fri–Sun; www.parcodeglietruschi.it).* Allow about two hours to explore the 180 or so caves, including the honeycomb cells or *colombari,* possibly used for raising pigeons, and the medieval ruins of the Aldobrandeschi castle. The caves were inhabited until the 18th century.

🚗 *Take SP12 for Sorano; follow signs straight to the Fortezza. Free parking.*

⑤ Sorano

Grosseto, Toscana; 58010
Enter the town through the huge Sorano **fortezza** (fortress), built by the Orsini lords, rulers until 1550. It is worth exploring the fortress – look for the frescoed room in the octagonal tower – and visiting the museum *(closed Mon).* Continue through the town's warren of lanes to a fortified outcrop, the Leopoldine Stone, and its terrace with superb panoramic views.

🚗 *Take SP4 south to Pitigliano. Walk – don't drive – into town; park on Piazza Garibaldi or Piazza del Mercato (paid).*

Above Restaurant in an idyllic location on the lake at Bolsena

EAT AND DRINK

BOLSENA

La Tavernetta *inexpensive*
Family-run place serving pizza and fish. *Corso Cavour 54, 01023; 0761 798 979; www.latavernettabolsena.com; closed Tue in winter*

AROUND GROTTE DI CASTRO

La Cantina del Mago *moderate*
Intimate cellar restaurant with seasonal chestnut ravioli and wild boar *ragù. Via F Annibale 5/A, Latera, 01010 (8 km/ 5 miles southwest on SS74); 333 321 0910; www.covodeibriganti.it*

SORANO

Fidalma *moderate*
A favourite with locals, with specialities such as *acquacotta* – a Tuscan soup. *Piazza Busatti 5, 58010; 0564 633 056; www.ristorantefidalma.com; closed Wed*

AROUND SORANO

La Vecchia Fonte *inexpensive*
Cosy family run restaurant serving traditional fish dishes and ricotta pasta. *Piazza della Repubblica 9, San Quirico, 58010; 0564 619 015; www.lavecchiafonte.com; closed Mon*

Above Pitigliano, once a refuge for Jews exiled from Rome

VISITING THE PARCO ARCHEOLOGICO CITTÀ DEL TUFA

Steps to tombs can be slippery; wear sturdy shoes for walking trails.
0564 614 074; www.parcodeglietruschi. it; open daily until sunset (winter: Sat & Sun only)

WHERE TO STAY

SOVANA

Sovana Hotel & Resort *moderate*
Well-conceived restoration of an old palazzo. Gardens overlook the Duomo.
Via del Duomo 66, 58010; 0564 617 030; www.hotelsovana.com

TERME DI SATURNIA

Terme di Saturnia *expensive*
One of Italy's most famous spa resorts offers guests total luxury.
Well-signposted in Saturnia, 58014; 0564 600 111; www.termedisaturnia.it

Below Tomb of Hildebrand, discovered in 1924, Parco Archeologico Città del Tufa

⑥ Pitigliano
Grosseto, Toscana; 58017

This is an evocative tufa town that appears to rise straight from the rock. Past a 16th-century aqueduct lies the 14th-century **Palazzo Orsini** which features a museum *(closed Mon)* displaying silverware, coins, wooden sculptures and textiles. Many Jews were attracted to Pitigliano because the ruling Orsini had a fairly relaxed attitude to them (unlike Rome): their history is covered in the **Synagogue and Jewish Museum** *(closed Sat & Mon)* behind the Duomo. Gourmets must try the prestigious Bianco di Pitigliano wine and olive oil, cellared in the tufa caves.

🚗 *Take SP46 Via Crocceria for Sovana, where there is paid parking up a paved road to the right of the town.*

⑦ Sovana
Grosseto, Toscana; 58010

This tiny town on a tufa outcrop dates back to the 7th century BC. Around 940, the Aldobrandeschi family made Sovana their seat of power. The most famous member of the family was Hildebrand (c.1020–85) who became the great reformer Pope Gregory VII. Visit the **Chiesa di Santa Maria**, in Piazza Pretorio, with its 8th-century pre-Romanesque marble ciborium (canopy over the altar), and the 11th-century **Cattedrale di SS Peter and Paul**, in Via del Duomo *(open daily)* with beautifully carved portals and 8th-century crypt.

🚗 *Take the road towards Saturnia. After a short distance the Parco Archeologico is across a stream with parking on the right.*

⑧ Parco Archeologico Città del Tufa
Sovana; 58010

The most important natural or historical site in the area of Sorano, San Quirico and Sovana, this is an Etruscan necropolis *(city of the dead)*. It is set so close to Sovana it is possible to imagine the funeral rites as the ancients made their way from the town down roads carved directly into the tufa, to these secret and ceremonial places of worship.

A one–two hour walking tour

On entering the park – the **ticket kiosk** ① is on the left – climb left up the slope to the **Tomb of the Demoni Alati** ② or Winged Demons (2nd–3rd century BC), still under excavation. It is hard to see, but the temple pediment has intricate and sophisticated carving. To the right is the monumental **Tomb of Hildebrand** ③ (3rd century BC), named after Sovana's most famous citizen. Originally carved out of the tufa with six columns across the front, and three on each side, sadly only one column remains. The monument would have been covered with polychromatic yellow, green and red plaster. To the right, a passage leads down to the underground tomb with its ceiling carved in tiers of rhomboids.
   Keep going right, along **Via Cava di Poggio Prisca** ④, an Etruscan road carved deep in the tufa. It was used by partisans during the war and "1945" is inscribed in the right wall. Nearby lies the **Tomb of Tifone** ⑤ (2nd century BC), very eroded but decorated at the top with a woman's head, wrongly thought to be a *tifone* (marine monster). Back at the main road, turn left for **Il Cavone Etrusco** ⑥, a deeply cut road still used by the locals and where rare black maidenhair ferns grow.
   At the main road, head right towards the ticket kiosk in the direction of Sovana and cross the stream. Then turn right off the road and cross another stream to the **visitor centre** ⑦. Use the stairs behind the centre to reach **Via Cava**

> #### What is Tufa?
> Tufa is a honey-coloured volcanic rock that is rigid but also relatively soft and light. The Etruscans and Romans found it a useful building material – it could be quarried, cut and carted quickly. It was thus ideal for a quick defensive wall that could be reinforced later with harder stone. The tufa landscape in this region is one of cultivated plateaus incised with ravines – some natural, others deeply cut, secret Etruscan roads leading to ancient religious sites.

di San Sebastiano ⑧ on the right, or **Tomb of the Siren** ⑨ to the left. The siren with a double tail was an Etruscan symbol used to ward off evil on the journey of the deceased.

🚗 *From the parking area, head west, continuing along the San Martino road SP22 which becomes the SP10 to Saturnia. The town is on the hill and the Terme are in the valley on the road to Manciano.*

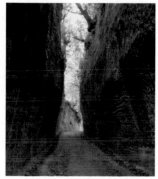

Above An ancient Etruscan road hewn, canyon-like, out of the soft rock in the Città del Tufa

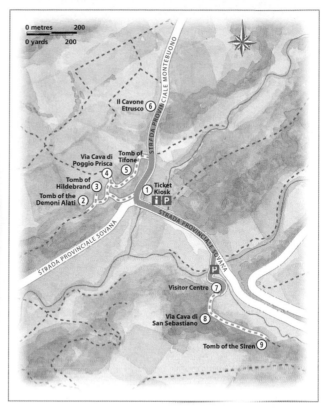

⑨ Terme di Saturnia

Grosseto, Toscana; 58014

The hot springs at Saturnia were created, so the legend goes, when the father of the gods, Saturn, threw his staff into the earth in a rage. Since time immemorial mere mortals have enjoyed the healing powers of these spa waters. Saturnia is in three parts: the old hill town – a good refreshment stop; the Terme Spa, founded in the 1800s and now a luxury resort, and

the open cascade, where you can don your bathing costume and take a warm sulphurous bath for free.

🚗 *Take the SP10, left for Montemerano towards Poderi di Montemerano. At Montemerano, circle to the northern side of town to a new car park near Via dell'ospedale.*

EAT AND DRINK

PITIGLIANO

Trattoria del Grillo *moderate*
In front of the 16th-century aqueduct, this cosy restaurant serves typically hearty Tuscan dishes.
Via Cavour 9, 58017; 0564 615 202; closed Tue and all July

TERME DI SATURNIA

I Due Cippi da Michele *expensive*
A national institution frequented by the well-heeled who stay at the nearby Terme Hotel and Spa. Classic quality Italian cuisine.
Piazza Veneto 26, 58014; 0564 601 074; www.iduecippi.com; closed Tue and 20 days Jan

Left The open cascade, Terme di Saturnia, where the water is a constant 37.5°C (99.5°F)

Eat and Drink: inexpensive under €25; moderate €25–€45; expensive over €45

Above Vine-trimmed piazza in quiet
Montemerano Above right Porto Santo
Stefano seen from the ferry to Isola Giglio

VISITING ISOLA DEL GIGLIO

Ferries sail from Porto Santo Stefano
to Giglio Porto every 90 minutes. In
summer cars need a permit so it is best
to leave it behind and park near Piazza
della Valle. In winter it is possible to take
a car. On Isola del Giglio, buses run every
40 mins (more often in August) from
Porto to Castello and Campese. Tickets
can be bought from the *Tabaccheria*
(tobacconist), Via Umberto I, 17.
www.giglioinfo.it; www.tiemmespa.it

WHERE TO STAY

AROUND MONTEMERANO

Albergo Poggio Bertino *inexpensive*
Mini-hotel with well-designed rooms,
run by a husband and wife.
*Loc. Pianetti 32, 58014 (take SP10
towards Saturnia; left after 3 km/2 miles);
0564 602 824; www.poggiobertino.com*

Le Macchie Alte *moderate*
This organic farm offers comfy rooms
and superb home-produced food.
*Poderi di Montemerano, 58014 (left off
SS332 S after 2 km/1 mile); 0564 620 470;
www.lemacchiealte.it*

MONTE ARGENTARIO

Hotel Baia D'Argento *expensive*
A comfortable 4-star hotel with sea
views, parking and a private beach.
*Pozzarello, Porto Santo Stefano, 58019;
0564 812 643; www.baiadargento.com*

Torre di Cala Piccola *expensive*
A luxurious retreat on the far west side
of the island with a private beach.
*Loc. Cala Piccola, Porto S Stefano, 58019
(follow coast road from the port); 0564
825 111; www.torredicalapiccola.com*

ISOLA DEL GIGLIO

Hotel Castello Monticello *moderate*
A conversion of a 1920s villa with sea
views and a shuttle bus to the beaches.
*Via Provinciale, Porto, 58013; 0564 809
252; www.hotelcastellomonticello.com*

⑩ Montemerano
Grosseto, Toscana; 58014
This castellated gem, built in 1200 by
the Aldobrandeschi and later made a
Sienese stronghold, is a maze of alleys
and pretty piazzas. Its 14th-century
Chiesa San Giorgio has the beautiful
Sienese *Madonna Enthroned* (1485)
and the *Madonna della Gattaiola*.

🚗 *Take the road to Manciano SS322 –
buy some pecorino – then right on SS74
to Albinia. Follow the signs all the way
to Porto Santo Stefano – pass over the
Via Aurelia autostrada, go on to Monte
Argentario, then turn right.*

Gourmet Maremma
Roman legionnaires valued the
hard, dry cheese – **pecorino** –
made from the Maremma sheep's
milk because it kept well on long
marches. Today's aged pecorino has
a slightly crumbly texture and an
almost salty taste – good with pears
and honey.
  Originally an Egyptian export,
bottarga is made in Orbetello – one
of the few places in Italy still making
it – by salting, pressing and aging
mullet roes for five months, and
then dipping in wax. Delicious when
grated over spaghetti with olive oil.

⑪ Monte Argentario and Isola del Giglio
Once an island, Argentario is now tethered to the mainland by two sand dunes
and a bridge. Unlike the rolling Maremma hills, Argentario peaks suddenly at
Punta Telegrafo (635 m/2,083 ft) and the coastline is punctuated by steep
cliffs and secluded beaches with a winding coast road. Isola del Giglio is a
small, picture-postcard-pretty island with a port, a castellated town and one
accessible beach. Popular in season with Italian holiday-makers, Giglio is largely
"undiscovered" despite being less than an hour by ferry from Porto Santo Stefano.

① Porto Santo Stefano
Grosseto, Toscana; 58019
The main port is divided in two by
the Fortezza Spagnola (1553), now
the **Museo del Mare** *(open daily in
summer, otherwise weekends only)* with
exhibits on shipbuilding and marine
archaeology. The first bay harbours
the fishing fleet, the ferry for Giglio
and stalls selling the day's catch, while
the second has a smart marina, bars
and seafood restaurants.
*Park in Piazza della Valle and take the
ferry to Giglio Porto (see panel, left).*

② Porto (Isola del Giglio)
Grosseto, Toscana; 58012
The entry point to Giglio is a crescent
of multicoloured houses, with a few
boats for hire and a small fishing fleet.

Look for fishermen cleaning their
catch on the wharves. At the
southeastern end stands the 16th-
century **tower** built to ward off pirates
such as Barbarossa who in 1544
absconded with 700 prisoners.
*Buses from Piazza G Rum Via di Rum.
Via di Castello goes to the old town.*

③ Castello (Isola del Giglio)
Grosseto, Toscana; 58012
Most of this unspoiled labyrinth of a
walled town was built after 1264 by
the Pisan governors and added to
by the Medici. The **Chiesa di San
Pietro Apostolo** has a silver relic of
Saint Mamiliano's arm, said to have
repulsed pirates in 1799.
*Buses stop in the car park in
Via Incrociata.*

④ Campese (Isola Giglio)
Grosseto, Toscana; 58012

The only large beach on the island is a sickle-shaped stretch facing west. With crystal clear water, it is excellent for swimming, sailing, snorkelling and diving. It offers amazing sunset views of the 17th-century **Torre Medicea**.

🚗 *To collect your car, take the bus to Giglio Porto and catch the ferry to Porto Santo Stefano. Drive east and follow the signs to Porto Ercole. Park off Via Ospizio or Piazza Vespucci.*

⑤ Porto Ercole
Grosseto, Toscana; 58018

Fortified by the Spanish in the 16th century, Porto Ercole's historic quarter lies behind the old **Porta della Rocca**, with the fortresses, **Rocca Spagnola** above and **Forte Filippo** across the harbour. The port is now a marina with a busy quayside. In the old town, explore the **Palazzo del Governatore** in the Piazzetta di Santa Barbara and the Spanish **Chiesa di Sant'Erasmo**, rumoured to be the burial place of Caravaggio who died nearby in 1610.

🚗 *Return north keeping the lagoon on the right. Where the road from Porto San Stefano meets, turn right to Orbetello. Park to the right of the town.*

⑥ Orbetello
Grosseto, Toscana; 58015

On a spit of land projecting into the lagoon, Orbetello is famous for its location, its fishermen who still use traditional methods and its *bottarga* – salted mullet roe. Note the **Molino Spagnolo** at the tip of the spit, the last of nine waterborne mills, and the **Cattedrale di Santa Maria Assunta** (Piazza Repubblica) (1375) with simple Tuscan Gothic lines. The lagoon also attracts water birds such as flamingos, spoonbills, widgeon and pintails.

Left Traditional shallow-water fishing boat and nets, Orbetello

GOURMET SHOPPING

La Casa del Formaggio
Sells local pecorino cheese, wines and other gourmet food products.
Via del Ponticino 40, Manciano, 58014; www.lacasadelformaggio.com

Orbetello Pesca Lagunare
The fishing cooperative sells *bottarga* and other products from the lagoon.
Via Giacomo Leopardi 9, Orbetello, 58015; www.orbetellopesca.it

EAT AND DRINK

MONTEMERANO

La Solina *moderate*
Family-run place serving homemade pasta and locally raised meat.
Loc. Poggio Bertino 18, 58014; 0564 602 986; www.lasolina.com; closed Wed, except in summer

Caino *expensive*
An unmissable dining experience from one of Italy's top chefs, Valeria Piccini.
Via della Chiesa 4, 58050; 0564 602 817; www.dacaino.it; closed Wed, Thu lunch

MONTE ARGENTARIO

I Pescatori *inexpensive*
Cheerful fishermen's restaurant serving simple seafood dishes. Try the *bottarga*.
Via Leopardi 9, 58015, Orbetello; 0564 860 611; www.ristoranteipescatori.it; closed Mon–Wed in winter

Antica Fattoria La Parrina *moderate*
An *agriturismo*, winery, farm shop and restaurant all rolled into one.
Via Aurelia (exit at km 146, 10 km/6 miles N from Orbetello) 58010; 0564 862 626; www.parrina.it; closed Mon

Il Pellicano *expensive*
Innovative cuisine at the resort of the same name, using local ingredients.
Loc. Sbarcatello, Porto Ercole, 58018 (along coast from port); 0564 858 111; www.pellicanohotel.com; open Apr–Oct

---

DAY TRIP OPTIONS

For day trips, Orvieto or Argentario both make good bases.

The pilgrim trail
Orvieto's ❶ spectacular Duomo was built for a miracle; explore the town, then join the pilgrims at Bolsena ❷ where the miracle happened. Sceptics may prefer a boat trip on the lake.

Leave Orvieto on the circular SS71, carry on south and follow the signs to Bolsena.

Tufa towns and tombs
History buffs will enjoy a day visiting the tufa towns Pitigliano ❻ and Sovana ❼ and then walking to and around the mysterious Parco Archeologico Città del Tufa ❽.

From Pitigliano take the Via Crocceria to Sovana; the Parco Archeologico is about a 10-minute walk northwest.

Island and lagoon
Winding, hilly Argentario ⑪ and the mirror-like lagoon of Orbetello ⑥ contrast nicely with each other. Birdwatchers may feel twitchy at Le Miniere which is WWF protected.

From Porto S Stefano, take the bridge to Orbetello. Crossing back, turn left to Porto Ercole and left at Strada Comunale di Feniglia for Le Miniere. From there, continue on the main road to Porto Ercole.

Gourmet Umbria

Spoleto to Preci

Highlights

- **Roman ruins**
  Wander the ancient streets of Spoleto and discover its Roman past

- **Religious Romanesque sites**
  Enjoy the sublime simplicity of stone arches and sculpted sanctuaries in remote valleys

- **Stunning mountain scenery**
  Cross the high plains of the Monti Sibillini for unique landscapes and a wonderland of wild flowers in spring

- **Gourmet delights**
  Visit the mountain-bound town of Norcia, celebrated across Italy for its fabulous food

Restaurants and shops lining Corso Sertoria with Porta Romana in the background, Norcia

Gourmet Umbria

Southeastern Umbria is dominated culturally by Spoleto, one of Italy's most beautiful towns, and geographically by the Apennine Mountains. The area is rich in both art and gastronomy. Roman remains and Romanesque architecture provide a special backdrop to sampling the region's recipes. The dense forests in the high country are the source of the sought-after and very expensive truffle, which is on the menu at many of the region's restaurants, and the pork butchers of Norcia are regarded as Italy's finest. The surrounding terrain is spectacular, sometimes surreal and wrapped in history.

M. Civitella 1103m
Croc
Ponte Nuovo
Mevale
Saccové
Cervara
Chiúsita
Corone
Pontechiúsita
S. Lázzaro 209
Roccan
Casali Belforte
Buggiano
Póggio di Croce
465
Triponzo
Montebuf
CERRETO DI SPOLETO 3
M. Aspro 1401m
M. Cavogna 1417m
Borgo Cerreto
Cortigno
Forsivo
Meggiano
Ponte
Biselli
UMBRIA 320
Corno
S. Giacomo
Perugia
Montefiorello
209 685
Nortosce
Maiano 3
Bazzano Inf.
M. Galenne 1217m
M. Galloro 1249m
Croceferro
Bazzano Superiore
Rocchetta
Pontebari
Eggi
Piedipaterno
S. Nicolò 3
Foca di Cerro
Grotti 395
209 685
VALLO DI NERA 2
685
Castèl S. Felice
SPOLETO 1
S. Anatólia di Narco
Ponte delle Torri
395
3
Monteluco
Vallócchia

0 kilometres 5
0 miles 5

KEY

Drive route

Above The impressive 12th-century Abbazia di San Eutizio, Preci, *see p153* **Below** Window display of Salumeria Padrichelli, packed with local produce, Spoleto, *see pp150–51*

ACTIVITIES

Enjoy an evening of culture at one of Spoleto's theatres, which have full programmes all year round, not just for the Festival

Stroll around the speciality food shops of Norcia, renowned for its charcuterie and legumes

Learn to hang-glide or para-sail in the high Monti Sibillini

Ramble across the gentle slopes and peaks of the Piano Grande for stunning views of the Monti Sibillini

Trek on horseback or pony across the plains of the Piano Grande near Castelluccio

PLAN YOUR DRIVE

Start/finish: Spoleto to Preci.

Number of days: 2–3, allowing half a day to explore Spoleto.

Distances: Spoleto to Preci 146 km (91 miles). Add 40 km (25 miles) from Preci back to Spoleto.

Road conditions: The roads are well maintained but they are mountainous and should be driven with great care. In winter snow chains are mandatory.

When to go: The best time is between May and September with a preference for late spring to catch the wild flowers. The weekends can get busy around Castelluccio in summer.

Opening hours: Museums are usually open daily 10am–6pm, though small ones close for lunch between 12:30pm and 3pm. Most are closed on Mondays. Shops tend to open 9am–1pm and 4–8pm, although most are shut on Monday mornings and Sundays. Food shops are closed on Thursday afternoons in Umbria although in tourist hot spots they remain open seven days a week. Churches tend to open 9am–12:30pm and 3:30–6pm.

Main market days: Spoleto: Fri in Piazza Garibaldi, Mon–Sat am in Piazza del Mercato; **Norcia:** Thu; **Visso:** Fri.

Shopping: Look out for truffles, salami from Norcia and Castelluccio lentils.

Major festivals: Spoleto: Festa dei Due Mondi (arts), Jun–Jul; **Cerreto di Spoleto:** Sagra del Ciarlatano (history and folklore), mid-Aug; **Norcia:** Black truffle festival, Feb; **Castelluccio:** La Fioritura (wild flowers in bloom), May–Jul.

DAY TRIP OPTIONS

It is possible to visit the area in a number of day trips. **Foodies** will enjoy exploring the delicatessens of Norcia and Castelluccio, while **sports enthusiasts** can spend time horse riding, hiking or mountain biking across the Piano Grande. For full details, *see p153*.

Left Palazzo Comunale and the Basilica di San Benedetto, Norcia, *see p152*

Above Vicolo di Volusio, dating from the 1st century AD, reflects Spoleto's Roman past

VISITING SPOLETO

Parking
The car park in Viale dei Cappuccini is on the southern edge of Spoleto, not far from the motorway, and is the most convenient for exploring the city.

Tourist Information
This well-run centre has lots of information on Spoleto and the area. *Piazza della Libertà 7; 06049; 0743 238 920; www.visitspoleto.it*

WHERE TO STAY

SPOLETO

Clitunno *inexpensive*
Stylish rooms in a historic palazzo. *Piazza Sordini 6, 06049; 0743 223 340; www.hotelclitunno.com*

Palazzo Leti *moderate*
Beautifully appointed rooms and excellent views. Good location just off Via delle Felici near the old Roman quarter. *Via degli Eremiti 10, 06049; 0743 224 930; www.palazzoleti.com*

Gattapone *expensive*
Below La Rocca in a quiet location with stunning views. *Via del Ponte 6, 06049; 0743 223 447; www.hotelgattapone.it*

VALLO DI NERA

Locanda Cacio Re *moderate*
The Cacio Re is an excellent base for exploring this part of the Nera Valley. *Località Casali, 06040; 0743 617 003; www.caciore.com*

❶ Spoleto
Perugia, Umbria; 06049

Spoleto sits serenely overlooking the broad Umbrian plain that bears its name. Its rich and varied history lies in the enormous pink and white blocks that have provided a base for the city since Etruscan times, as well as in its Roman ruins, Romanesque churches and Renaissance art. Famous for its thriving cultural festival season, the Festa dei Due Mondi draws an international crowd. This walk takes visitors to the places that make Spoleto one of the most picturesque and historic cities in Italy.

A three-hour walking tour

Spoleto is a pleasant town to wander at virtually any time of day. From the car park at Viale dei Cappuccini it is a gentle walk up to town past the Parco Chico Mendez. On reaching Piazza della Libertà visitors will find the **Teatro Romano** ① *(open daily)*. This splendid Roman theatre is linked to the **Museo Archeologico Nazionale** ② *(Via Sant'Agata 18; open daily)*. The museum has Roman statuary and other artifacts from Spoleto and nearby. Back in the piazza, turn right onto Via F Brignone and head uphill past Piazza della Fontana. Take the next left onto Via Arco di Drusus and the great **Arco di Drusus** ③, the original triumphal arch into Roman Spoleto, will come into view. Close by the church of **Sant' Ansano** ④ is built on the ruins of a Roman temple, parts of which can be seen in its crypt. The road leads to **Piazza del Mercato** ⑤, the old Roman forum. This lively

Cheese with truffles

piazza holds a market *(Mon–Sat am)* of mostly fruit and vegetables. Turn right onto Via del Municipio for the **Casa Romana** ⑥ *(closed Tue)*. Dating back to the 1st century AD, this building is believed to have been the house of Vespasia Polla, the mother of Emperor Vespasian (9–79 AD) as the mosaic floors indicate a wealthy owner.

Turn right onto Via Aurelio Saffi for the Romanesque **Chiesa di Sant' Eufemia** ⑦ and the Museo Diocesano *(closed Mon & Tue)*. The 12th-century church is unique in Umbria, in that it has a separate gallery for women. The museum houses a *Madonna and Child* by Filippino Lippi and a bust of Pope Urban VIII by Lorenzo Bernini. Spoleto's crown jewel is the Duomo, **Santa Maria Assunta** ⑧ *(open daily)*, best approached by continuing past Sant' Eufemia and turning left. The steps down to Piazza del Duomo allow for a stunning view of the majestic

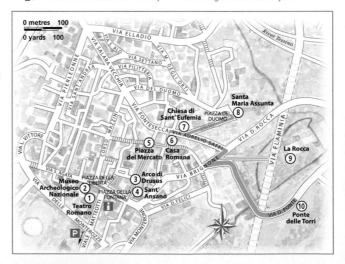

building with its Romanesque exterior and huge bell tower. Inside, paintings by Pinturicchio and Fra Lippo Lippi are on display, as is Lippi's tomb.

Head back onto Via Aurelio Saffi and then turn left up to the ticket office for the steep walk to **La Rocca** ⑨ (closed Mon). The huge fortress is divided into two large and elegant courtyards and it is easy to see why it was used effectively as a prison until 1982. Highlights inside include 15th-century frescoes in the *camera pinta* (painted room). The views from the fortress are spectacular and behind it is the **Ponte delle Torri** ⑩. Turn left on leaving La Rocca and follow Via del Ponte for a pleasant circular walk. The walk back to the car park is straight-forward and downhill.

Just outside the town is one of Italy's oldest churches, the **Basilica San Salvatore** (4th–5th century AD), which is one of the most perfect examples of Lombard architecture, combining features of Roman temples and Paleo-Christian churches.
🚗 *From Spoleto join the SS3 towards Perugia. Take the turn for Norcia onto the SS685. Turn left onto the SS209/685 and eventually take a right for Vallo di Nera. Park at Piazza Santa Maria.*

② **Vallo di Nera**
Perugia, Umbria; 06040
Perched above the river it previously stood guard over, this beautifully preserved town has all the elements of a medieval village. Its streets are narrow and winding, the remains of the castle portray a military past and the open-air washbasins testify to the communal nature of the people who still live here. Its three churches retain

an air of solemnity. The 13th-century **Chiesa di Santa Maria** houses 14th-century frescoes of Christ and the Virgin Mary painted by Cola di Pietro and Francesco di Antonio. The **Chiesa di Santa Caterina** has two vertically aligned church bells and only the apse and side walls remain of the **Chiesa di San Giovanni Battista**.
🚗 *Drive back and continue along the SS209/685. About 1.5 km (1 mile) past Borgo Cerreto there is a very hard left-hand turn to the road up to Cerreto di Spoleto. Be careful as this is a very dangerous turn.*

Ponte delle Torri
This spectacular bridge, with its ten arches is 230 m (775 ft) long and 70 m (230 ft) high. There was probably a Roman aqueduct on the site that was augmented in the Middle Ages. The architect Gattapone, who built La Rocca (1359–70), is generally credited with the current span, providing both a road and a watercourse.

Above left View of Spoleto and the surrounding hills from La Rocca *Above right* The courtyard of honour in La Rocca, Spoleto

Below left Detail of the beautiful Romanesque façade of Spoleto's Duomo *Below right* The castellated village of Vallo di Nera

OUTDOOR ACTIVITIES IN THE PIANO GRANDE

Halfway across the **Piano Grande** is a small cluster of huts and a parking area for the camper vans of holiday-makers and hang-gliders. Also here is **Sibillini's Ranch**, where horses and ponies are available for trekking across the plain. *www.castellucciodinorcia.it*

WHERE TO STAY

CERRETO DI SPOLETO

Casa Vacanza Piantamori *inexpensive*
The old Palazzo Argentieri is now a pleasant hotel and restaurant.
Piazza Pontano, 06040; 0743 922 250; www.casapiantamori.com

NORCIA

Grotta Azzurra *moderate*
This historic family-run hotel with a fine restaurant is a good place to try truffle-based dishes and *cinghiale* (wild boar).
Via Alfieri 6; 06046; 0743 816 513; www.hotelgrottaazzurra.com

Palazzo Seneca *expensive*
This elegant hotel can organize cooking classes and truffle hunts.
Via Cesare Battisti 12, 06046; 0743 817 434; www.palazzoseneca.com

AROUND NORCIA

Fonte Antica *inexpensive*
Family-run *agriturismo* in Campi. Rustic rooms and delightful countryside views.
Via Vissana 7, Campi, 06046 (10 minutes' drive from Norcia along the SP476); 0743 828 523; www.fonteantica.com

Below left Salami at Brancaleone da Norcia **Below right** Panoramic view of Norcia **Below bottom** Piazza Pontano in Cerreto di Spoleto

③ Cerreto di Spoleto
Perugia, Umbria; 06041

This area was originally dominated by the Romans who built roads through these mountainous valleys. The old part of Cerreto (called Borgo Cerreto) straddles the main road, but high on a cliff directly above is the little town of **Cerreto di Spoleto**, with splendid views and an elegant piazza. Much of the town dates back to the 12th century. The 15th-century frescoes by an unknown local painter in the **Chiesa di San Giacomo** tell the stories of St John and St Catherine.

🚗 *Return to SS209/685, turn right onto SS320, which becomes SS396 to Norcia.*

④ Norcia
Perugia, Umbria; 06046

Sitting on the high plains of the Apennines, Norcia can seem very isolated. Historically the birthplace of Saints Benedict and Scholastica, today the town is renowned for dried and cured meats. The word *norcineria* is used all over Italy to mean "specialist pork butcher". Allow enough time to browse the wonderful food shops, looking out for Brancaleone da Norcia in particular. The main square, **Piazza San Benedetto** is flanked by the **Palazzo Comunale** (1490) and opposite, La Castellina, which houses the **Museo Civico Diocesano** *(closed Mon in winter)*. Originally a fortress built for Pope Julius III in the 1550s, the museum has a good collection

The Sacred Salamis of Norcia

Italians refer to the products of the pork butchers of Norcia in a manner verging on veneration. Look out for: *Salsiccia Rustica*, wild boar sausage; *Salami al Cinghiale e tartufo nero*, salami made from boar and black truffle; *Coglioni di Mulo*, a soft salami; *Salame spalmare*, a spreadable salami and *Corallina di Norcia*, so called because of the colour provided by the chilli flavouring.

of early and Renaissance art, as well as sculpture and polychrome votive statuary. The Gothic **Basilica di San Benedetto** (1389) is built in the shape of a Latin cross with an ogival portal.

🚗 *Take the SP476 and turn left for Castelluccio and the SS685. At the roundabout, take the 2nd exit onto the SP477 to the pass. The car park is on the right as the valley plain comes into view.*

⑤ The Pass above the Piano Grande
Perugia, Umbria; 06046

It is well worth stopping at the pass above the Piano Grande for its stunning scenery. The view of this windswept prairie against the backdrop of the impressive massifs of the Monti Sibillini is breathtaking. The area is also famous for its variety of wild flowers in spring. It is a great place to stop for a picnic on the grass or a ramble over the gentle hills nearby.

🚗 *Follow the SP477 to Castelluccio. Parking is on the right as the road crests.*

6 Castelluccio
Perugia, Umbria; 06046

Originally a collection of shepherds' huts, this small stone town still reflects its utilitarian rural background. There is little of architectural beauty but plenty of character. Much of the town was covered in political graffiti in the 1950s and some remains today. Old ladies sit on doorsteps sorting the lentils for which Castelluccio is famous. The lentils are grown on the wide plain below the town and are known throughout Italy as Castelluccio lentils. The **Chiesa di San Maria Aussuta** *(often closed)* houses a sculpture of the *Madonna* (1499) attributed to Giovanni Antonio di Giordano. The edge of town near the road can become crowded with weekend adventurers who use the valley for hang-gliding, para-sailing and horse riding.

🚗 *Take SP477, becoming SP136 then SP134, to Visso. Turn right at Via G Rosi, and park in Piazza Garibaldi.*

7 Visso
Macerata, Le Marche; 62039

Located in steep mountainous terrain, Visso sits at the confluence of three rivers, one of which flows through the middle of town via a raised canal. The main square **Piazza dei Martiri Vissani** is lined with 15th and 16th-century buildings with both rounded and pointed Gothic arches. Look out for the 12th-century Romanesque-Gothic **Collegiata di S Maria** *(open daily)* with its elegant portal, a gigantic 14th-century fresco of St Christopher and a 14th-century carved stone baptistry. Nearby **Piazza**

Capuzi complete with shops and bars, leads into the medieval streets with portals and windows carved by local craftsmen.

🚗 *Leave Visso heading west. Follow signs to Terni/Norcia/Cascia turning left onto SP209. Take a left onto SP476 and after 5km (3 miles) arrive at Preci. Stay on the SP476 towards Pièdivalle, turn left for the Abbey, where there is ample parking.*

Clock face, Palazzo Comunale, Norcia

8 Abbazia di San Eutizio, Preci
Perugia, Umbria; 06047

Despite its interesting past the real reason for coming to Preci is to see the **Abbazia di San Eutizio** *(open daily, 10am–6pm)* just along the road. Preci was destroyed twice during wars in the 16th century only to bounce back when a medical school with illustrious graduates, one of whom removed a cataract for England's Queen Elizabeth I, was established here. The Abbey dates from the late 12th-century and is a remarkable religious shrine to the Benedictine monks who kept the faith in the worst years of the early Middle Ages.

Above left Stone Gothic mullion windows, Abbazia di San Eutizio **Above right** Sweeping view of Castelluccio from the Piano Grande

EAT AND DRINK

NORCIA

Dal Francese *inexpensive*
Typical trattoria serving good regional cuisine. *Via Riguardati 16; 06046; 0743 816 290; www.ristorantedalfrancese norcia.it; closed Fri except summer*

Ristorante Beccofino *moderate*
Here, the Battilocchi family serves local dishes, with an emphasis on truffles. *Piazza S Benedetto 12, 06046; 0743 816 086; www.ristorantebeccofino norcia.com; closed Tue*

Brancaleone da Norcia
Shop selling delicious salamis, cold meats and truffles. *Corso Sertorio 17; 06046; www.brancaleonedanorcia.it*

VISSO

La Filanda *moderate*
Sample local goodies here, such as freshwater fish. *Via Pontelato 4, 62039; 0737 972 027; www.lafilanda-visso. com; closed Wed*

Hotel Ristorante Elena *moderate*
Restaurant specializing in fare from Le Marche, including trout, river prawns and hare. *Via G Rossi 20; 62039; 0737 9277; www.hotelristorantelena.com; closed Tue except for hotel guests*

DAY TRIP OPTIONS

From Spoleto any of the stops along this drive make an easy day trip. The SS209/685 is the main road following the course of the River Nera.

A gourmet trail

Head to Norcia 4 for a morning of browsing the speciality meat shops, for which the town is famous. After lunch at one of the many restaurants, head to Castelluccio 6, where there

are shops selling a great selection of pulses, lentils, beans and pasta mixes.

From Spoleto head north and follow directions to Norcia via SS209/685 and SP320 and SP396. From Norcia follow the SP476 then SP477 to Castelluccio.

Activities at the Piano Grande

The stunning terrain of the Piano Grande 5 makes for an ideal day out for those who enjoy outdoor

activities. The middle of the plain is perfect for horse riding, whereas Castelluccio 6 and the pass above the valley 5 are the best options for walking, mountain biking, hang-gliding and para-sailing. The pass is also an ideal place for a picnic lunch.

From Spoleto follow directions to Piano Grande and then Castelluccio. From Castelluccio follow the signs for Norcia. Both routes take visitors to the pass.

Eat and Drink: inexpensive, under €25; moderate, €25–€45; expensive over €45

In the Heart of Umbria

Lago Trasimeno to Trevi

Highlights

- **Turning point in history**
  View the battle site where Hannibal defeated a Roman army on the northern shores of Lago Trasimeno

- **The splendours of Deruta**
  Admire the vast array of beautiful majolica ware in the many potters' shops and studios

- **World-renowned wines**
  Visit the superb wine museum at Torgiano and sample one of Italy's finest reds at Montefalco

- **The treasures of Spello**
  Walk the winding streets of an old Roman town and reassess great Renaissance master Pinturicchio

Vineyard owned by the Lungarotti family of wine makers, Torgiano

In the Heart of Umbria

Starting at the magnificent lakeside fortress, the Rocca del Leone at Castiglione del Lago, this drive skirts the great Lago Trasimeno. Surrounded by olive groves and studded with towers and forts protecting the ancient pathways of armies and pilgrims, the route around the lake is particularly picturesque. The tour then heads to Deruta, the heart of the world-famous majolica ceramics, and on to the wine and olive areas of central Umbria before reaching Roman ruins and Renaissance masterpieces from Spello to Trevi.

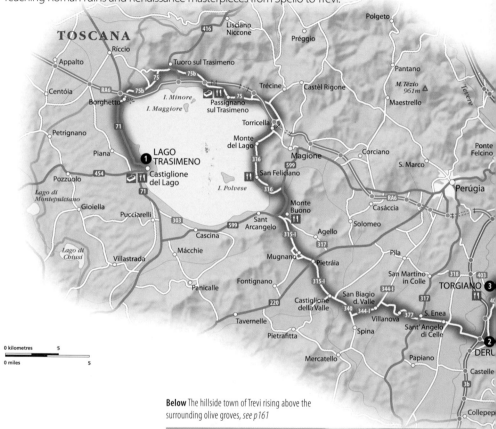

Below The hillside town of Trevi rising above the surrounding olive groves, *see p161*

ACTIVITIES

Enjoy paddling in the water in the Lido at Castiglione del Lago

Take a ferry to an island on Lago Trasimeno and enjoy a picnic lunch

Stroll through the ancient towns of Bettona and Bevagna

Enjoy a tasting of one of the finest Umbrian wines in Montefalco

Learn about Umbrian olive oil at the museum in Trevi

Above Expansive view across Lago Trasimeno from the ramparts of Castiglione del Lago's medieval fortress, *see p158*

KEY

═══ Drive route

Piccione

Bosco
318

Pieve S. Nicolò

Petrignano *Palazzo* *Piano d. Pieve*

estrada 147

Bastia U. *Assisi* *Armenzano*

S. Maria d. Àngeli *Monte Subasio*

Chiásci

Ú M B R I A

Topino

4 BETTONA 75 **11**

403

Urvinum Hortense *Cannara* **5 SPELLO**

410 *Grotta di Pale*

Cullemáncio 403 *Véscia*

Cantalupo *Fiamenga* 316 *Foligno*

BEVAGNA *Scandolaro*

11 6 *S. Eráclio* 3

Gualdo Cattáneo

316 443 444

Ponte di Ferro 422 *Montepennino* **MONTEFALCO**

Bastardo **7 11** 3

San Fortunato **8 TREVI**

444 447

Fabbri

445 *Tempietto d. Clitunno*

451 447 *Castèl San Giovanni* *Pissignano* *Fonti d. Clitunno*

Giano dell' Umbria *Castèl Ritaldi* *Campello sul Clitunno*

Terzo la Pieve

Uncinano

PLAN YOUR DRIVE

Start/finish: Lago Trasimeno to Trevi.

Number of days: 3 days.

Distance: 130 km (80 miles).

Road conditions: Generally excellent. Between Spello and Montefalco road signage can be confusing.

When to go: The area around Lago Trasimeno is buzzing in the high summer months, but quiet in winter. The other areas are excellent all year.

Opening times: Museums open Tue–Sun but are closed 12:30–3pm. Shops are generally open from 9am–1pm and 4–8pm, although they are closed all day Sunday and Monday mornings. Churches open daily, 9am–12:30pm and 3:30–6pm.

Main market days: Castiglione del Lago: Wed; Passignano sul Trasimeno: weekly market, Sun (Mar–Sep) or Fri (Oct–Feb); flea market, every 3rd weekend of the month; Deruta: Tue; Spello: Wed; Bevagna: Market of the Gaite, fabulous medieval market in June.

Shopping: Look out for majolica ware, for which the region is famous, as well as Umbrian olive oil and the Sagrantino di Montefalco wine.

Major festivals: Castiglione del Lago: Kite Festival, Apr–May; Tulip Festival, Apr; Passignano sul Trasimeno: Palio delle Barche (boat race), Jul; Bettona: Festa di S Crispolto (religious procession), May; Goose Festival, end Jul–Aug; Spello: Infiorata del Corpus Domini (floral carpet), May–Jun; Montefalco: Agosto Montefalchese, Aug; Sagrantino Wine Festival, Sep; Trevi: Ottobre Trevano (a month of celebrations), Oct; Frantoi Aperti (olive oil festival), Nov–Dec.

DAY TRIP OPTIONS

Food- and wine-lovers will delight in the opportunity to sample the wines and olive oil of Umbria. **History enthusiasts** can visit the site where Hannibal vanquished a Roman army and will be fascinated by the many Roman antiquities in this region. For full details, *see p161*.

VISITING LAGO TRASIMENO

Tourist Information
Piazza Mazzini 10, Castiglione del Lago, 06061; 075 965 2484; www. lagotrasimeno.net

Parking
There is paid parking on the northern side of Castiglione del Lago on Via Belvedere and at Piazza Trento e Trieste in Passignano sul Trasimeno.

Ferry services around the lake
During the warmer months regular ferries run across Lago Trasimeno to the islands from Castiglione del Lago, Passignano sul Trasimeno and San Feliciano. Timetables are posted at the piers where the ferries dock, and tickets are for sale nearby. A one-way trip usually takes between 20 minutes and half an hour. *www.umbriamobilita.it*

Fishing boats for hire
Fishing boats can be hired for 4 hours for two people or larger boats for up to ten with demonstrations of fishing techniques for 3 hours. The meeting point is in front of the Fishermen's Cooperative on the lakefront at San Feliciano. *075 847 6005 (book ahead); www.pescatoridel trasimeno.com*

WHERE TO STAY

AROUND LAGO TRASIMENO

Miralago *moderate*
Rooms overlook the lake and the town.
Piazza Mazzini 6, Castiglione del Lago; 06061; 075 951 157; www. hotelmiralago.com

Hotel La Torre *moderate*
This family hotel is only a few steps from the palazzo and the *rocca*. Breakfast pastries are baked on the premises.
Via Vittorio Emanuele 50, Castiglione del Lago, 06061; 075 951 666; www.latorretrasimeno.com

Hotel Lido *moderate*
On the shore of the lake in the heart of the town. Bike hire for guests, pool and car park.
Via Roma 1, Passignano sul Trasimeno, 06065; 075 827 219; www.hotellido perugia.com

BETTONA

La Corte di Bettona *moderate*
Right inside the old town, this restored former pilgrim *hospitale* has 39 comfortable rooms and suites.
Via Santa Caterina 2, 06084; 075 987 114; www.relaisbettona.com

Right The pretty town of Passignano sul Trasimeno, perched on the edge of Lago Trasimeno **Far right** Fishing boats lining the water's edge, San Feliciano, Lago Trasimeno

① Lago Trasimeno
Perugia, Umbria; 06061

From Roman times through the medieval period, Lago Trasimeno was an important way point for armies. Hannibal defeated a Roman army on the lake's northern shore in 217 BC and Crusaders, en route to the Holy Land, paused at the 13th-century fortress of Castiglione del Lago. Today, the lake is a regional nature reserve and its surrounding towns make it a popular holiday destination.

Surrounded by water on three sides, **Castiglione del Lago** is a unique hill town which seems to float ethereally above a distant strand. Enter the town through Porta Fiorentina into Piazza Mazzini, the main square, with its specialist food shops and restaurants. The main concourse, Via V Emanuele, leads to Piazza Gramsci and the **Palazzo della Corgna** *(open daily)*. Named for the Della Corgna family who ruled here for nearly a hundred years (1550–1643), the palazzo is now effectively a small museum. The interior is lavishly frescoed with scenes from history and the life of the Della Corgna family. A covered walkway links the palazzo to the **Rocca del Leone** (fortress), which is inset into the walls of the castle. This resilient pentagon-shaped structure with five towers and three gates was designed in 1247 and widely regarded as one of the most impregnable fortresses of its day. Its ramparts provide views across the lake and from the tower, a bird's-eye view of the town and countryside.

In the summer concerts are staged in the natural amphitheatre of the ruins.

On the northern shore of the lake is **Passignano sul Trasimeno**, with an old quarter above the more modern town below. The lakeside offers pleasant walks as well as restaurants and bars. In the square opposite the park and pier, shops spill their majolica ware across the pavement.

Isola Maggiore (accessible by ferry) is home to a small village where visitors head for lunch at one of the restaurants. Other attractions include the **Museo del Merletto** (Lace Museum) *(open daily in summer)* and the 18th-century **Palazzo Capitano del Popolo** *(closed to the public)* with mullion windows and a clock tower.

San Feliciano on the eastern shore of the lake is a picturesque fishing village. Its **Museo della Pesca** *(closed Mon)* offers an insight into the once thriving local fishing industry.

🚗 *From the Via Belvedere, head west downhill, turn right into Via Firenze which becomes Via Trasimeno. Take SR71 to Borghetto, right on SS75 bis and follow to Passignano on SS75. Right on the SP316 for Toricella, continue past San Feliciano. Join SS599, turn left for SP315-I towards Mugnano/Castiglione della Valle/Marsciano. Turn left on SP340 towards San Biagio della Valle/Perugia. Left on SP344, right for Villanova, then left on SP377 towards Sant'Angelo di Celle, passing under SS3b/E45 motorway for Deruta. Follow signs to "centro" and park at Porta San Michele.*

② Deruta

Perugia, Umbria; 06053

The premium Italian centre for majolica (brightly glazed pottery), old Deruta sits on a small hill overlooking a sea of shops and studios, all devoted to its production. The Piazza dei Consoli makes up the main street to the old town. At its end the 14th-century Romanesque **Chiesa di San Francesco** *(open daily)* has an early fresco and a 19th-century majolica of the patron of potters, Saint Catherine of Alexandria. The **Museo Regionale della Ceramica** *(open daily)* houses an exceptional collection of ceramics.

🚗 *From the car park head north, turn right on Via Tiberina and continue as the road becomes Via Roma/SP400, following signs for Torgiano. At the T-junction, turn left for Torgiano on SP403, cross the river and take 3rd left up Via Olivello. Park in Piazza Matteotti.*

Majolica of Deruta

Works in terracotta have been found in this region since the Etruscan era. In the 14th and 15th centuries increased trade brought Arabian techniques of glazing from Spain. The earliest works were in green and brown, then yellow, blue and orange. The oldest family pottery in the world is Ubaldo Grazia Maioliche Artistiche Artigianali, which has been operating for 500 years. Tours can be taken of the workshop in Via Tiberina 181 *(closed Sun).*

③ Torgiano

Perugia, Umbria; 06089

Originally a small defensive outpost on the river plain below Perugia, Torgiano is easy to explore. It has achieved international fame in the world of wine thanks mainly to the Lungarotti family of wine makers and their superb private **Museo del Vino** *(Corso V Emanuele 11; open daily)*. This comprehensive exhibition includes everything imaginable to do with wine – from Roman and Etruscan artifacts to 18th-century etchings on the perils of drinking.

🚗 *Leaving Piazza Matteotti, turn right at SP403/Viale Giuseppe Mazzini for Bettona. On arriving at the walls, bear left to park on the eastern side of town.*

Majolica rondels on a building in Deruta

④ Bettona

Perugia, Umbria; 06084

Known as the "Balcony of Umbria" Bettona has wonderful views across the valley towards the Apennine Mountains. On the approach to town there are heavily weathered Etruscan walls, with one curvaceous stone on the northern wall, known as the "Nun's bum". Enter through a covered passageway in the bastion and **Chiesa of San Crispolto** *(open daily),* passing the cloister and into the town. In Piazza Cavour, the **Palazzetto del Podestà** *(open daily)* houses the **Pinacoteca** (Civic Gallery), with works by Perugino.

🚗 *Head northwest around the walls, take the first right at Via del Colletto to Passaggio. Turn right at Via Perugia/SP403 towards Perugia. Turn left onto Via Collemancio/SP412 for Cannara. Go through town and cross the river. Turn right at Via Sant'Angelo towards Spello on SP410. Turn right and pass under the motorway. Right at Via Centrale Umbra, sharp left at the roundabout, and first right. The car park is at Via Martin Luther King.*

Above left Detail of the Town Hall decorated with majolica tiles, Deruta **Above** Tree-lined avenue leading to Lago Trasimeno
Left Display of distinctive earthenware pottery for sale, Torgiano

EAT AND DRINK

AROUND LAGO TRASIMENO

Da Settimio *moderate*
This is where the locals go for lake fish.
Lungolago A Alicata 1, San Feliciano, 06063; 075 847 6000; closed Wed

Monna Lisa *moderate*
Serves many local specialities, such as *tegamaccio*, a soup made with lake fish.
Via del Forte 2, Castiglione del Lago, 06061; 075 951 071; www.ristorante monnalisa.com; closed Wed

Trattoria del Pescatore *moderate*
This old building was once a mill run by Capuchin friars. Specializes in fish dishes.
Via San Bernardino 5, Passignano sul Trasimeno, 06065; 075 829 6063; www. delpescatore.com; closed Tue

DERUTA

Locanda del Bracconiere *moderate*
Rustic food such as *pappardelle del Bracconiere* (pasta with wild boar sauce).
Via Borgo Garibaldi 8, 06053; 075 972 353; closed Mon dinner

TORGIANO

Tre Vaselle *expensive*
One of the best restaurants in Umbria, with many specialities of the region.
Via Garibaldi 48, 06089; 075 988 0447; www.3vaselle.it

BETTONA

Poggio degli Olivi *moderate*
A delightful agriturismo serving its own pork, olive oil and produce.
Loc. Montebalacca, Passaggio di Bettona, 06080; 347 377 9804; www. poggiodegliolivi.it; closed Wed

SHOPPING FOR MAJOLICA

In Deruta, Piazza dei Consoli has plenty of shops with upmarket fine ware and more affordable ceramics. *Ubaldo Grazia* in *Via Tiberina 181* is a good place to order a complete dinner set.

Eat and Drink: inexpensive, under €25; moderate, €25–€45; expensive, over €45

Above Two 12-sided towers flank the Porta
Venere Roman gate, Spello

VISITING SPELLO

Parking
Park at Via Martin Luther King.

Tourist Information
Piazza Matteotti 3, 06038; 0742
301009; www.prospello.it

WHERE TO STAY

SPELLO

Terme Francescane *moderate*
This spa hotel offers various mud
treatments. It also has a romantic
restaurant on an island in the lake.
Via delle Acque, 06038; 0742 301186;
www.termefrancescane.com

BEVAGNA

Il Chiostro di Bevagna *inexpensive*
Good value in the heart of Bevagna.
Corso G Matteotti 107, 06031; 0742 361
987; www.ilchiostrodibevagna.com

MONTEFALCO

Hotel Degli Affreschi *inexpensive*
Simple rooms close to old town centre.
Corso Mameli 45, 06036; 0742 378 150;
www.hoteldegliaffreschi.it

❺ Spello
Perugia, Umbria; 06038

The walled town of Spello rises steeply on the extreme southern flank
of Monte Subasio. Built almost entirely from pink and white stone
quarried from the mountain, this Roman and medieval town has
many delights, not least of all the works of the early 16th-century
artist, Pinturicchio.

A two-hour walking tour

From the northern end of the car park
walk left along Via Sant'Anna to the
Porta Consolare ①, a huge triple
vaulted Roman gate dating from the
Augustan period of the 1st century AD.

Bend to the left at Via Consolare and
pause at the 14th-century **Cappella
Tega** ② to view highly coloured cross
vaults. The road then becomes Via
Cavour and on the right is Spello's
cathedral, the **Chiesa di Santa Maria
Maggiore** ③ *(open daily)*. Inside is the
Baglioni Chapel, covered with narrative
frescoes painted by Pinturicchio in
1501. On each side of the altar are
frescoes by Perugino (1521).

Continue up Via Cavour to the
Chiesa di Sant'Andrea ④ *(open
daily)*. On the right of the transept is
Pinturicchio's *Madonna with Child
and Saints* (1508). Via Cavour leads
into Piazza della Repubblica, where
the 13th-century **Palazzo Comunale**
⑤ *(open daily)* stands. In the entrance
hall are Roman decorative figures
and the front of a sarcophagus. On
the left-hand side of the road, now
Via Garibaldi, is **Palazzo Urbani** ⑥
the new Municipal seat, and on the
right, the **Chiesa di San Lorenzo** ⑦
(open daily). Continue straight to enter

the town's ancient defences through
an arch up Via Torre di Belvedere.
Look out for medieval buildings such
as the **Bibi House** ⑧ on the
immediate right and the 13th-
century **Chiesa di San Martino** *(open
daily)* ⑨. Proceed up to Piazza
Belvedere with superb views across
the valley to Assisi. The **Chiesa di San
Severino** ⑩ *(open daily)* and a Roman
gate, **Porta dell'Arce** ⑪, can also be
found here. Take Via Arco Romano to
S Maria di Vallegloria and turn right
back into the old quarter along Via
Giulia to the remains of another
Roman arch **Arco di Augusto** ⑫.
Return to Via Giulia and complete the
loop back to Via Garibaldi, turning right
down Via Catena, then Via Scalette
into Via Torri di Properzio for the most
impressive of Spello's gates, the **Porta
Venere** ⑬. Turn left down Via Tornetta,
left along Via Centrale Umbra to **Porta
Urbica** ⑭, and follow the wall along
Via Roma back to Porta Consolare.

🚗 *From the car park turn right, then
left on Via Centrale Umbra towards
Foligno. Pass under the motorway and
left at Via Firenze. At the roundabout,
take the SS316 to Bevagna. Turn right
around the parkland, then left to park
at Piazzale Minolfo Masci.*

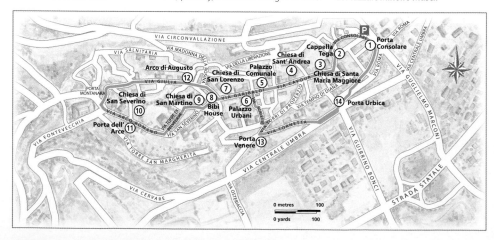

Where to Stay: inexpensive, under €100; moderate, €100–€200; expensive, over €200

⑥ Bevagna
Perugia, Umbria; 06031

The historian Livy first mentions Bevagna in 308 BC. Roman mosaics of fabulous sea creatures adorn the floor of what was a bathing complex, visible from outside Via Porta Guelfa 7; buy tickets at the Museo Civico *(Corso G Matteotti 70)*. The remains of the Roman theatre are reflected in the little house and underground passages in Via Anfiteatro. Around the main square, Piazza Silvestri, stand three beautiful Romanesque churches: **San Silvestro, San Michele** and **SS Domenico e Giacomo** and the Gothic **Palazzo dei Consoli** *(all open daily)*.

🚗 *Back on the SS316 follow signs for Montefalco. Turn left on the SP443, which becomes the SP444 at Montepennino. At Montepennino turn right to stay on this road leading into Viale della Vittoria to the walls of Montefalco. Park in this street or Borgo Garibaldi.*

⑦ Montefalco
Perugia, Umbria; 06036

All roads in this impressively walled town lead up to the central Piazza del Comune. Visit the **Museo Civico** *(open daily)* in the former Chiesa di San Francesco on Via Ringhiera Umbra. Due west is the main street, Corso G Mameli, with an array of bars and shops, the beautiful **Chiesa di Sant' Agostino** and the swallow-tailed **Torre di Sant' Agostino**. Montefalco is a centre for weaving with several boutiques selling exceptional linens. Sagrantino di Montefalco, one of Italy's finest red wines, is widely available in the town.

🚗 *Leave Montefalco on Via della Vittoria, following signs for Trevi.*

Continue on the SP445 (after a short distance road numbers cease) to Fabbri. After Fabbri, at a T-junction, turn left onto the SP447 and then follow signs to Trevi all the way up the hill. Once in town, park in Piazza Garibaldi.

⑧ Trevi
Perugia, Umbria; 06039

Just inside the gate of this rugged hill town, along Via Roma to Piazza Mazzini, is the information office and town hall *(closed Mon)*. The highest point of Trevi is occupied by the **Duomo San Emiliano** *(open daily)* with its magnificent 11th-century façade. The **Complesso Museale San Francesco**, including the fascinating **Museo della Civiltà dell'Ulivo** (olive oil museum) *(closed Mon)*, are all located in the former Franciscan convent in Largo Don Bosco on the northern edge of the old town.

Close to Trevi, there is a splendid natural fountain and springs at **Fonti del Clitunno** *(open 8:30am–8pm in summer)*. To reach it follow Via Flaminia/SS3 to Pissignano. Shortly thereafter, the font is on the right.

Above Detail from the marble portal of the 13th-century Chiesa di San Michele, Bevagna

Left The tranquil gardens of Fonti del Clitunno, near to Trevi

---

DAY TRIP OPTIONS

Visitors with a passion for food and wine can sample the region's delicious produce – an ideal day out for those based in Spello or Montefalco. History enthusiasts will enjoy the second option, easily undertaken from Lago Trasimeno or Bevagna.

Umbrian wine and oil

The hillsides around Lago Trasimeno and the Appenine mountains of Umbria are covered with olive trees and grape vines. Visit the excellent wine museum at Torgiano ③, the olive oil museum in Trevi ⑧, followed by wine-tasting at Encoteca Federico II in Montefalco ⑦ and then dinner at Enoteca l'Alchimista.

From Spello take the SP410 towards Cannara, continue through the town and cross the river to take the SP403 towards Bettona and follow to Torgiano.

Roman history

View the site of Hannibal's famous victory over the Romans on the northern shores of Lago Trasimeno ①, then on to Spello ⑤ to visit the Roman gates and finally Bevagna ⑥ to view the remains of the ancient Roman theatre and mosaics.

Follow the driving directions from Lago Trasimeno to Spello and then on to Bevagna. It is also possible to reverse the itinerary and start at Bevagna.

Eat and Drink: inexpensive, under €25; moderate, €25–€45; expensive, over €45

Castelli Romani

Frascati to Rocca Priora

Highlights

- **Roman ruins**
  Walk among Roman remains in the moody, volcanic hillsides of Tusculum or admire the ancient tombs, baths and ruins in Albano Laziale

- **Panoramic lake and city views**
  Enjoy stunning views over Rome – twinkling at night, majestic by day – as well as lake vistas from the Castelli Romani's crater-edged towns

- **Magnificent villas**
  Marvel at the castles and aristocratic villas built as summer residences by statesmen, feudal lords and popes

- **Local flavours**
  Feast on herb-roasted pork, wood-fired country breads, local chestnuts, wild strawberries and chilled Frascati wine

The hill town of Rocca di Papa basking in the evening sun

Castelli Romani

Twenty kilometres (12 miles) southeast of Rome the ancient Roman road, Via Tuscolana, begins its gentle climb through the sloping forests of the Colli Albani. In the Middle Ages these hills were fortified with castles and the 13 Castelli Romani villages are chiselled into the landscape of the long-extinct Vulcano Laziale at altitudes of up to 900 m (2,959 ft). Rome's nobles, Vatican officials and the Pope have been finding summer refuge in the chestnut- and oak-covered hills for centuries. Roman roads run through the hills dotted with farms, vineyards, elegant villas, wild flowers and strawberry stalls. During harvest time, the area bustles with activity as the grapes for the excellent Colli Albani and Frascati DOC white wines are harvested.

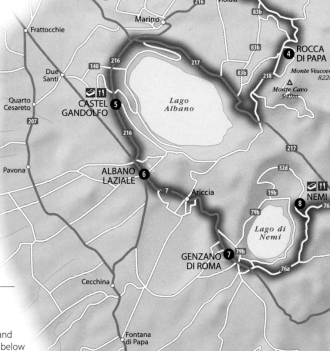

Above Enjoy a stroll in the Colli Tuscolani, near ancient Roman ruins, see *p167*

ACTIVITIES

Walk the 10-km (6-mile) circumference around the clear waters of Lago Albano

Picnic at night on Frascati's Belvedere and enjoy the twinkling panorama of Rome below

Take a cycle ride in the Colli Tuscolani

Wine and dine in typical Roman *cantine* and *osterie*

Take the picturesque train ride from Frascati to Rome and back in a day

Tour the wineries between Frascati and Grottaferrata

KEY

Drive route

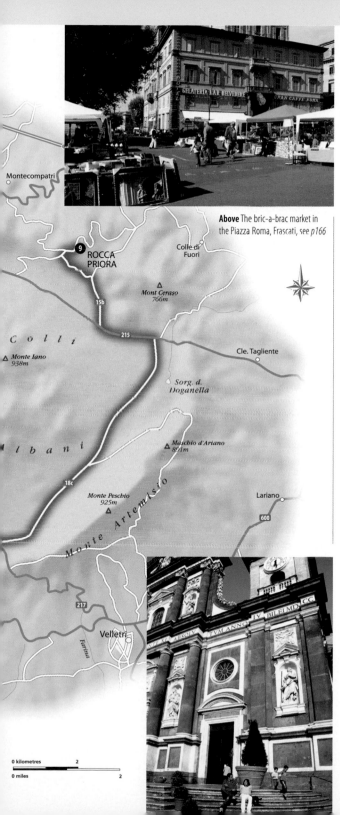

Above The bric-a-brac market in the Piazza Roma, Frascati, see *p166*

PLAN YOUR DRIVE

Start/Finish: Frascati to Rocca Priora.

Number of days: 3, allowing a day and a half to tour Lago Albano and Lago Nemi, half a day in Frascati, and a day of eno-gastronomy or walking in the Parco Regionale di Castelli Romani.

Road conditions: Generally excellent roads with a few winding climbs and descents. Best to avoid town centres.

Distance: 60 km (37 miles).

When to go: The weather is mild year-round. Summer weekends are the busiest time and the narrow roads are likely to become congested.

Opening times: Most museums open 9am–7pm and often close Mon and Sun afternoon, with shorter hours in winter. Churches can be unpredictable, and usually close noon–3 or 4pm.

Main market days: Frascati: Wed; Grottaferrata: Mon; Rocca di Papa and Castel Gandolfo: Fri; Albano Laziale: Thu; Genzano: Tue; Nemi: Sat.

Major festivals: Frascati: Carnevale Tuscolano (folkloric festival), Feb; Festa delle Ville Tuscolana (summer festival of entertainment, mostly at Villa Torlonia), Jun–Aug; Festa della Cortesia, last weekend in Oct for the end of the wine harvest; **Grottaferrata:** Fiera di Grottaferrata, late Mar/early Apr; **Castel Gandolfo:** Sagra delle Pesche (peaches), last weekend Jul; **Genzano:** Infiorata (flowers), 2nd weekend Jun, **Nemi:** Sagra delle Fragole di Nemi (strawberries), first Sun in Jun; **Rocca Priora:** Sagra dell'Agnello, late Aug; Sagra del Fungo Porcino (mushrooms), Sep.

DAY TRIP OPTIONS

From Frascati, visit **Roman remains**, and a magnificent **fortified monastery**; admire the view from tiny **hilltop towns** and **walk** to the top of a **mountain** – then enjoy a glass of **wine**. From Nemi, pack some **strawberries** and see a **papal palace**, **Bernini masterpieces** and **grand villas** all with perfect **lake views**; have a **swim** and finish off with a tour of **Roman ruins**. For full details, *see p169*.

Left The 17th-century Cattedrale di San Pietro Apostolo, Frascati, *see p166*

Above War memorial in front of the Villa Aldobrandini, Frascati

VISITING FRASCATI

Getting There and Parking
From Rome, pass through Cinecittà then take Via Tuscolana, continue briefly on Via Anagnina, then the SS215. The main car park is at Piazza Marconi.

Visitor Information
General tourist information at Frascati Point, *Piazza Marconi, 00044; 06 9401 5378; www.frascati.lazio.it.* Parco Regionale dei Castelli Romani – best for outdoor activities, *Villa Barattolo, Via Cesare Battisti 5, 00040, Rocca di Papa.*

WHERE TO STAY

FRASCATI

Hotel Cacciani *moderate*
This family-run hotel combines good facilities with old-world charm. There is an excellent restaurant *(see right)* and most rooms have great views of Rome. *Via A Diaz 13, 00044; 06 940 1991; www.cacciani.it*

Hotel Flora *expensive*
Housed in part of a 19th-century palazzo, this hotel is in an excellent location in the centre of Frascati. *Viale Vittorio Veneto 8, 00044; 06 941 6110; www.hotel-flora.it*

GROTTAFERRATA

Tenuta Cusmano *moderate*
This impeccably run country villa is next to the owner's organic winery. Rooms are classy and there are tennis courts and a pool in the beautiful grounds. *Via Anagnina 20, 00046; 06 941 3264; www.tenutacusmano.it*

Park Hotel Villa Grazioli *expensive*
This 4-star Relais & Chateaux hotel is in a 16th-century cardinal's villa, with paintings by Italian masters such as Ciampelli. There is also a swimming pool. *Via Umberto Pavoni 19, 00046; 06 945 4001; www.villagrazioli.com*

❶ Frascati
Roma, Lazio; 00044

The biggest and best-known of the Castelli Romani towns, Frascati's elegant gardens and villas are gently landscaped into a hill, while the town's heart is a hive of winding narrow streets. To the uninformed, Frascati may be synonymous with cheap *vino* but the town actually thrives on the high reputation of its wines, especially the fruity white Frascati Superiore. Join the locals in their ritual evening stroll and enjoy the breathtaking views of Rome twinkling in the distance.

A one-hour walking tour

The vast **Piazza Marconi** ① climbs 200 m (656 ft) up the hill towards the stately Villa Aldobrandini backed by dense forest. It is a major commuter hub with a car park at its centre.

Walk down the centre of the piazza past the war memorial, Monumento ai Caduti, and cross over to **Piazza Roma** ②, where locals meet outside the cluster of café-bars and *gelateria*. From here, take Via Cesare Battisti and Via Palestro to Piazza San Pietro. This animated city square is graced by the Baroque façade of the 17th-century **Basilica Cattedrale di San Pietro Apostolo** ③ *(open daily)*. Its harmonious two-tone towers and spires with inset rose windows and statuettes were created by Girolamo Fontana who started work in 1694. Pass by the monument to Fontana on the way to the adjoining Piazza Gesù and the ornate little 17th-century

Chiesa del Gesù ④ *(open daily)* with an interior of frescoes, carved wood and a cobalt-coloured dome. Every Sunday evening from October to June there are free concerts.

From Piazza Gesù, turn right into Via Cairoli, to head to Via Olmo and go along Via Vivario Santa Maria. This leads to the bejewelled 18th-century **Chiesa di Santa Maria in Vivario** ⑤ with its Romanesque bell tower.

Head to **Piazza San Rocco** ⑥ and take Via Ludovico Micara to **Piazza Giuseppe Mazzini** ⑦. On the way there are stalls selling *porchetta* (pork roasted with herbs) and bakeries with breads and pizzas hot from wood-fired stoves. Enjoy an urban picnic at the tables provided by a *fraschetta* – bars that serve their wine while visitors can eat their own food. Walk along Via Ajani and turn right on Via C Battisti to the paved **Belvedere** ⑧ at the base of Piazza Marconi. It offers

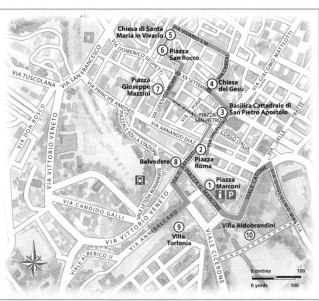

stunning 180-degree panoramas of the countryside and Rome below. For some greenery, cross the piazza to the **Villa Torlonia** ⑨ park. Damaged in World War II, all that remains of the palazzo are a few sandstone fountains.

Cross back over the piazza to **Villa Aldobrandini** ⑩ *(closed Sat & Sun; Via Cardinal Massai 18; 06 942 1434)*. This Neo-Classical masterpiece was built in 1550 and Pope Clement VIII acquired the property for his nephew, Cardinal Pietro Aldobrandini. Only the lovely gardens are open to the public. Return to Piazza Marconi and the car park.

🚗 *From Piazza Marconi follow signs for "tuscolo" Via Catone, then fork uphill towards Villa Aldobrandini and the road becomes the SP73b. Follow the signs to Tusculum. The car park is at the end of the road.*

② Tusculum
Roma, Lazio; 00044

The Via del Tuscolo winds its way up towards Monte Tuscolo and the Colli Tuscolani. The name comes from the pre-Etruscan civilization, Tusculum, which existed in the hills around 380 BC. From the car park, walk over to the site where a Roman amphitheatre has been uncovered. The forests of the Colli Tuscolani and Colli Albani lie on the western confines of the Parco

Regionale dei Castelli Romani. Visitors come here for the amphitheatre, the views and the forests.

🚗 *Continue on the SP73b and turn right into the SS215, the Via Tuscolana. Grottaferrata is not signposted so head for Rome until reaching a major crossing, go round the lights heading for Rome/Albano Laziale, then follow signs to the centre and signed parking.*

③ Grottaferrata
Roma, Lazio; 00046

The streets of this well-heeled town link elegant parks and piazzas against a backdrop of vineyards and the woods of the Parco Regionale dei Castelli Romani. The main draw is the Byzantine **Monastero Esarchico Santa Maria di Grottaferrata** *(Corso del Popolo 128)*. Also referred to as the Abbazia Greca di San Nilo, it was founded in 1002 by Byzantine Greek Orthodox monks from Calabria, led by San Nilo di Rossano and his disciple San Bartolomeo. Its 13th-century bell tower is beautifully decorated with polychrome ceramic tiles. The monastery's impressive 15th-century fortifications – walls, moats and battlements – are all intact.

🚗 *Take SS216 then SS218 towards Rocca di Papa. Continue on SS218 which leads directly to the town's main square.*

EAT AND DRINK

FRASCATI

Osteria Ristorante Zaraza' *moderate*
Excellent quality, top-level ingredients and generous portions of regional food served in an elegant setting. Splendid views from the terrace.
Viale Regina Margherita 45, 00044; 06 942 2053; closed Sun eve and Mon

Ristorante Cacciani *expensive*
Swish family restaurant where seasonal produce infuses traditional cooking: dishes range from grilled steaks to stockfish ravioli with chickpea cream.
Via Armando Diaz 13, 00044; 06 940 1991; www.cacciani.it; closed Sun eve and Mon

Other options
The **Cantina da Santino** *(Via Pietro Campana 27, 00044; 06 9429 8110; www.cantinadasantino.it)* serves the family's wine at wooden tables with BYO snacks. **Cantina Simonetti** *(Piazza San Rocco 4, 00044; 347 630 0269; www.cantinasimonetti.com; open Sat & Sun, evenings Tue–Fri; closed in winter)* is a traditional *fraschetta*, with local wines, meats and cheeses. For good coffee and ice cream, try **Bar degli Specchi** *(Via Cesare Battisti 3, 00044; 06 942 0293; www.bardeglispecchi.it; closed Mon)*

GROTTAFERRATA

Taverna Passamonti *inexpensive*
A welcoming ristorante-pizzeria, with an open hearth and a patio on the square. Menu includes bruschetta, mushroom and bean soup and pizza.
Largo Passamonti 2, 00046; 06 945 9917; closed Tue

Il Canneto *moderate*
A popular restaurant, opened by a former cyclist, with cycling memorabilia on its walls. Hearty home-made dishes of pasta, meat, *porcini* mushrooms and *panna cotta* (cooked creamy custard).
Via della Cavona 12, 00046; 06 9431 5466; closed Mon

Above Ancient stone drinking fountain in Rocca di Papa

WHERE TO STAY

CASTEL GANDOLFO

Hotel Castel Gandolfo *moderate*
Small, welcoming hotel a few steps from the papal palace in the old town centre. Views of the lake from some guest rooms and from the roof terrace. *Via de Zecchini 27, 00040; 06 936 0521; www.hotelcastelgandolfo.com*

NEMI

Il Cortile B&B *inexpensive*
Ideal for those seeking lakeside calm in a tiny medieval town; there are two rooms, each with its own bathroom, in a small courtyard off the main street. The building was restored using local stone and is filled with antiques and paintings. *Corso Vittorio Emanuele 8, 00040; 06 936 8147; www.mammamaria.org/bb_english.htm*

Below One of the highest of the Castelli Romani, Rocca di Papa

4 Rocca di Papa
Roma, Lazio; 00040

Five centuries before Vatican officials chose Castel Gandolfo to be their summer residence, Pope Eugenio III used to stay here – hence the name. The second highest of the hill towns, it stands like a stone thimble among the hills of the Parco Regionale dei Castelli Romani. The 14th-century medieval quarter has the **Chiesetta del Crocefisso** at its centre. Lower down is the oldest Castelli Romani town square, Piazza Vecchia. The lively main square, Piazza della Repubblica, is known as "Rocca di Papa's living room" and is home to the Duomo, the 1664 **Chiesa dell'Assunta** *(open daily)*, rebuilt after an earthquake in 1806. On Monte Cavo's slopes, the **Convento di Palazzolo** is built over a Roman settlement with views over Lago Albano. There are signposted walks in the woods nearby.

🚗 *Follow signs to Via dei Laghi/Albano Laziale, continuing on the SS218. Turn right into the SS217 towards Roma/Marino. Near Marino turn left by traffic lights onto the SS216, follow the brown signs to the lake and Castel Gandolfo.*

5 Castel Gandolfo
Roma, Lazio; 00040

On the western rim of Lago Albano, Castel Gandolfo is named after the Gandolfi family who built the 12th-century fortress, later restored by the bishop of Albano. In 1608, Pope Clement VIII transformed it into the **Palazzo Pontifico**. The palace has been used ever since as the papal summer residence. Admire its façade from the **Piazza della Libertà**, home to two Bernini masterpieces: the 1659 fountain inspired by Rome's San Pietro

and the Chiesa di S Tommaso di Villanova. The Corso della Repubblica leads on to **Piazza Cavalletti** where there is the Belvedere, a viewpoint over Lago Albano and the entrance to the 17th-century **Villa Barberini** *(not open to the public)*, the pope's residence. Above the city on Via Ercolano, there are several remarkable villas and the **Parco Archeologico degli Ibernesi**, around the ruins of the 1st-century AD Villa di Domiziano. Nearby stands Villa Torlonia – a Vatican property – with a Classical façade, Doric columns and a wide terrace. Below town, take a swim in Lago Albano or hire a sun lounger or pedalo. If it is not warm enough, consider walking the 10-km (6-mile) circuit of the lake.

🚗 *Continue on the SS216. In Albano Laziale, turn left into the SS7 just before Piazza Giuseppe Mazzini. Park near the Piazza to walk around the town or continue into the centre.*

Above Castel Gandolfo sitting proudly on the volcanic rim of Lago Albano

6 Albano Laziale
Roma, Lazio; 00041

Built on the site of a 2nd-century AD Roman fort, Albano Laziale has some remarkable Roman ruins. Follow the marked Circuito Monumentale around the ancient sites, starting at the Rome end of the city on Via Appia, and the 14-m (46-ft) high gate, Porta Praetoria. Off the main avenue, Corso Matteotti, in the historic centre are the amazing ruins of an ancient complex of Roman baths built by Caracalla, the **Terme di Cellomaio**. Next to the complex is the white marble Romanesque **Chiesa di San Pietro Apostolo** with its 13th-century frescoes. Via de Gasperi leads to Piazza Sabatini and the **Cattedrale di San Pancrazio** *(open daily)*, built on the foundations of an ancient basilica. Above town, a

remarkable 3rd century Roman **Anfiteatro Severiano** has been excavated. Built into a rocky bank, the amphitheatre was 22 m (72 ft) high and seated 10,000 spectators.

🚗 *Take the Borgo Garibaldi to SS7 and then Via Appia Nuova. Follow signs for Ariccia and Genzano. Park on-street.*

❼ Genzano di Roma
Roma, Lazio; 00040

Sitting above the volcanic Lago di Nemi, Genzano di Roma is most famous for its June flower festival *(see p165)*, when its streets are covered in petals. **Palazzo Sforzo Cesarini** is the main attraction in the medieval centre on Piazza del Palazzo Ducale. Next door is the 19th century English-style garden **Parco Sforza Cesarini** *(open Sat am & Sun)*. The town also has many artisan bakeries. Try the wood-fired *pane casereccio di Genzano* or traditional biscuits such as *bussolani* and *tozzetti*.

🚗 *Take the SS7, then the SP76a, following the signs to Nemi. Park on the main road, the centre is pedestrian only.*

❽ Nemi
Roma, Lazio; 00040

Perched on the crater rim above Lago di Nemi, this pastel-coloured town is famous for its strawberries and flowers grown around the lake.

From the lower square, Piazza Roma with its fountain of the goddess Diana, walk up Corso Vittorio Emanuele to the **Palazzo Ruspoli** with its medieval tower *(not open to the public)* at the top of town. In the main street, ice-cream stalls are piled high with strawberries and *norcinerie* (butchers' shops) have every sort of cured meat strung from their ceilings.

🚗 *Take the SP76a, turn right into the Via del Laghi towards Velletri, then left into the SP18c towards Artena. Rocca Priora is also signed as Vivaro. At the SS215, turn left towards Frascati/Rocca Priora, then follow the signs, turning right into the SP15b (SP80b).*

❾ Rocca Priora
Roma, Lazio; 00040

The highest of the Castelli towns at 786 m (2,580 ft), Rocca Priora forms a natural podium over the Colli Albani region. Start down at the town's medieval gate and hike up through the narrow streets and curved terraces of the coloured houses. Christmas decorations festoon the main street and square all year round. Explore Piazza Umberto, with its 1880 **Castello Savelli** (now the town hall) and 15th-century **Chiesa dell'Assunta**. The best views are from the adjacent Piazza Zanardelli which looks out into the valley and over the town of Montecompatri below.

Above left Tables lining the street outside a bar-*gelateria*, Nemi **Above centre** Nemi's pastel-coloured houses in the evening sun **Above right** Strawberries and cherries for sale, Nemi

EAT AND DRINK

CASTEL GANDOLFO
Ristorante La Gardenia *moderate–expensive*
Incredible lake location and a range of aromatic dishes: tagliatelle with prosciutto and zucchini; lemon-scented *raviolini* and rocket salad with orange. *Via Bruno Buozzi 4, 00040; 06 936 0001; www.ristorantelagardenia.it; closed Mon*

Antico Ristorante Pagnanelli *expensive*
There is a theatrical edge to the setting suspended over the lake. Much of the produce comes from the family farm and the menu of seasonal regional cuisine is topped off by its wine cellar. *Via Antonio Gramsci 4, 00040; 06 936 0004; www.pagnanelli.it; closed Tue Nov–Apr*

NEMI
Bar Belvedere *inexpensive*
Nestled into the cliff-side under a sweep of sunshades this place has incredible views. The great ices and snacks are simply the icing on the cake. *Via Belvedere Dante Alighieri 3, 00040*

La Pergola *moderate*
A pretty tavern with splendid lake views from the terrace. Rustic fare reigns supreme, especially game and grilled meat, but there are pizzas, too. *Piazza del Mercato 7, 00040; 06 936 8171; www.lapergola.altervista.org; closed Tue*

DAY TRIP OPTIONS
There are few standout highlights here; just the sublime combination of hilltop towns, woods, lakes and fine views.

Picnic in the hills
Based in Frascati ❶, stock up on goodies for a picnic. Make a quick

visit to Tusculum ❷ and Grottaferrata ❸ before heading to Rocca di Papa ❹ for a picnic and a walk in the Parco Regionale dei Castelli Romani.

Follow the first part of the main drive. Return on a more direct route to Frascati using the SS218 to shorten it slightly.

A circuit of the lakes
From Nemi ❽, pack food and head for Castel Gandolfo ❺ to walk around the lake or go for a swim. Return via Roman Albano Laziale ❻.

Take SS217 and SS216 to Castel Gandolfo. Loop back on the SS216, SS7 and SP76a.

Eat and Drink: inexpensive, under €25; moderate, €25–€45; expensive, over €45

DRIVE **16**

Abruzzo: Mountains and Sea

Gran Sasso to Termoli

Highlights

- **Gran Sasso and Campo Imperatore**
  Explore vast meadows and mountain peaks with ancient livestock paths and modern ski trails

- **Historic Sulmona**
  Stroll around this scenic town and visit the nearby sanctuary of Hercules Curino

- **Guardiagrele**
  Sample delicious gourmet cuisine and shop for handmade crafts

- **Trabocco Coast**
  View curious fishing wharves along the Adriatic coastline and swim in the clear waters of the Tremiti Islands

The port of San Domino, the largest of the idyllic Tremiti Islands

Abruzzo: Mountains and Sea

Abruzzo is a region that is almost two-thirds mountainous parkland – ideal for hiking, horse riding or, in winter, skiing on the Gran Sasso or Maiella ranges. It also boasts a lovely stretch of Adriatic coastline and is home to scenic stone villages, ancient monasteries and castles, as well as the fine medieval town of Sulmona. Guardiagrele has long been a centre for skilled artisans working in gold, lace, textiles and other materials, traditions that are being continued today. Gourmands will delight in Abruzzo's outstanding restaurants and superb local wines like Montepulciano d'Abruzzo and Trebbiano.

ACTIVITIES

Climb Gran Sasso's highest peak, Corno Grande, at 2,912 m (9,554 ft)

Stroll around historic Sulmona and sample the local speciality, *confetti* (crunchy sugar-coated almonds)

Hike or horseback ride through the pine and fir forests of the Maiella Mountains

Shop for traditional crafts in Guardiagrele

Relax on the lovely beaches around the historic port of Termoli

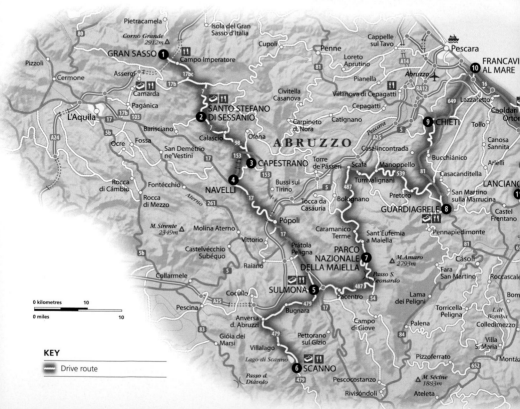

KEY

Drive route

Above The Maiella Mountains provide fertile ground for vineyards such as those of the Zaccagnini winery at Bolognano, *see p177* Left Sulmona, *see p176*

Above Baroque fountain in the central Piazza Garibaldi, Sulmona

PLAN YOUR DRIVE

Start/finish: Gran Sasso to Termoli.

Number of days: 4, allowing for a day on the Tremiti Islands.

Distance: 381 km (237 miles).

Road conditions: Well maintained.

When to go: Spring and summer are the best times to visit when the wild mountain flowers are in bloom. Skiing from Nov/Dec up to May.

Opening times: Museums and shops open 9am–1pm and 4–7pm, closing earlier on Sun and in winter. Many are closed on Mon. Churches are usually open daily from 7am–12.30pm and 3–7pm – avoid visiting during services.

Main market days: Sulmona: Wed and Sat mornings, Piazza Garibaldi, local produce; Guardiagrele: Periodic craft fairs for gold, ceramics and textiles.

Major festivals: Around Abruzzo: many food and drink festivals, Jun–Aug, **Sulmona:** Procession of the fleeing Madonna, Easter morning; Italian Film Festival, Nov. **Termoli:** St Basso Feast Day, 3 Aug.

DAY TRIP OPTIONS

Energetic explorers combine a day in **Sulmona** with a trip to the **Maiella Mountains** and a spa treatment at Caramanico Terme. **Families and beach lovers** will enjoy the Trabocco Coast and the beautiful **Tremiti Islands**. For full details, *see p179*.

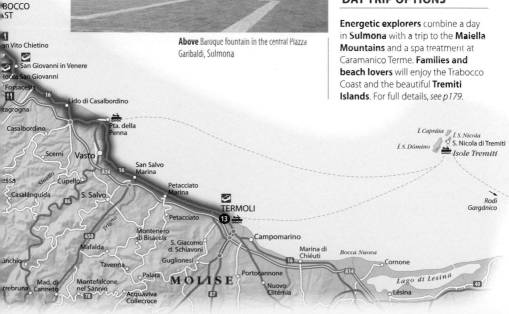

Above A hostel in the Gran Sasso mountain range

GETTING TO GRAN SASSO AND CAMPO IMPERATORE

From Sulmona drive north (towards L'Aquila) on the SS17 to Camarda then Assergi. Take Autostrada A24, which tunnels under the Gran Sasso and exits at Isola del Gran Sasso d'Italia, near Corno Piccolo. Return to Camarda along the same road and from here proceed to Campo Imperatore.

WHERE TO STAY

AROUND GRAN SASSO

Elodia Relais and Park *moderate*
Stylish country inn with nine spacious rooms. Discount for lunch or dinner at the excellent restaurant nearby.
*Via Valle Per Chiana, Camarda; 67100
0862 606 830; www.elodia.it*

SANTO STEFANO DI SESSANIO

Sextantio Albergo Diffuso *expensive*
Innovative, luxurious hotel housed in carefully restored medieval buildings. Breakfast with local jams and breads. Wine bar and restaurant serve typical dishes made from local produce.
Via Principe Umberto, 67020; 0862 899 112; www.sextantio.it

① Gran Sasso
Abruzzo; 67100
Camarda is the gateway to the Gran Sasso d'Italia (Big Rock of Italy) mountain range and national park, and Campo Imperatore. Excellent restaurants in the area such as Elodia *(see left)* also attract visitors here. Ten minutes' drive north at Assergi, the *funivia* (cable car) glides up the mountain to **Campo Imperatore**.

The Gran Sasso massif is southern Italy's top ski destination. During the summer take an invigorating hike over its rounded limestone mountains or make the guided climb up central Italy's highest mountain, **Corno Grande**, standing at 2,912 m (9,554 ft). For information contact Gran Sasso Tourist Centre *(0862 605 21, www.gransassolagapark.it)*.

🚗 *In summer take SS17bis southeast, then turn sharp right on SP7 to Santo Stefano di Sessanio. Continue towards the tower. Park on the road before the entrance to the Sextantio hotel. Santo Stefano is closed to traffic.*

In winter (Oct–May) the road is closed. Take SS17bis south to Pagánica, bear left on SP103 and turn left on SS17 to Barisciano. Turn right on SP7 and head north to Santo Stefano di Sessanio.

② Santo Stefano di Sessanio
Abruzzo; 67020
The road from Campo Imperatore to Santo Stefano di Sessanio curves around mountain tops past small lakes, sheep and cattle tracks until the fortified town comes into view, silhouetted on a hill-top. Constructed around the year 1000,

Above The road to Campo Imperatore winds its way past the impressive Corno Grande

in later centuries the town belonged for a time to the Medici family. Almost completely abandoned in the mid-20th century, the small town was restored by a Milanese investor using traditional building methods, such as the forked trunk of a chestnut tree as a roof support. This preserved the town's ancient patina and cleverly hid energy-efficient modern comforts.

It is possible to watch artisans make soap, candles and textiles, sample herbal teas and learn about herbal remedies. Santo Stefano's Ensemble in Residence plays a series of classical and modern concerts, a conscious decision to avoid folk clichés and emphasize quality.

Look for similar careful restoration in **Calascio** *(67020 Calascio)*, another Gran Sasso town that also originated around 1000 and claims to have Italy's highest fortress, the Rocca Calascio, with four round towers that

Below The small hill town of Barisciano close to Santo Stefano di Sessanio

Where to Stay: inexpensive, under €100; moderate, €100–€200; expensive, over €200

Above Dusk settles on the quiet streets of Santo Stefano dsi Sessanio

were added in the 15th century. Also restored by the owner of Sextantio *(see left)*, Rocca Calascio was one of the locations used for the films *Ladyhawke* and *The Name of the Rose*.

🚗 *From Santo Stefano take the SP7 southeast, continue through Rocca Calascio to the SP8a/SP98 then take the SP72 to Capestrano.*

3 Caspestrano
Abruzzo; 67022
Named for the Franciscan friar San Giovanni Capestrano, born here in 1386, Capestrano sits on the crest that divides the Navelli plain and the Ofena basin. In the main piazza the cathedral stands opposite the Castello Piccolomini-Medici, which now serves as the city hall. The funerary statue, *Warrior of Capestrano*, was discovered here by a farmer in 1934. Dating from the 6th century BC it is now the centrepiece of Chieti's Archaeological

Museum *(see p178)*, and has become the symbol of Abruzzo.

🚗 *From Capestrano, go back up the SP72, then head southwest on the SS153 towards Navelli.*

4 Navelli
Abruzzo; 67020
This hilltop town is famed for its precious saffron, produced by the crocus flowers that bloom on the wide Navelli plain. The town itself has changed little over the centuries. No bars, shops, or trattorias interrupt the stone houses. Stairways and stone walkways pass under diagonal rustic arches. Some homes have courtyards that are home to chickens, roosters and other animals. The tourist office is located in the piazza at the base of town, near the local coffee bar.

🚗 *From Navelli head southeast on the SS17 towards Sulmona. At the south end of town, near Via Circ. Orientale, there is a covered car park.*

EAT AND DRINK

AROUND GRAN SASSO
Ostello di Campo Imperatore *inexpensive*
Part of the Hotel Campo Imperatore, this 1930s rustic bar serves simple fare. With outside tables and a casual ambience it is the perfect place for hikers to share information and swap stories.
Loc. Campo Imperatore, 67010 Gran Sasso d'Italia; 0862 400011; www. hotelcampoimperatore.com; closed mid-Sep–mid-Nov

Elodia Restaurant *moderate*
One of the area's best restaurants. Specialities include tasty dishes of lamb, pork, beef and wild boar.
Via Valle Per Chiana, Camarda; 0862 606 830; www.elodia.it

Hotel Cristallo *moderate*
Enjoy spectacular panoramic views as you dine on traditional Italian fare.
Fonte Cerreto, L'Aquila, 67010; 0862 606 678 ; www.hotelcristallolaquila.it

Other options: Ristoro Mucciante *inexpensive*
On route from Campo Imperatore to Santo Stefano (SS17bis), this wooden store with picnic tables sells pecorino and ricotta cheese, cured meats and pasta, plus soda, beer and wine.
Loc. Madonnina, 67023; 0862 938 357; open daily Apr–Dec, Sat & Sun Feb–Mar

SANTO STEFANO DI SESSANIO
Lo Stemmo del Cavaliere *inexpensive*
Serves delicious *gnocchi allo zafferano* (pasta dumplings with saffron), lentil soup and a variety of main dishes from locally sourced meat and vegetables.
Via della Giudea, 67020; www. ostellodelcavaliere.it; closed Thu

Below The high peaks and beautiful countryside of the Gran Sasso

Above The road into Sulmona, framed by the peaks of the Maiella Mountains

VISITING SULMONA

Parking
Park in the covered car park near Via Circ. Orientale, Sulmona, 67039

Tourist Information
Corso Ovidio 208, Sulmona, 67039; 0864 773 088; www.abruzzoturismo.it

VISITING PARCO NAZIONALE DELLA MAIELLA

Tourist Information
Book for hiking trips in the Maiella Mountains at the visitor centre.
Paola Barrasso, Via del Vivaio; Caramanico Terme, 085 922 343; www.parcomajella.it

WHERE TO STAY

SULMONA

Ovidius Santacroce *inexpensive*
Across from San Panfilo cathedral, this modern family hotel is at the edge of Sulmona's historic centre and has Wi-fi, a bar and restaurant.
Via Circ. Occidentale 177, 67039; 0864 538 24; www.hotelovidius.it

SCANNO

La Dimora di d'Annunzio B&B *inexpensive*
Charming rooms decorated by local artist, behind the cathedral under the arch.
Vico De Angelis 2, 67038 Scanno; 0864 747 942; www.ladimoradidannunzio.it

GUARDIAGRELE

Villa Maiella *inexpensive*
Large attractive rooms, delicious breakfast buffet and restaurant meals.
Strada Sette Dolori 30, 66016; 0871 809 319; www.villamaiella.it

❺ Sulmona
Abruzzo; 67039

Situated at the foot of the Maiella Mountains, between two national parks, Sulmona is renowned for its *confetti* (crunchy sugar-coated almonds) and its master goldsmiths. The central square is one of the region's most picturesque, framed by a stunning medieval aqueduct.

A one-hour walking tour

From the car park walk north on Corso Ovidio, the town's main shopping street. At Piazza Carmine turn right under the arches of the medieval aqueduct, **Acquedotto Medievale** ①, into grand **Piazza Garibaldi** ②. The piazza hosts a bustling morning market *(Wed, Sat)*. On the northern side of the square is the Fontana del Vecchio, the Old Man Fountain, built in 1474 and said to represent Solimo, the mythical founder of Sulmona. Admire the deeply recessed portals adorning the nearby Chiesa di San Francesco della Scarpa. Return to Corso Ovidio and continue north, past Piazza XX Settembre with its **statue of Ovid** ③. Stop at **Rapone Confetti** ④ to try the *confetti* flavoured with Navelli saffron, then pause to look at the jewellery displayed in Camillo Canale. Further along is the **Complesso SS. Annunziata** ⑤ *(closed Sun–Mon)*, the city museum housed in the former church. The

Sulmona confetti *shop*

nearby **Caffè Ovidio** ⑥ *(Corso Ovidio 224)* is a good place to have a coffee and a quick bite to eat. Continue on to Viale Roosevelt to the 8th-century **Cattedrale di San Panfilo** ⑦. The façade has Romanesque bas-reliefs and a 1391 Gothic portal, and inside are fragments of 15th-century frescoes and a 12th–17th-century crypt. Return on Corso Ovidio, turn left onto Via Solimo. Visit **Mirella's** ⑧, a tiny shop selling beautiful hand-embroidered linens. Turn right and follow Via Gramsci to the **Teatro Comunale** ⑨. Take Via Antonio de Nino back towards Corso Ovidio and retrace your steps to the car park.

A short drive from the centre of Sulmona (follow signs on SS17), on the slopes of Monte Morrone, is the **Sito Archeologico Ercole Curino** (sanctuary of Hercules Curino). One of the region's most important archaeological sites, it has magnificent views over the valley.
🚗 *Take the SR479 to Scanno.*

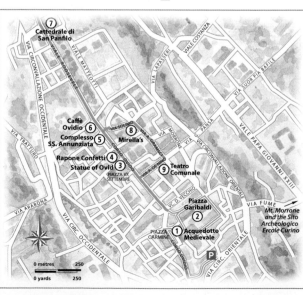

⑥ Scanno

L'Aquila, Abruzzo; 67038

This well-kept medieval hill-town, on a rocky spur by a clear mountain lake, is extremely popular, especially in the summer. The lake is perfect for canoeing or windsurfing. Scanno retains a medieval feel with its narrow alleys, courtyards and Renaissance churches, the most important of which is **Santa Maria della Valle** (open daily). The medieval fountain **Fontana Sarracco** with its Romanesque arches has become one of the town's symbols. Artisans still practise crafts such as lacemaking in styles particular to Abruzzo. The **Museo della Lana** (open daily Jul–Aug and most weekends) explores the art of woolmaking.

🚗 *Return to Sulmona on SR479. Take SP13a east to Pacentro and continue on SR487 to Caramanico Terme. Park next to the Tourist Information Centre at Corso Bernardi 39 or on Via Vivaio.*

⑦ Parco Nazionale della Maiella

Pescara, Abruzzo; 65023

The rounded Maiella Mountains are part of the enormous Parco Nazionale della Maiella. The forested peaks and valleys of the national park offer abundant opportunities for walking, climbing, cycling, and spotting birds and wildlife. Abruzzo's highest ski lift ascends 1,650 m (3,280 ft) to Guado di Coccia for winter skiing and summer hiking along trails in the Maiella massif.

Caramanico Terme is a pretty spa town situated at the confluence of the Ofento and Orta rivers. The health benefits of its sulphur-rich waters

Above Colourful plants decorate the balcony of a house in Guardiagrele

have been known since the 16th century (www.termedicaramanico.it).

🚗 *From Caramanico Terme, take the SR487 north to Scafa, and turn right onto the SS5. Turn right again, following signs for Turrivalignani and Manoppello, then for Serramonacesca, Pretoro and Guardiagrele.*

⑧ Guardiagrele

Chieti, Abruzzo; 66016

Set on a forested slope, Guardiagrele is a major centre for crafts. Artisans still ply their trade in copper, iron, gold, wool, ceramics and textiles. The church of **Santa Maria Maggiore**, (open daily) with its Gothic portal, also has a museum in its crypt.

The area around Guardiagrele is a good place to sample Abruzzo wines, from the robust red Montepulciano to whites like Trebbiano, Passarino and Pecorino. Wineries require appointments, so be sure to pre-book.

🚗 *Take the SS81 north to Chieti.*

EAT AND DRINK

SULMONA

Ristorante Clemente *moderate*
Sample delicious traditional dishes such as antipasto of aubergine *involtini*, warm sheep's milk ricotta and homemade pasta, complemented by local wines.
Vico Quercia 5, 67039; 0864 210 679; closed Sun, Mon, Thu

SCANNO

Gli Archetti *moderate*
Mountain cuisine, specialities include local meat and game, alongside tempting homemade pastas.
Via Silla 8, 67038; 0864 74645; www. gliarchetti.it; open Sat & Sun Nov– Mar; closed Jan

GUARDIAGRELE

Anello Bar Trattoria *inexpensive*
Try local wines such as Masciarelli's trademark Montepulciano d'Abruzzo with traditional dishes.
Via Anello 114, 66016; 0871 83271; closed Mon; booking required

Villa Maiella Ristorante e Albergo *moderate*
One of Abruzzo's best chefs concocts delicious local specialities such as lamb with saffron sauce and *coniglio farcito* (stuffed rabbit).
Via Sette Dolori 30, 66016; 0871 809 319; www.villamaiella.it; closed Sun eve, Mon, Jan

WINE TASTING IN GUARDIAGRELE

Taste the local grapes at Zaccagnini winery (*Contrada Pozzo, Bolognano; 65020; 085 888 0195; www. zaccagninivini.it*), between Caramanico Terme and Guardiagrele. Or at Mascerelli winery (*Via Gamberale 1; 66010; Casacanditella/Semivicoli; 0871 85241/82333; www.masciarelli.it*) in San Martino sulla Marrucina.

Above Sulmona's central square, the picturesque Piazza Garibaldi

Eat and Drink: inexpensive, under €25; moderate, €25–€45; expensive, over €45

Above Boys out fishing at Lago Angelo, near Chieti

VISITING THE TRABOCCO COAST

Progetto Mare
Book fishing, boat and scuba trips.
*Via Frentana 92, Marina San Vito
Chietino; 0872 618 665; 339 392 1211;
www.progettomare.it*

Visiting the Tremiti Islands
Several companies run ferries from
Termoli to the islands, including
Tirrenia. Check timetables at *www.
tirrenia.it* or contact the captain of
Termoli port: *0875 706484*

WHERE TO STAY

AROUND FRANCAVILLA AL MARE

Agriverde *inexpensive*
This organic farm and winery is in the
hills near Ortona. Comfortable rooms
in a 19th-century house.
*Via Stortina 32a, Caoldari di Ortona,
66020 (off the SS16 towards Termoli);
0859 032 101; www.agriverde.it*

TRABOCCO COAST

Valle di Venere Hotel & Ristorante
inexpensive
Friendly family-run hotel rooms and
apartments.
*Villa S Maria 5, San Giovanni in Venere,
Fossacesia, 66022; 0872 608 291;
www.valledivenere.com*

Rifugiomare B&B *inexpensive*
Set in olive trees and a pleasant walk
to the beach. Very small, with shared
bathrooms; book the more spacious
matrimoniale (double bed) room.
*Contrada Piane Favaro 179, Rocca San
Giovanni, 66020; 0872 608 112;
www.rifugiomare.it*

TERMOLI

Residenza Sveva Albergo Diffuso
inexpensive
These simply furnished but
comfortable rooms are available
throughout Termoli's historic centre.
*Piazza Duomo 11, 86039; 0875 706 803;
www.residenzasveva.com*

Where to Stay: inexpensive, under €100; moderate, €100–€200; expensive, over €200

⑨ Chieti
Chieti, Abruzzo; 66100
A modern city with good shopping,
Chieti also has some Roman ruins
such as the theatre *(on Via Zecca)* and
temples from Emperor Nero's reign.
Teatro Marrucino is a lovely 19th-
century theatre on Largo G Valignani.
   Chieti has two impressive
archaeological museums. **Museo
Archeologico Nazionale d'Abruzzo**
(closed Mon, Villa Comunale 2)
contains some of Abruzzo's most
important finds, including a famous
bronze statue called the *Warrior of
Capestrano*. The archaeological
complex and user-friendly museum,
La Civitella *(closed Mon, Via G Pianell,
www.lacivitella.it)* houses local
bronzes and ceramics.
🚗 *Take the SS649 east towards
Francavilla al Mare. Follow the
signs to the Museo Michetti,
where there is a car park.*

⑩ Francavilla al Mare
Chieti, Abruzzo; 66023
Francavilla al Mare is one of
Abruzzo's most charming seaside
resorts and a cultural centre. Perched
on a hill overlooking the sea is the
Museo Michetti *(closed Mon, Sat–Sun
am)*. Paolo Michetti's two grand
paintings are reason enough to
stop here. His painting of the Serpari
procession combines the exoticism
of Cocullo's annual May snake
procession, which has pagan origins,
and the 19th-century Orientalists'
use of light in painting. The
museum continues to collect the
works of his contemporaries, and
modern art.
🚗 *From Francavilla al Mare SS16 south
to San Vito Chietino, SP81/SP82
southwest to Lanciano. Car park is at
Ripa Civitanova near Largo Appello.*

⑪ Lanciano
Chieti, Abruzzo; 66034
Lanciano's four quarters radiate out
from the central Piazza del Plebescito.
In the piazza is the imposing
Cattedrale di Santa Maria del Ponte
which was built atop a Roman bridge.
Art-lovers will delight in the **Casa
Museo Federico Spoltore**, dedicated
to Spoltore (1902–88). Following his
death, the artist's house was
transformed into a museum *(Via
Federico Spolotre 4)*, lovingly
maintained with the painter's original
furnishings and housing examples of
his work. The Cistercian-Gothic church
of Santa Maria Maggiore, built in 1227,
has medieval figures on the façade.
Inside is a processional silver cross
sculpted by Nicola da Guardiagrele,
the 15th-century sculptor honoured
with one-man shows in Rome and
Florence during 2008 and 2009.
🚗 *From Lanciano return to San Vito
Chietino and the Trabocco Coast.*

Above Detail from a temple reconstruction at the
museum La Civitella, Chieti

Trabocchi
The origins of these strange fish-
catching structures are not clear.
Some hypothesize that immigrants
built them in the late 1600s. Others
date their system of engineering
to the 8th century. *Trabocchi*
have wooden beams and nets with an
intricate system of weights and
balances to scoop up fish, while
staying connected to land. Fragile
as they look, they can withstand
violent storms. A special law
now preserves some 20 remaining
trabocchi dotted along the coast.

⑫ Trabocco Coast

Chieti, Abruzzo; 66026

The Trabocco Coast extends from Ortona south to Vasto and is less than an hour's drive from the Maiella Mountains. Along the coastal road there are examples of the vanishing, *trabocchi*. Laws to help preserve these ancient fishing wharfs have allowed them to be developed into museums, observation points or summer dining spots. At **San Vito Chietino** a surviving *trabocco* sits on an open beach. Others are in secluded coves such as the one near **Fossacesia**.

Near Fossacesia is the **Abbazia San Giovanni in Venere** *(open daily)*. The name translates as St John in Venus, indicating the presence of an earlier temple. This Benedictine monastery and church dates from the 6th century. The church has 13th-century frescoes and a crypt with Roman columns. **Vasto** and other coastal towns are famous for the dish of *brodetto*, a stew of fish, seafood and peppers.

🚗 *From San Vito Chietino go south on SS16. Take Via Strada Statale Lanciano Fossacesia Est. Right on SP106/Via SP San Giovanni in Venere and park below the abbey. Continue south on SS16 to Termoli. Park at the port.*

⑬ Termoli

Molise; 86039

Once an ancient fishing port, Termoli is now a popular resort with several lovely beaches, such as Spaiggia di Sant'Antonio, north of the town's walls. Termoli's historic centre is enclosed by a wall and many of the houses have been restored. In the central square, the Romanesque **Duomo** *(open daily)* is dedicated to St Mary of Purification and houses 12th–13th-century relics of the city's patron saints – Bassus and Timoteus.

Termoli's port has year-round ferry services to the nearby **Tremiti Islands** *(see left)*. The islands are very popular with Italians. Santo Domino has a sandy beach and is good for swimming. Close to Termoli port there's a fish market every morning.

Climb the flight of steps from the port to explore Termoli's **Castello Svevo** *(open daily)*. Built in the 11th century it was later extensively renovated by Frederick II (1194–1240), after it was damaged during an attack by the Venetian fleet. The castle was once part of a wider fortification system, including a wall surrounding the entire city, but today only one tower remains.

Above left The Museo Michetti at Francavilla al Mare **Above right** An ancient *trabocco* survives at Fossacesia

EAT AND DRINK

AROUND CHIETI

La Lanterna *moderate–expensive*
This pink villa excels at fish antipasto. The wine cellar has a stunning Valentini Montepulciano d'Abruzzo.
Via Valignani 18, Villanova di Cepagatti, 65012 (off the SS81); 085 977 1700; closed Mon

TRABOCCO COAST

L'Angolino da Filippo *moderate–expensive*
Excellent fish restaurant near the beach. Dishes include tuna with pistachios and cuttlefish in ink with potatoes.
Via Sangritana 1, Marina di San Vito Chietino, 66038; 0872 616 32; closed Mon

Castello di Septe *moderate*
Medieval castle hotel and restaurant with traditional cuisine. Breakfast buffet.
Loc. Castello di Sette 20, Mozzagrogna; 66030; 0872 578 635/578 940; www. castellodisepte.com

Trabocco Pesce Palombo *expensive*
Dine on a trabocco. Fixed menu of fresh fish. *SS 16, Loc. Fuggitella, Fossacesia, 66022; 0872 608 574; open for dinner & Sun lunch in summer only; www.traboccopescepalombo.it*

DAY TRIP OPTIONS

Based in Francavilla al Mare or anywhere along the Trabocco Coast, Termoli is within easy reach. The medieval town of Sulmona sits between two national parks and is also easily accessible from the coast.

Medieval sights and mountains
Stroll along Sulmona's ❺ Corso Ovidio, shop for hand-crafted gold jewellery and sample the delicious *confetti*. After lunch take the

scenic drive into the Maiella Mountains ❼ for a hike or a ride up Abruzzo's highest ski lift. Finish the day at Caramanico Terme with a relaxing treatment at one of the town's spas.

Sulmona is easily accessed from the SS17. Take the SP13a east towards Pacentro and the SR487 curving north along the San Leonardo Pass towards Santa Eufemia a Maiella. Continue to Caramanico Terme.

Coast and Tremiti Islands
Drive along the Trabocco Coast ⑫ to view the trabocchi and visit the abbey of San Giovanni in Venere. At Termoli 13 ⑬ take the ferry to the Tremiti Islands for a seafood lunch and a swim in the clear waters.

The SS16 runs south along the coast from Francavilla al Mare to Termoli. From Termoli's port it takes an hour to reach the Tremiti Islands. See left for details of ferry services.

Eat and Drink: inexpensive, under €25; moderate, €25–€45; expensive, over €45

Neapolitan Riviera

Naples to Grotte dell'Angelo

Highlights

- **Elegant Naples**
  Visit the top destination for the Grand Tourists of the 18th and 19th centuries

- **Ancient Roman towns**
  Wander the ancient towns of Pompeii and Herculaneum, frozen in time

- **Ravello – a mountain arts festival**
  Explore this old sea power, which now puts on one of Italy's great arts festivals

- **Delicious local produce**
  Sample wine, mozzarella and limoncello liqueur

- **Greek temples by the sea**
  Marvel at Greek temples in Paestum that date from the 6th century BC

The magnificent shopping arcade Galleria Umberto I, Naples, built in 1884

Neapolitan Riviera

Travellers seeking sun, sea and superb cuisine have come to Naples and the Amalfi coast ever since Roman emperors first made the place fashionable. And today, the bustling city of Naples provides lively street scenes that unfold under castles, palaces and in piazzas. The coast, however, offers a more relaxing world of dramatic vistas of towering cliffs set against an expanse of glittering blue sea. In pretty coastal towns serene cafés are draped in cascading flowers and citrus scents and medieval alleyways are a temptation to explore. Finally, if the heat gets too much, there is always the chance for a refreshing dip in the sea, perhaps under the unflinching gaze of some magnificent Greek temples.

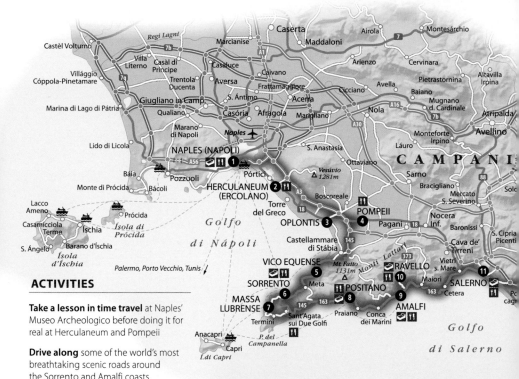

ACTIVITIES

Take a lesson in time travel at Naples' Museo Archeologico before doing it for real at Herculaneum and Pompeii

Drive along some of the world's most breathtaking scenic roads around the Sorrento and Amalfi coasts

Swim beneath the cliffs and sun on beaches in Positano and Amalfi

Listen to a concert in Ravello on a stage that uses the sea as a backdrop

Visit a working buffalo farm in Paestum, and try *bufala* (buffalo milk) ice cream and mozzarella

Go diving in the bay of Naples and see the incredible Parco Sommerso di Baia

Below The stunning Amalfi coastline bathed by the Tyrrhenian Sea, *see p188*

Above Glorious view from the terrace of the Rossellini Restaurant, Ravello, *see p189*

KEY

━━ Drive route

PLAN YOUR DRIVE

Start/finish: Naples to Grotte dell'Angelo.

Number of days: 4 with a day in Naples to explore the city and an island or archaeological site.

Distance: 249 km (155 miles).

Road conditions: Well-paved and signposted, some hairpin bends. Petrol stations are few, so fill the tank before departure. On narrow roads, buses and large vehicles have precedence.

Opening times: Museums and shops in southern Italy tend to open 9am–7pm or later, closing earlier on Sun and in winter. Many places also close 1–4pm for lunch and are closed Mon. Churches usually open daily 7am–12:30pm and 4–7pm; avoid visiting during services.

When to go: Swimming season is May–Oct. Jul–Aug is the busiest for the coast. Winter is often sunny, but some coastal establishments only open Easter–Oct.

Main markets: Naples (Montesanto): Mercato Alimentare della Pignasecca, food market on Via Marina; Mercato del Pesce di Porta Nolana, fish market near Piazza Garibaldi; **Naples (Poggioreale):** clothes and shoes market; **Amalfi:** Wed.

Major Festivals: Naples: 1st Sun of May and 19 Sep, The Miracle of San Gennaro; May, Maggio dei Monumenti (special events at historic sites, open May & Jun); **Sorrento:** May, lemon festival; **Massa Lubrense:** Jun, lemon festival; Sep, Festival della Tarantella; **Positano:** 14 August, Sbarco dei Saraceni (recalling the Saracen invasion); Aug 15, Feast of Assumption of Mary; **Amalfi:** Jun/Jul, Chamber Music Festival along coast; **Caserta (Belvedere di San Leucio):** Sep, Leuciana Festival; **Ravello:** May–Oct, Ravello Arts Festival.

DAY TRIP OPTIONS

History enthusiasts can begin in **Naples** with the **Palazzo Reale**, grand castles and **Museo Archeologico**, and then visit **Herculaneum** and **Pompeii**. **Sybarites** can take their pleasure on a winding coastal road to the cliffside towns of hard-to-leave **Positano**, pretty **Amalfi**, cultural **Ravello** and scientific **Salerno**. For full details, *see p189*.

Above The remarkable worked stone façade of Chiesa del Gesù Nuovo, Naples

VISITING NAPLES

Parking
On Autostrada A3, follow signs to Porto and Via Volta. Brin public parking (24 hrs) is at the corner of Via Volta and Via Brin. It is best not to drive in Naples.

Tourist Information
Piazza del Gesù Nuovo, 081 551 2701; Via S Carlo 9, 081 402 394; or *Via S Lucia 107, 081 245 7475, www.inaples.it*

VISITING THE ANCIENT SITES

A special ticket allows visits to the five ancient sites – Pompeii, Herculaneum, Oplontis, Stabia, and Boscoreale. Plan at least a full day for a brief visit to all five. Visit also *www.pompeiisites.org*.

Ercolano Tourist Office
Via IV Novembre, 80056; 081 788 1243

WHERE TO STAY IN NAPLES

Palazzo Alabardieri *moderate*
Elegant retreat with helpful staff in Naples' chic Chiaia neighbourhood near Piazza del Plebiscito.
Via Alabardieri 38, 80121; 081 415 278; www.palazzoalabardieri.it

Costantinopoli 104 *moderate*
This 19th-century villa in the centre has a small garden pool and is a 5-minute walk to the archaeological museum. Set in a quiet courtyard.
Via S. Maria di Costantinopoli 104, 80138; 081 557 1035; www.costantinopoli104.it

Posillipo Dream *inexpensive*
Set in Posillipo in Naples' west end, with views of the Phlegreian Fields and the islands of Nisida, Procida and Ischia. Also offers cooking courses.
Via Manzoni 214/O, Parco Flory Palazzina 4b, 80123; 081 575 6000; www.posillipodream.it

❶ Naples (Napoli)

Campania; 80121

The beauty of Naples lies in its grand castles, palaces and churches, in the splendour of its blue boat-filled bay and in the history of its ancient ruins. It is easy to see why the city has been a chic destination for centuries. However, Naples can be a challenging place; be aware that it is notorious for pick pockets and the traffic is anarchic. If it gets too much, get away from it all on a spa-covered island or by hiking up a volcano. Nowhere else is such variety so close and accessible.

A two-hour walking tour

From the car park follow the coastal road west around the bay to **Castel dell'Ovo** *(open daily)* ❶. The Santa Lucia neighbourhood resembles a film set with its restaurants, marina, and sailing club, and Vesuvius as the backdrop. Head up Via Chiaramonte to **Piazza dei Martiri** ❷ for a glimpse of Naples' contemporary art scene at Alfonso Artico and Gallery Navarra, then head northeast on Via Chiaia past **Galleria Fonti** ❸. Via Chiaia is a key area for *la passeggiata*, the ritual walk at dusk in one's finery before a night out. Entering the grand **Piazza Plebiscito** ❹, admire its central church San Francesco di Paola *(open daily)* inspired by Rome's Pantheon. Enjoy a cappuccino or *caffé shakerato* (iced coffee) at Gran Caffè Gambrinus looking at the Royal Palace. Built in the early 17th century by Domenico Fontana, the Palazzo Reale *(closed Wed)* was home to the Bourbon and Savoy families. Highlights include the Hercules Salon, Throne Room, 1768

A poster advertising Navigazione Generale

Court Theatre and the National Library with its beautiful illuminated medieval manuscripts. From Piazza Plebiscito, walk past the famous opera house (seats 3,000) **Teatro San Carlo** *(Via San Carlo 101–3)* ❺, and through the magnificent 1884 glass-roofed shopping arcade, Galleria Umberto I, to exit on Via Toledo. **Gay-Odin Cioccolateria** ❻, still in its original location *(Via Toledo 427)*, makes delicious chocolates. Turn right at Via Benedetto Croce to **Santa Chiara** *(closed Sun)* ❼ – named after Clare, the companion of St Francis to whom Robert of Anjou dedicated its construction in 1310. The church cloister is brightened by 18th-century majolica tiles and its Museo dell'Opera *(open daily)* holds the royal tombs of the wide-ranging medieval Angevin dynasty – and ruins of Roman baths. The Piazza del Gesù Nuovo has the imposing façade of Chiesa Gesù Nuovo, studded with hundreds of small pyramids. Further along are several pastry shops, such as **Scaturchio**

Below The twin peaks of Vesuvius' volcano, seen from the pretty marina at the Castel dell'Ovo at dusk

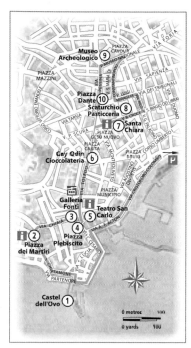

② Herculaneum (Ercolano)

Napoli, Campania; 80056

Named after Hercules, this ancient Roman town was destroyed by Vesuvius in AD 79 – the same blast that engulfed Pompeii with rocks and ash. Herculaneum was entombed in superheated mud, preserving plants and textiles. At the **Herculaneum Archaeological Excavations** (*Ercolano Scavi, Corso Resina; open daily; www.Pompeiisites.org*), pick up a map and visit the **House of Neptune and Amphitrite** for its luminous mosaics, while the shop next door still has wooden shelves and ceramic jugs. Recent excavations have revealed some delightful frescoes in the **Papyri Villa**.

To visit Vesuvius from Ercolano, follow signs in town for "Vesuvio". The scenic drive through vineyards – the ash has made the soil very fertile – with great views of the Bay of Naples, takes about 20 minutes to reach the car park at the top. It is possible to walk the 4 km (2½ miles) up to the volcano's steaming 600-m (1,970-ft) wide crater in about three hours.

🚗 *Return to the Autostrada A3; take the Torre Annunziata Nord for Oplontis.*

③ Oplontis

Torre Annunziata, Campania; 80058

A suburb of Pompeii, Oplontis was also destroyed by Vesuvius. Now overrun by Torre Annunziata, Oplontis merits a detour to see the remains of the huge villa and gardens of Emperor Nero's wife, Poppaea Sabina. Villa Poppaea (*Via Sepolcri 1; 081 862 1755; open daily*) is one of the grandest and best-preserved villas from the first century AD with delightful *trompe l'oeil* frescoes, fine mosaics and brilliant Pompeii-red walls. Slightly scruffy Torre Annunziata gets its name from the towers built to warn against Saracen raids and a chapel of the Virgin Mary.

🚗 *Take the A3 towards Salerno and turn off on Pompei Ovest – follow signs to the archaeological site. There are several well-marked car parks.*

Above The ruins of Herculaneum with Vesuvius looming ominously behind

EAT AND DRINK

NAPLES

Pizzeria Sorbillo *inexpensive*
Naples' most famous pizzeria, Sorbillo is always packed with diners who come for excellent pizza at a reasonable price.
Via dei Tribunali 28, 80139; 081 446 643; www.accademiadellapizza.it

Umberto Ristorante e Pizzeria *inexpensive–moderate*
Founded in 1916, this restaurant serves superb food – both traditional and with modern twists. Don't miss the delicious Neapolitan antipasto. Attentive service
Via Alabardieri 30/31, 80121; 081 418 555; www.umberto.it; closed Mon

Trattoria Nennella *inexpensive–moderate*
A hospitable trattoria with traditional Neapolitan food. The simple but good house wine matches the food brilliantly.
Via Lungo Teatro Nuovo 103, 80121; 081 414 338; closed Sun

Other options
Try superb *gelato* and sweets such as *sfogliatella* (cone-shaped layers of pastry filled with lemon cream), or artichoke *torte* at **Scaturchio Pasticceria** (*Piazza San Domenico Maggiore 19, 80134; 081 551 6944; www.scaturchio.it*).

HERCULANEUM (ERCOLANO)

Viva lo Re Enoteca *moderate*
Pleasant wine bar serving hearty food just a few steps from the entrance to Herculaneum, by the Miglio D'Oro hotel.
Corso Resina 261, 80056; 081 739 0207; www.vivalore.it; closed Sun eve & Mon

---

Pasticceria ⑧. At Piazzetta Nilo, turn left onto Via Nilo, then left towards Piazza Luigi Miraglia. Follow Via Costantinopoli with its artisan shops to Piazza Museo Nazionale and the **Museo Archeologico** (*closed Tue*) ⑨. Marvel at Greek, Egyptian and Etruscan art and the best finds from Pompeii, Herculaneum and other ancient cities. This is perfect preparation for visits to Pompeii and other archaeological sites. Return on Via Toledo, past **Piazza Dante** ⑩, to Piazza Plebiscito.

🚗 *Take A3 Autostrada to Ercolano exit. Follow signs to Ercolano Scavi (Archaeological Excavations). The car park is on Via Alveo (off Via Resina).*

Day Trip to Ischia

Ischia's main attractions are its spas and beaches, so enjoy a massage, a mud pack or just have a swim. **Parco Idrotermale Negombo di Lacco Ameno** (*Via San Montano; 081 986 1527; open Apr–Oct*) is a thermal park with plenty of spas. However, for a natural spa beach, try **Maronti Beach**, south of Barano. For food, head to **Sant'Angelo** – choose the restaurant with the best catch that day. Several ferries leave from Naples' port. No tourist cars allowed in high season, so use the island's taxis.

Above Lively bronze statuette in the House of the Faun, Pompeii **Right top** The Sacrarium of the Lares, home to Pompeii's guardian deities **Right below** The amphitheatre at Pompeii, the oldest in the Roman world **Bottom right** Vico Equense, up on the cliffs above the sea

BOAT TRIPS FROM SORRENTO

Check boat schedules at Marina Piccola. Simply admire the fabulous coastline from the sea, or rub elbows with the jet set and explore Capri. Take the funicular up to Capri's main square and stroll along lanes lined with jewel-box villas.

WHERE TO STAY

SORRENTO

Grand Hotel Excelsior Vittorio
expensive
Dramatically set on top of tuff cliffs and part of the town square this grand hotel was built over an ancient Roman villa.
Piazza Tasso 34, 80067; 081 807 1044; www.exvitt.it

Hotel Bellevue Syrene Sorrento
expensive
Built in 1750, it has frescoes and a terrace overlooking the Bay of Naples.
Piazza della Vittoria 5, 80067; 081 878 1604; www.bellevue.it

POSITANO

Hotel Poseidon *moderate–expensive*
As well as attentive service and private terraces with bay views, guests here can enjoy literary events and concerts.
Via Pasitea 148, 84017; 089 811 111; www.hotelposeidonpositano.it

Hotel Palazzo Murat *expensive*
The 18th-century wing is filled with antiques and there is a small garden and patio for breakfast and concerts.
Via dei Mulini 223, 84017; 089 875 177; www.palazzomurat.it

④ Pompeii
Campania; 80045
When Vesuvius erupted in AD 79 the port and its 20,000 inhabitants were perfectly preserved by the volcano's ashes. **Pompeii** *(open daily)* has transfixed visitors since its discovery in the 18th century. Exquisite mosaics and wall paintings among the ruins of theatres, shops, homes and temples offer total immersion into the Roman world. Visit the site when it opens in the morning, or in mid-afternoon when the breeze picks up and the crowds are gone. Near the centre and unmissable **Forum** and theatres, the **Lupanare Brothel** displays frescoes showing the speciality of each worker. A bakery even has charred remains of some bread. Once inside the site, try to get away from the crowds by walking to **Villa dei Misteri** – about 10 minutes or so from the Forum, but worth the walk to see the mysterious tale displayed in a private villa. The

luminous figures in a fresco on the villa's interior walls are shown on the famous Pompeii-red background. An adolescent girl is prepared for some initiation rite, perhaps to enter the cult of Dionysus or Orpheus.

🚗 *Take Via Plinio to A3 Autostrada, exit Castellammare di Stábia. Follow signs for SS145 to Vico Equense. Follow signs to "centro" – park at Piazza Mercato.*

⑤ Vico Equense
Campania; 80069
Originally located on the shoreline, the people of Vico Equense moved to the clifftop when pirates and weather made life below too risky. Visit the **Antiquarium** *(Corso G. Filangieri 98; open Mon, Wed & Fri am, Tue & Thu pm)* for a good pre-Roman archaeological collection from more than 200 necropoli discovered in the area. Children will enjoy the **Museo Mineralogico Campano** *(Via San Ciro 2; closed Mon and Sun am)* with its glowing minerals, dinosaur eggs and fossils. Church buffs can admire the colourful majolica dome of **SS Ciro e Giovanni** *(Via San Ciro, Piazza Umberto)* dedicated to the town's patrons, and the 14th-century red and white Gothic-Baroque **Annunziata Cathedral** *(Via Vescovado)*, poised dramatically at the edge of the cliffs. Enjoy a "pizza metro", cut to the size you want (the town claims it as its own invention). Head for the beaches at the base of the cliffs, or soak in mineral springs in **Scrajo Terme** *(SS145; 081 801 5731; closed weekends)*. For some exercise, take the SS269 via Moiano up to the village of Monte Faito, through forests and past farm hamlets to trails on Monte Faito (1,131 m/3,732 ft) – the highest peak in the Monti Lattari,

Where to Stay: inexpensive, under €100; moderate, €100–200; expensive, over €200

Above View over Sorrento, known as the city of orange and lemon groves

with views of the bay, Vesuvius and a 10th-century castle built by the Duke of Sorrento.

🚗 *Take SS145 to Sorrento. Park on Via Cocumella for access to the beach.*

⑥ Sorrento

Campania; 80067

Captivating the visitor with stunning views, Sorrento is infused with the perfume of its citrus trees, a constant reminder to sample the local liqueur, Limoncello. Walk the cliff paths for panoramic sea views or mingle with the locals in their *passeggiata* down at the port, or swim and sunbathe. If the walk back up is too steep, for a small fee, take the elevator to Piazza Vittoria. The **Museobottega della Tarsialignea** *(Palazzo Pomarici Santomasi, Via San Nicola 28; closed Sun)* tells the story of Sorrento's famous *intarsio* (inlaid wood). See it in the choir stalls in the medieval **Cattedrale di San Filippo e Giacomo** *(Corso Italia 1; open daily)* and in the **Museo Correale di Terranova** *(Via Correale 50 ; closed Tue)*. Browse the shops that line the narrower streets parallel to Corso Italia. Sorrento's patron saint, Anthony, has a basilica on **Piazza Sant'Antonino** that was built around the year 1000, probably over an ancient temple.

🚗 *Take SS145 to Massa Lubrense then to Sant'Agata Sui Due Golfi. Pay for on-street parking in Sant'Agata.*

⑦ Massa Lubrense

Campania; 80064

A headland comprising 18 villages, Massa Lubrense is more rustic than its glamorous neighbours. At its tip is Punta della Campanella, probably once the site of a Greek temple. Hike here from the towns of Termini or

Nerano over patches of Roman road. The point takes its name from the lighthouse, built in 1335 (modified 1566) with a bell *(campana)* to warn of pirates. Gourmets head for Don Alfonso at **Sant'Agata Sui Due Golfi**, a town on a crest with views of the gulfs of Naples and Salerno. An hour's hike up to the Benedictine monastery grounds, **Monastero del Deserto** *(Via Deserto 23; monastery not open to visitors)* offers fabulous views of the two bays.

🚗 *From Sant'Agata Sui Due Golfi take SS145, becoming SS163 to Positano. There are two car parks on Via Pasitea.*

⑧ Positano

Salerno, Campania; 84017

The pastel houses that tumble down Positano's natural basin are bathed in fennel and citrus scents from the tiers of gardens and terraces. At the Tourist Office *(Via del Saracino 4)*, pick up a map before admiring the **Duomo** and its colourful majolica dome; inside, the Black Madonna recalls the Byzantine era. For locals and visitors, however, Positano is about style and relaxation, so enjoy both while people-watching in a café such as **La Sirenuse** *(Via C. Colombo 30, 84017)*. Legend has it that the **Li Galli** rocks in the bay were the haunt of the Sirens whose singing lured sailors to their doom. The Sirens may be gone (as have the rocks' other famous inhabitants, dancers Leonide Massine and Rudolph Nureyev), but it is possible to take a boat trip from a beach kiosk and enjoy a relaxing visit to the islets – now a nature reserve – and a refreshing swim.

🚗 *Take SS163 to Amalfi and park at Piazza Flavio Gioa by the marina.*

EAT AND DRINK

POMPEII

Il Principe Ristorante *expensive*
Taste delicious ancient Roman cuisine or contemporary regional dishes.
Piazza Bartolo Longo 8, 80045; 081 850 5566; www.ilprincipe.com; closed Sun eve & Mon

VICO EQUENSE

Torre del Saracino *expensive*
Gourmet dining in the restaurant of award-winning chef Michele Deleo.
Via Torretta 9, Marina di Equa, 80069; 081 802 8555; www.torredelsaracino.it; closed Sun eve & Mon

SORRENTO

Zi'Ntonio *inexpensive–moderate*
Friendly seafood restaurant on marina.
Via L. De Maio 11, Via Marina Grande 180, 80067; 081 878 1623; www.zintonio.it

Il Buco di Aversa Giuseppe *expensive*
One of Sorrento's classic restaurants, in the arches under the Basilica.
Rampa Marina Piccola 5, 80067; 081 878 2354; www.ilbucoristorante.it; closed Wed, Jan

AROUND MASSA LUBRENSE

Don Alfonso 1890 *expensive*
Lunch or dinner at Don Alfonso is a must for gourmets worldwide. The cooking showcases the intense flavour of local ingredients
Corso Sant'Agata 11/13, Sant'Agata Sui Due Golfi, 80064 (just off SS145 on Massa Lubrense road); 081 878 0026; www.donalfonso.com; closed Mon & Tues; mid-Jun–15 Sep; closed lunch

POSITANO

Buca di Bacco *moderate*
Set on the beach next to the port, tables overlook the parade of visitors while the cuisine spotlights catch from the sea.
Via Rampa Teglia 4, 84017; 089 875 699; www.bucadibacco.it; closed winter

Above The pastel houses of Positano tumbling down the cliff to the sea

Eat and Drink: inexpensive, under €25; moderate, €25–€45; expensive, over €45

Above left The Duomo at Amalfi, its mosaics gleaming in the sun **Above right** Tiers of houses overlooking the seafront at Amalfi

WHERE TO STAY

AMALFI

Hotel Luna Convento *moderate*
Set into the cliff over the sea, the 13th-century monastery has a Moorish-inspired cloister, a terrace and a pool.
Via P. Comite 33, 84011; 089 871 002; www.lunahotel.it; closed Jan–Feb

Santa Caterina *expensive*
This family-run hotel pampers guests with a spa (try the lemon massage) and an elevator down to its own lido.
Via Amalfitana 9, 84011; 089 871 012; www.hotelsantacaterina.it

RAVELLO

Hotel Giordano *expensive*
Once the owner's family villa, it has 17 guest rooms and a lovely terrace view.
Via S. Chiara 2, 84010; 089 857 255; www.villamaria.it

Palazzo Sasso *expensive*
One of Europe's great hotels – staff ratio is 90 to 100 guests. Take a sauna, steam bath, massage and beauty treatments.
Via San Giovanni del Toro 28, 84010; 089 818 181; www.palazzosasso.com

SALERNO

Villa Lupara *moderate*
Take a dip in the chromotherapy pool set amidst vineyards with sea views only 4 km (2 miles) from Salerno's centre.
Via Fossa Lupara, Loc. Croce/Salerno, 84125; 089 228 798; www.villalupara.it; closed Jan–Mar

PAESTUM

Azienda Agrituristica Seliano *inexpensive*
Close to the Greek temples of Paestum, this friendly farm has superb food and offers cooking lessons.
Via Seliano, 84063; 082 872 3634; www.agriturismoseliano.it; closed Jan–Feb

Right The shady garden at the elegant Hotel Villa Maria, Ravello

⑨ Amalfi
Salerno, Campania; 84011

Once a mighty maritime republic, Amalfi has plenty to see. The 15th-century watchtower, **Torre di San Francesco** (known as Torre Saracena) now hosts a romantic restaurant. The **Duomo** glitters when the sun strikes the gold mosaics on its pediment and pointed arches throw *chiaroscuro* (light and shade) to the cathedral's portico. Uphill, the **Supportico Rua Nova Mercantorum**, tunnels that led to Arab baths in the 12th century, now offers a shady, alternative parallel to the high street. The **Museo della Carta** in Valle dei Mulini (*Via delle Cartiere; open daily; Nov–Feb: closed Mon*) tells the story of Amalfi's famous papermaking industry. Nearby, the **Cooperativa Amalfitana** (*Via delle Cariere 55/57*) sells the favourite local tipple, limoncello, by the bottle.

🚗 *Take the SS163 and turn left up the SS373 to Ravello. Park after the tunnel.*

⑩ Ravello
Salerno, Campania; 84010

Ravello's mountaintop perch means that it lacks the beaches of Positano and Amalfi, but this suits locals and visitors alike who prefer its arts scene

away from the crowds of the coastal towns. Not so in the 12th century, when Ravello was a major trader with the Orient – a history reflected in its Moorish architectural details. The town's many steps keep the pace leisurely but reward the effort with stunning sea views. The summer arts festival attracts a sophisticated audience for quality dance, music and drama, **Ravello Festival** (*www.ravellofestival.com*). Ravello has many deluxe hotels and fine dining to match – among Europe's best. Ravello's main sight is the cathedral **Santa Maria Assunta** (*open daily*) dedicated to the town's patron saint, Pantaleone, with its 1179 bronze door. Next to the Duomo, **Villa Rufolo** (*Piazza Duomo; open daily*) has Moorish influences and a lush garden.

🚗 *Return to the SS163 coastal road to Salerno. On Lungomare Trieste, park at Piazza della Concordia.*

⑪ Salerno
Salerno, Campania; 84121

A bustling major port, Salerno's pretty and quiet medieval centre is reached via Porta Nova. **Villa Comunale** (*open daily*), the town garden by the lovely theatre, is the ideal spot to freshen up with a lemon *granita*. The cathedral, **Duomo di San Matteo** (*Piazza Alfano I; open daily*), has a courtyard built using 28 Roman columns and its 11th-century bronze door was cast in Constantinople. Beautifully carved medieval ivory panels make a visit to **Museo Diocesano** (*San Matteo; open am daily*) worthwhile. Above town, the massive **Castello Arechi**, its long and turbulent history reflected in its mix of architectural styles, commands the 300-m (984-ft) hill along with the **San Liberato Monastery**, both offering stunning views. The elevator,

Far left One of the buffalo that provide milk to make mozzarella in Paestum **Left** The remains of the grand Temple of Ceres/Athena at Paestum

EAT AND DRINK

AMALFI

Gran Caffè Tea Room *inexpensive*
A tradition since 1936, stop for a light lunch with good salads and sandwiches. *Viale delle Repubbliche Marinare 37/38, 84011; 089 871 047; www.bargran caffeamalfi.it; closed Mon & Nov–Jan*

Torre Saracena *moderate*
Dine in a romantic setting atop a 15th-century watchtower above the sea *Via Pantaleone Comite 33, 84011; 089 871 002; closed Tue (except Jul–Aug), Jan–Mar*

RAVELLO

Rossellinis Restaurant *expensive*
Gourmets love this elegant, award-winning spot in the Palazzo Sasso *Via S. Giovanni del Toro 28, 84010; 089 818 181; www.palazzosasso.com; closed Jan–Apr*

SALERNO

Antica Pizzeria Vicolo della Neve *inexpensive*
Meat, vegetables and pizza all baked in the oven are specialities along with the reasonable Aglianico red wine. *Vicolo della Neve 24, 84100; 089 225 705; www.vicolodellaneve.it; open eves only; closed Wed*

Trattoria del Padreterno *moderate*
Serving only excellent fish. Sit outdoors in the piazza and people-watch. *Piazza Flavia Gioia 12, 84121; 089 239 305; closed Tue*

PAESTUM

Ristorante Nettuno *moderate*
Near the Temple, of Neptune or Zeus, this eatery offers seafood and local wine. *Zona Archeologica, Via Nettuno 2, 84047; 0828 811 028; open lunch only, closed Mon*

Ascensore Comunale, ascends to **Giardino di Minerva** *(Via Ferrante Sanseverino 1)* a medieval medical garden and a reminder that Salerno once housed one of Italy's first schools for surgeons. Stop by the port to watch ships or take a sea excursion to nearby coastal towns and islands.

🚗 *Head south on Lungomare Trieste to the SS18 then continue south all the way to Paestum. Lots of parking on site.*

⑫ Paestum

Salerno, Campania; 84063
Three majestic Greek temples, better preserved than most in Greece, can be found in the **Area Archeologica** *(Via Magna Grecia 919; open daily)*. The **Temple of Ceres** (500 BC), originally attributed to the goddess of agriculture and fertility, has been more recently identified with Athena, the goddess of wisdom. Proximity to the sea may have influenced the naming of the **Temple of Neptune** (450 BC), but current theories favour Zeus, the mightiest of the Greek gods. Paestum's **Basilica** (550 BC), the oldest and best-preserved temple, was dedicated to the goddess Hera, wife of Zeus, and has nine tapered columns in the front

and 18 on the side. On site, the **Museo Archeologico Nazionale di Paestum** *(closed first and third Mon of each month)* has interesting frescoes from the **Tomb of the Diver** found here in 1968.

It is also interesting to visit **Azienda Barlotti**, a mozzarella factory *(Via Torre di Paestum)* that makes and sells superb mozzarella as well as salami, other cheeses, and luscious rich ice cream made from *bufala* milk.

🚗 *Take SS18 north, turn right (east) onto SS166, then take SS19 (north) to Pertosa-Grotte dell'Angelo.*

⑬ Grotte dell'Angelo

Salerno, Campania; 84030
Near the Tanagro river east of the Monti Alburni, at Pertosa lie the **Grotte dell'Angelo** (Angel Caves) *(open daily; www.grottedellangelo.sa.it)*. Tours take visitors around the caves that were first inhabited in the Neolithic Age. Take a boat across a lake before exploring the tunnels filled with stalactites and stalagmites, crystal formations, and into a cavernous hall 40 m (131 ft) high. Learn more about the caves at Pertosa's **Museo di Speleologia** *(Tourist Information Centre, Via Santa Maria; 0975 392 232 98)*.

DAY TRIP OPTIONS

The driving is quite uncomplicated on this trip – it is basically following the coastal road – so day trips really depend on personal preferences. Naples requires a day, including a visit to an ancient site – more if there is a wish to see the other ancient sites – but the laidback traveller could spend a lazy day in each of the coastal towns, or tick them all off in a day's driving. The best solution, of course, lies somewhere in between.

An educational trip

Get the benefit of the Grand Tour and see magnificent churches and royal palaces of Naples ❶ before studying the past in the Museo Archeologico. For an ancient history field trip, head to Herculaneum ❷ and Pompeii ❹ with a detour up Vesuvius, for any geology students.

Straightforward driving – pick up the Autostrada A3 near Naples' train station and follow the signs to Herculaneum (Ercolano) and Pompeii.

A coastal idyll

This day is all about pleasure – start at lemon-scented Positano ❽ for a boat trip and swim. Avoid the lure of the Sirens and head to pretty Amalfi ❾ for lunch and a post-prandial stroll overlooking the sparkling sea. Next stop, Ravello ❿, for a touch of highbrow culture before reaching Salerno ⑪ in time for *la passeggiata* and a stroll around its historic centre.

Follow the winding SS163 along the coast with stunning views all the way.

DRIVE **18**

The Heel of Italy

Alberobello to Gallipoli

Highlights

- **Fairytale Alberobello**
  Wander around this magical town
  with its whitewashed limestone *trulli*
  made using prehistoric techniques

- **Baroque splendour of Lecce**
  Admire Lecce's Baroque architecture
  with extravagant flourishes made
  possible by the soft golden sandstone

- **Primitivo wines**
  Drink the world-famous, robust red
  wines made from the locally grown
  Primitivo grape (also called Zinfandel)

- **Splash in the Adriatic or Ionian**
  Swim in the sea from tiny private
  coves or join the see-and-be-seen set
  on expansive sandy beaches

A clutch of the extraordinary dwellings –
trulli – of Alberobello

The Heel of Italy

Bathed in an ivory light, Puglia radiates warmth all year round. Phoenicians, Greeks and Romans, medieval Crusaders and pilgrims have all been drawn here by its easy access to the East. The rest of the world is now also catching on to the lure of Puglia's mild climate, sandy beaches, clean water and superb full-bodied red wines. This drive enables visitors to marvel at the monuments left behind from previous ages, including the magical clusters of ancient domed dwellings, or *trulli*, of Alberobello and Locorotondo; the vast pre-Roman necropolis at Manduria; and especially the fanciful Baroque façades of Lecce, Otranto, Martina Franca and Ostuni, some carved in local golden limestone.

[Map of Puglia region showing Bari, Mola di Bari, Monópoli, Alberobello, Locorotondo, Martina Franca, Ostuni, Manduria, Táranto, Matera, Basilicata, and Golfo di Taranto with numbered stops 1–5]

ACTIVITIES

Marvel at the circular domed houses in Alberobello, Italy's magical centre of the *trulli*

Sleep in a domed *trullo* or in a *masseria*, a fortified farm

Taste some Primitivo red wine in Manduria

Take a dip at San Cataldo on the way to Otranto

Look east in Otranto, the crossroads to the Holy Land during the Crusades

Take a thermal bath at Santa Cesarea Terme, a spa resort set on the beautiful Adriatic Coast

Relax on the beach at Capo Santa Maria di Leuca

Stroll up the main boulevard to the beautiful port and beaches of Gallipoli

Below Ancient well in an olive grove in the countryside on the way to Lecce, *see p196*

Above Elaborate obelisk of Sant'Oronzo in Piazza della Libertà, Ostuni, *see p195*

PLAN YOUR DRIVE

Start/finish: Alberobello to Gallipoli.

Number of days: 3, allowing half a day to explore Lecce.

Distance: Approx. 261 km (162 miles).

Road conditions: Well-paved and signposted. Avoid busy periods by travelling during non-peak hours.

When to go: July and August are the busiest months for the coast. Winter is often sunny, but some coastal places are only open from Easter to October.

Opening times: Museums and shops in southern Italy tend to open 9am–7pm or later, closing earlier on Sun and in winter. Many places will also close between 1–4pm for lunch, and will be closed on Mon. Churches are usually open daily from 7am–12:30pm and 4–7pm – avoid visiting during services.

Main market days: Ostuni: antique market, every 2nd Sun; Lecce: antique market, every last Sun; Otranto: Wed am, Via Calamari car park; Gallipoli: Mercato Ittico fish market, daily am.

Shopping: Fans of everything vinous can enjoy excellent Primitivo in Manduria and a variety of good wines in Locorotondo. Visitors should also look out for local olive oil in Martina Franca, and papier mâché and wicker crafts in Otranto.

Major festivals: Alberobello: Aug, Città dei Trulli; Carpino: 7 days early Aug, Folk Festival; Locorotondo: 16 Aug, St Rocco; Martina Franca: 11 Nov, St Martin's Feast Day; Ostuni: 25–27 Aug, St Oronzo; 3 Feb, San Biagio; Manduria: 12 Mar & 2–3 Sep, St Gregory; Lecce: Dec, Fiera dei Pupi (papier mâché); Otranto: Aug, Santi Martiri Idruntini (Feast of Martyrs); Gallipoli: 19 Jan, St Sebastian; 23 Jul, Feast St Cristina.

DAY TRIP OPTIONS

Two possible options – drive the *Strada dei Trulli* through a **fairytale landscape** to see **whitewashed houses**, **splendid churches** and **basilicas** and taste good **wines**. Or see the gold magnificence of Lecce's **carved stone buildings** and **piazzas**, **coastal roads**, **beaches** on two different **seas** and **ancient artifacts** in a **civic museum**. For full details, *see p197*.

VISITING ALBEROBELLO

Parking
There is a car park with meters on Via Indipendenza – uses coins or buy a car parking card from *tabacchi* (no charge for overnight parking 10pm–9am).

Tourist Information
Piazza Ferdinando IV; 080 432 5171; and Pro Loco at *Via Montenero 1; 080 432 2822; www.prolocoalberobello.it.*

WHERE TO STAY

ALBEROBELLO

Trullidea *inexpensive–moderate*
Rent a rustic but cosy *trullo*, with cooking facilities. One even has a pool. *Via Monte San Gabriele 1, 70011; 080 432 3860; www.trullidea.it*

AROUND LOCOROTONDO

Agriturismo Masseria Marzalossa *inexpensive–moderate*
This 17th-century manor house with pool is set in lemon and olive groves. *C da Pezze Vicine 65, Fasano, 72015 (SS172dir to Fasano, right on SP1bis); 080 441 3780; www.marzalossa.com*

Agriturismo Masseria Maccarone *inexpensive–moderate*
Gracious 17th-century manor house with some frescoed ceilings. *C da Carbonelli 29, Fasano, 72015 (SS172dir to Fasano, across SS16); 080 482 9300/9176; www.masseria maccarone.it; closed Jan–Apr*

Agriturismo Masseria San Domenico *expensive*
Luxuriously remodelled 15th-century watchtower with private beach. *Strada Litoranea 379, 72015, Savelletri di Fasano (on coast); 080 482 7769; www.imasseria.com; closed Jan–Mar*

Below The light and elegant Piazza Plebiscito, Martina Franca **Below right** The pretty white walls and narrow streets of Locorotondo

① Alberobello
Bari, Puglia; 70011
The *Strada dei Trulli* (SS172) weaves past Alberobello, Locorotondo and Martina Franca, all dotted with cylindrical houses with cone-shaped roofs (*trulli*). There are over 1,000 *trulli* scattered throughout Puglia, with white walls and slate roofs often daubed with mystical symbols. The Trulli Capital, however, is Alberobello with most examples in its hilly Rione Monti and Aia Piccola neighbourhoods. In town, **Museo del Territorio** (*Piazza 27 Maggio, closed Mon)* is made up from a few *trulli* linked together and shows how they were built and furnished with local crafts. Nearby Piazza Pagano is close to the heart of Aia Piccola. Peek through gaps in the houses to see the *trulli* in Rione Monti. For other views, go down Via Galilei, towards Via Brigata Regina and then into Rione Monti and along Via Monte San Michele.

🚗 *Take the SS172 and head southeast to Locorotondo. Park alongside the road going uphill towards the town.*

② Locorotondo
Bari, Puglia; 70010
On a ridge above the Valle d'Itria, Locorotondo affords an expansive view of farmland dotted with *trulli*. Enter the historic centre along Via Garibaldi or the ancient gate, Porta Nuova. The circular town plan follows the hill contours with whitewashed houses winding round in narrow streets.

Poster advertising pasta, Puglia

Locorotondo's main church, **Chiesa Madre San Giorgio Martire**, built 1790–1825 is dedicated to George, the town's dragon-slaying patron saint. Inside, one of the chapels has 14th-century stone bas-reliefs. The 15th-century nobleman the Prince of Taranto built the church **Santa Maria la Greca** in Romanesque-Gothic style. Below town, stop at the winery, **Cantina Sociale** *(Via Madonna della Catena 99; 080 431 1644)*, to pick up some good wine. They have plenty to choose from, but support the patron saint with the Casale San Giorgio, an IGT (certified local) red made from Negroamaro and Primitivo grapes. They also make champagne-method wines with a southern twist that blends Verdeca, Bianco d'Alessano and Fiano grapes.

🚗 *Drive south on SS172. Near Via Valle d'Itria, on the right, there is a car park outside the city gate by Piazza Roma.*

The Ancient *Trulli* of Puglia
The *trulli* are made from limestone using an ancient dry-stone technique. The oldest examples date from the 16th century, but most were rebuilt from the 18th century onwards with mortar. Roofs are often cone shaped, but can be pyramids or domes, with a stone pinnacle. Clusters of *trulli* have often been formed into larger structures. The interiors have arched niches used for sleeping or cooking and may even have a temporary second floor constructed. Some are used for tourist accommodation.

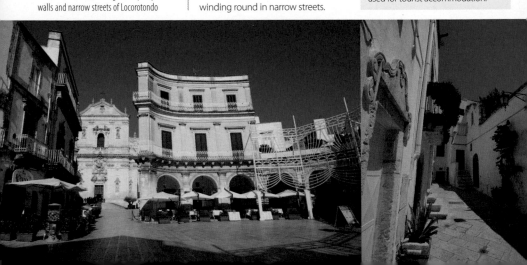

③ Martina Franca
Taranto, Puglia; 74015

A stroll around elegant Martina Franca reveals a fine architectural heritage. Near Piazza Plebiscito, the Baroque façade of 18th-century **Basilica di San Martino** *(Via Masaniello 1; open daily)* shows St Martin sharing his cloak with a beggar. Inside has treasures too, such as the beautiful font and painting of *The Last Supper.* Alongside several Gothic and Baroque churches, **Chiesa del Carmine** (1728–58) shows the lighter touch of architect Francesco Borromini. Next door, the **Villa del Carmine** has good views of the Valle d'Itria. The 1668 **Palazzo Ducale** *(Piazza Roma)*, now a city hall, has frescoes in the Sala dell' Arcadia by 18th-century artist Domenico Carella. End the visit with a drink at Bar Tripoli on Piazza Garibaldi, a historic 19th-century bar, or shop for L'Acropoli di Puglia cold-pressed olive oil made from Coratina olives.

🚗 *Head back to Locorotondo on SS172 then east SP134/SP11 to Cisternino and SP17 to Ostuni. Park on-street outside the city gate.*

④ Ostuni
Brindisi, Puglia; 72017

With ancient close-packed white houses around cool courtyards and winding narrow alleyways, Ostuni is a town worth exploring. At its heart, the elevated **Duomo** *(open daily)* stands out as one of the few buildings that is not whitewashed. Built from 1435–95, the late-Gothic cathedral has a fine rose window, original roof design and a yellow ceramic-tiled dome. In the same square is the 18th-century **Palazzo Vescovile**, with pretty loggia, which incorporates part of a 1198 castle. The **Museo delle Civiltà Preclassiche della Murgia Meridionale** *(Via Cattedrale 15; open daily am)* was an 18th-century monastery but now houses the skeleton of a 25,000-year-old woman among other prehistoric finds. **Chiesa di San Francesco** on Piazza della Libertà is one of Ostuni's oldest churches and has a Baroque monument to St Oronzo outside.

🚗 *Take SP22 southwest towards Céglie Messápica, SP26 to Francavilla Fontana, then the SP54/SP96 to Manduria. Park near the main square, Piazza Garibaldi.*

⑤ Manduria
Taranto, Puglia; 74024

The Messapians (an ancient tribe) colonized the area around Manduria in 1000 BC and thrived until defeated by the Romans in the 3rd century BC. Evidence of their culture is on display in the museum **Oltre Le Mura** *(Via Omodei; closed Mon)*, whose collection includes burial artifacts of jewellery, weapons and vases. The Messapian necropolis at **Parco Archeologico delle Mura Messapiche** *(Via Sant'Antonio; closed Mon)* is also worth a visit. This museum contains some 1,200 tombs dating from the 6th–2nd centuries BC. Step forward a thousand years with a visit to the **Duomo Santissima Trinita** *(Via Marco Gatti 8; open daily)*. Under the Gothic-Renaissance rose window is a tableau of the Trinity, with the Holy Father holding the dead Christ. Inside, mask motifs represent the Four Ages of Man, while the women carved into the 17th-century pulpit represent the Four Ages of the World. Manduria's main highlight, however, is its hefty purple wine, Primitivo, named because the grapes ripen early. Primitivo wines are readily available – local ones to try include Pervini, Sinfarosa, Masseria Pepe and Tenuta Pozzopalo.

🚗 *Take SS7ter east to Lecce. Enter on Via Taranto, go south on Viale dell' Università, left onto Viale Gallipoli and look for parking on the right, or try the on-street parking near the Castello.*

Above left Quiet corner in the whitewashed town of Ostuni **Top right** Unusual *trulli* houses, Alberobello **Above right** Elaborate fanlight, Martina Franca

EAT AND DRINK

ALBEROBELLO

Ristorante Casanova *moderate*
Set under the arches of an ancient olive oil mill, this restaurant serves dishes such as creamy *burratine* cheeses and *fava* bean purée with chicory.
Via Monte San Gabriele 16, 70011; 080 432 3292; www.casanovailristorante. it

MARTINA FRANCA

Il Ritrovo degli Amici
moderate–expensive
Delicious traditional cuisine served in elegant surroundings.
Corso Messapia 8, 74015; 080 483 9249; www.ilritrovodegliamici.it

OSTUNI

Osteria del Tempo Perso *moderate*
Traditional Pugliese cuisine: *orecchiette* and other dishes make good use of fresh vegetables, seafood and meat.
Via F Tanzarella 47, 72017; 0831 304 819; www.osteriadeltempoperso.com; closed Mon

MANDURIA

Osteria dei Mercanti *moderate*
Excellent traditional cuisine, friendly atmosphere, and good Primitivo wine by the carafe in Manduria's historic centre. Serves pizza in the evening.
Via S G Laciata 7, 74024; 099 971 3673; closed Mon

Eat and Drink: inexpensive, under €25; moderate, €25–€45; expensive, over €45

Right Remains of Roman amphitheatre in Lecce's Piazza Sant'Oronzo

VISITING LECCE

Parking
On-street parking near the Castello.

Tourist Information
APT Lecce *Via Monte San Michele 20; 0832 314 117; www.pugliaturismo.com* and **IAT Lecce** *Via V Emanuele 24; 0832 248 092; www.viaggiareinpuglia.it.*

WHERE TO STAY

LECCE

Patria Palace Hotel *moderate*
Baroque palazzo facing Santa Croce with spa and roof garden. Restaurant Atenze serves traditional cuisine. *Piazzetta Riccardi 13, 73100; 0832 245 111; www.patriapalacelecce.com*

OTRANTO

Hotel Palazzo Papaleo *moderate–expensive*
Beautifully furnished rooms, excellent service and a spa make this hotel a sumptuous retreat in the town centre. *Via Rondachi 1, 73028; 0836 802 108; www.hotelpalazzopapaleo.com*

GALLIPOLI

Hotel Palazzo del Corso *expensive*
Luxurious hotel on the town's main street – fine textiles and antiques, and a roof garden with views of the harbour. *Corso Roma 145, 73014; 0833 264 040; www.hotelpalazzodelcorso.it*

⑥ Lecce
Lecce, Puglia; 73100

The Baroque of Lecce is the most exuberant in Italy, the city's soft, golden sandstone carved into the flights of fancy of its 17th-century architects. The vast Piazza Duomo is stunning but it is the detailed façades of churches such as Santa Croce that create the over-the-top splendour. The interiors are worth exploring, too, but a walk through town, admiring the exteriors, is a must.

A two-hour walking tour

From the car park at the Castello, walk along Viale Francesco Lo Re to start at the **Museo Provinciale Sigismondo Castromediano** ① *(Viale Gallipoli 28; 0832 307 415; open daily, closed Sat–Sun pm)*. The museum has objects dating from the Bronze Age and an excellent collection of Attic vases. North on Viale Francesco Lo Re, the ancient Porta San Biagio leads to the 1539-49 **Castello** ②, commissioned by Charles V and built over an earlier Norman castle. West of the castle, **Piazza Sant'Oronzo** ③ is home to a bronze statue of patron St Oronzo on one of the Roman-era Appian Way's final mile markers. It was erected in the 1600s as thanks for deliverance from the plague. Next to the column, the elliptical Roman amphitheatre, dating to Emperor Hadrian's era, is set below street level. Walk north of the amphitheatre between Palazzo Carafa and head west on Via Vittorio Emanuele II, past an ornate church dedicated to St Irene. Stop to admire the **Piazza del Duomo** ④ and the grand cathedral *(open daily)*, Bishop's Palace, and Seminary. Built around 1100, the Duomo's present look is 17th-century – designed by Giuseppe Zimbalo, who also designed the five-storey bell tower. Continue on Via Emanuele, which becomes Via G Libertini, with the Baroque churches of **Santa Teresa** ⑤, the **Chiesa del Rosario** (Holy Rosary) ⑥ and **Sant'Anna** ⑦ built in the 1600s and 1700s. Head back to Piazza Sant' Oronzo, pass the north side of the Municipio and continue to **Basilica di Santa Croce** ⑧, perhaps Lecce's most famous Baroque building. Cross over to the **Giardini Pubblici** ⑨, turn right on Viale Francesco d'Assisi to return to the car park. On the way to Otranto, stop for a swim at the beach of San Cataldo. 🚗 *From the car park take the SP364 to San Cataldo, then the SP366 to Otranto. The car park is below Otranto's Castello.*

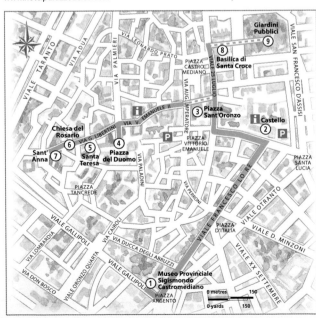

⑦ Otranto

Lecce, Puglia; 73028

Enter the historic centre through the town gate Porta Terra. The 153/ **Castello Aragonese** *(open daily Jul–Aug)* is a pentagonal castle with cylindrical towers. The Romanesque **Annunziata Cathedral** *(open daily)* was built in 1088 – do not miss the fanciful 12th-century floor mosaics, nor the remains of the 800 martyrs of the 1480 invasion by the Turks. **Museo Diocesano** *(Piazza Basilica 1; closed Mon)* displays religious sculpture carved in Lecce stone, some dating to the 15th–16th centuries. In town, look out for papier-mâché, stone or wicker crafts, as well as local wines and olive oil. The drive to Capo passes the spa at **Santa Cesarea Terme** *(www.termesantacesarea.it)* – stop off for a wine-and-honey facial.

🚗 *From the car park head south on SP358 to Leuca. Look for signs for Faro – follow the SS275. Park northeast of the lighthouse on Via Panoramica or on the SS275.*

⑧ Capo Santa Maria di Leuca

Lecce, Puglia; 73040

Where the "earth ends", Capo Santa Maria di Leuca is surrounded by sheer windswept cliffs and sandy beaches. West of the lighthouse is a Roman column and monumental staircase.

To the northeast is a sanctuary to Santa Maria de Finibus Terrae, probably built over an ancient Roman temple of Minerva. The nearby village of Marina di Leuca makes for a nice stroll.

🚗 *Head north on SS274 to Gallipoli. Park on the side streets of Corso Roma.*

⑨ Gallipoli

Lecce, Puglia; 73014

A good spot to begin exploring the place the Greeks called *Kallipolis* (Beautiful City), is on **Corso Roma** at the port where it becomes a bridge linking to the old town. Nearby is a Greco-Roman fountain (3rd century BC) and the 17th-century **Chiesa del Canneto** built over ruins of a Templar church. Across the bridge the **Castello Angioino** has a square plan with four towers. The 17th-century **Cattedrale di Sant'Agata** *(open daily)* is splendid but no longer has its saint's relic, Agatha's breast. Smaller Baroque churches are hidden away in the old city centre – an ideal spot for lunch or a moonlit dinner overlooking the sea. **Museo Civico** *(Via Antonietta De Pace 118; 0833 264 224; www.museocivicogallipoli. it; closed Mon)* has artifacts from Messapian, Roman and medieval ages. Enjoy the aquamarine sea at one of the town's sandy beaches. Lungomare Lido San Giovanni has a lovely pine forest across the road from the beach.

Above left Pretty beach at San Cataldo, near Lecce **Above right** Bauxite lake on the way to the coast, reflecting the red hues of the mineral, Otranto

EAT AND DRINK

LECCE

Cucina Casereccia Le Zie *moderate*
Serves traditional Pugliese pasta, beans, vegetables and meat dishes. *Viale Colonnello Costadura 19, 73100; 0832 245 178; www.lezie.it; closed Sun eve & Mon*

Alle Due Corti *moderate*
No-frills decor and a menu in dialect means authentic dishes like crispy pasta or casseroles with rice and mussels. *Corte dei Giugni 1, 73100; 0832 242 223; www.alleduecorti.com; closed Tue*

OTRANTO

Ristorante Peccato di Vino *moderate*
Delicious updates on Pugliese cuisine (potatoes layered with mussels and rice) and a good wine selection. *Via Rondachi 7/9, 73028; 0836 801 488; www.peccatodivino.com; closed Tue*

GALLIPOLI

Ristorante Roof Garden *moderate*
An unpretentious eatery serving simple Italian fare and great pizzas. *Corso Roma 62, 73014; 0833 263 303*

Il Bastione *moderate–expensive*
Romantic harbour setting and a really superb cuisine that is creative and traditional. *Riviera Nazario Sauro 28, 73014; 0833 263 836; www.ristorante ilbastionegallipoli.com*

DAY TRIP OPTIONS

This drive can be broken into two day trips – one inland for those based in Alberobello, and one coastal for those staying in Lecce.

Follow the Strada dei *Trulli*
Based at Alberobello ❶, marvel at the extraordinary clusters of domed *trulli* and discover their history in the Museo

del Territorio. Then head off to Locorotondo ❷, admiring the *trulli* dotted landscape on the way. In town, see the cathedral dedicated to St George. Last stop, Martina Franca ❸ and its fantastic architectural heritage, especially the Baroque basilica of the town's patron saint, Martin.

Simply take the SS172 all the way.

Coast to Coast
Start at Lecce ❻, a golden Baroque fantasy before hitting the coast at San Cataldo for a dip in the Adriatic; head down to historic Otranto ❼, then west across the heel to Gallipoli ❾ for a tour and swim in the Ionian Sea.

Take SP364 then SP366 to Otranto, then SS16 to Maglie then SP361 to Gallipoli.

Eat and Drink: inexpensive, under €25; moderate, €25–€45; expensive, over €45

The Gargano Promontory

Castel del Monte to Lésina

Highlights

- **Medieval Trani**
  Wander this historic town, once the haunt of pilgrims and Knights Templar

- **Margherita di Savoia**
  Get a taste of this salt town – in the museum, in a spa and on your food

- **The Archangel Michael**
  Descend to the grotto where he appeared – it became one of the most important pilgrim sites in the world

- **Péschici**
  Explore the narrow streets of this coastal town founded by the Slavs

- **Lido del Sole**
  Set yourself free in this magical place where land and sea are barely distinct

The town and castle of Péschici built into the cliffs above the Adriatic Sea

The Gargano Promontory

The "spur" of Italy's "boot", the Gargano Promontory (Promontorio del Gargano) has a wealth of attractions. This drive begins inland, south of the Gargano at Castel del Monte, with sweeping views and the mystery of Frederick II's octagonal castle. It then heads to the coast and the medieval town of Trani, where pilgrims flocked on their way to the Holy Land, along with their protectors, the Knights Templar. The route then takes visitors north to Barletta, the site of Italy's most famous duel, and to the salty town of Margherita di Savoia before eventually curving around the rugged promontory coast with its pretty towns, Vieste and Péschici, and the shady Foresta Umbra further inland. The drive ends along the scenic road between Lido del Sole and Lésina.

Above Whitewashed houses carved of rock are built on top of each other, Péschici, *see p205*

ACTIVITIES

Explore the castle built by Frederick II at Castel del Monte

Stroll through Trani's luminous streets to the cathedral at the edge of the sea and dine at the port

Soak in thermal waters at Margherita di Savoia

Descend to the grotto of Archangel Michael at Monte Sant'Angelo

Take a boat trip to the Tremiti Islands from Vieste

Hike through woods and see the deer in the Foresta Umbra

Bike or drive across flat Lido del Sole and take a dip in the sea

Above Stretch of sandy coastline at Péschici, *see p.205*

PLAN YOUR DRIVE

Start/finish: Castel del Monte to Lésina.

Number of days: 3, plus optional 1-day excursion to the Tremiti Islands.

Distance: Approx. 257 km (160 miles).

Road conditions: Well paved, though not always signposted. Country roads are narrow, so be sure to stay to the right to avoid encounters around bends. Watch out for slow moving tractors.

When to go: August is the most crowded time. Moderate winters make for pleasant touring of hill towns.

Opening times: Museums open in the morning and again in the afternoon – and many close on Mondays. Shops typically open 9am–1pm, then reopen from 3pm to 7 or 8pm. Many shops are closed on Monday mornings and Saturday afternoons. Churches close noon to 4pm or later, and discourage visits during Mass.

Main market days: Trani: Tue; Barletta: Sat; Monte Sant'Angelo: Sat; Vieste: Mon, every two weeks; Péschici: 1st & 3rd Sat of month; Lésina: 1st & 3rd Mon of month.

Shopping: Look out for Castel del Monte DOC wines in Corato (5 km/ 3 miles from Castel del Monte).

Major festivals: Barletta: Disfida (Duel), Feb; Trani: Speedboat Championship, Jul; Vieste: St George's Festival, Apr; Santa Maria di Merino Feast Day, May; Falò di Sant'Antonio, Jun; Péschici: St Elia Profeta Feast Day, Jul; Jazz Festival, Aug.

DAY TRIP OPTIONS

Explore the area as a tour or also as a series of day trips. **Families** with young children will enjoy **feeding deer** at their Foresta Umbra compound or **swimming** along the coast at Vieste. **History enthusiasts** will enjoy a visit to Castel del Monte, and the Museo Civico e Pinacoteca at Barletta, while **wine-lovers** will want to sample Castel del Monte DOC **wines** at an *enoteca*. For those who want to **relax**, Terme di Margherita di Savoia is ideal. For full details, *see p205*.

VISITING CASTEL DEL MONTE

From Andria take the SS170d to Castel del Monte. Park in the castle's assigned car park, then transfer by shuttle bus 10am–1:30pm and 2:30–7pm.

WHERE TO STAY

TRANI

Hotel Regia *moderate–expensive*
Intimate hotel at the edge of the water near Trani's cathedral. It also has an excellent restaurant, and some of the tables have a view of the port. Guest rooms overlook the port, sea or cathedral. *Piazza Duomo 2, 70059; 0883 584 444; www.hotelregia.it*

Hotel San Paolo al Convento *expensive*
This 15th-century former convent at Trani's port is now a comfortable hotel. *Via Statuti Marittimi 111, 70059; 0883 482 949; www.sanpaolo alconvento.it*

MONTE SANT'ANGELO

Palace Hotel San Michele *moderate*
A former convent converted into a hotel set in tranquil gardens. Facilities include a swimming pool and fitness centre. *Via Madonna degli Angeli, 71037; 088 456 5653; www.sanmichelepalace.it*

Below left Elaborate town gate, Barletta **Below centre** The luminous façade of Cattedrale San Nicola Pellegrino, Trani **Below right** Imposing exterior of the 13th-century octagonal Castel del Monte

① Castel del Monte
Foggia, Puglia; 70031
The Holy Roman Emperor Frederick II constructed the 13th-century octagonal fortress at Castel del Monte *(closed 1 Jan, 25 Dec)* out of huge blocks of limestone rich in quartz. A UNESCO World Heritage Site, the eight-towered building intrigues tourists and scholars alike for its mathematical forms and eclectic mix of architectural styles. Fragments of decorative elements hint at the past richness of bas-reliefs, frescoes and mosaics. Be sure to try the local Castel del Monte DOC wine made in Corato, 5 km (3 miles) northeast. Look for the *trulli (see p194)* that dot the fields and olive groves on the road to Barletta.

Bronze detail, Cattedrale, Trani

🚗 *Take the SS170d to Andria then head to Trani on the SP130. Look for "centro" signs and head for the Marina. Park at Piazza Manfredi near the castle.*

② Trani
Bari, Puglia; 70059
A thousand years ago, Trani's port bustled with pilgrims and Crusaders on their way to the Holy Land. Today the harbour is still the main point of interest. At the water's edge stands the magnificent 11th-century **Cattedrale San Nicola Pellegrino** *(Piazza Duomo; open daily)* dedicated to the pilgrims' saint. Nearby, Frederick II's **Castello Svevo** *(Piazza Manfredi; open daily)* was periodically modified to keep up with changing weapons technology. Tour the courtyards and salons to see remains of medieval frescoes. The **Museo Diocesano** *(Piazza Duomo; open*

am; also pm in summer) reveals Trani's religious heritage with finds from the 4th century BC to a 14th-century carved ivory altar. Walk down medieval Via Ognissanti to **Chiesa di Ognissanti** *(open rarely)*, a 12th-century Templar church built as part of a hospital. Note the sculpture of the Annunciation in the lunette above the door. Further along the street, visit the grand 1456 late-Gothic **Palazzo Caccetta** *(open daily)*. The public gardens at **Villa Comunale** *(Piazza Plebiscito; open daily, 9am– 8pm)* which face the sea are worthy of a visit, as is the **Mercato Ittico** (fish market) at Piazza Longobardi.
For the more adventurous, visitors can kayak, sailboat, or scuba dive at **Lega Navale Italiana** *(Molo San Antonio; 0883 448 32)*. The Sant'Antonio dock is also a good place to find a boat for a local excursion along the coast.
An ideal spot to have a coffee is at one of the cafés at the port, or find a bar and sip the sweet local wine, Moscato di Trani DOC.

🚗 *Take SS16 Adriatica, the coastal road, north. Park on the street near the castle or in Piazza della Disfida.*

③ Barletta
Bari, Puglia; 70051
Just outside the town gate by the sea, Emperor Frederick II's castle stands sentry. Built in 1233 over a Norman fortress, the castle now hosts the **Museo Civico e Pinacoteca** *(Piazza Castello; closed Mon)*, displaying archaeological artifacts, ceramics, stone tablets with medieval inscriptions and a bust of Frederick II.

Santa Maria Maggiore (*Via Duomo 38; open daily*), Barletta's cathedral, dates from the 6h century, and was built over an even older Roman temple. Here too are traces of the Knights Templar. **Basilica del Santo Sepolcro** (*Via Sant'Antonio*) offered prayer and hospitality to Crusaders. Outside stands the Colossus of Heraclius, an early medieval bronze statue of an emperor in battledress.

Cantina della Disfida (*closed Mon*) was probably the site of the challenge for the famous duel in 1503. Thirteen pairs of French and Italian knights fought each other after insults were thrown – the Italians won. The duel is re-enacted every February.

A few doors away in **Palazzo della Marra** (*Via Cialdini*) climb upstairs to a loggia with sea views and on to **Pinacoteca Giuseppe de Nittis** (*closed Mon pm*), a museum dedicated to the local Impressionist artist (1846–84).

🚗 *Take the SS16 north, then the SS159.*

④ Margherita di Savoia
Foggia, Puglia; 71044

Margherita is all about salt. The town developed as a result of the salt flats that stretch along the coast north of Barletta – the salt works date as far back as the 3rd century BC. Visitors should enjoy the health benefits of the mineral salts on the beach at the **Lido Terme** near Lungomare Colombo. Or take the spa waters at **Terme di Margherita di Savoia** (*Piazza Libertà 1; Apr–early Dec, closed Sat pm & Sun*).

For some culture, visit the **Pinacoteca Comunale Francesco Galante Civera** (*Corso Vittorio Emanuele; open summer, daily; winter, Mon–Fri am*) in a fortified 17th-century manor. This museum is dedicated to the local early-1900s artist, Civera, known for his pictures of fishermen, and life around the salt flats.

The story of salt continues at the **Museo Storico della Salina di Margherita di Savoia** (*Corso Vittorio Emanuele 99; www.museosalina.it; open summer, daily; winter, Mon–Fri am*). The salt marshes are also great for watching ducks, waders and other birds, especially from August to March.

🚗 *SP141/SS159 then SS89 north. After Manfredonia, take the SS272 left. Park at Zona Castello, Viale Madonnina, Via Carlo d'Angiò and Piazza Ciro Angelillis.*

⑤ Monte Sant'Angelo
Gargano, Foggia; 71037

Perched on a rocky spur, the town of Monte Sant'Angelo commands great views over the surrounding Foresta Umbra. It was put on the pilgrim map after Archangel Michael was said to have appeared to a grotto here in AD 493. The **Sanctuario di San Michele** (*Via Reale Basilic; open daily*) has a shrine to St Michael – its bronze doors were cast in Constantinople in 1076. The building has a genuine cave chapel and other shrines including a 16th-century statue of Michael in Carrara marble and Frederick II's 1228 Silver Cross, said to contain a piece of the True Cross. Near the grotto stands the irregularly shaped **Castello Normanno Svevo Aragonese** (*open daily*) and the large pentagonal **Torre dei Giganti**.

🚗 *Take the SS89dirb to the coastal road SP53, then north to Vieste. Follow signs to "centro". Park off Viale XXIV Maggio at Via Jenner/Via Enrico Fermi.*

Above Monte Sant'Angelo, gracefully tracing the curve of the mountainside

EAT AND DRINK

AROUND CASTEL DEL MONTE
La Bottega dell'Allegria *moderate*
Corato is the heart of Castel del Monte DOC winemaking. Winemakers come to this eatery for the food and wine. *Via Imbriani Matteo Renato 49, Corato, 70033 (take the SS170dir south 100 m/ 100 yards, turn left onto SP234 and left again after 12 km/7 miles onto SP238); 080 872 2873; closed Mon*

La Locanda di Beatrice *moderate*
A popular restaurant for dining on traditional Pugliese dishes with good local wines. *Strada Provinciale 231, Corato, 70033 (follow directions to Corato above); 080 872 4122; www.locandadibeatrice.it; closed Mon*

TRANI
Osteria Corteinfiore *moderate*
Traditional, well-prepared food makes this a favourite of local winemakers. *Via Ognissanti 18, 70059; 0883 508 402; www.corteinfiore.it; closed Mon, 2 wks Jan*

Below Trani's pretty harbour at dusk with the Cattedrale San Nicola Pellegrino in the background

Eat and Drink: inexpensive, under €25; moderate €25–€45; expensive, over €45

Above A view across Vieste's rooftops towards the sea Below One of the sandy beaches at Vieste, along the Gargano Promontory

VISITING VIESTE

Parking
There is a car park at the corner of Via Jenner and Via Enrico Fermi.

Tourist Information
There is an office in *Piazza Kennedy, 71019; 0884 708 806 (Oct–May closed Sun); www.viaggiareinpuglia.it.*

WHERE TO STAY

VIESTE

Village Camping Spiaggia Lunga *inexpensive–moderate*
Campsite with 3-room bungalows on a huge sandy beach. Watersport options. *Litoranea Vieste-Péschici km 7, 71019; 0884 706 171; www.spiaggialunga.it; closed winter (open from Apr)*

FORESTA UMBRA

Hotel de Ginestre *moderate*
A spa, pool, and modern comforts near the forest entrance. *Località Mandrione (3km off the SP52bis); 0884 707 663; www.hotelginestre.it*

PESCHICI

Villa Passiaturo *inexpensive*
Great breakfasts and sea views. Rooms are simply furnished in a modern style. *Via G Libetta 30, 71010; 0884 963 040; www.villapassiaturo.it; closed Dec–Apr*

⑥ Vieste
Foggia, Puglia; 71019
One of Italy's easternmost towns, Vieste is an excellent base for exploring the Gargano Promontory. The medieval clifftop town is good for a pleasant stroll, while down below visitors can relax on the beach and enjoy a full array of water sports. Vieste is also handy for the Tremiti Islands *(see p179)*, with their sandy beaches and pretty coves.

A two-hour walking tour
Begin the walk from the car park at Via Jenner and Via Enrico Fermi. Head south towards Lungomare Enrico Mattei and turn left onto Viale Federico II di Svevia. Pass by the angular 13th-century **Castello di Vieste** ① *(closed)*. Turn right onto Piazza Castello for a sweeping vista, taking in the 26 m (85 ft) rock in the sea (said to be a fisherman petrified by grief on losing his wife) and the sandy beach Spiaggia della Scialara di Castello. On the far side of Piazza Castello, a flight of steps leads to Piazza Duomo and the 11th-century **Cattedrale dell'Assunta** ② *(open daily)*. The statue Madonna of Merino is of the city's patron saint and the central nave has a trompe l'oeil effect.

On exiting the cathedral, turn left on Via Duomo. The **Museo Civico** ③ *(Via Celestino V 78; closed Sun)* displays archaeological finds including ceramics, arrowheads, and inscriptions from the 4th–1st centuries BC. Near the cathedral, look for Chianca Amara, a stone jutting out of a wall near some steps that was the site of beheadings during a siege in 1554. Carry on down Via Duomo. On the left the longer flight of steps leads to Via Seggio becoming Via Carlo Matrolla and Via

Pola. Bear right slightly on Via San Francesco leading to the promontory **Punta di San Francesco** ④. The 1438 church and convent complex rises up as if carved out of the rock. Continue to the right by the park next to the sea. Return along Via Pola to the grand Piazza Vittorio Emanuele II. Before reaching the piazza, on the left is a museum dedicated to the mollusc. **Museo Malacologico** ⑤ *(Via Pola 8; open Jun–Sep, daily)* offers 11,500 specimens from "every sea on earth". Cross to Piazzale Kennedy where the tourist information office is located and head along Viale Italia for the **Giardini Pubblici di Marina Piccola** ⑥ with views of a small island, Scoglio di Santa Eufemia, once dedicated to the goddess Venus Sosandra. To carry on down to the **Porto Turistico Aurora** ⑦, continue north. Otherwise return to the car park by heading south on Corso Tripoli, then take Via Vittorio Veneto. Conclude the visit to Vieste with an afternoon at one of its 17 beaches.

🚗 *From the car park head out of town, then onto the SP52. Then take the SP52bis and follow signs for Foresta Umbra. Park near the Corpo Forestale Visitor Centre or Bar Forest.*

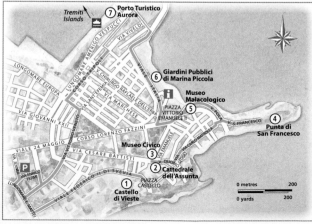

Visiting Isole Tremiti

Pristine water and an unspoiled setting draw scuba divers, swimmers and picnickers on day trips. There are four islands but **San Nicola** and **San Domino** are the ones to visit. San Nicola was the administrative centre and has a medieval abbey and fort. San Domino has woods, grottoes and more visitor facilities. Two ferries leave from the main jetty at **Vieste**. In summer, there are also boats going to the islands from other smaller coastal towns. Boats leave Vieste at 9:10am and leave Tremiti at 5:10pm to return to Vieste. Book at the jetty.

7 Foresta Umbra
Parco Nazionale del Gargano; 71018
Foresta Umbra (Shady Forest) offers visitors an ideal respite from the sun under arcades of oak, larch, maple, and ash trees. From the **Corpo Forestale Visitor Centre** there are hiking trails into the woods – yellow signs on trees or rocks mark the paths. The forest hosts a variety of wildlife including deer, a rare wild cat (*felix silvestris*), tortoises, snakes and plenty of birds such as woodpeckers, owls and even an eagle or two. With more than one third of Italy's flora, the wood is a botanist's dream.
📷 *From the Visitor Centre take SP144 north past Vico del Gargano to the coastal SS89, then head east. Follow signs for "centro" and park on-street.*

8 Péschici
Foggia, Puglia; 71010
Perched on a rocky cliff by the sea, Péschici was founded by Slavs around AD 970. Built onto the rocks above the coast, the 10th-century **Castello di Péschici** (*Piazza Castello; open daily*) has rooms full of medieval and Renaissance torture devices. In town, woodcarver **Nicola Priaci** (*located near the terrace by Torre Calalunga*) makes

bowls and other objects carved from a variety of woods. On the coastal spur east of town, dine al fresco next to a *trabocco (see p178)*. Further east, watchtowers dot the coast such as **Torre Calalunga** on the highest point between Cala Lunga and Baia di Turco.
📷 *Return to SS89 west to Lido del Sole then the SP41 and SP40 to Lésina.*

9 Lido del Sole to Lésina
Lésina, Puglia; 71010
The sparsely inhabited coastal area, unspoiled beaches and nature attract surprisingly few visitors to **Lido del Sole**. The drive from Lido del Sole to Lésina crosses a flat, sandy narrow strip of land with fragrant pine forests barely separating the Adriatic Sea from **Lago di Varano**. Swimmers opt for the lovely long deserted stretches of beach on the opposite side of the road with several camp sites. Back on the mainland at **Torre Mileto** the next strip of land that separates the sea from **Lago di Lésina** is so thin it is not open to car traffic. The road skirts to the south of the lake. Bird-watching is best in winter when the bird population is greater. Lésina is the main town next to the lake and still retains some of its medieval core.

Above left The rocky coastline near Péschici, Gargano Promontory **Above right** Wooden getty heading out to Lago di Lésina

EAT AND DRINK

VIESTE

Il Desiderio Rosticceria *inexpensive*
Good local food is served at this friendly carry-out with outside tables.
Via Cesare Battisti 143, 71019

Locanda al Dragone *moderate*
Set in a natural grotto in Vieste's historic centre. The speciality is fish.
Via Duomo 8, 71019; 0884 701 212 ; www.aldragone.it; closed Nov–Mar, Tues Apr–May

AROUND FORESTA UMBRA

Options in Vico del Gargano
Vico is a modest town at the northern park entrance, close to Péschici. Il **Trappeto Cantina Ristorante Pizzeria** (*Via Casale 168, 71018; 347 915 3363; www.cantinailtrappeto.it*) has a warm, rustic setting in a former olive oil mill. **La Corte Federiciana Ristorante** (*Piazza Castello, 71018*) is in Frederick II's castle in the town centre.

PESCHICI

Trabucco Da Mimí Ristorante *inexpensive*
Romantic atmosphere by the sea. Friendly waiters serve excellent seafood.
Località Punta San Nicola, 71010; 0884 962 556; www.altrabucco.it

DAY TRIP OPTIONS
The first of these day trips is within easy access of Péschici and the second trip is ideal for those based in Trani.

Forest and beaches
Spend the morning at the Foresta Umbra 7 and feed the deer in their compound (marked "*daini*"). Enjoy a

picnic lunch before heading to Vieste 6 for an afternoon on the beach.

From Péschici take the SS89 and the SP144 for the Foresta Umbra. Take the SP52bis and SP52 for Vieste.

History, wine and a spa
Begin by exploring Castel del Monte 1, then head to a winery at Corato to

sample Castel del Monte DOC wines. Spend the afternoon visiting Barletta's Museo Civico e Pinacoteca 6 and end the day by taking the spa waters at Terme di Margherita di Savoia 4.

From Trani take the SP130 and SS170d for Castel del Monte. Follow the SP234 and SP238 for Corato. Barletta is off the SS16 and Margherita di Savoia is off the SS159.

Eat and Drink: inexpensive, under €25; moderate €25–€45; expensive, over €45

Echoes of Greece

Vibo Valentia to Reggio di Calabria

Highlights

- **Tropea's green and blue sea**
  Swim in clear waters that sparkle in gemlike hues of jade, aquamarine, turquoise and sapphire

- **La Costa Viola**
  Marvel at the violet-coloured light and water seen from the terraces in Nicotera as Stromboli lights up

- **Scilla**
  Sample the delicious local seafood and take a fishing trip along the coast

- **The Greek bronzes of Riace**
  Admire some of the most splendid bronze sculptures of ancient Greece in Reggio's archaeological museum

Tropea's clifftop houses overlooking its white sandy beach and clear seas

Echoes of Greece

The Romans called southern Italy and Sicily "Magna Graecia", or Greater Greece because of the many Greek colonies there. Even today there are tiny villages in remote areas where an ancient Greek language is still alive. The toe of Italy's "boot" is one of its most rugged and least explored regions. On the beautiful coast, Tropea attracts the jet set with its white sandy beaches, while further south, Nicotera and the Costa Viola (Violet Coast) offer purple hues and pristine water in scenic coves off the beaten path. Scuba divers will delight in Scilla, where two seas meet in the Strait of Messina – resulting in a rich marine life, while history buffs will appreciate the astonishing Greek statues found in Riace, now in Reggio.

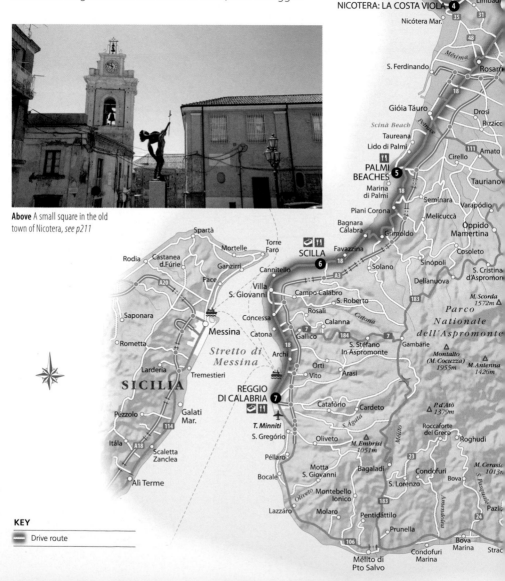

Above A small square in the old town of Nicotera, see p211

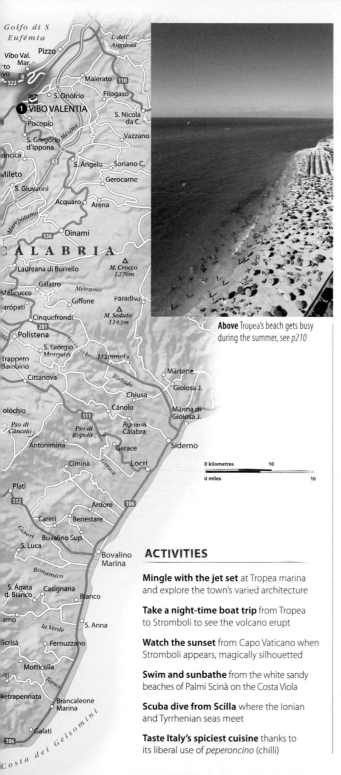

Above Tropea's beach gets busy during the summer, see p210

PLAN YOUR DRIVE

Start/finish: Vibo Valentia to Reggio di Calabria.

Number of days: 3–4 with a day exploring Tropea.

Distance: Approx. 129 km (80 miles).

Road conditions: Generally well-paved and signposted, although some coastal roads are winding and narrow. Avoid busy periods by travelling during non-peak hours.

When to go: July and August are the busiest months along the coast. Winter is often sunny, but some coastal places are only open from Easter to October.

Opening times: Museums and shops in southern Italy tend to open 9am–7pm or later, closing earlier on Sun and in winter. Many places will also close between 1–4pm for lunch, and are closed on Mon. Churches are usually open daily from 7am–12:30pm and 4–7pm – avoid visiting during services.

Main market days. Vibo Valentia: Sat; **Vibo Valentia Marina:** Mon; Tropea: Sat; Nicotera: Sun.

Major festivals: Regional: Estate Vibonese, throughout the province of Vibo Valentia, Aug; **Tropea:** Sagra del Cammello (camel festival), May; Ricadi: Sagra della Cipolla Rossa (red onion festival), Aug; **Palmi:** Festa della Madonna dell'Alto Mare, last Sun in Jul; Madonna of the Holy Letter Procession, last Sun in Aug; San Rocco Feast Day, Aug; **Reggio:** Festa della Madonna della Consolazione, Sep.

ACTIVITIES

Mingle with the jet set at Tropea marina and explore the town's varied architecture

Take a night-time boat trip from Tropea to Stromboli to see the volcano erupt

Watch the sunset from Capo Vaticano when Stromboli appears, magically silhouetted

Swim and sunbathe from the white sandy beaches of Palmi Scinà on the Costa Viola

Scuba dive from Scilla where the Ionian and Tyrrhenian seas meet

Taste Italy's spiciest cuisine thanks to its liberal use of *peperoncino* (chilli)

DAY TRIP OPTIONS

From Tropea enjoy a **swim** and **tasty seafood** before heading to Capo Vaticano for a **hike** and **views** of Stromboli volcano. From Scilla enjoy the quiet **sandy stretches** of Palmi Scinà **beach** and then see the **riches of the sea** by **boat** or by **scuba dive**. At Reggio admire the **ancient Greek bronze statues**. For full details, see p213.

VISITING TROPEA

Parking
Park on-street or follow signs to car parks on Via Campo, off Lungomare Marina del Covento and west of Mare Piccolo. There is also off-peak parking in Piazza Vittorio Veneto near the centre.

Tourist Information
The tourist information office can help with booking a boat trip to the Aeolian islands *(see pp222–3)*, a day trip around Stromboli or just a cruise to see the volcano at night. They should also be able to advise on where to book a diving trip.
Piazza Ercole, 89861; 0963 61475; www.prolocotropea.eu

WHERE TO STAY

VIBO VALENTIA

Hotel Risorgimento *inexpensive*
Modern, clean hotel within easy walking distance of the castello.
Largo Diano 2, 90000; 0963 41125; www.hotelresidencerisorgimento.it

TROPEA

B&B De Medici *inexpensive–moderate*
Modern, light-filled rooms are clean and simply furnished with wrought iron beds and colourful bedspreads.
Via Dardano 8, 89861; 0963 613 61; www.bbdemedici.com

B&B Donna Ciccina *moderate*
In the centre of town, some of the spacious rooms have wood beam ceilings and terrace views.
Via Pelliccia 9, 89861; 0963 62180; www.donnaciccina.com

❶ Vibo Valentia
Vibo Valentia, Calabria; 89900

Vibo Valentia is the provincial capital of the province (of the same name). Its inland location makes it quieter than the coastal towns. According to legend, this is where the god of the Underworld, Hades, snatched Persephone as she gathered flowers and took her to his underground kingdom. The remains of 6th-century temple foundations dedicated to Persephone have been identified at Vibo Valentia (known as Hipponion at the time). Objects related to her cult are on display in the **Castello Normanno Svevo** *(open daily)* built by the Count of Sicily, Ruggero the Norman, around 1070 and modified from the 12th–18th centuries. The castle's **Museo Archeologico** *(closed Mon)* also displays votive offerings found locally. There are panoramic views from the battlements. The nearby Roman port of Vibo Valentia Marina is now mostly used by cargo ships and boats to the Aeolian Islands *(see pp222–3)*. By the port stand the ruins of the 1442 **Castello di Bivona**, built to protect against pirates.

🚗 *Take the SS18 northeast, then turn left onto the SS182 and left onto the SS522 (SP6) to Tropea, turning right onto the SP17.*

❷ Tropea
Vibo Valentia, Calabria; 89861

Tropea rises from steep cliffs along the stunning Briatico coastline serrated with small inlets and underwater reefs. Famous for its red onions, the town nevertheless attracts the chic and the glamorous with the natural beauty of intense aquamarine sea and white sandy beaches. The small marina has boats for excursions to volcanic Stromboli and other romantic islands, and the Aspromonte Mountains form a picturesque backdrop to the east. Up on the cliffs, Tropea's town architecture reveals medieval Norman and Arab touches as well as a more austere Baroque style than that of Rome or Naples.

A one-hour walking tour

If parked at Piazza Vittorio Veneto, walk north to **Corso Vittorio Emanuele** ①, Tropea's major promenade street, lined with shops and coffee bars. Turn left onto Via Caivano, then left again to **Largo Rota** ②, a quiet piazza with residential buildings and a good restaurant, Taverna L'Antica Grotta *(see right)*. Back on Corso Emanuele, take a right at Via Roma to reach **Largo Duomo** ③ *(open daily)*, Tropea's Norman-style cathedral built in about 1100 with a Swabian portico added in the 13th-century. Three palazzos in the square have interesting architectural details: D'Quino has balconies in *petto d'oca* (goose breast) style and Barone and Zinnato have granite portals. Back to Corso Vittorio Emanuele and the tourist information office *(see left)* at **Piazza Ercole** ④, housed in a palace that was once the ancient seat of a noble family. Opposite the tourist office is a *gelateria*, worthy of a visit. During the day, the town centre is likely to be quiet as most people will be on the beach. Many will stay there for lunch, too, so it is a good time to eat in one of Tropea's fine restaurants.

The Corso concludes at **Largo Migliarese** ⑤, a square high above the sea with uninterrupted views

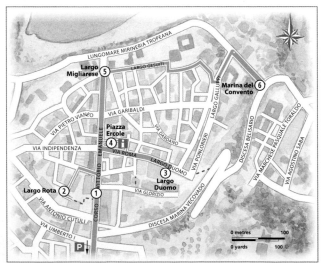

over the marina, the sandy beaches each side, the distant Aeolian Islands and mountains of Aspromonte. On the north side of the square, take the steps down to the beaches. Follow Largo Gesuiti, turn left from Largo Galluppi and then turn right to reach the **Marina del Convento** ⑥ – popular for sun-bathing and swimming.

🚗 *Take Via Libertá forking right onto SP22. Follow the coast and continue to San Nicolo, turning right on Loc. Capo Vaticano Faro. Follow signs for the "Faro" (lighthouse).*

❸ Capo Vaticano
Vibo Valentia, Calabria; 89865

On top of a dramatic promontory, the lighthouse of Capo Vaticano has excellent walking trails around its base with marvellous sea vistas of the Tyrrhenian Coast and Aeolian Islands. Down below the lighthouse, translucent waters and pleasant coves invite swimmers to take a dip and sun themselves on boulders. Even if the day is hazy, prepare for the sunset. The light creates dramatic effects as the sun sinks behind the volcanic islands and Stromboli magically lights up.

A long flight of stone steps near the lighthouse leads down to the water. Keen scuba divers might want to see a sunken World War II ship in Riaci Bay, the remains of an ancient Roman port in Formicoli or Secca del Monaco in Grotticelle Bay with a steep drop-off of 80m (262ft).

🚗 *Drive back to SP22 turning right to Panaia, and take the SP23. Park on the street below the Castello; you may need to buy a ticket if on a meter.*

Right Panoramic sea view from the top of the cliffs at Capo Vaticano **Far right** Long sandy strip of beach running from Nicotera Marina

❹ Nicotera: La Costa Viola
Vibo Valentia, Calabria; 89844

The first town on the Violet Coast, Nicotera merits a little exploration before heading to the beach. Wander the narrow alleys of the **Ghetto**, the former Jewish quarter, pausing on terraces along the way to look down on the purple-violet hues of the sea, which gave the coast between Nicotera and Scilla its name. The **Castello Ruffo's** museums *(open daily am)* have exhibits of local mineralogy and archaeology. For a swim, try one of the bathing spots at **Nicotera Marina** – there is no danger these days from the type of Saracen attack that led to the town being abandoned in the 9th century.

The vibrant colours along this coast become especially evident at sunset when violet, red and orange all appear, mingling and shifting position as the sun moves. On the drive to Palmi, stop at the yellow church of Santa Maria delle Scale to admire the spectacular view.

🚗 *Take the SP30 to Rombiolo, then take the SP33 right to the SS18 and head south towards Palmi. For Scinà, turn right before Palmi on the Contrada San Francesco.*

Above left The Castello Normanno Svevo in the centre of Vibo Valentia **Above centre** The marina and Tyrrhenian Sea seen from cliffs of Tropea town **Above right** Santa Maria delle Scale beside the road from Nicotera to Palmi

EAT AND DRINK IN TROPEA

Taverna L'Antica Grotta *inexpensive*
Sit inside a cavern dug into the cliffs or outside in the scenic piazza to enjoy delicious traditional Tropean specialities including home-made pasta
Largo Rota 9, 89861; 349 316 1056

Caffè del Corso *inexpensive*
The coffee is good, but the big draws are the ice cream and anything made with almonds – the excellent biscuits and delicious cakes.
Corso Vittorio Emanuele 14, 89861; 0963 666 100; closed Tue in winter

Torre Galli Resort & Restaurant *inexpensive–moderate*
Situated just outside Tropea, this sea resort has a pleasant restaurant and rooms set among olive and lemon groves. Take the Strada Provinciale Tropea (SP17) for 4 km (2 miles) and turn left at the fork for Brattirò.
SP Tropea; San Rocco Moccina 1, 89862; Drapia; 0963 67254 ; www.torregalli.it

VISITING SCILLA

Diving
Scilla Diving Centre can organize trips for divers of all abilities (*Via Annunziata, 89058; 0965 754585; www.scilladiving.it; open Jun–Sep*).

Boat Trips
Francesco Arena is part of a collective of fishermen that runs boat trips to places of interest (*Via Salita de Zerbi 17, 89058; 33914 37799*).

WHERE TO STAY

SCILLA

Le Piccole Grotte B&B *inexpensive*
Attractive rooms in the picturesque fishing area of town. Rooms have private bathrooms and some have a balcony or terrace overlooking the sea. Fishing trips can be arranged. *Via Grotte 10, Chianalea, 89058; 0965 754 881; www.lepiccolegrotte.it*

Villa Paladino *inexpensive–moderate*
This B&B is in converted railway quarters, set in an olive grove that overlooks the sea. *Via Oliveto, Chianalea, 89058; 0965 790585; www.villapaladino.it*

AROUND SCILLA

Castello Altafiumara *expensive*
This luxurious 18th-century Bourbon fortress is 11 km (7 miles) from the centre of Reggio di Calabria. Set in beautiful parklands, it looks out over the sea and has a private beach, swimming pool, gym and restaurant. Take the coastal road SS18 south towards Villa San Giovanni and follow the signs for the castello. *Santa Trada di Cannitello, Villa San Giovanni, 89010; 0965 759 804; www.altafiumarahotel.it*

Below The pastel houses of Chianalea perched over the sea at Scilla

Above Scilla's Castello Ruffo houses a lighthouse overlooking the Strait of Messina

⑤ Palmi beaches
Reggio Calabria, Calabria; 89015
Sitting below wooded Monte Sant' Elia, Palmi's main attraction is its location on a long strip of unspoiled beaches. The surrounding forest reaches almost to the sea and high reed beds add to the sense of seclusion. Tucked away along the shore are a few well-hidden motels and camp sites. To go with the vivid colours, the air is filled with the sweet scent of oranges, jasmine, bergamot and wild oregano. North of town, **Scinà beach** has few facilities – a restaurant and snack shop – but is all the better for that. It forms part of a long sandy beach running all the way to Palmi.

Ravaged over the years by pirates and earthquakes, Palmi town has lost most of its 10th-century architecture. There is, however, a folk museum and **L'Antiquarium Comunale** with artifacts from the 5th century BC to 11th century AD. In the bay near the Lido sits the photogenic **Scoglio dell'Ulivo**, a magnificent boulder with an olive tree on it.

As in the rest of southern Italy, religious festivals are important in Palmi. The July Festa della Madonna dell'Alto Mare is a procession taking a revered statue of the Virgin to sea. On 16 August each year, Rocco, the town's patron saint is celebrated with a feast day of a procession of *mbuttari* who carry the saint's statue followed by *spinati* (penitents). The women wear a crown of thorns while the men flagellate and mortify themselves with ropes and branches.

🚗 *Take the SS18 south along the coast to Scilla. Park on-street near the beach.*

⑥ Scilla
Reggio Calabria, Calabria; 89122
According to Greek legends, Scilla was the place where jealous Circe turned the beautiful nymph Scylla into a fearsome sea monster. The town now sits behind a mighty fortress looking over the sea to Sicily. **Castello Ruffo**, on a rocky outcrop, was a 9th-century monastery before being transformed into a fort by the local noble family of Ruffo in 1255 and remodelled again in 1542. It is now home to a lighthouse *(closed)*. The castle's terrace affords a good view of the Strait of Messina. Next to the castle, the narrow alleys and stairways of the **Chianalea** ("galley deck") **quarter** wind past pretty fishermen's houses. The San Giorgio quarter of town is home to the city hall and in PiazzaSan Rocco, the **Chiesa San Rocco** is dedicated to Scilla's patron saint. During the summer the beach area near Marina

Where to Stay: inexpensive, under €100; moderate, €100–€200; expensive, over €200

Far left The undeveloped sandy beach at Scinà, about 2 km (1 mile) north of Palmi
Left Stall displaying the excellent produce of sunny Calabria

---

Greek: the Calabrian Language
In the south of Calabria and in the Parco Nationale dell' Aspromonte, a few villages are struggling to keep alive the ancient language, Grecanico. This Greek language has been linked by studies with the ancient Greek tongue dating as far back as the 7th century BC. The language has been dying out since the 16th century and was all but eradicated by Mussolini. Today, it is known only by a few elders.

Grande attracts sunbathers and swimmers working up an appetite for seafood dining in the nearby restaurants. Under the castle sits the **Chiesa dello Spirito Santo**, with a notable Baroque façade that has survived earthquakes and storms; inside is a Venetian 16th-century organ.

Scuba divers like Scilla for the rich variety of marine life thriving in the strong currents – sea scorpions, wrasse and sea horses. To view wildlife up close, arrange to go diving; or join a boat trip along the coast to learn about traditional fishing, visit a cave or two and get a good fish lunch, too *(see left)*.

🚗 *Continue south on the SS18 towards Villa S Giovanni to reach Reggio di Calabria.*

⑦ Reggio di Calabria
Reggio Calabria, Calabria; 89122
Not the prettiest of cities, Reggio, founded by the Greeks in the 8th century BC, draws most visitors thanks to its **Museo Nazionale** *(open daily; Piazza De Nava, Reggio di Calabria; www.museonazionalerc.it)*. This excellent museum contains two of the best ancient bronzes in the world. The 2-m (6-ft) tall male statues made by a Greek sculptor in the 5th century BC were found underwater off the Riace coast in 1972. The bodies are bronze with copper inlaid eyelashes, nipples and lips, silver teeth and eyes of ivory and glass. Near the museum, Reggio's port has ferries making the 40-minute trip to Messina. Reggio's formidable **Castello** *(closed Mon)* was built in 534–9 as a Byzantine fort, with two towers added during the Aragonese reign in the 15th century. The **Duomo** *(open daily)*, rebuilt after the 1908 earthquake devastated the city, has an impressive façade and many gold treasures inside.

EAT AND DRINK

PALMI
Scinà 015 Ristoclub
inexpensive–moderate
Good food, sophisticated atmosphere, just steps from Scinà's unspoiled beach. There is summer courtyard dining and a fire for winter. Excellent *pappardelle mare e monti* (pasta ribbons with shrimp and porcini mushrooms). *Contrada Scinà; 89015; 0966 479 015; www.scina015.it; closed Wed in winter*

SCILLA
Bleu de Toi *moderate*
Set in an old fisherman's *borgo* (neighbourhood), this place specializes in Calabrese seafood and fish, with a good choice of local wines. The small interior expands outdoors on a wooden pier over the water. *Via Grotte 40, Chianalea; 89058, 0965 790 585; www.bleudetoi.it; closed Tue except Jul & Aug*

REGGIO DI CALABRIA
Baylik *moderate*
Close to the port, the aptly named Baylik (Turkish for fish) specializes in fish and offers some innovative versions of old favourites, such as *penne alla carbonara* with smoked swordfish instead of bacon. *Vico Leone 1, 89121; 0965 48624; info@baylik.it; closed Mon*

DAY TRIP OPTIONS
There is not a lot of driving for these trips, so just relax and enjoy the day.

Stromboli adventure
At Tropea ②, mingle with the jet set, swim and enjoy a seafood lunch. Set off for Capo Vaticano ③ and a cliff walk with views of Stromboli. Back to Tropea ② for a night boat to fiery Stromboli.

Follow the coastal road SP22.

La Costa Viola
Based at Scilla ⑥, head up the Violet Coast to Palmi Scinà ⑤ for a quiet swim, to admire the colour of the light and take a brief wander around town. Head back to Scilla ⑥ to go on a diving trip or to take a short ride in a boat along the coast to see if the colours look any different from a seaborne perspective.

Follow the coastal road SS18.

The real Greek
Explore the city of Reggio di Calabria ⑦ and visit the Museo Nazionale with its collection of locally found Greek artifacts including the two bronze warriors. Return to Scilla ⑥ for dinner in one of the restaurants serving local seafood and fish in the Chianalea neighbourhood.

Reggio di Calabria is easily accessed from the SS18.

Eat and Drink: inexpensive, under €25; moderate €25–€45; expensive over €45

Rome
Foggia
Naples • • Bari
• Taranto

Tyrrhenian Sea

Palermo • Reggio di Calabria
Catania •

Ionian Sea

Sicily's Volcanoes

Taormina to the Aeolian Islands

Highlights

- **Medieval Taormina**
  Visit the jewel of the Ionian coast, a perfectly preserved town with awe-inspiring views

- **Volcanic scenery**
  Witness unusual landscapes, from a gorge cut through lava to the most active volcanoes in Europe

- **Local artisan foods**
  Indulge in almond wine, pistachio cake and the sweetest strawberries

- **Aeolian paradise**
  Escape to these mythic islands for spectacular swimming

A view of Taormina, as Mount Etna lets off steam in the distance

Sicily's Volcanoes

Sicily sits on the fault line of the European and African tectonic plates, whose jostlings have created a chain of volcanoes, most famously Mount Etna. This is a tour through some of the most dramatic landscapes in southern Europe: active volcanoes and volcanic islands; amazing rock formations created by a river forging through a gorge of solidified lava; hot springs, steaming sulphurous fumeroles and black beaches. Food- and wine-lovers will find that the fertile volcanic soil produces some of Italy's best wine, cheese, fruits and nuts.

AEOLIAN ISLANDS

Alcudi Porto
Isola Alicudi

Filicudi Porto
Isola Filicudi

S. Marina Salina
Isola Saline

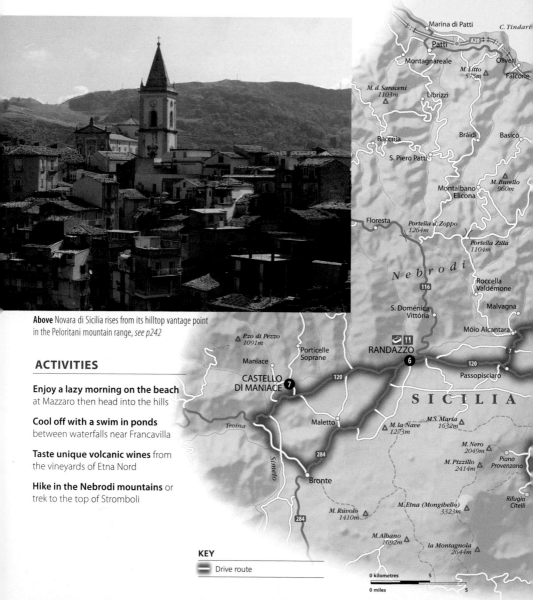

Above Novara di Sicilia rises from its hilltop vantage point in the Peloritani mountain range, *see p242*

ACTIVITIES

Enjoy a lazy morning on the beach at Mazzaro then head into the hills

Cool off with a swim in ponds between waterfalls near Francavilla

Taste unique volcanic wines from the vineyards of Etna Nord

Hike in the Nebrodi mountains or trek to the top of Stromboli

Marina di Patti
C. Tindari
Patti
Montagnareale
Oliveri
M. Litto 575m
Falcone
M. d. Saraceni 1103m
Librizzi
Raccúia
Bráidi
Basicò
S. Piero Patti
Montalbano Elicona
M. Burello 960m
Floresta
Portella d. Zoppo 1264m
Portella Zilla 1104m
Nebrodi
Roccella Valdémone
116
Malvagna
S. Doménica Vittória
Móio Alcántara
Pzo di Pezzo 1091m
Porticelle Soprane
RANDAZZO
Maniace
6
120
CASTELLO DI MANIACE
7
120
Passopisciaro
Troina
Maletto
S I C I L I A
M. la Nave 1273m
M.S. Maria 1632m
284
M. Nero 2049m
Piano Provenzano
Simeto
M. Pizzillo 2414m
Bronte
Rifugio Citelli
M. Rúvolo 1410m
M. Etna (Mongibello) 3323m
284
M. Albano 1692m
la Montagnola 2644m

KEY

Drive route

0 kilometres   5
0 miles   5

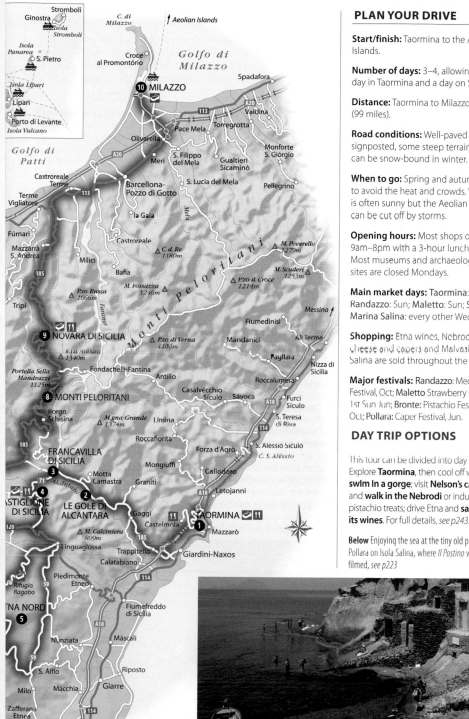

PLAN YOUR DRIVE

Start/finish: Taormina to the Aeolian Islands.

Number of days: 3–4, allowing half a day in Taormina and a day on Salina.

Distance: Taormina to Milazzo 159 km (99 miles).

Road conditions: Well-paved and signposted, some steep terrain. Etna can be snow-bound in winter.

When to go: Spring and autumn to avoid the heat and crowds. Winter is often sunny but the Aeolian Islands can be cut off by storms.

Opening hours: Most shops open 9am–8pm with a 3-hour lunch break. Most museums and archaeological sites are closed Mondays.

Main market days: Taormina: Wed; Randazzo: Sun; Maletto: Sun; Santa Marina Salina: every other Wed.

Shopping: Etna wines, Nebrodi cheese and capers and Malvasia from Salina are sold throughout the area.

Major festivals: Randazzo: Medieval Festival, Oct; Maletto Strawberry Festival, 1st Sun Jun; Bronte: Pistachio Festival, Oct; Pollara: Caper Festival, Jun.

DAY TRIP OPTIONS

This tour can be divided into day trips. Explore **Taormina**, then cool off with a **swim in a gorge**; visit **Nelson's castle** and **walk in the Nebrodi** or indulge in pistachio treats; drive Etna and **sample its wines**. For full details, see p243.

Below Enjoying the sea at the tiny old port of Pollara on Isola Salina, where *Il Postino* was filmed, see p223

Above Street scene in the old town, Castiglione **Top right** Rifugio Citelli, Etna Nord **Right** Castiglione di Sicilia tumbling down from its hilltop perch

WINE TOURS

To organize a tour of one of Etna's vineyards, contact **Frank Cornellisen** on *392 976 9728* or see *www.passo pisciaro.com* for producer **Andrea Franchetti**. Another rising star is **Alberto Ajello** on *348 701 6773*.

WHERE TO STAY

CASTIGLIONE DI SICILIA

Hotel Federico II *inexpensive*
Family-run hotel in a converted 13th-century palazzo just off the main square. Great views from roof terrace.
Via Maggiore Baracca 2, 95012; 0942 980 368; www.hotelfederico secondo.com

ETNA NORD

Rifugio Ragabo *inexpensive*
Simple clean rooms in a pine chalet. Guided treks can be organized to the Grotta del Gelo, year-round ice cave.
Pineta Bosco Ragabo, Linguaglossa, 95015; 095 647 841; www.ragabo.it

RANDAZZO

Parco Statella *moderate*
An 18th-century villa with horse riding and sports in extensive grounds, ideal for children.
2 km (1 mile) from Randazzo on SS187, direction Linguaglossa, 95036; 095 924 036; www.parcostatella.com.

Where to Stay: inexpensive, under €100; moderate, €100–€200; expensive, over €200

④ Castiglione di Sicilia
Catania, Sicilia; 95012
A splendid little town clustered below a restored castle, be sure to see the turban-domed bell tower belonging to the **Chiesa di Sant'Antonio Abate**, and the remains of Byzantine frescoes in the **Chiesa di San Nicola** *(open daily)*. In the valley below is a beautifully-preserved 8th-century Byzantine church built of lava, known as **La Cuba** for its perfect symmetry. Just behind it, a path leads to the River Alcantara and the waterfalls and pools known as **Piccole Gole**.

🚗 *Take SP71, turn left on SS120 to Linguaglossa. Drive through town and follow brown signs for Etna Nord. Road forks after Rif. Ragabo: straight on for Rif. Citelli; right to Piano Provenzana.*

⑤ Etna Nord
Catania, Sicilia; 95015
Mount Etna is at its most spectacular in winter, when the peak is covered in snow. As you drive, look out for lumps of solidified lava emerging through the undergrowth. The ski resort of **Piano Provenzano** was devastated in the 2002 eruption – the scorched skeletons of trees still protrude from a river of solidified lava – but still affords excellent views across the Nebrodi mountains. From the battered-looking building of **Rifugio Citelli** the views are even better. It is possible to organize treks from here.

🚗 *Follow signs for Milo, S Alfio then take SP59 to Linguaglossa. Follow SS120 to Randazzo. Follow signs for Centro. Turn right at the Santa Maria church, following signs to the San Giorgio e il Drago restaurant. Park in the piazza outside.*

Wines of Etna

Mineral-rich volcanic soil, extreme temperatures and low yields combine to lend a fascinating richness and complexity to the wines grown on Etna. In the vanguard are Andrea Franchetti, a Tuscan who produces the award-winning Passopisciaro, and Belgian Frank Cornellissen who has developed a cult following by spurning the use of sulphates.

⑥ Randazzo
Catania, Sicilia; 95036
Built entirely of lava, the medieval town of Randazzo has miraculously escaped Etna's eruptions but not the bombing in World War II. Its meticulously restored centre holds

Above Skeletal trees poke above the solidified lava flow of a recent eruption, Mount Etna

some striking churches, such as Santa Maria, its nave soaring between columns of black lava, and San Martino, whose exquisitely patterned bell tower dominates the town. Opposite is a castle tower housing the **Museo Vagliasindi** *(open daily)*, whose most prized exhibits are ancient Greek vases from the nearby necropolis of Tissa.

📷 *Take SS120 towards Castello di Maniace (Castello di Nelson).*

Above Nave of the chapel in Castello di Maniace in the Nebrodi mountains

⑦ Castello di Maniace

Catania, Sicilia; 95034

Maniace is a little green paradise at the foot of the Nebrodi mountains. On entering the village, note the mellow stone walls of the **Castello di Maniace** *(closed Mon)*, a 12th-century Benedictine monastery given by Bourbon King Ferdinand to Vice Admiral Horatio Nelson, in gratitude for British help in repressing the revolution of 1799 in Naples. Nelson never actually visited, but his descendent, Alexander Hood, gave it the air of an English country house.

Nelson was given the honorary title Duke of Bronte after the handsome, lava-built town of **Bronte**, which lies close by and is well worth a detour. Surrounded by groves of pistachio trees, the town is a fine place to sample local specialities such as pistachio ice cream, pistachio cake, or pistachio *arancini*. The town's nominal similarity with the literary Brontë sisters is no coincidence. Born Patrick Prunty, their father was an admirer of Nelson and changed his

name in the great man's honour. Also worth a stop is the town of **Maletto**, famous for the sweetest strawberries in Sicily. The strawberry festival is in June with processions through the streets.

📷 *At a T-junction after the Castello, follow signs to Bronte. Turn right onto SS120 and then almost immediately left to Bronte. From Bronte take the SS284, passing Maletto on the left, and drive back through Randazzo to join the SS120. At Passopisciaro turn left for Móio Alcantara, SP7, then take the SS185 towards Novara di Sicilia.*

Walking in the Nebrodi

The Castello di Maniace is also seat of a Parco di Nebrodi office (095 690 018) which has leaflets about marked walks and sells the detailed and reliable Il Parco di Nebrodi map. One of the loveliest itineraries is an 18-km (11-mile) trek past a dozen mountain *sorgente* (springs). The first part of the walk, up to the Sorgente Farina, Sorgente Fanusa and the Rifugio Donnavida, can be covered in less than an hour. The walk begins at Piazza San Gabriele in the Contrada Petrosina, about 2 km (1 mile) from the Castello.

⑧ Monti Peloritani

Messina, Sicilia; 98030

A magnificent stretch of road takes you through the Monti Peloritani range, a landscape of oaks and pines with fractured limestone bluffs. The road passes abandoned mining settlements with unforgettable views of Etna and springs where the locals stock up on mountain water.

📷 *The SS185 continues through the 1,125-m (3,691-ft) pass of Sella Mandrazzi before descending to Novara. There is a free car park on the left before you enter the town.*

Above A ripening cluster of pistachio nuts in one of the many groves surrounding Bronte

Above Pantiled roofscape of Maletto, famous for the sweetest strawberries in Sicily

EAT AND DRINK

CASTIGLIONE DI SICILIA

Alcantara Formaggi
Artisan factory run by father and son, producing unpasteurized cheeses, mostly of sheeps' milk. Sample oven-baked ricotta and *pecorino ubriaco* (drunken sheeps' cheese), pecorino covered with the skins of grapes left over after pressing for wine.
Via Federico II 105, 95012; 0942 984 268; closed Sun

Dispensa dell'Etna *inexpensive*
Wine bar and restaurant with an abundant range of locally produced wines, liqueurs, preserves and other delicious foodstuffs.
Piazza Sant'Antonio 2, 95012; 0942 984 258; www.ladispensadelletna.eu; closed Fri in winter

AROUND ETNA NORD

Buy some good local meat, cheese, vegetables and fruit before you leave Castiglione or Linguaglossa and enjoy a picnic at one of the picnic sites with barbecues along the road.

RANDAZZO

Pasticceria Gelateria Santo Musumeci
This bar opposite the church of Santa Maria serves ice creams and cakes made of local almonds, hazelnuts and pistachios.
Piazza Santa Maria 9–10, 95036; 095 921 196; closed Tue, except in Aug

San Giorgio e Il Drago *moderate*
Cosy trattoria housed in a 19th-century wine cellar. Home-made pasta with wild asparagus in spring, dishes using *porcini* mushrooms collected from the woods of Etna in the autumn.
Piazza San Giorgio 28, 95036; 095 923 972; closed Tue and 20 days in Jan

Eat and Drink: inexpensive, under €25; moderate, €25–€45; expensive, over €45

Above Thirteenth-century clifftop castle in the *Borgo* (upper town) of Milazzo

VISITING THE AEOLIAN ISLANDS

Ferry and hydrofoil services
Car ferries and hydrofoils run year-round to the Aeolian Islands from Milazzo and (less frequently) Messina: **Siremar** *(090 928 3242; www.siremar.it)*; **Ustica Lines** *(090 928 7821; www.usticalines.it)*.

Tourist Information
Offices at *Malfa, 090 984 43 26* and *Leni, 090 980 92 25*. Seasonal office in *Santa Marina* (near Pasticceria Matarazzo).

Boat Trips
Salina has ferry and hydrofoil links with all the Aeolian Islands *(Mario Zaia; 090 986 315)*. For private boat trips, contact *Alessio Follone; 333 578 6725*; for Stromboli treks, *Magmatrek; 090 986 5768; www.magmatrek.it*.

WHERE TO STAY

NOVARA DI SICILIA

B&B Sganga Kondé King *inexpensive*
Huge rooms with magnificent views in an 18th-century palazzo.
Via Nazionale 162, 98058; 0941 650 526

MILAZZO

Hotel Cassisi *inexpensive*
Elegant and intimate family-run hotel furnished in Japanese minimalist style.
Via Cassisi 5, 98057; 090 922 9099; www.cassisihotel.com

Petit Hotel *moderate*
Italy's only eco-hotel with energy-saving lights and organic breakfast.
Via dei Mille 37, 98057; 090 928 6784; www.petithotel.it

THE AEOLIAN ISLANDS (SALINA)

Capo Faro *moderate*
Hip hotel with rooms in tastefully restored Aeolian houses on a vineyard.
Via Faro 3, Malfa, 98050; 090 984 4330; www.capofaro.it; open Apr–Oct

Signum *expensive*
Bijou hotel with infinity pool where you can watch Stromboli erupt on horizon.
Via Scalo 15, Malfa, 98050; 090 984 4222; www. hotelsignum.it; open Apr–Oct

Where to Stay: inexpensive, under €100; moderate, €100–€200; expensive, over €200

---

⑨ Novara di Sicilia
Messina, Sicilia; 98058
Novara di Sicilia is a splendidly sited town, spilling down a mountainside around a rocky bluff topped by a church. The old centre is still cobbled, and either side of the main street a tangle of steep, mossy-stepped streets twist and turn between abandoned stone houses. Novara is a lively town, with plenty of

---

⑪ The Aeolian Islands
Messina, Sicilia; 98050
Named after Aeolus, the Greek God of the winds, the volcanic, seven-island archipelago of the Isole Aeolie is a UNESCO World Heritage Site.

Salina
Salina is the greenest of the Aeolian Islands; its twin peaks (each an extinct volcano) are cloaked with Mediterranean maquis and crowned with deciduous and pine forest. Centrally located, Salina is also a convenient base for day trips to the other islands of the archipelago.

① Santa Marina Salina
The main port of the island cascades down the lower slopes of Monte Fossa delle Felci, dominated by the sand-coloured dome of the **Chiesa dell'Immacolata** *(open daily)*. There is a single traffic-free street, Via Risorgimento, along which modish boutiques occupy the ground floors of grand 19th-century townhouses, built with fortunes made selling sweet Malvasia wine to the British. Be sure to drop in on Pasticceria Matarazzo for a pastry with Malvasia.
🚗 *Head towards Lingua (3 km/2 miles). The road crosses two gullies forged by lava. Drive into Lingua; continue until road ends at car park.*

---

local produce to be sampled. Prime among these is *maiorchino*, an aged sheeps' cheese with the texture of Parmesan but more pungent. Teams race through the streets with a wheel of cheese several times a year.
🚗 *The SS185 continues with views to the sea, the scythe-shaped Capo di Milazzo and the Aeolian Islands. The road joins the coastal SS113 near Terme Vigliatore. Turn right, following signs for Milazzo through Barcellona.*

⑩ Milazzo
Messina, Sicilia; 98057
Milazzo is the main port for the Aeolian Islands. Modern and functional around the port, the main street, Corso Umberto I, is a pleasant place to shop or stroll while waiting for a ferry. With time to spare, head for the upper town to visit the fortified citadel, dominated by a newly restored 13th-century castle.

Above Sand-coloured Chiesa dell'Immacolata behind the small harbour, Santa Marina Salina

---

Trips to the Outer Islands
The many rocky islets off **Panarea** are great for swimming, and from the stunning cove of Cala Junco visitors can climb to see the remains of a Bronze Age village. The island is also a favourite haunt of the fashion crowd and has many stylish boutiques and bars. For something more adventurous book a trek up the volcano of **Stromboli**, timed to arrive at the summit just before sunset. Or head for the beautiful island of **Filicudi**, best explored by foot on its network of mule tracks.

② Lingua

Dominated by an old lighthouse, Lingua sits beside the salt lagoon or "salina" for which the island is named. Salt was extracted here until the 1960s, for export and for the salting of fish and capers. These days people visit for the *granite* at Da Alfredo on the little seafront piazza *(open Easter–Nov)*. The stony beach below the piazza is a popular place to swim. From the car park in Lingua a well-marked path leads to the isolated house of **Paolo Noce**, used by a local family in the autumn for the olive harvest, from where there are constantly changing views of all the Aeolian Islands. Particularly lovely in late afternoon (but bring a torch for the descent), the walk is relatively undemanding and takes 40 minutes each way, with a steepish climb of 20 minutes up steps to begin with, then fairly flat.

🚗 *Drive back through Santa Marina, following signs to Malfa. Shortly after*

Malfa the road forks and the right branch hairpins down to Pollara.

③ Pollara

Known for its black beaches, the startling rock formation of the *Perciato* and for its lively caper festival, the remote hamlet of Pollara gained worldwide fame as the main location for the film *Il Postino*.

🚗 *Beyond the junction for Pollara the road continues along to Valdichiesa.*

① Valdichiesa

Planted with Malvasia vines, Valdichiesa is the lush valley in the saddle between Salina's two mountains. From the church of Madonna del Terzito there is a 10-km (6-mile) walk to the summit of **Monte Fossa delle Felci**. Continuing, the road passes through the village of **Leni**, which spills down a ridge high above the sea, and then hairpins down to the tiny fishing port of **Rinella**.

Beautifully preserved Greek funerary vase

Above left A colourful window box in the pretty hamlet of Lingua **Above** The clear waters off Pollara beach are ideal for a swim

EAT AND DRINK

NOVARA DI SICILIA

Bar Angelina
Family-run bar producing its own *dito di apostolo* (ricotta-stuffed wafer).
Via Nazionale 151, 98058; 0941 650100; closed Mon in winter

Macelleria Antonella
Salami and *maiorchino* cheese.
Largo Bertolami, Via Nazionale 384, 98058; 0941 650 692; closed Sat pm, Sun

THE AEOLIAN ISLANDS (SALINA)

Alfredo in Cucina *inexpensive*
Famous for its fig, mulberry and prickly-pear *granite*. Great for lunch too.
Via Marina Garibaldi, Lingua, 90019; 090 984 3307; www.alfredoincucina.com

Pasticceria Matarazzo *inexpensive*
Known for its chocolate croissants and almond, pistachio and pine-nut pastries.
Via Risorgimento 119/A, Santa Marina, 98050; 090 984 3000

Portobello *moderate*
Try hard-fried scorpion fish.
Via Bianchi 1, Santa Marina, 98050; 090 984 3125; open mid-Mar–mid-Nov

---

DAY TRIP OPTIONS

Those staying around Messina and Catania will find the A18 offers quick access to Taormina.

Cool off in the gorge

Spend the morning taking in the sights and café scene of Taormina ❶. Cool off with an afternoon's paddle in the Alcantara Gorge surrounded by amazing volcanic rock formations ❷.

Take the SS185 which connects with the A18 west of Taormina. From the Tyrrhenian side it is quickest to loop

round on the A20/A18. Access the gorge at Motta Camastra to reach waterfalls and ponds for swimming.

Etna adventure

Follow the Etna Nord ❺ circuit for eerie volcanic landscapes and splendid views. Picnic on Etna or lunch in Castiglione ❹, then embark on a trek organized by Rifugio Ragabo or arrange a tour and tasting with one of Etna's up-and-coming wine makers.

Get there via the A18 and SS120 or A20 and SS185.

Nelson's castle

Visit a little part of England at the Castello di Maniace ❼ given to Admiral Nelson, Duke of Bronte, the starting point for a leisurely walk or energetic trek past springs in the Monti Nebrodi. Alternatively, head to Nelson's ducal town of Bronte and indulge in the pistachio delights of its *pasticcerie* – then pop into Maletto if strawberries are in season.

Skirt the edge of Etna on the SS120 and loop round on the SS284 for Castello, Bronte and Maletto.

Eat and Drink: inexpensive, under €25; moderate, €25–€45; expensive, over €45

- Rome
- Foggia
- Naples
- Bari
- Taranto

Tyrrhenian Sea

- Palermo
- Reggio di Calabria
- Catania

Ionian Sea

Sicilian Baroque

Noto to Necropoli di Pantalica

Highlights

- **Baroque jewel**
  Visit the south's most perfectly
  preserved Baroque town, Noto

- **Flight of flamingoes**
  Spot flamingoes, herons, storks and
  pelicans in a coastal nature reserve of
  salt lagoons and sand dunes

- **Artists on the beach**
  Join the artists of the Gruppo di Scicli
  for an early morning walk along the
  unspoiled sands of Sampieri

- **Archaeological gems**
  Discover Sicily's ancient Greek past –
  the ruins of Akrei and its wonderfully
  preserved theatre

Film-set perfection of the main square in Ragusa
Ibla, flanked by the Duomo di San Giorgio

Sicilian Baroque

In 1693, in the wake of a mighty eruption of Etna, this corner of Sicily was devastated by an earthquake. Towns were rapidly rebuilt out of the glowing local limestone – apricot gold in Noto, almond cream in Modica – in a style of Baroque that ranges from the muscular geometry of Noto's cathedral to flights of grotesque fancy twisting and turning around balconies in Scicli. The area is equally rich in natural treasures: there are several nature reserves with quiet sandy beaches, offshore islands and, inland, dramatic limestone gorges honeycombed with caves, inhabited from prehistoric times until the earthquake made life too precarious.

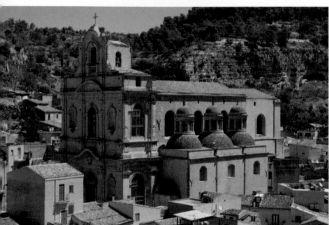

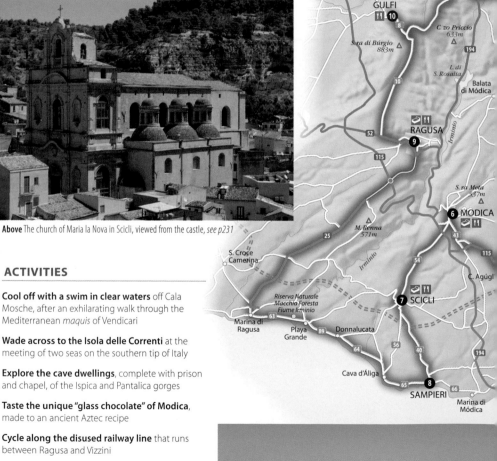

Above The church of Maria la Nova in Scicli, viewed from the castle, *see p231*

ACTIVITIES

Cool off with a swim in clear waters off Cala Mosche, after an exhilarating walk through the Mediterranean *maquis* of Vendicari

Wade across to the Isola delle Correnti at the meeting of two seas on the southern tip of Italy

Explore the cave dwellings, complete with prison and chapel, of the Ispica and Pantalica gorges

Taste the unique "glass chocolate" of Modica, made to an ancient Aztec recipe

Cycle along the disused railway line that runs between Ragusa and Vizzini

Right Quiet beach next to dunes in the Riserva Naturale Macchia Foresta Fiume Irminio, *see p231*

KEY

━━━ Drive route

0 kilometers   5

0 miles   5

PLAN YOUR DRIVE

Start/finish: Noto to Necrópoli di Pantalica.

Number of days: 4–5, allowing half a day in Noto and a day to explore the Riserva Naturale l'Oasi di Vendicari.

Distance: About 250 km (155 miles).

Road conditions: Well-paved roads but signage can be difficult.

When to go: Spring and autumn avoids the heat and crowds, but winter can be nice too. In August, towns empty as everyone heads to the beach.

Opening times: Most shops open 9am–1pm, then from around 4pm (winter) or 5pm (summer) until 8pm; closed on Sundays. Most museums and archaeological sites are closed on Mondays. Churches tend to open 7am–12:30pm and 4–7pm, but hours for smaller churches may vary.

Main market days: Noto: Mon am; Modica: antiques market 4th Sun of month; Scicli: general market Tue am.

Shopping: Food-lovers should seek out sundried tomatoes from Pachino, Bonajuto chocolate from Modica and sample rival vegetable pies from Ragusa Ibla and Palazzolo Acreide. Art lovers can pick up an original print or lithograph by one of the Gruppo di Scicli.

Major festivals: Modica: Vasa Vasa, Easter; Scicli: Uomo Vivo (man alive), Easter; Cavalcata di San Giuseppe, Sat closest to Mar 19; Madonna delle Milizie, May; **Donnalucata:** San Giuseppe Squid Festival, Mar 19; **Chiaramonte Gulfi:** Carnevale, Feb; **Palazzolo Acreide:** Carnevale, Feb.

DAY TRIP OPTIONS

Visitors can divide the tour into a series of day trips. Spend a day **by the sea** at Cala Mosche; pack a picnic lunch of local bread pasties and head off to find **ancient cave dwellings**; take a whistlestop tour of stunning **Baroque townscapes**. For full details, see p233.

Above The façade of the restored Duomo in Noto, glowing in the evening light

VISITING NOTO

Parking
Follow signs for Centro Storico, and park on the road to Largo Porta Nazionale.

VISITING RISERVA NATURALE L'OASI DI VENDICARI

Main entrance and information point at Pantano Grande. Entry to park is free but there is a small fee for parking. *Open daily 7am–8pm (summer) or 6:30pm (winter)*

WHERE TO STAY IN NOTO

La Fontanella *moderate*
This restored 19th-century palazzo on the edge of the old town has 9 rooms and 4 suites.
Via Rosolino Pilo 3, 96017; 0931 894 735; www.albergolafontanella.it; closed Jan–Mar

① Noto
Siracusa, Sicilia; 96017
Noto is the apogee of Sicilian Baroque and its newly restored centre is as perfect as a stage set. Much of Noto's charm lies in the local limestone from which it is built, the hues varying from gold to apricot ice cream depending on the light. Unfortunately, this stone is also friable (and thus fragile), leaving the city vulnerable to the quakes and tremors to which the region is prone. In 1996 the dome of the cathedral collapsed and the restoration, painstakingly undertaken stone by stone, has recently been completed.

Work began on Noto in 1703, ten years after the original town – now known as Noto Antica – was destroyed by the earthquake. To see the best of the town, walk along the main street, **Corso Vittorio Emanuele**, passing through the imposing **Porta Reale**. On the left is the church of **Santa Chiara** *(open daily)*, built on an unusual elliptical plan, and beyond, the theatrical central square, **Piazza Municipio**, where a magnificent flight of steps rises to the muscular Baroque **Duomo** *(open daily)*, its

Above Arcaded and balconied stone façade of the Palazzo Ducezio, Noto

interior serene and flooded with light from the rebuilt dome. Opposite the Duomo, is the elegant **Palazzo Ducezio**, Noto's town hall. Walk alongside the Duomo to **Palazzo Trigona**, with its curvaceous balconies, where steps lead up past more fine Baroque buildings to Noto Alta, the upper town, and the church of **Santa Maria di Gesù** *(rarely open to the public)*, from where there are views of the surrounding countryside.

🚗 *Follow signs for Siracusa, then Siracusa/Pachino on the SP15. Right on the SP19 for Pachino, following signs for Portapalo. Look for sign for Cala Mosche on the walls. Slow for sharp left turn.*

② Riserva Naturale l'Oasi di Vendicari
Siracusa, Sicilia; 96017
This enchanting coastal nature reserve has well-marked paths to unspoiled beaches of white-gold sand, and a chain of salt lakes that between October and March attract over 200 species of migratory birds, including flamingoes, herons, cranes, black storks and pelicans.

A one-hour walking tour
Leave the main car park, turn left. Visitors can pick up free large scale maps from the information booth.

Below Cala Mosche beach and bay, Riserva Vendicari **Below right** Conehead thyme, a typical *maquis* plant found at Riserva Vendicari

Follow the path straight ahead, stopping off to observe the birds on the **Pantano Grande** ① lake from the hide on the left. The path continues along duckboards through a forest of bamboo down to the coast, emerging on a fine beach of pale gold sand dominated by the ruins

Maquis flora

Among the typical plants of the Mediterranean maquis to look out for are species such as *Juniperus macrocarpa*, a rare type of juniper bush, and *Coridothymus capitatus*, or conehead thyme, whose nectar is the prime ingredient in Hyblaean honey, renowned since antiquity.

museum is
the **Villa Co**
panoramic
🚗 **Wind up**
following si
the SP57, th
SP124 to Pa

⑪ Palaz

Siracusa, Sic
A slightly ra
whose roots
times, Palaz
undergoing
is well worth
Baroque chi
Addolorata,
barley sugar
acanthus lea
restrained **Sa**
Paolo whose
concealed b
worth seeing
Antonino U
glorious folk
collections o
ceramics, agi
reconstructe
Sicily's rural p
ruins of ancie
small but ma
theatre, whic
occasional pe

DAY TRIP
To break up
Modica or S
between th

By the seas
Spend a mc
Cala Mosch
Noto. Enjoy
tuna marina
head for the
at the south

of an **abandoned *tonnara*** ②, or tuna processing plant, dating back to the 1920s and built by the Florio family, who invented canned tuna. The lakes were used to provide salt for the preserving of tuna.

The path then follows the coast, with more views over Pantano Grande, and its smaller sister lake, **Pantano Piccolo** ③, to the stunning cliff-hugged bay of **Cala Mosche** ④, one of the most beautiful bays in Sicily and a popular location for film shoots. Until recently, turtles would nest on the beaches, but local fondness for turtle soup led to their disappearance. Projects are underway to encourage the turtles back to Vendicari. From here the walk can be extended to take in the **Agriturismo Cala Mosche** ⑤, about 1 km (half a mile) away along a clearly marked path across typical Mediterranean maquis.

🚗 **Continue on the SP19 following signs for Marzamemi. Parking is available on both sides of the town.**

③ Marzamemi

Siracusa, Sicilia; 96018
Once an important centre for tuna fishing, Marzamemi retains an evocatively decayed maritime

complex of 19th- and early 20th-century tuna factory, warehouses and a lichened church, all built of mellow local limestone. A *tonnara* at nearby Pachino houses La Cialoma restaurant, owned by the niece of the last *rais*, a name for the head tuna fisherman that goes back to Arab times. "La Cialoma" was the song traditionally sung to round fishermen up for the *mattanza*, or tuna slaughter, held in May and June, when tuna were trapped in a complex system of nets, before being stabbed to death.

🚗 **Follow signs for Pachino. Left on SR6, cross SR8, right to Capo delle Correnti.**

Below Remnants of the old tuna factory and church in Marzamemi's old town

EAT AND DRINK

NOTO

Costanzo *inexpensive*
One of the most famous *gelaterie* (ice cream parlours) in Sicily, with flavours such as jasmine and rose evoking the island's Arabic heritage.
Via Spaventa 7, behind Palazzo Ducezio, 96017; 0931 835 243; closed Wed

RISERVA NATURALE L'OASI DI VENDICARI

Agriturismo Cala Mosche *inexpensive*
This holiday farm house produces its own vegetables, lemons and oil. Food in its restaurant includes local cheese, fish and game. Rooms available.
Cala Mosche entrance, 96017; 347 858 7319; closed Nov–Mar

AROUND MARZAMEMI

L'Alimentare Scimonello
Pachino tomatoes are famous and it is worth stopping at this grocery shop to buy sundried tomatoes, local chillies, pine nuts, almonds and dried fruit.
Piazza Vittorio Emanuele, 96018, Pachino (4 km/2 miles from Marzamemi), 96018; 0931 846 305; closed Sun

La Cialoma *inexpensive*
Set in a picturesque old *tonnara* and run by the niece of the last *rais*, this restaurant specializes in fresh local fish.
Piazza Regina Margherita 23, Pachino, 96018; 0931 841 772; www.lacialoma.it; closed Tue eve

Eat and Drink: inexpensive, under €25; moderate, €25–€45; expensive, over €45

Above The
San Giorgio

VISITING

Tourist Inf
AAPIT, Via
la Rocca),
ragusaturi
9am–1:30p
& 4–6pm

WHERE

RAGUSA

Le Chicche
Stylish little
roof terrace
of Ibla's Du
Via Salita S
239 180; w

PALAZZO

Anapama
Three inviti
converted
foot of the
by lush gard
pool fed by
bikes for gu
available to
Contrada F
or 331 786

Right View of
out to the dist
preserved med
Chiaramonte

DRIVE **23**

Sardinia: Capital to Coast

Cagliari to Cala Gonone

Highlights

- **Seaside capital**
  Explore Cagliari, the walled "city of water and light", spectacularly perched over the Bay of Angels

- **Su Nuraxi**
  Be amazed by this prehistoric settlement – the most complete Nuraghic complex in Sardinia

- **Wild Gennargentu**
  Escape to Sardinia's highest and most dramatic mountain scenery, once the home of bandits

- **Idyllic beaches**
  Cast away to beautiful coves, secret grottos and visions of paradise in the unspoiled Golfo di Orosei

The Castello district of Cagliari, surrounded by ancient city walls

Above Café-bar in a shaded shopping arcade along Via Roma, Cagliari

VISITING CAGLIARI

Parking
The most central car parks are south of Via Roma on the waterfront between Piazza Deffenu and Piazza Matteotti.

Tourist Information
Piazza Matteotti 9, 09124; 070 669 255; Mon–Fri 8:30am–1.30pm & 2:30–7:30pm, Sat & Sun 8:30am–7:30pm (closes earlier out of season).

WHERE TO STAY IN CAGLIARI

Hotel AeR Bundes Jack Vittoria
moderate
In a splendid location on Via Roma, this family-run 2-star hotel has a pleasantly faded elegance. Rooms are simple, spotless and air-conditioned. Sea-facing rooms have balconies and are available for a supplement.
Via Roma 75, 09124; 070 657 970; www.hotelbjvittoria.it

T Hotel *expensive*
Cagliari's first designer hotel is a tower of glass and steel where warm, sunny colours are tempered with ice-cool blues and greens to great effect. The T Bistrot is a popular meeting place and serves a good Sunday brunch. The hotel also has a stylish and well-equipped beauty and wellness centre with indoor pool and gym.
Via dei Giudicati 66, 09131; 070 474 00; www.thotel.it

Other options
Set in an old historical building in the convenient Marina area **Quattro Mori** *(moderate)* is a 3-star hotel with pleasant, comfortable rooms and a good restaurant *(Via Giovanni Maria Angioy 27; 070 668 535; www. hotel4mori.it)*. Close to Poetto Beach, the **Hotel Calamosca** *(moderate)* overlooks a cove with direct access to beaches *(Viale Calamosca 50, 01926; 070 371 628; www.hotelcalamosca.eu)*

Right Arch of the Bastione San Remy, Cagliari, built in the early 1900s

❶ Cagliari

Sardegna; 09100

Big, bustling Cagliari has been Sardinia's capital since at least Roman times and is the island's biggest port. It has an enviable setting overlooking the beautiful Golfo degli Angeli (Bay of Angels), and its historic heart – the Castello – is cradled by ancient ramparts which enclose some beautiful architectural gems and historical treasures. Beneath the citadel walls, the vibrant Marina quarter is a tangle of tiny streets bursting with tantalizing shops, restaurants and bars.

A two–three hour walking tour

This walk is best undertaken in the morning. Leave the car at the car park by the waterfront and there is the option of a steepish walk up to the Castello or the shuttle bus no. 7 from Piazza Matteotti (twice-hourly).

Start from **Bastione San Remy** ❶ at Piazza Costituzione. On the terrace of the Bastione is the Caffè degli Spiriti – a glorious spot for taking in the views over something long and cool. Heading north, walk up Via del Fossario to Piazza Palazzo, the heart of the Castello district, and to the **Cattedrale di Santa Maria** ❷ *(open daily)*. Admire the restored Pisan Romanesque façade and the elaborate Gothic/Baroque interior – do not miss the crypt under the altar.

Head north again and turn right into **Piazzetta Mercede Mundula** ❸ for views over the Bay of Cagliari. Continue up Via Pietro Martini to the Piazza Indipendenza and the medieval **Torre di San Pancrazio** ❹, a symbol of the city *(closed Mon)*. A

Roman glass vase, Museo Archeológico

stiff climb to the top is rewarded with views over the bay. Go through the archway to the Piazza dell' Arsenale and the Cittadella dei Musei (Citadel of Museums). Of the four museums here, the **Museo Archeologico** ❺ is the highlight *(closed Mon)*, giving a fascinating insight into Sardinia's past with artifacts from prehistoric to Roman times. Turn right out of the museum and exit Porta Cristina. Turn right along Viale Buon Cammino then cross over the road with Via Anfiteatro on your left and carry on along Viale Buon Cammino, keeping the Roman amphitheatre on your left. Turn left at the next junction down Viale Frà Ignazio da Laconi to arrive at the entrance to the 2nd-century AD **Anfiteatro Romano** ❻ *(closed pm & all day Mon)*. Once the site of gladiatorial contests seating 10,000 spectators, it is now used for summer concerts. Keep following the road down and turn left, still on Via Frà Ignazio da Laconi to *ingresso* no.11 for the **Orto**

Botanico ⑦ *(closed Mon & Sun pm)*. These gardens are pleasantly green and shady with a collection of over 500 species of Mediterranean and tropical plants.

After the gardens, continue along Via Frà Ignazio da Laconi and turn left into Via Portoscalas past Chiesa di San Michele before feeding left into Corso Vittorio Emanuele II. Then turn right into Largo Carlo Felice and down to **Via Roma** ⑧ and left to the car parks. This last part of the walk passes through a good shopping area with delicatessens (Jenna e Lua), designer shops (Loredana Mandas) and large department stores (La Rinascente) – keen shoppers should explore further.

From Cagliari, head southeast on Via Roma and continue along Viale Armando Diaz on to Ponte Vittorio. Fork left at Viale Poetto and then turn left at Via Lungo Saline which then becomes Via dell'Ippodromo. Left at the end leads to another Viale Poetto, where there are car parks.

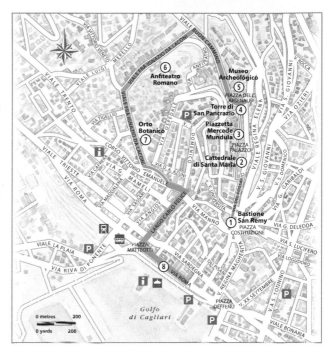

② Poetto
Cagliari, Sardegna; 09126

Backed by saltwater lagoons that are frequented by pretty flamingoes, Poetto's 6-km (4-mile) stretch of soft white sand is the perfect spot for basking in the sun and swimming. Parasols and loungers are available for daily rental from about €10 each and it is also possible to indulge in all kinds of watersports here. There are plenty of waterside cafés and bars and in high summer there is an open-air cinema and concert area.

Marina Piccola, at the southern end, is the liveliest part and the posing point for the local well-heeled fashionistas. It can get quite crowded around the marina, so it is best to head further east where there is more space. The Sella del Diavolo (Devil's Saddle) is the impressive rocky promontory visible to the south.

Leaving Poetto, head north towards the SS131 (Circonvallazione Quadrifoglio), follow signs to Oristano/Sassari for 38 km (24 miles) and then signs for Sanluri.

EAT AND DRINK CAGLIARI

Al Porto *moderate*
Atmospheric trattoria in the historic centre specializing in traditional seafood and fishy delights.
Via Sardegna 44, 09124; 070 663 131; closed Mon

Dal Corsaro *expensive*
One of Cagliari's top gourmet finds, this is a firm fixture on the culinary scene. The elegant family-run restaurant is set near the waterfront. Booking is advised.
Viale Regina Margherita 28, 09124; 070 664 318; www.dalcorsaro.com; closed Sun, 2 wks Jan

Other options
With lovely views over the city walls, **Caffè Librarium Nostrum** *(Via Santa Croce 33, 09124; 346 522 0212; www. caffelibrarium.com)* serves good snacks. A modern bar, **De Candia** *(Via Marco de Candia 1–3, Bastione San Remy, 09124)* has outside tables and also serves food. There is live music in summer.

Left Vast expanse of white sand, Poetto Beach, Cagliari

Eat and Drink: inexpensive, under €25; moderate, €25–€45; expensive, over €45

Above A trompe l'oeil mural within a mural on a wall in central Fonni

WHERE TO STAY

SU NURAXI

Hotel Su Nuraxi *inexpensive*
Conveniently located for visits to Su Nuraxi and with views across golden wheat fields to the nuraghe, this hotel (with a popular restaurant) is simply furnished but very welcoming.
Viale Su Nuraxi 6, Strada Provinciale Barùmini-Tuili (immediately after the Nuraghic village) 09021; 070 936 8519; www.hotelsunuraxi.it

FONNI

Cualbu *moderate*
This 50 bedroom modern hotel is good value with plenty of space and well-appointed rooms. The gardens are verdant and relaxing and there is a swimming pool. The elegant restaurant specializes in traditional, meaty Sardinian cuisine.
Viale del Lavoro 19, 08023; 0784 57054; www.hotelcualbu.com

③ Sanluri
Campidano, Sardegna; 09025
Set in the island's most fertile region, Sanluri is famous for having the only continuously inhabited medieval castle in Sardinia, the Castello di Eleonora d'Arborea, named after a warrior queen who fought against the Catalan-Aragonese in the 15th century. Today it is the home of the counts of Villa Santa but within lies the **Museo Risorgimentale** *(closed Mon & Sat)* full of military artifacts, rich furnishings and assorted objects of interest, including Napoleon's wife Josephine's wine glasses, marked with a "J". There are stupendous views from the castle roof and on a clear day it is possible to see the Castello di San Michele in Cagliari, some 40 km (25 miles) away.
🚗 *From Sanluri, follow signs to Villamar, then take the SS197 north to Barùmini (Su Nuraxi). Turn left off the SS197 onto the SP47, then right onto the SP44 – site of Su Nuraxi. There is a car park at the site.*

④ Su Nuraxi
Barùmini, Sardegna; 09021
Standing stately and alone on the hillside, this is Sardinia's largest, most important Nuraghic complex. Its origins are estimated to date to 1500 BC and the archaeological remains are extraordinarily well preserved. It was only discovered in 1949 by the Sardinian archaeologist Giovanni Lilliu when heavy rains revealed stoneworks under what had been thought to be just another

Nuraghi
The Nuraghic people built many prehistoric stone villages in Sardinia from about 1800 BC but left no written records. Shrouded in mystery, around 7,000 of these circular beehive-like Nuraghic dwellings dot the countryside, usually located in panoramic spots – probably for defensive purposes. Su Nuraxi, meaning literally "The Nuraghe", is described by UNESCO as the finest and most complete example of this remarkable form of prehistoric architecture. A popular Sard saying is, "a modern builder guarantees his work for five years, but the Nuraghic builder guaranteed his for 5,000".

hillock. The central tower, constructed from hewn basalt blocks – transported by unknown means from 10 km (6 miles) away – served as a fortress with a tower at each of its four corners and an encircling fortified wall. Originally 18 m (60 ft) high, the tower has lost 5 m (15 ft) in height, but is still impressive. From the top there are excellent views of the whole village of 200 beehive-shaped buildings – including a flour mill and bakery – which now form a UNESCO World Heritage Site *(open 9am–dusk daily; guided tours on the half hour)*. Take heed, the terrain is fairly tough so sturdy shoes and good mobility are required.
🚗 *From Su Nuraxi take the SS197 for a short way then bear left onto the SS128. At Lago di Gusana bear right on the SS389d to Fonni – there is parking on the street, but not in the old town.*

Right Ancient remains of the central tower and village of Su Nuraxi **Far right** Sweeping views from the Su Nuraxi site over to the hill of Las Plassas

Where to Stay: inexpensive, under €100; moderate, €100–€200; expensive, over €200

Above View over the hills and gorgeous countryside around Fonni

⑤ Fonni
Nuoro, Sardegna; 08023

From 1,000 m (3,280 ft), Sardinia's highest village, Fonni, looks out over vineyards and cork forests to the Gennargentu Mountains. It is a splendid starting point for hiking in the area and there is also skiing in winter. The less active might prefer to explore the 17th-century **Basilica della Madonna dei Martiri** *(open daily)* an elaborate study in Baroque. The revered image of the Madonna, said to be made from the crushed bones of martyrs, draws pilgrims – their huts *(cumbessias)* surround the church in Piazza Europa.

🚗 *From Fonni head north on the SS389 to Mamoiada. Park in the Piazza Europa.*

⑥ Mamoiada
Nuoro, Sardegna; 08024

This is the town of *mamuthones* (pagan costumed figures), which erupts at Carnival time, when men clad in fearsome wooden masks and shaggy sheepskins parade the streets. The spectacle is re-enacted on 17 January for the Festa di Sant'Antonio: the sinister figures are on display at the excellent **Museo delle Maschere** *(Piazza Europa 15, 08024; closed Mon)*

🚗 *From Mamoiada follow the SP22 southeast to Orgòsolo. Park at the entrance to the town (on-street parking) from where there is easy access to the Corso Rebubblica.*

⑦ Orgòsolo
Nuoro, Sardegna; 08027

Once famous for its bandits, Orgòsolo is now better known for its murals, which are everywhere. Satirical, comic, political, folkloric, or even brutalist, they have turned the town into an open-air art museum. They first started appearing in 1975 when a local art teacher and his pupils painted satirical and political murals to commemorate the 30th anniversary of Liberation and Resistance. On 15 August the Festa dell'Assunta – one of the most colourful and spectacular processions of the region – takes place here.

19th-century carnival mask, Mamoiada

🚗 *From Orgòsolo head north on the SP58 then take the SP22 to Nuoro.*

Below Mural of Luigi Pintor, founder of communist daily *Il Manifesto*, Orgòsolo

Above Traditional architectural detail in Fonni's old town

EAT AND DRINK

AROUND SU NURAXI

Sa Lolla Ristorante/Albergo
moderate
Set in a rustic country house, this restaurant (which is also a pleasant hotel) serves traditional Sard and Italian cuisine and specializes in local seasonal dishes.
Via Cavour 49, Barumini, 09021 (in the village beneath the Su Nuraxi archaeological site); 070 936 8419; www.wels.it/salolla; closed Mon

ORGÒSOLO

Ai Monti del Gennargentu
moderate
Outside Orgòsolo in a rural location set among oak trees, this is a highly regarded rustic restaurant with rooms. It features traditional mountain fare, perfect after building up a healthy appetite in this area so well known for its excellent walking and outdoor pursuits.
Località Settiles (5 km/3 miles south of Orgòsolo in the direction of Montes), 08027; 0784 402374; www.aimontidelgennargentu.it

Other options
Fonni has a couple of good-value pizzerias **Carlo Loddo** *(Via Bruncuspina 4, 08023; 0784 58543)* and **Il Pergolato** *(Via Roma 10, 08023; 0784 58455)*. For more traditional cuisine with a local flavour try **Ristorante Il Cinghialetto** *(Via Grazia Deledda 115, 08023; www.ilcinghialetto.it)*, which also has some rooms.

Above The 7-m (23-ft) statue of *Il Redentore* on Monte Ortobene, inaugurated in 1901

VISITING NUORO

Parking
The old centre in the northeastern part of town is best avoided and the Corso Garibaldi at its heart is pedestrianized. However, the Museo del Costume is in the southeastern part of the town, where there is paid on-street parking.

WHERE TO STAY

AROUND NUORO

Hotel Su Gologone *moderate*
Set in magnificent scenery, this hotel, one of Sardinia's most beautiful, offers a swimming pool, beauty centre and excursions; most rooms have balconies. *Loc. Su Gologone, Oliena, 08025 (SS129 towards Dorgali; Oliena signed on right); 0784 287 512; www.sugologone.it; closed Jan–Mar*

MONTE ORTOBENE

Casa Solotti *inexpensive*
Friendly, family-run B&B with quiet and comfortable rooms in pleasant gardens. Breakfasts include home-made goodies. *Monte Ortobene, 08100; 0784 33954; www.casasolotti.it*

CALA GONONE

Hotel Pop *inexpensive*
Friendly, family-run hotel by the sea with an outdoor terrace and restaurant. *Via Marco Polo 2, 08022; 0784 93185; www.hotelpop.it*

Hotel Costa Dorada *moderate*
This charming hotel overlooking the bay has a vine-clad terrace, lovely gardens and a boat for excursions. *Lungomare Palmasera 45, 08020; 0784 93332; www.hotelcostadorada.it; open Mar–Oct*

⑧ Nuoro
Nuoro, Sardegna; 08100
The capital of its eponymous province, Nuoro is steeped in traditions which, in the mountains, are still very much a part of daily life. The town may not be especially pleasing to the eye, but it has a strong café culture around the old centre (Piazza San Giovanni and Corso Garibaldi). Try the old-style Bar Majore *(see right)* or enjoy the terrace of Bar Nuovo *(Piazza Mazzini)*. Nuoro is also the birthplace of the writer Grazia Deledda, the first Italian woman to win the Nobel Prize for Literature (1926). Her former home is now the **Museo Deleddiano** *(Via Grazia Deledda 53; closed Mon & Sun pm)*. However, the highlight of the town (and where there is on-street parking) is the **Museo del Costume** *(Via A Mureu 56; open daily)* with over 7,000 items of local crafts and costumes. Do not miss the Tavola degli Antichi *(Via Trieste 70)*, it is an Aladdin's cave of gourmet treats such as almond biscuits and honey.

🚗 *From Nuoro go east on Corso Garibaldi (SS129) to Via Manzoni (SP 22), then right at Via Monte Ortobene (SP42). Park at the designated car park and follow the dusty track and 49 steps up to Il Redentore.*

⑨ Monte Ortobene
Nuoro, Sardegna; 08100
Just east of Nuoro, Monte Ortobene (955 m/3,130 ft) is topped with an impressive brass statue, *Il Redentore* (*Christ the Redeemer*) by the sculptor Vincenzo Jerace. On 29 August each year a procession climbs up the mountain as the climax of the 10-day

Optional Trip to Tiscali

One of the most extraordinary sights on the island, Tiscali is a huge cave that houses the remains of a Nuraghic village buried inside Monte Tiscali. Originally there were more than 60 circular huts dating from the 1st millennium BC. The dwellings remained inhabited until medieval times and the site was rediscovered only in the 19th century. Monte Tiscali is 515 m (1,690 ft) high and the terrain is rough, so sturdy footwear is a necessity. Take a guide *(see left)* and allow a full day. Remember to bring sunscreen, water and a hat, too.
Drive from Dorgali following the signs for Hotel Su Gologone, about 7 km (4 miles) east of Oliena, just off the Oliena–Dorgali road to reach the start of the walk.
Walk from here following the signpost for Valle Lanaittu and then the red marker signs to Tiscali.

festival Sagra del Redentore. The mountain affords breathtaking views and the wooded slopes are a great favourite for picnics.

🚗 *Head northwest on Via Monte Ortobene (SP42), then take SS129; go right on SP38 and right on SS125, then continue on Via Lamarmora for a few km into Dorgali and park on-street for the Tourist Information Centre.*

⑩ Dorgali
Nuoro, Sardegna; 08022
Lying about 9 km (6 miles) inland from the Golfo di Orosei, Dorgali is at the heart of one of the best areas for the Cannonau wines. Sample the rich reds (and whites) and learn a bit more about wine making at the

Above View over the town of Dorgali towards the Monti del Gennargentu

Where to Stay: inexpensive, under €100; moderate €100–€200; expensive over €200

Above left Marina in a spectacular setting at Cala Gonone **Above right** The clear waters of Cala Luna beach, only accessible by boat

Enotec Vinarius *(Via Tola 2; 0784 96793)* and Cantina di Dorgali *(Via Piemonte 11; 0784 96143)*. There is also the small **Museo Archeologico** *(Via Vittorio Emmanuele; closed Mon)* with an important collection of pieces from Nuraghic sites. Dorgali is a good base for treks or excursions to the Gola Su Gorroppu and Monte Tiscali.

🚗 *From Dorgali take Via Lamarmora to the SS125 west and follow signs for Ristorante Albergo Sant'Elene (see right). Past the hotel, follow signs for Tiscali along an unsurfaced road for 4 km (2 miles) and turn left at the sign to Gorroppu and the car park. Then it is a 2-hour walk to the Flumineddu river and the start of the gorge.*

⑪ Gola Su Gorroppu
Nuoro, Sardegna; 08020

This spectacular gorge is carved out of limestone and framed by soaring 400 m (1,300 ft) cliffs. Depending on how full the Flumineddu river is, it is possible to walk along the riverbed, picking your way over the boulders. Note that the whole length is about 8 km (5 miles) – proper equipment

and a guide is needed to venture a long way inside. In the autumn and winter the waters in the river can become torrential. However, this is one of southern Europe's deepest and most magnificent gorges and worth an excursion. Guided tours cost about €35 a head, with a packed lunch.

🚗 *Return to Dorgali then go south on the SS125, turning left into a mountain tunnel before a series of hairpin bends leads to Cala Gonone (waterfront parking).*

⑫ Cala Gonone
Nuoro, Sardegna; 08020

Framed by soaring mountains like a vast amphitheatre, Cala Gonone on the Golfo di Orosei is a pretty resort with good beaches. However, a short boat ride away are the truly idyllic beaches of Cala Luna, Cala Fuili and Cala Cartoe. Nearby, too, is the Grotta del Bue Marino – the most dramatically beautiful of the many caves on this coastline. Bue marino is the local name for the monk seal and this was one of its last hiding places – it has not been seen since 1992. Boat trips can be booked from any of the small kiosks that line the little port.

Festival outfit, Museo del Costume, Nuoro

VISITING GOLA SU GORROPPU AND MONTE TISCALI

Both these excursions really should be undertaken with an experienced guide.
Cooperativa Ghivine
Via Montebello 5, Tiscali, 08022; 0784 96721; www.ghivine.com

EAT AND DRINK

NUORO

Bar Majore *inexpensive*
Nuoro's oldest café is ornately decorated. Its central location makes it the perfect spot for people-swatching.
Corso Garibaldi 71, 08100

AROUND DORGALI

Ristorante Albergo Sant'Elene *inexpensive–moderate*
Glorious terrace views are accompanied by excellent regional cuisine.
Località Sant'Elene, 08022, 3 km (2 miles) off SS125 from Dorgali; 0784 94577; www.hotelsantelene.it; closed Mon (except in summer) and Jan

CALA GONONE

Ristorante Al Porto *moderate*
Seafood delights and the Sardinian speciality *bottarga*, dried fish roe.
Piazza del Porto 2, 08022; 078 493 185; www.hotelpop.it

DAY TRIP OPTIONS
Cagliari is an obvious base for day trips with Nuoro being good for access to the mountains. Dorgali is the best place to organize a trip into the gorge.

Mini "Capital and Coast"
Spend the morning exploring the historical highlights of Cagliari ❶, then enjoy a long, slow traditional Italian lunch at Al Porto *(see p239)* before heading for the pillow-soft

sands of Poetto Beach ❷ for some well-deserved rest and relaxation.

Drive southeast on Via Roma – there are car parks on the Lungomare.

The real Sardinia
Some say it is in the mountains that the real Sardinia can still be found, so start at Nuoro ❽ to learn about the local customs. Next see Orgòsolo's ❼ famous murals and the sinister costumes at Mamoiada ❻ before

returning to Nuoro for the traditional sport of people-watching in a café.

Orgòsolo is on the SP22 and the SP58 from Nuoro; Mamoiada is on the SS389.

Simply gorgeous
For spectacular scenery, take the sheer walls of the gorge and clear waters of the Flumineddu. Take a tour of the Gola Su Gorroppu ⑪ from Dorgali ❿.

Dorgali is on the SS125. The tour is best organized with a guide – see above.

Sardinia's Coral and Emerald Coasts

Bosa to Olbia

Highlights

- **Coral Coast capital**
  Stroll around Alghero, surrounded by towers and fortifications

- **Sardinia's second city**
  Be immersed in Sassari's sophisticated café society, complete with fascinating *centro storico*

- **Arcipelago della Maddalena**
  Escape to these dreamy islands with Caribbean-blue seas

- **Costa Smeralda**
  Sparkling like a precious jewel, this coastline is a fascinating one to explore and is the perfect spot to see and be seen

View of Castelsardo and its citadel from across the port

Sardinia's Coral and Emerald Coasts

A beautiful stretch of coastal road leads from charming little Bosa to Alghero – both seaside resorts and picturesque walled medieval towns with a distinctive Spanish flavour following the Spanish conquest of Sardinia in the 14th century. The route then goes inland to the old university town of Sassari. Continuing along the northern coast, Castelsardo is famous for its imposing medieval citadel and handicrafts, while inland the mountain town Aggius is cradled by cork woods and nearby is the moonscape Valle della Luna. Back on the coast, the Arcipelago della Maddalena is a vision of paradise, and the Costa Smeralda has hidden gems.

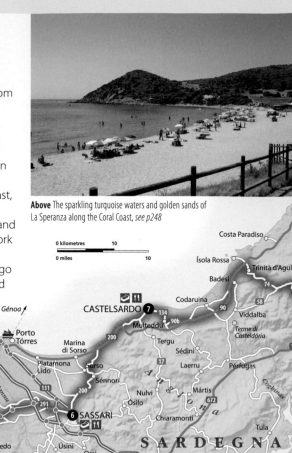

Above The sparkling turquoise waters and golden sands of La Speranza along the Coral Coast, *see p248*

0 kilometres   10

0 miles   10

Costa Paradiso

Ísola Rossa

Trinità d'Agult

Badesi

74

Génoa

CASTELSARDO **7** 134

Codaruina

90

58

Viddalba

Múltèddu

90b

Terme di Castcldória

Pozzo S. Nicola

Porto Tórres

Marina di Sorso

200

Tergu

Sédini

Platamona Lido

Sorso

Laerru

Pérfugas

Palmádula

131

200

Sénnori

Nulvi

Mártis

672

Argentiera

Mannu

291

Osilo

Chiaramonti

Tula

Porto Ferro

291

6 SASSARI

S A R D E G N A

55b

Olmedo

Usini

Ploaghe

Sant'Antíoco di Bisárcio

Fertília

127b

Fertília

Ossi

Uri

Florínas

597

Tramaríglio

55

4

Necrópoli Anghelu Rúiu

131

CAPO CACCIA AND GROTTA DI NETTUNO **5**

NURAGHE DI PALMAVERA

3 ALGHERO

Íttiri

Árdara

Chilivàni

199

105

Síligo

Ozieri

LA SPERANZA **2**

292

Villanova Monteleone

Thiesi

Mores

Ittireddu

Romana

105

Monteleone Rocca Dória

ACTIVITIES

KEY

Drive route

105

Montresta

Tirso

Capo Marárgiu

19

49

1 BOSA

Bosa Marina

Modolo

Porto Alabe

Follow the wine route around Bosa and Alghero

Delve deep into Neptune's grotto where fantastical stalactites and stalagmites seem to come to life

Be part of Sassari's sophisticated café culture

Walk over the lunar landscape of the Valle della Luna

Gaze out over the Straits of Bonifacio to Corsica from the watchtower at Santa Teresa di Gallura

Beg or borrow a boat to discover the jewel-like seas and pearly-white sands of the Costa Smeralda

Below A view of Alghero's atmospheric *centro storico* across the bustling marina, see pp248–9

PLAN YOUR DRIVE

Start/finish: Bosa to Olbia.

Number of days: 4, allowing half a day to explore Alghero.

Distance: Bosa to Olbia 286 km (178 miles).

Road conditions: Generally well paved and signposted with some steep terrain around Valle della Luna. The scenic coastal roads, particularly around the Costa Smeralda, get very busy in high season.

When to go: May, June and September are ideal months. July and August are busy and best avoided.

Opening hours: Shops tend to open Mon–Sat 9am–1pm and 4–7pm or 8pm. Churches are usually open 8am–noon and 4–7pm. Museum opening times vary enormously, but usual hours are 9am–1pm and 4–7pm or 8pm. Many museums are closed on Mondays. Archaeological sites are generally open from 9am to one hour before sunset.

Main market days: Alghero: Wed; Sassari: Mon–Sat; Olbia: Tue.

Shopping: Look out for deep red coral jewellery, straw-woven baskets, *bottarga* (Sardinian caviar) and delicious Sardinian wines including Malvasia di Bosa and Tanca Farrà.

Major festivals: Bosa: Festa di Santa Maria del Mare, Aug; Festa di Nostra Signora di Regnos Altos, Sep. Alghero: International Summer of Music Festival, Jul–Aug. Sassari: Cavalcata Sarda (medieval pageant), May; I Candelieri (candle procession), Aug.

DAY TRIP OPTIONS

This drive is easily divided into three sections. The medieval seaside town of Alghero and the vineyards that surround it should satisfy **culture-** and **wine-lovers**. Those with an interest in **history** and **rock formations** will find Nuraghe di Palmavera and the Grotta di Nettuno fascinating and **families** with children will enjoy island-hopping in the Arcipelago della Maddalena. For full details, *see p253*.

Above left Houses and fishing boats line the banks of the Temo river, Bosa **Above right** Villa Las Tronas, one of the most lavish and expensive hotels in Alghero

VISITING ALGHERO

Parking
The largest, most convenient car parks are north and south of Via Garibaldi next to the port.

Tourist Information
Piazza Porta Terra; 079 979 054; www.comune.alghero.ss.it; open 8am–8pm Sat–Sun.

WHERE TO STAY

BOSA

Corte Fiorita *inexpensive–moderate*
Three historic buildings in the town centre have been converted into a hotel with tastefully decorated rooms. Breakfast is served in a courtyard garden. *Lungo Temo de Gasperi 45, 08013; 078 537 7058; www.hotel-bosa.it*

ALGHERO

Agriturismo Vessus *inexpensive*
Situated just outside Alghero and set among olive groves and flower-filled gardens, this charming hotel has rooms located around the swimming pool. The restaurant specializes in seasonal and home-grown produce. *Located on the SS292 towards Villanova Monteleone, 07041; 079 973 5018; www.vessus.it; restaurant open Jun–Sep for dinner*

Villa Las Tronas *expensive*
Alghero's most luxurious hotel is perched on a private promontory with splendid sea views. Elegant interiors as well as a saltwater swimming pool and beauty centre. *Lungomare Valencia 1, 07014; 079 981818; www.hotelvillalastronas.it*

❶ Bosa

Nuoro, Sardegna; 08013

Overlooked by the **Castello dei Malaspina** *(open daily)*, this pretty town hugging the banks of the Temo river, was originally founded by the Carthaginians and has a medieval centre full of narrow, cobbled alley-ways. Bosa is surrounded by vineyards and is on the *Strada della Malvasia di Bosa* – the wine route of delicious golden Malvasia dessert wine – for which the town is famous. (Visit the Tourist Office at Via Azuni, 5; tel 0785 376107 for information on the wine route.) Many artists live here and some of the old medieval houses are being lovingly restored.

From Bosa go west to pick up the Viale Alghero, then turn right onto the SP49 (later the SP105) towards Alghero. 8 km (5 miles) south of Alghero is La Speranza. Park next to the beach.

❷ La Speranza

Sassari, Sardegna; 07019

The coastal road from Bosa to Alghero is one of the island's most scenic – skirting gorgeous inlets and coves. La Speranza is one of the more accessible and beautiful beaches along this road, backed by rugged landscape. There is a resident colony of rare griffon here. Parasols can be hired on the beach and there is a good restaurant and bar.

Continue along the SP105 in the direction of Alghero.

Sardinian Wines

Malvasia white grapes proliferate around Bosa and the sweet wine Malvasia di Bosa is one of Sardinia's highest-quality wines. Cannonau vines are planted at the Sella e Mosca estate near Alghero and there are some delicious wines produced from these grapes. The estate also makes the award-winning Tanca Farrà wine, which is a blend of Cannonau and Cabernet Sauvignon grapes.

❸ Alghero

Sassari, Sardegna; 07041

The island's most picturesque medieval seaside town, Alghero has a distinctive Catalan character. Following the Catalan-Aragonese invasion of Sardinia, Alghero underwent total Hispanicization and became known as "little Barcelona". The old town is the perfect place for a stroll to sample delicious local seafood and wines. It is also known for its deep red coral, unique to this coastline, which is intertwined with intricate filigree work to make jewellery.

A two–three-hour walking tour

Early in the morning is the best time of day to explore the old town. Leave the car at the portside car park just off Via Garibaldi, (north of the centre) which is well-placed for the old town. Walk along the water-front and, after the Bastione della Maddalena (an old fort), turn left into the main square, **Piazza Civica** ①. This lively piazza, known as *Il Salotto* (the dining room), is fitted with shops and restaurants. Marogna at no. 34 is the best place for coral jewellery and at no. 23 is Il Ghiotto, an Aladdin's cave of Sardinian gourmet delights.

Walk along Via Manno at the western side of the piazza, which leads into Piazza Duomo. The **Cattedrale di Santa Maria** ② *(open daily)* has a white Neo-Classical façade flanked by four large columns and topped by an impressive octagonal

Where to Stay: inexpensive, under €100; moderate, €100–€200; expensive, over €200

Above A typical cobbled street in Alghero's historic centre

campanile. Originally founded in the 16th century, the oldest parts of the cathedral are an example of the pure Catalan-Gothic style, while the transformations in the interior and on the façade date from the 18th century. From Via Roma, behind the cathedral, turn right onto Via Carlo Alberto and a short way down on the left arrive at **Chiesa di San Francesco** ③ *(open*

Mon–Sat). This is one of Alghero's landmarks, recognizable by its stately pointed Aragonese tower. Built between the 15th and 16th centuries, this church has a beautiful star-studded vault in the presbytery, an 18th-century marble altar and a simple, yet lovely cloister, where in summer *al fresco* concerts are staged. Continue down Via Carlo Alberto, taking time to browse along Alghero's main shopping hub, brimming with boutiques and jewellery shops. On the left is the 17th-century **Chiesa di San Michele** ④ *(open daily)*. This Jesuit church is remarkable for its glistening ceramic dome that pierces Alghero's skyline. Inside is elaborate stucco, fine altar paintings and a sculpture of St Michael slaying the dragon. Retrace your steps up Via Carlo Alberto and right onto Via Gilbert Ferret, then left onto Via Simon and up to the **Torre di Porta Terra** ⑤ on your right *(open daily in summer)*. Originally the main gate to the walled town, this tower is now an interpretation centre and from the terrace there are magnificent views.

🚗 *Leaving Alghero follow signs to Fertilia (west) and take the SS127 bis for Nuraghe di Palmavera. There is a rough off-road car parking area.*

EAT AND DRINK

BOSA

Borgo Sant'Ignazio *inexpensive*
Atmospheric bistro serving lobster and Sardinian desserts. Try the local Malvasia wine. *Via Sant'Ignazio 33, 08013; 0785 374129; closed Tue*

ALGHERO

Trattoria Al Refettorio *moderate*
Wine bar and restaurant with outside seating. Fresh fish and local specialities. *Vicolo Adami 47, 07041; 079 973 1126; www.alrefettorio.it; open Wed–Mon*

Angedras Restaurant
moderate–expensive
This minimalist-style restaurant features seafood tasting platters. Excellent home-made pasta and Sardinian desserts. *Via Cavour 31, 07041; 079 9735034; www.angedrasrestaurant.it*

Other options
For a great spot for an *aperitivo* with free tastings of typical Sardinian fare try **Il Ghiotto (di Roberto Peana)**, *inexpensive (Piazza Civica 23, 07041; 079 974820; closed Mon)*. Overlooking the port, **Café Latino**, *inexpensive (Bastioni Magellano10, 07041; 079 976541; closed Tue)* is perfect for a long cool drink and tasty snacks. A short distance from Alghero is **Sella e Mosca** *(Localita I Piani, 07041; 079 997700; www.sellaemosca.com; closed Sun)* known for their award-winning wines. Visit the wine cellars and give in to temptation in the *enoteca* (wine shop).

Above Medieval buildings tightly packed together, Alghero

Eat and Drink: inexpensive, under €25; moderate, €25–€45; expensive, over €45

Above Incredible stalactites and stalagmites reflecting in a lake, Grotta di Nettuno

WHERE TO STAY

SASSARI

Hotel Vittorio Emanuele *moderate*
A fully restored former palazzo in the centre of town. The rooms are pleasingly furnished and the rustic stone cellar is an ideal spot for wine-tasting. *Via Mannu 5, 07100; 0784 98879; www.subarchile.it*

CASTELSARDO

Hotel Riviera da Fofò *moderate*
Set on the road across from the beach, with lovely views of the old town. Rooms are comfortable and modern and some have balconies.
Via Lungomare Anglona 1, 07031; 079 470 143; www.hotelriviera.net

AGGIUS

Il Muto di Gallura *moderate*
Set between Aggius and Tempio Pausania, this *agriturismo* is an attractive rustic stone-built farmhouse with outdoor swimming pool. The restaurant serves typical Sardinian food.
Località Fraiga, 07020; 079 620 559; www.mutodigallura.com

④ Nuraghe di Palmavera
Sassari, Sardegna; 07041
One of the largest Nuraghic villages in the area, Nuraghe di Palmavera *(open daily)* consists of a complex nuraghe – the so-called palace – surrounded by about 50 circular huts. The main tower of the nuraghe, whose dome-shaped ceiling is still intact, dates back to 1100 BC. The site shows the different phases of the life and organization of the tribal community that once lived here. The highlight is the **Capanna delle Riunioni** (Reunion Hut) where political debates and gatherings of magical-religious cults were held. For more on nuraghe, *see p240.*

🚗 *Continue along the SS127 bis, then take the SP55 to Capo Caccia. There is a designated car park.*

⑤ Capo Caccia & Grotta di Nettuno
Sassari, Sardegna; 07041
The limestone headland Capo Caccia, to the west of Alghero, is a panoramic spot with sweeping views over the

cape. Around the headland is the **Grotta di Nettuno** – the mythical cave of Neptune and nymphs. A steep series of 654 steps leads down to the cave, bathed in shimmering colours and bristling with stalactites and stalagmites contorted into fantastical shapes such as the Great Organ. Tours *(run daily Apr–Sep)* leave on the hour and last 45 minutes. Note that in rough weather high waves close off the grotto. As an alternative to driving, take a boat from Alghero town port (1 hour).

🚗 *From the car park at Capo Caccia, follow the SP55, then turn left at SP55 bis and after 9 km (6 miles), bear left onto the SS291 through to Sassari. In Sassari follow signs to the local bus station at Mostra Artiginiato and the car park alongside at Emiciclo Garibaldi.*

⑥ Sassari
Sassari, Sardegna; 07100
Second only to Cagliari in terms of size, this is Sardinia's oldest university town. Its medieval heart is a labyrinth of narrow streets and picturesque little piazzas. The 15th-century **Duomo di San Nicola** *(open daily)* on Piazza Duomo is a splendid example of Baroque architecture. Inside the striking choir is the work of 18th-century Sardinian artists. The main road, Corso Vittorio Emanuele II, is full of palazzos – some crumbling, others lovingly restored, with beautiful wrought-iron balconies and Gothic windows. The renovated Liberty-style **Teatro Cívico** *(open Tue–Sat; 079 232182)*, is a treasure with its refurbished ceiling frescoes by the same craftsmen who restored Venice's La Fenice. As well as staging concerts

Right The impressive Baroque façade of Duomo di San Nicola, Sassari **Far right** The simple, Gothic nave of Duomo di San Nicola, Sassari

and plays, this is where local dignitaries meet before I Candelieri festival, celebrating the town's deliverance from plague, (see p247) in August. Opposite at no. 42, the 15th century **Casa di Re Enzo** has a gorgeous frescoed interior and is now a good Goldenpoint lingerie and swimwear shop. The centre of café society is a short stroll away along Via Roma. Worth a visit is the elegant **Caffè Italiano** at no. 38/40, and **Barberry's** at no. 18 is popular late at night.

🚗 *Head north on SS200 to Castelsardo. Park in central Piazza Pianedda. Avoid driving into the old city.*

7 Castelsardo
Sassari, Sardegna; 07031
Translated literally as Sardinian Castle, this citadel, spectacularly perched on a rocky outcrop, started life in the 12th century as a Genoese cliff city (Castel Genoese), then became Castel Aragonese in the 14th century under the Spanish and finally Castelsardo in the 18th century. A climb up the steep steps and lanes of the medieval old city rewards with magnificent views from the top of the castle. Inside **Museo dell'Intreccio** (open daily) is a museum dedicated to straw-weaving (l'intreccio) for which the town is famous. In the medieval centre visitors can buy handmade baskets

and watch local women weaving them outside their doorways.

🚗 *From Castelsardo take the SS134, turn left onto SP90 bis, then SP90, following signs for Trinità d'Agultu, then follow the SP74 and SP27 to Aggius.*

8 Aggius & Valle della Luna
Olbia-Tempio, Sardegna; 07020
Set in a splendid panoramic position in the mountainous Gallura countryside, amid cork-oak forests and granite boulders, this hill village is known for its choral music and for its handicrafts, especially woven carpets. The **Museo Etnografico** (open daily mid-May–mid-Oct) on Via Monti di Lizu off Via Roma, gives a fascinating insight into the local traditions and crafts. A short distance northwest of Aggius is the Valle della Luna – an extraordinary lunar landscape where huge granite boulders are strewn in twisted shapes. From Aggius, take a left signposted towards Trinità d'Agultu to drive through the Valle della Luna. The road eventually leads to the coast.

🚗 *Bear northeast on the SP27, left at SS133, left at the SP5 signed to Aglientu, right at the SP90, and keep following the coastal SP90 road to Santa Teresa. The main car park is at the northern end on Via Verdi, close to the Spiaggia Rena Bianca.*

Straw-woven baskets, Castelsardo

Above right The main nuraghe surrounded by circular huts, Nuraghe di Palmavera
Above left Bizarre rock formations on the hills behind the village of Aggius

EAT AND DRINK

SASSARI

Bar Caffè Florian *inexpensive*
Great for immersing in Sassari's café society this stylish, arty bar has tables that spill out onto the pavement.
Via Roma 6, 07100

Ristorante Liberty *moderate*
A former Liberty-style palazzo, this elegant restaurant looks out onto a piazza in the old town. The restaurant also owns the wine and piano bar alongside with an atmospheric tasting cellar.
Piazza N Sauro 3, 07100; 079 236361; www.ristoranteliberty.com; closed Mon

CASTELSARDO

La Guardiola *moderate*
Located just below the castle with a splendid dining terrace overlooking the sea. The specialities are fish and seafood.
Piazza Bastione 4, 07031; 079 470755; www.ristorantelaguardiola.com; open daily Jun–Sep, closed Mon, Oct–May

Where to Stay: inexpensive, under €100; moderate, €100–€200; expensive, over €200

Above left La Maddalena town nestled at the foot of a hill, Arcipelago della Maddalena
Above right Bassa Trinita beach with unusal rock formations, Arcipelago della Maddalena

VISITING ARCIPELAGO DELLA MADDALENA

Ferry information
Car and foot passenger ferries depart from the port at Palau every 20 mins in summer (once an hour after midnight) and hourly in winter. *www.saremar.it*

WHERE TO STAY

CANNIGIONE

Hotel Baja *moderate*
Close to the seafront, this hotel is white and minimalist. Good restaurant, outdoor swimming pool and fitness centre. *Via Nazionale, 07020; 0789 892041; www.hotelbaja.it; open Apr–Sep*

PORTO CERVO

Cervo Hotel *expensive*
Understated elegance at this hotel in the heart of Porto Cervo. *La Piazzetta, 07021; 0789 931 111; www. starwoodhotels.com; open May–Sep*

Below Al fresco dining, La Maddalena, Arcipelago della Maddalena

⑨ Santa Teresa di Gallura
Olbia-Tempio, Sardegna; 07028
On the northern tip of Sardinia, this is an attractive and popular seaside resort surrounded by beautiful beaches. It is also the main departure port for Corsica and, in summer, regular ferry trips to the Maddalena Islands. The town's hub is **Piazza Vittorio Emanuele**, lined with bars and restaurants and the site of the Tourist Information Centre. From here a short walk up Via del Mare leads to the **Torre de Longosardo** *(open daily Jun–Sep)*, a 16th-century Spanish watch-tower affording splendid views over the Straits of Bonifacio to Corsica. To the west of the tower, a path leads down to the lovely main beach, **Spiaggia Rena Bianca**. Lying 4 km (2 miles) to the west of Santa Teresa is the spectacular granite headland, Capo Testa flanked by glorious beaches.
🚗 *Head out of town on the SP90, then go left on the SS133 bis to Palau. Ferries leave from the port at Palau.*

Red geraniums potted in an urn

⑩ Arcipelago della Maddalena
Olbia-Tempio, Sardegna; 07024
The ferry crossing from Palau to La Maddalena takes 20 minutes. This is the only town on the seven islands of the archipelago and it is an atmospheric spot full of piazzas and cobbled streets. The Chiesa di S Maria Maddalena on Via Baron Manno houses the **Museo Diocesano** *(open Tue–Sun)* and exhibits include silver candlesticks and a crucifix that were gifts from Horatio Nelson when he was aboard HMS *Victory* here between 1803 and 1805. Look out for **Sardegna da Mangiare Da Bere** (Piazza Garibaldi), a shop selling Sardinian specialities from cheese and salami to *bottarga* (tuna caviar) and cakes. At the eastern end of the island a causeway links to the island of Caprera – the home and burial place of Giuseppe Garibaldi (1807–82). It is a pleasant place to walk around, though keep an eye out for the wild boar that roam freely. There are boat trips from Palau to the other islands including little Budelli, renowned for its beautiful **Spiaggia Rosa** (pink beach).
🚗 *From Palau take SP123, follow signs to Capo d'Orso that lead to a car park.*

⑪ Capo d'Orso
Olbia-Tempio, Sardegna; 07021
Some 6 km (4 miles) east of Palau is the Capo d'Orso, an extraordinary bear-shaped rock – one of many of the fantastically formed, weather-sculpted rocks along this coastline.

To reach it walk through the gate from the car park and follow the marked path to the headland.

🚗 *From Capo d'Orso take the SP123 then the SP121 south along the coast to Cannigione. There is parking along the main street set back from the port.*

⑫ Cannigione

Olbia-Tempio, Sardegna; 07021
This vibrant seaside town has a very pretty marina. Much more low-key than the Costa Smeralda resorts, it is popular with families and has good bars, restaurants and hotels, making it an ideal base for exploring the area.

🚗 *Out of Cannigione go east towards Via Nazionale and follow signs for Baia Sardinia to pick up the SP59, which winds along the coast.*

⑬ Porto Cervo

Olbia-Tempio, Sardegna; 07021
Porto Cervo is the capital of the Costa Smeralda – the "millionaire's playground" with a coastline stretching 56 km (35 miles) with more than 80 sandy beaches, little coves and bays. The waters here really do sparkle like precious jewels while the pseudo Moroccan/ Mediterranean town is awash with smart bars, restaurants and designer shops. Its **Piazzetta** is at its heart and is the perfect place to see the time-honoured *passeggiata* when people parade to see and be seen or to indulge in a cocktail at sunset on the terrace of the Cervo Hotel.

🚗 *Leave Porto Cervo heading southwest on the SP59 and follow signs to Olbia on the SP94, SP73 and SS125. There are three car parks near the port, off the main road Via Genova.*

Above The golden sands and sparkling water of Princess Beach, Costa Smeralda

COSTA SMERALDA

This area was undeveloped until the 1960s when the Aga Prince Kharim IV came across the beautiful stretch of coast and decided to make it into a "millionaire's paradise". One of the best ways to explore the stunning beaches is by boat, though many are also accessible by foot and road. West of the Cala di Volpe bay, Capriccioli and Romazzino beaches with their eponymous, hugely expensive hotels, are great places to wander.

⑭ Olbia

Olbia-Tempio, Sardegna; 07026
Although this is Sardinia's busiest passenger port, the old part of the town around Corso Umberto is crammed with attractive piazzas, bars and restaurants. The main sight is the **Basilica di San Simplico** *(open daily)*, dating back to the 11th–12th-centuries. The church is dedicated to Olbia's patron saint and is Gallura's most important medieval church.

EAT AND DRINK

LA MADDALENA

La Grotta *moderate*
Family-run restaurant where the signature dish is lobster. *Via Principe di Napoli 3, 07024; 0789 737228; www.lagrotta.it; open daily May–Sep*

CANNIGIONE

L'Ancora *inexpensive–moderate*
A wood-burning pizza oven, freshest fish and delectable meat dishes make this restaurant a favourite. Good local wines and *mirto* – the Sardinian myrtle berry liqueur. *Località Micalosu, 07021; 0789 86086; www.lancoraristorante.it*

PORTO CERVO

Tanit *expensive*
Perched over an exclusive marina, this chic restaurant serves gourmet cuisine. *Poltu Quatu (east of Baia Sardinia and west of Porto Cervo); 0789 955008; open daily in summer*

DAY TRIP OPTIONS

Most sights along this drive are in easy reach if you are based at Alghero or along the Costa Smeralda.

History and wine tasting

Spend the morning wandering Alghero's compact *centro storico* ❸ and lunch at one of the restaurants at Piazza Civica. In the afternoon head for the *Strada della Malvasia di Bosa* ❶ or visit the Sella e Mosca vineyard and sample their wines.

From Alghero take the SS127 bis a few km up the road from Necropoli Anghelu Ruiu to the vineyard, 079 997 700; www.sellaemosca.com.

Prehistoric huts and mythical caves

Visit the nuraghic village at Nuraghe di Palmavera ❹. Afterwards head to the Capo Caccia and the Grotta di Nettuno ❺ to view fantastical stalactites and stalagmites.

From Alghero follow the signs to Fertilia (west) and then take the SS127

bis. To reach the Capo Caccia continue along the SS127 bis, then take the SP55.

Island-hop around the Arcipelago della Maddalena

Families will enjoy island-hopping in the Arcipelago della Maddalena ❿. Explore the cobbled streets of La Maddalena before heading to Budelli for a relaxing afternoon on the idyllic Spiaggia Rosa beach.

Ferries to La Maddalena leave the port at Palau every 20 minutes in summer.

Eat and Drink: inexpensive, under €25; moderate, €25–€45; expensive, over €45

Acknowledgments

Dorling Kindersley would like to thank the many people whose help and assistance contributed to the preparation of this book.

Main Contributors

Ros Belford is a travel writer and broadcaster specializing in Sicily.

Judy Edelhoff is a freelance photographer, writer and broadcaster who has travelled all over Italy. She has written on travel, art, food and wine.

Adele Evans has travelled extensively around Italy, and has written numerous travel articles for magazines, newspapers and guidebooks.

Tamara Thiessen is a Sydney-Paris based writer and photographer. She has contributed to magazines and newspapers worldwide, as well as many guidebooks.

Christine Webb, a former art director and magazine designer, left her native Australia in 2000 for Italy, where she works as a freelance journalist and photographer.

Marius Webb is a freelance travel writer based in Tuscany. He and Christine have contributed to many guides to Italy including *Best of Tuscany 2008* and *Time Out Italy 2008*.

Celia Woolfrey is a journalist, former *Guardian* gardening columnist and co-author of the *Rough Guide to Italy*, where she has travelled from the Alps to the heel of the boot.

Fact checker
Jo-Ann Titmarsh

Proofreader
Debra Wolter

Indexer
Hilary Bird

Special Assistance
John Bleasdale, Dr Paolo Diamante at Automobile Club d'Italia, Sabina Fata, Stefania Gatta, Richard Land, Janice Marini Cossetti, Cristina Murroni, Cristiano Rigon, Deborah Soria, Susanna Soria, Jo-Ann Titmarsh.

Photography
Judy Edelhoff, Tony Souter, Tamara Thiessen, Christine Webb, Marius Webb, Celia Woolfrey.

Additional Photography
Sarah Ashton, Demetrio Carrasco, Steve Gorton, Paul Harris and Anne Heslope, John Heseltine, James McConnachie, Roger Moss, Kim Sayer.

Revisions Team
John Bleasdale, Imogen Corke, Cristina Dainotto, Peter Douglas, Carly Madden, Nicola Malone, Alison McGill, Alessandra Pugliese, Susana Smith, Sands Publishing Solutions, Lucy Richards, Rebecca Winke.

Picture Credits
t=top; tl=top left; tr=top right; c=centre; cl=centre left; cr=centre right; bl=bottom left; br=bottom right.

Every effort has been made to trace the copyright holders of images, and we apologize in advance for any unintentional omissions. We would be pleased to insert the appropriate acknowledgments in any subsequent edition of this publication.

The Publishers would like to thank the following individuals, companies and picture libraries for their kind permission to reproduce their photographs:

4Corners Images: SIME/Guido Baviera 202bl; SIME/Riccardo 198–9. **akg-images**: 26–7. **Alamy Images**: imagebroker/Martin Moxter 13tc; Jon Arnold Images Ltd/Doug Pearson 234–5; Jijo Kunily 15tc; Homer W Sykes 203tr. **Banca Popolare – Volksbank**: 15tl. **Corbis**: AgStock Images/Ed Young 221br; Atlantide Phototravel/Guido Cozzi 170–1; John Heseltine 194c; JAI/Walter Bibikow 204tl; David Lees 184c; Starlight/Roger Ressmeyer 185tr; Swim Ink 2, LLC 218c. **DK Images**: Gary Ombler/Crown Copyright. Reproduced with the permission of the Controller of HMSO 13tl. **Getty Images**: DEA/R. Carnovalni 205tr; Gallo Images/Travel Ink 17bl; Iconica/Petr Svarc 66tl; The Image Bank/ Grant Faint 8; The Image Bank/Jeremy Woodhouse 1; The Image Bank/Walter Bibikow 212bl; Lonely Planet Images/David Tomlinson 10tl; Lonely Planet Images/Richard Nebesky 5br; Panoramic Images 10br; Photographer's Choice/Richard Adams 203bl; Photographer's Choice/ Grant Faint 12bl; Photographer's Choice/Vincenzo Lombardo 10bl; Reportage/Bruno Morandi 13tr; Stone/Michael Busselle 9br; Stone/Stephen Studd 13br. **UniCredit Group**: 14bl. **Christine Webb**: 2–3, 5tc, 5bc, 6cl, 6bl, 7br, 16bl, 17t, 18tl, 18bl, 19bl, 23bl, 24bl, 25bl, 27c, 98–9, 100cl, 101tl, 102tc, 102tr, 102c, 102bl, 103tl, 104tl, 104tcb, 104bl, 112c, 113tl, 113tr, 113bc, 113br, 114tl, 114tc, 114bl, 114bc, 115tr, 115c, 115bl, 116tl, 116cr, 116bl, 117tl, 117tc, 117c, 118–19, 120cl, 120br, 122tl, 122c, 122br, 123tr, 124tl, 124tr, 125tl, 125tc, 126–7, 128cl, 129tl, 130tl, 130br, 132tl, 132tr, 132br, 133tl, 133tc, 133tr, 134tl, 134tc, 134crb, 134br, 135tr, 135clb.

Sheet Map
Front: **Getty Images**: Photographer's Choice/Maremagnum

Jacket
Front: **Corbis**: JAI/Walter Bibikow.
Spine: **Corbis**: JAI/Walter Bibikow t.
Back: **Alamy Images**: Tom Mackie c; **DK Images**: Tamara Thiessen cl; Celia Wolfrey cr.

All other images are © Dorling Kindersley. For further information see www.dkimages.com.

SPECIAL EDITIONS OF DK TRAVEL GUIDES

DK Travel Guides can be purchased in bulk quantities at discounted prices for use in promotions or as premiums.

We are also able to offer special editions and personalized jackets, corporate imprints, and excerpts from all of our books, tailored specifically to meet your own needs.

To find out more, please contact:
(in the United States) **SpecialSales@dk.com**
(in the UK) **travelspecialsales@uk.dk.com**
(in Canada) DK Special Sales at **general@tourmaline.ca**
(in Australia) **business.development@pearson.com.au**

Phrase Book

IN EMERGENCY

Help!	Aiuto!	eye-yoo-toh
Stop!	Fermate!	fair-mah-teh
Call a doctor.	Chiama un medico	kee-ah-mah oon meh-dee-koh
Call an ambulance.	Chiama un' ambulanza	kee-ah-mah oon am-boo-lan-tsa
Call the police.	Chiama la polizia	kee-ah-mah lah pol-ee-tsee-ah
Call the fire brigade.	Chiama i pompieri	kee-ah-mah ee pom-pee-air-ee
Where is the telephone?	Dov'è il telefono?	dov ch eel teh-leh-foh-noh?
The nearest hospital?	L'ospedale più vicino?	loss-peh-dah-leh-pee-oo vee-chee-noh?

COMMUNICATION ESSENTIALS

Yes/No	Sì/No	see/noh
Please	Per favore	pair fah-vor-eh
Thank you	Grazie	grah-tsee-eh
It's a pleasure	Prego	preh-goh
Excuse me	Mi scusi	mee skoo-zee
Hello	Buon giorno	bwon jor-noh
Goodbye	Arrivederci	ah-ree-veh-dair-chee
Good evening	Buona sera	bwon-ah sair-ah
morning	la mattina	lah mah-tee-nah
afternoon	Il pomeriggio	eel poh-meh-ree-joh
evening	la sera	lah sair-ah
yesterday	ieri	ee-air-ee
today	oggi	oh-jee
tomorrow	domani	doh-mah-nee
here	qui	kwee
there	la	lah
What?	Quale?	kwah-leh?
When?	Quando?	kwan-doh?
Why?	Perchè?	pair-keh?
Where?	Dove?	doh-veh?

USEFUL PHRASES

How are you?	Come sta?	koh-meh stah?
Very well, thank you.	Molto bene, grazie.	moll-toh beh-neh grah-tsee-eh
Pleased to meet you.	Piacere di conoscerla.	pee-ah chair eh dee coh-noh-shair-lah
See you later.	A più tardi.	ah pee-oo tar-dee
That's fine.	Va bene.	va beh-neh
Where is/are …?	Dov'è/Dove sono …?	dov-eh/doveh soh-noh?
How long does it take to get to …?	Quanto tempo ci vuole per andare a …?	kwan-toh tem-poh chee voo-oh-leh pair an-dar-eh ah …?
How do I get to …?	Come faccio per arrivare a …?	koh-meh fah-choh pair arri-var-eh ah …?
Do you speak English?	Parla inglese?	par-lah een-gleh zeh?
I don't understand.	Non capisco.	non ka-pee-skoh
Could you speak more slowly, please?	Può parlare più lentamente, per favore?	pwoh par-lah-reh pee-oo len-ta-men-teh pair fah-vor-eh?
I'm sorry.	Mi dispiace.	mee dee-spee-ah-cheh

USEFUL WORDS

big	grande	gran-deh
small	piccolo	pee-koh-loh
hot	caldo	kal-doh
cold	freddo	fred-doh
good	buono	bwoh-noh
bad	cattivo	kat-tee-voh
enough	basta	bas-tah
well	bene	beh-neh
open	aperto	ah-pair-toh
closed	chiuso	kee-oo-zoh
left	a sinistra	ah see-nee-strah
right	a destra	ah dess-trah
straight on	sempre dritto	sem-preh dree-toh
near	vicino	vee-chee-noh
far	lontano	lon-tah-noh
up	su	soo
down	giù	joo
early	presto	press-toh
late	tardi	tar-dee
entrance	entrata	en-trah-tah
exit	uscita	oo-shee-ta
toilet	il gabinetto	eel gah-bee-net-toh
free, unoccupied	libero	lee-bair-oh
free, no charge	gratuito	grah-too-ee-toh

MAKING A TELEPHONE CALL

I'd like to place a long-distance call.	Vorrei fare una interurbana.	vor-ray far-eh oona in-tair-oor-bah-nah
I'd like to make a reverse-charge call.	Vorrei fare una telefonata a carico del destinatario.	vor-ray far-eh oona teh-leh-fon-ah-tah ah kar-ee-koh dell dess-tee-nah-tar-ree-oh
I'll try again later.	Ritelefono più tardi.	ree-teh-leh-foh-noh pee-oo tar-dee
Can I leave a message?	Posso lasciare un messaggio?	poss-oh lash-ah-reh oon mess-sah-joh?
Hold on.	Un attimo, per favore	oon ah-tee-moh, pair fah vor-eh
Could you speak up a little please?	Può parlare più forte, per favore?	pwoh par-lah-reh pee-oo for-teh, pair fah-vor-eh?
local call	telefonata locale	te-leh-fon-ah-tah loh-cah-leh

SHOPPING

How much does this cost?	Quant'è, per favore?	kwan-teh pair fah-vor-eh?
I would like …	Vorrei …	vor-ray
Do you have …?	Avete …?	ah-veh-teh…?
I'm just looking.	Sto soltanto guardando.	stoh sol-tan-toh gwar-dan-doh
Do you take credit cards?	Accettate carte di credito?	ah-chet tah -teh kar-teh dee creh-dee-toh?
What time do you open/close?	A che ora apre/ chiude?	ah keh or-ah ah-preh/kee-oo-deh?
this one	questo	kweh-stoh
that one	quello	kwell-oh
expensive	caro	kar-oh
cheap	a buon prezzo	ah bwon pret-soh
size, clothes	la taglia	lah tah-lee-ah
size, shoes	il numero	eel noo-mair-oh
white	bianco	bee-ang-koh
black	nero	neh-roh
red	rosso	ross-oh
yellow	giallo	jal-loh
green	verde	vair-deh
blue	blu	bloo

TYPES OF SHOP

antique dealer	l'antiquario	lan-tee-kwah-ree-oh
bakery	il forno /il panificio	eel forn-oh /eel pan-ee-fee-choh
bank	la banca	lah bang-kah
bookshop	la libreria	lah lee-breh-ree-ah
butcher	la macelleria	lah mah-chell-eh-ree-ah
cake shop	la pasticceria	lah pas-tee-chair-ee-ah
chemist	la farmacia	lah far-mah-chee-ah
delicatessen	la salumeria	lah sah-loo-meh-ree-ah
department store	il grande magazzino	eel gran-deh mag-gad-zee-noh
fishmonger	il pescivendolo	eel pesh-ee-ven-doh-loh
greengrocer	il fruttivendolo	eel froo-tee-ven-doh-loh
grocery	alimentari	ah-lee-men-tah-ree
hairdresser	il parrucchiere	eel par-oo-kee-air-eh
ice-cream parlour	la gelateria	lah jel-lah tair-ree-ah
market	il mercato	eel mair-kah-toh
newsstand	l'edicola	leh-dee-koh-lah
post office	l'ufficio postale	loo-fee-choh pos-tah-leh
shoe shop	il negozio di scarpe	eel neh-goh-tsioh dee skar-peh
supermarket	il supermercato	eel su-pair-mair-kah-toh
tobacconist	il tabaccaio	eel tah-bak-eye-oh
travel agency	l'agenzia di viaggi	lah-jen-tsee-ah dee vee-ad-jee

SIGHTSEEING

art gallery	la pinacoteca	lah peena-koh-teh-kah
bus stop	la fermata dell'autobus	lah fair-mah-tah dell ow-toh-booss
church	la chiesa	lah kee-eh-zah
	la basilica	lah bah-seel-i-kah
closed for holidays	chiuso per le ferie	kee-oo-zoh pair leh fair-ee-eh
garden	il giardino	eel jar-dee-no
library	la biblioteca	lah beeb-lee-oh-teh-kah
museum	il museo	eel moo-zeh-oh
railway station	la stazione	lah stah-tsee-oh-neh
tourist information	l'ufficio di turismo	loo-fee-choh dee too-ree-smoh

STAYING IN A HOTEL

Do you have any vacant rooms?	Avete camere libere?	ah-veh-teh kah-mair-eh lee-bair-eh?
double room	una camera doppia	oona kah-mair-ah doh-pee-ah
with double bed	con letto matrimoniale	kon let-toh mah-tree-moh-nee-ah-leh
twin room	una camera con due letti	oona kah-mair-ah kon doo-eh let-tee
single room	una camera singola	oona kah-mair-ah sing-goh-lah
room with a bath, shower	una camera con bagno, con doccia	oona kah-mair-ah kon ban-yoh, kon dot-chah
porter	il facchino	eel fah-kee-noh
key	la chiave	lah kee-ah-veh
I have a reservation.	Ho fatto una prenotazione.	oh fat-toh oona preh-noh-tah-tsee-oh-neh

EATING OUT

Have you got a table for…?	Avete una tavola per … ?	ah-veh-teh oona tah-voh-lah pair …?
I'd like to reserve a table.	Vorrei riservare una tavola.	vor-ray ree-sair-vah-reh oona tah-voh-lah
breakfast	colazione	koh-lah-tsee-oh-neh
lunch	pranzo	pran-tsoh
dinner	cena	cheh-nah
The bill, please.	Il conto, per favore.	eel kon-toh pair fah-vor-eh
I am a vegetarian.	Sono vegetariano/a.	soh-noh veh-jeh-tar-ee-ah-noh/nah
waitress	cameriera	kah-mair-ee-air-ah
waiter	cameriere	kah-mair-ee-air-eh
fixed price menu	il menù a prezzo fisso	eel meh-noo ah pret-soh fee-soh
dish of the day	piatto del giorno	pee-ah-toh dell jor-no
starter	antipasto	an-tee-pass-toh
first course	il primo	eel pree-moh
main course	il secondo	eel seh-kon-doh
vegetables	il contorno	eel kon-tor-noh
dessert	il dolce	eel doll-cheh
cover charge	il coperto	eel koh-pair-toh
wine list	la lista dei vini	lah lee-stah day vee-nee
rare	al sangue	al sang-gweh
medium	al puntino	al poon-tee-noh
well done	ben cotto	ben kot-toh
glass	il bicchiere	eel bee-kee-air-eh
bottle	la bottiglia	lah bot-teel-yah
knife	il coltello	eel kol-tell-oh
fork	la forchetta	lah for-ket-tah
spoon	il cucchiaio	eel koo-kee-eye-oh

MENU DECODER

l'acqua minerale gassata/ naturale	lah-kwah mee-nair-ah-leh gah-zah-tah/ nah-too-rah-leh	mineral water fizzy/ still
agnello	ah-niell-oh	lamb
aceto	ah-cheh-toh	vinegar
aglio	al-ee-oh	garlic
al forno	al for-noh	baked
alla griglia	ah-lah greel-yah	grilled
l'aragosta	lah-rah-goss-tah	lobster
arrosto	ar-ross-toh	roast
la birra	lah beer-rah	beer
la bistecca	lah bee-stek-kah	steak
il brodo	eel broh-doh	broth
il burro	eel boor-oh	butter
il caffè	eel kah-feh	coffee
i calamari	ee kah-lah-mah-ree	squid
i carciofi	ee kar-choff-ee	artichokes
la carne	la kar-neh	meat
carne di maiale	kar-neh dee mah-yah-leh	pork
la cipolla	la chip-oh-lah	onion
i contorni	ee kon-tor-nee	vegetables
i fagioli	ee fah-joh-lee	beans
il fegato	eel fay-gah-toh	liver
il finocchio	eel fee-nok-ee-oh	fennel
il formaggio	eel for-mad-joh	cheese
le fragole	leh frah-goh-leh	strawberries
il fritto misto	eel free-toh mees-toh	mixed fried dish
la frutta	la froot-tah	fruit
frutti di mare	froo-tee dee mah-reh	seafood
i funghi	ee foon-ghee	mushrooms
i gamberi	ee gam-bair-ee	prawns
il gelato	eel jel-lah-toh	ice cream

l'insalata	leen-sah-lah-tah	salad
il latte	eel laht-teh	milk
lesso	less-oh	boiled
il manzo	eel man-tsoh	beef
la melanzana	lah meh-lan-tsah-nah	aubergine
la minestra	lah mee-ness-trah	soup
l'olio	loh-lee-oh	oil
il pane	eel pah-neh	bread
le patate	leh pah-tah-teh	potatoes
le patatine fritte	leh pah-tah-teen-eh free-teh	chips
il pepe	eel peh-peh	pepper
la pesca	lah pess-kah	peach
il pesce	eel pesh-eh	fish
il pollo	eel poll-oh	chicken
il pomodoro	eel poh-moh-dor-oh	tomato
il prosciutto cotto/crudo	eel pro-shoo-toh kot-toh/kroo-doh	ham cooked/cured
il riso	eel ree-zoh	rice
il sale	eel sah-leh	salt
la salsiccia	lah sal-see-chah	sausage
le seppie	leh sep-pee-eh	cuttlefish
secco	sek-koh	dry
la sogliola	lah soll-yoh-lah	sole
gli spinaci	lyee spee-nah-chee	spinach
succo d'arancia/ di limone	soo-koh dah-ran-chah/ dee lee-moh-neh	orange/ lemon juice
il tè	eel teh	tea
la tisana	lah tee-zah-nah	herbal tea
il tonno	eel ton-noh	tuna
la torta	lah tor-tah	cake/tart
l'uovo	loo-oh-voh	egg
vino bianco	vee-noh bee-ang-koh	white wine
vino rosso	vee-noh ross-oh	red wine
il vitello	eel vee-tell-oh	veal
le vongole	leh von-goh-leh	clams
lo zucchero	loh zoo-kair-oh	sugar
gli zucchini	lyee dzu-kee-nee	courgettes
la zuppa	lah dzu-pah	soup

NUMBERS

1	uno	oo-noh
2	due	doo-eh
3	tre	treh
4	quattro	kwat-roh
5	cinque	ching-kweh
6	sei	say-ee
7	sette	set-teh
8	otto	ot-toh
9	nove	noh-veh
10	dieci	dee-eh-chee
11	undici	oon-dee-chee
12	dodici	doh-dee-chee
13	tredici	tray-dee-chee
14	quattordici	kwat-tor-dee-chee
15	quindici	kwin-dee-chee
16	sedici	say-dee-chee
17	diciassette	dee-chah-set-teh
18	diciotto	dee-chot-toh
19	diciannove	dee-chah-noh-veh
20	venti	ven-tee
30	trenta	tren-tah
40	quaranta	kwah-ran-tah
50	cinquanta	ching-kwan-tah
60	sessanta	sess-an-tah
70	settanta	set-tan-tah
80	ottanta	ot-tan-tah
90	novanta	noh-van-tah
100	cento	chen-toh
1,000	mille	mee-leh
2,000	duemila	doo-eh mee-lah
5,000	cinquemila	ching-kweh mee-lah
1,000,000	un milione	oon meel-yoh-neh

TIME

one minute	un minuto	oon mee-noo-toh
one hour	un'ora	oon or-ah
half an hour	mezz'ora	medz-or-ah
a day	un giorno	oon jor-noh
a week	una settimana	oona set-tee-mah-nah
Monday	lunedì	loo-neh-dee
Tuesday	martedì	mar-teh-dee
Wednesday	mercoledì	mair-koh-leh-dee
Thursday	giovedì	joh-veh-dee
Friday	venerdì	ven-air-dee
Saturday	sabato	sah-bah-toh
Sunday	domenica	doh-meh-nee-kah

GENERAL DRIVING INDICATIONS

Compulsory stop

Your route has priority

Your route no longer has priority

You have priority at the next junction

Give way to incoming traffic

No overtaking

Roundabout

No access for vehicles over 3.5 m in height

...f speed limit

Obligatory minimum distance of 70 m

Minimum speed limit

Residential area with special speed limit

...of bends

Slippery road

Risk of strong crosswinds

Risk of rockfalls

...ows

Road narrows on the left

Level crossing with barrier

Level crossing with no barrier

Children crossing, or school

Pedestrian crossing

Road works

Driver's Phrase Book

SOME COMMON ROAD SIGNS

accendere i fari	headlights on
attenzione	watch out, caution
autostrada	motorway (with toll)
banchina non transitabile	soft verge
caduta massi	falling rocks
centro	town centre
code	traffic ahead
controllo automatico della velocità	automatic speed monitor
cunetta o dosso	ditch
deviazione	diversion
disporsi su due file	two-lane traffic
divieto di accesso	no entry
divieto di fermata	no stopping
divieto di transito	no thoroughfare
dogana	customs
escluso residenti	residents only
fine del tratto autostradale	end of motorway
ghiaccio	ice
incrocio	junction
incrocio pericoloso	dangerous junction/ crossroads
informazioni turistiche	tourist information
lavori in corso	roadworks
nebbia	fog
non oltrepassare	no access
pagare qui	pay here
parcheggio a giorni alterni	parking on alternate days
parcheggio a pagamento	paying car park
parcheggio custodito	car park with attendant
parcheggio incustodito	unattended car park
pedaggio	toll
pedoni	pedestrians
pericolo	danger
pista ciclabile	bicycle trail
rallentare	reduce speed
scuola	school
senso unico	one way
sosta vietata	no parking
sottopassaggio	subway
strada a fondo cieco	dead end
strada camionabile	route for heavy vehicles
strada ghiacciata	ice on road
strada statale	main road
strada sdrucciolevole	slippery road
strada secondaria	secondary road
strada statale	main road
uscita camion	works exit
veicoli lenti	slow lane
zona a traffico limitato	restricted traffic area
zona pedonale	shopping centre

DIRECTIONS YOU MAY BE GIVEN

a destra	right
a sinistra	left
dritto	straight on
giri a destra	turn right
giri a sinistra	turn left
il primo/la prima a destra	first on the right
il secondo/la seconda a sinistra	second on the left
vada oltre …	go past the …

THINGS YOU'LL SEE

acqua	water
area di servizio	service area
aspirapolvere	vacuum cleaner
autolavaggio	car wash
autorimessa	garage (for repairs)
benzina	petrol
benzina senza piombo	unleaded petrol
benzina super	4-star petrol
casello autostradale	motorway toll booth
cera per auto	car wax
code	traffic queue
deviazione	diversion
gasolio	diesel oil
gommista	tyre repairs
guidare a passo d'uomo	drive at walking speed
liquido tergicristallo	windscreen washer liquid
olio	oil
raccordo autostradale	motorway junction
spegnere il motore	turn off engine
spingere	push
stazione di servizio	service station
tirare	pull
uscita	exit
vietato fumare	no smoking

THINGS YOU'LL HEAR

Vuole una macchina con il cambio automatico o manuale?
Would you like an automatic or a manual?

Esibisca la patente, per favore?
May I see your licence, please?

Mi fa vedere il passaporto, per favore?
May I see your passport, please?

USEFUL PHRASES

Could you check the oil/water level, please?
Potrebbe controllare il livello dell'olio/dell'acqua, per favore?
potreb-be kontrol-lare eel leevel-lo del ol-yo/del akwa pair fah-vor-eh

Fill it up, please!
Faccia il pieno, per favore!
facha eel p-yeno pair fah-vor-eh

I'd like 35 litres of 4-star petrol, please.
Mi dia trentacinque litri di super, per favore.
mee dee-a trentacheenkwe leetree dee soopair pair fah-vor-eh

Do you do repairs?
Effettua riparazioni?
ef-fet-too-a reeparatz-yonee

Can you repair the clutch?
Può ripararmi la frizione?
pwo reepararmee la freetz-yone

There is something wrong with the engine.
C'è qualcosa che non va nel motore.
cheh kwalkoza ke non va nel motore

The engine is overheating.
Il motore si surriscalda.
eel motore see soor-reeskalda

I need a new tyre.
Ho bisogno di una gomma nuova.
o beezon-yo dee oona gom-ma nwova

Can you replace this?
Può sostituirlo?
pwo sosteetoo-eerlo

The indicator is not working.
La freccia non funziona.
la frech-cha non foontz-yona

How long will it take?
Quanto tempo ci vorrà?
kwanto tempo chee vor-ra

Where can I park?
Dove posso parcheggiare?
dove pos-so parkej-jare

I'd like to hire a car.
Vorrei noleggiare una macchina.
vor-ray nolej-jare oona mak-keena

I'd like an automatic/a manual.
Vorrei una macchina con il cambio automatico/manuale.
vor-ray oona mak-keena kon eel kam-bee-o owtomateeko/ manwale

How much is it for one day?
Quanto costa per un giorno?
kwanto kosta pair oon jorno

Is there a mileage charge?
C'è un supplemento per il chilometraggio?
cheh oon soop-plemento pair eel keelometraj-jo

When do I have to return it?
Quando devo riportarla?
kwando devo reeportarla

Where is the nearest petrol station?
Dov'è la stazione di servizio più vicina?
doveh la statz-yone dee sairveetz-yo p-yoo veecheena

How do I get to …?
Come faccio per arrivare a …?
koh-meh fah-choh pair arri-var-eh ah

Is this the road to …?
È questa la strada per …?
eh kwesta la strada pair

Which is the quickest way to …?
Qual' è la strada più breve per …?
kwal eh la strada p-yoo breve pair

USEFUL WORDS

automatic	**con il cambio automatico**	*kon eel kam-bee-o owtomateeko*
bonnet	**il cofano**	*kofano*
boot	**il portabagagli**	*portabagal-yee*
brake	**il freno**	*freh-no*
breakdown	**il guasto**	*gwa-sto*
car	**l'automobile, la macchina**	*ow-toh-moh-beeleh, mak-keena*
car ferry	**il traghetto**	*traget-to*
car park	**il parcheggio**	*parkej-jo*
clutch	**la frizione**	*freetz-yone*
crossroads	**l'incrocio**	*een-kro-cho*
drive	**guidare**	*gwee-dar-eh*
engine	**il motore**	*mo-tor-eh*
exhaust	**lo scappamento**	*skap-pamento*
fanbelt	**la cinghia della ventola**	*cheeng-ya del-la ven-to-la*
garage (for repairs)	**l'autorimessa**	*ow-toh-ree-mes-sa*
gear	**il cambio, la marcia**	*kam-bee-o, mar-cha*
gears	**le marce**	*mar-cheh*
headlights	**i fari**	*far-ee*
indicator	**la freccia**	*frech-cha*
junction	**l'incrocio**	*een-kro-cho*
licence	**la patente**	*pa-ten-teh*
lorry	**il camion, l'autocarro**	*kam-yon, ow-toh-kar-ro*
manual	**con il cambio manuale**	*kon eel kam-bee-o man-wah-leh*
mirror	**lo specchietto**	*spekk-yet-to*
motorcycle	**la motocicletta**	*moto-chee-klet-ta*
motorway	**l'autostrada**	*ow-toh-strada*
motorway entry	**raccordo di entrata**	*rak-kor-do dee en-tra-ta*
motorway exit	**raccordo di uscita**	*rak-kor-do dee oo-shee-ta*
number plate	**la targa**	*tar-ga*
petrol	**la benzina**	*bendz-eena*
petrol station	**la stazione di servizio**	*statz-yone dee sair-veetz-yo*
rear lights	**i fari posteriori**	*far-ee post-airy-oree*
ring road	**raccordo anulare**	*rak-kordo anoolareh*
road	**la strada**	*stra-da*
spare parts	**i pezzi di ricambio**	*petzee dee ree-kam-bee-o*
spark plug	**la candela**	*kan-deh-la*
speed	**la velocità**	*ve-loh-chee-ta*
speed limit	**il limite di velocità**	*lee-mee-teh dee ve-loh-chee-ta*
speedometer	**il tachimetro**	*tak-ee-me-tro*
steering wheel	**il volante**	*vo-lan-teh*
traffic lights	**il semaforo**	*seh-ma-foro*
trailer	**il rimorchio, la roulotte**	*ree-mork-yo, roo-lot*
transmission	**la scatola del cambio**	*ska-toh-la del kam-bee-o*
tyre	**la gomma**	*gom-ma*
van	**il furgone**	*foor-gon-eh*
warning sign	**il triangolo**	*tree-angolo*
wheel	**la ruota**	*rw-oh-ta*
windscreen	**il parabrezza**	*para-bretza*
windscreen wiper	**il tergicristallo**	*tairjee-kreestal-lo*

Road Sign

SPEED LIMITS AND

Give way

Junction gives priority to traffic from the right

80

Speed limit

End o

WARNING SIGNS

Unspecified danger

Successio

Speed bumps

Road nar

Steep descent

Wild anima

Driver's Phrase Book

SOME COMMON ROAD SIGNS

accendere i fari	headlights on
attenzione	watch out, caution
autostrada	motorway (with toll)
banchina non transitabile	soft verge
caduta massi	falling rocks
centro	town centre
code	traffic ahead
controllo automatico della velocità	automatic speed monitor
cunetta o dosso	ditch
deviazione	diversion
disporsi su due file	two-lane traffic
divieto di accesso	no entry
divieto di fermata	no stopping
divieto di transito	no thoroughfare
dogana	customs
escluso residenti	residents only
fine del tratto autostradale	end of motorway
ghiaccio	ice
incrocio	junction
incrocio pericoloso	dangerous junction/ crossroads
informazioni turistiche	tourist information
lavori in corso	roadworks
nebbia	fog
non oltrepassare	no access
pagare qui	pay here
parcheggio a giorni alterni	parking on alternate days
parcheggio a pagamento	paying car park
parcheggio custodito	car park with attendant
parcheggio incustodito	unattended car park
pedaggio	toll
pedoni	pedestrians
pericolo	danger
pista ciclabile	bicycle trail
rallentare	reduce speed
scuola	school
senso unico	one way
sosta vietata	no parking
sottopassaggio	subway
strada a fondo cieco	dead end
strada camionabile	route for heavy vehicles
strada ghiacciata	ice on road
strada statale	main road
strada sdrucciolevole	slippery road
strada secondaria	secondary road
strada statale	main road
uscita camion	works exit
veicoli lenti	slow lane
zona a traffico limitato	restricted traffic area
zona pedonale	shopping centre

DIRECTIONS YOU MAY BE GIVEN

a destra	right
a sinistra	left
dritto	straight on
giri a destra	turn right
giri a sinistra	turn left
il primo/la prima a destra	first on the right
il secondo/la seconda a sinistra	second on the left
vada oltre ...	go past the ...

THINGS YOU'LL SEE

acqua	water
area di servizio	service area
aspirapolvere	vacuum cleaner
autolavaggio	car wash
autorimessa	garage (for repairs)
benzina	petrol
benzina senza piombo	unleaded petrol
benzina super	4-star petrol
casello autostradale	motorway toll booth
cera per auto	car wax
code	traffic queue
deviazione	diversion
gasolio	diesel oil
gommista	tyre repairs
guidare a passo d'uomo	drive at walking speed
liquido tergicristallo	windscreen washer liquid
olio	oil
raccordo autostradale	motorway junction
spegnere il motore	turn off engine
spingere	push
stazione di servizio	service station
tirare	pull
uscita	exit
vietato fumare	no smoking

THINGS YOU'LL HEAR

Vuole una macchina con il cambio automatico o manuale?
Would you like an automatic or a manual?

Esibisca la patente, per favore?
May I see your licence, please?

Mi fa vedere il passaporto, per favore?
May I see your passport, please?

USEFUL PHRASES

Could you check the oil/water level, please?
Potrebbe controllare il livello dell'olio/dell'acqua, per favore?
potreb-be kontrol-lare eel leevel-lo del ol yo/del akwa pair fah-vor-eh

Fill it up, please!
Faccia il pieno, per favore!
facha eel p-yeno pair fah-vor-eh

I'd like 35 litres of 4-star petrol, please.
Mi dia trentacinque litri di super, per favore.
mee dee-a trentacheenkwe leetree dee soopair pair fah-vor-eh

Do you do repairs?
Effettua riparazioni?
ef-fet-too-a reeparatz-yonee

Can you repair the clutch?
Può ripararmi la frizione?
pwo reepararmee la freetz-yone

There is something wrong with the engine.
C'è qualcosa che non va nel motore.
cheh kwalkoza ke non va nel motore

The engine is overheating.
Il motore si surriscalda.
eel motore see soor-reeskalda

I need a new tyre.
Ho bisogno di una gomma nuova.
o beezon-yo dee oona gom-ma nwova

Can you replace this?
Può sostituirlo?
pwo sosteetoo-eerlo

The indicator is not working.
La freccia non funziona.
la frech-cha non foontz-yona

How long will it take?
Quanto tempo ci vorrà?
kwanto tempo chee vor-ra

Where can I park?
Dove posso parcheggiare?
dove pos-so parkej-jare

I'd like to hire a car.
Vorrei noleggiare una macchina.
vor-ray nolej-jare oona mak-keena

I'd like an automatic/a manual.
Vorrei una macchina con il cambio automatico/manuale.
vor-ray oona mak-keena kon eel kam-bee-o owtomateeko/ manwale

How much is it for one day?
Quanto costa per un giorno?
kwanto kosta pair oon jorno

Is there a mileage charge?
C'è un supplemento per il chilometraggio?
cheh oon soop-plemento pair eel keelometraj-jo

When do I have to return it?
Quando devo riportarla?
kwando devo reeportarla

Where is the nearest petrol station?
Dov'è la stazione di servizio più vicina?
doveh la statz-yone dee sairveetz-yo p-yoo veecheena

How do I get to …?
Come faccio per arrivare a …?
koh-meh fah-choh pair arri-var-eh ah

Is this the road to …?
È questa la strada per …?
eh kwesta la strada pair

Which is the quickest way to …?
Qual' è la strada più breve per …?
kwal eh la strada p-yoo breve pair

USEFUL WORDS

automatic	**con il cambio**	*kon eel kam-bee-o*
	automatico	*owtomateeko*
bonnet	**il cofano**	*kofano*
boot	**il portabagagli**	*portabagal-yee*
brake	**il freno**	*freh-no*
breakdown	**il guasto**	*gwa-sto*
car	**l'automobile,**	*ow-toh-moh-beeleh,*
	la macchina	*mak-keena*
car ferry	**il traghetto**	*traget-to*
car park	**il parcheggio**	*parkej-jo*
clutch	**la frizione**	*freetz-yone*
crossroads	**l'incrocio**	*een-kro-cho*
drive	**guidare**	*gwee-dar-eh*
engine	**il motore**	*mo-tor-eh*
exhaust	**lo scappamento**	*skap-pamento*
fanbelt	**la cinghia**	*cheeng-ya del-la*
	della ventola	*ven-to-la*
garage (for repairs)	**l'autorimessa**	*ow-toh-ree-mes-sa*
gear	**il cambio,**	*kam-bee-o,*
	la marcia	*mar-cha*
gears	**le marce**	*mar-cheh*
headlights	**i fari**	*far-ee*
indicator	**la freccia**	*frech-cha*
junction	**l'incrocio**	*een-kro-cho*
licence	**la patente**	*pa-ten-teh*
lorry	**il camion,**	*kam-yon,*
	l'autocarro	*ow-toh-kar-ro*
manual	**con il cambio**	*kon eel kam-bee-o*
	manuale	*man-wah-leh*
mirror	**lo specchietto**	*spekk-yet-to*
motorcycle	**la motocicletta**	*moto-chee-klet-ta*
motorway	**l'autostrada**	*ow-toh-strada*
motorway entry	**raccordo di**	*rak-kor-do dee*
	entrata	*en-tra-ta*
motorway exit	**raccordo di**	*rak-kor-do dee*
	uscita	*oo-shee-ta*
number plate	**la targa**	*tar-ga*
petrol	**la benzina**	*bendz-eena*
petrol station	**la stazione**	*statz-yone dee*
	di servizio	*sair-veetz-yo*
rear lights	**i fari posteriori**	*far-ee post-airy-oree*
ring road	**raccordo anulare**	*rak-kordo anoolareh*
road	**la strada**	*stra-da*
spare parts	**i pezzi di**	*petzee dee*
	ricambio	*ree-kam-bee-o*
spark plug	**la candela**	*kan-deh-la*
speed	**la velocità**	*ve-loh-chee-ta*
speed limit	**il limite**	*lee-mee-teh dee*
	di velocità	*ve-loh-chee-ta*
speedometer	**il tachimetro**	*tak-ee-me-tro*
steering wheel	**il volante**	*vo-lan-teh*
traffic lights	**il semaforo**	*seh-ma-foro*
trailer	**il rimorchio,**	*ree-mork-yo,*
	la roulotte	*roo-lot*
transmission	**la scatola**	*ska-toh-la del*
	del cambio	*kam-bee-o*
tyre	**la gomma**	*gom-ma*
van	**il furgone**	*foor-gon-eh*
warning sign	**il triangolo**	*tree-angolo*
wheel	**la ruota**	*rw-oh-ta*
windscreen	**il parabrezza**	*para-bretza*
windscreen wiper	**il tergicristallo**	*tairjee-kreestal-lo*

Road Signs

SPEED LIMITS AND GENERAL DRIVING INDICATIONS

Give way

Compulsory stop

Your route has priority

Your route no longer has priority

You have priority at the next junction

Junction gives priority to traffic from the right

Give way to oncoming traffic

No overtaking

Roundabout

No access for vehicles over 3.5 m in height

Speed limit

End of speed limit

Obligatory minimum distance of 70 m

Minimum speed limit

Residential area with special speed limit

WARNING SIGNS

Unspecified danger

Succession of bends

Slippery road

Risk of strong crosswinds

Risk of rockfalls

Speed bumps

Road narrows

Road narrows on the left

Level crossing with barrier

Level crossing with no barrier

Steep descent

Wild animals

Children crossing, or school

Pedestrian crossing

Road works